DEATH AND DYING:
Principles and Practices
In Patient Care

DEATH

and DYING

PRINCIPLES AND PRACTICES
IN PATIENT CARE

RICHARD G. BENTON
University of Texas Medical School at Houston

 VAN NOSTRAND REINHOLD COMPANY
NEW YORK   CINCINNATI   ATLANTA   DALLAS   SAN FRANCISCO
LONDON   TORONTO   MELBOURNE

Van Nostrand Reinhold Company Regional Offices:
New York   Cincinnati   Atlanta   Dallas   San Francisco

Van Nostrand Reinhold Company International Offices:
London   Toronto   Melbourne

Copyright © 1978 by Litton Educational Publishing, Inc.

Library of Congress Catalog Card Number: 77-18265
ISBN: 0-442-20708-5

Manufactured in the United States of America

Published by Van Nostrand Reinhold Company
450 West 33rd Street, New York, N.Y. 10001

Published simultaneously in Canada by Van Nostrand Reinhold Ltd.

15 14 13 12 11 10 9 8 7 6 5 4 3 2

Library of Congress Cataloging in Publication Data

Benton, Richard G.
   Death and dying.

   Includes bibliographical references and index.
   1. Terminal care.   2. Death.   I. Title.
R726.8.B46   616.07   77-18265
ISBN 0-442-20708-5

Foreword

In recent years, the subject of dying and death has become a major topic of conversation. Those of us who have been dealing with death for years have long recognized our inadequate training. DEATH AND DYING: PRINCIPLES AND PRACTICES IN PATIENT CARE, will go a long way in dealing with that inadequacy. It will be of invaluable help to the nurse, medical student, health-related social worker, and other health-related professionals in their experiences involving death.

The subject of dying, and what constitutes a legal death, has become one of the most controversial issues in medicine today. In the past, our final act with destiny caused little comment outside the circle in which we were known. Someone died, mourners claimed the body, and the person was quietly laid to rest.

Dying is no longer a simple affair, as Dr. Benton clearly illustrates in his book. Cessation of breath and pulse is not necessarily an indication of death. If the EEG shows that there are still active brain waves, then life can be maintained indefinitely by the life support equipment found in most hospitals. The major questions today are when is it ethical to pull the life support equipment? Who is allowed to make that decision? What role does the physician, the nurse, the family, and, indeed, the patient, play in the decision? DEATH AND DYING attempts to answer these questions and poses possible solutions to the problems.

The controversial issue of organ transplants and a sudden pronouncement of death is another topic causing much discussion. As Dr. Benton asks, if the organs are needed, will this inspire the physician to pronounce the patient dead? On the other hand, if there is no immediate use for the organs, might the patient still be considered alive? Chapter 2 will be of particular interest to those working in the intensive care units.

Chapter 3, which deals with the dying child, will prove to be one of the best, most informative discussions written on the subject. There is little doubt but that the dying child presents the most difficult death of all. It creates an emotional turmoil in even the most hardened professional. Personal emotions must be dealt with as well as those of the child and parents. The medical staff must provide support to the grieving parents and assist them toward their acceptance of the child's death. And what about the child? What are his or her feelings? This chapter will be invaluable to young nurses or medical students facing their first dying child.

With death comes the inevitable question, "Why did he or she die?" If there is no apparent reason, then the answer can only be resolved through an autopsy. Unfortunately, the public is still skeptical about autopsies. DEATH AND DYING helps nurses alleviate some of that skepticism. With a greater understanding of the autopsy procedure, the nurse will be able to calm and reassure the family when the need for an autopsy arises.

Dr. Benton's text does not confine its study of death and dying to modern times, but covers the entire scope of recorded civilizations. Here you will find the beliefs and traditions as practiced long ago. Many of our present day customs can be related to some of those ancient beliefs. Dr. Benton has researched his material thoroughly, making Chapter 5 a fascinating one for the reader.

Other interesting and controversial subjects covered in this book include euthanasia and cryonics. Does anyone have the right to practice euthanasia, more popularly known as "mercy killing"? Where does the patient stand in "the right to die" dilemma? If the patient has a "living will" giving specific instructions regarding his or her death, will it be honored? On the subject of cryonics, is it possible to return a frozen body to a living state? If so, how would one adapt to society after an absence of a hundred years? These are only a few of the questions posed by Dr. Benton in his discussion on euthanasia and cryonics. It gives the readers a lot to think about and helps us to formulate our own ideas.

A study of this book will provide the future nurses a clearer understanding of the process of dying and death. It will assist us in coping with our own emotions involving death, and, it is hoped, guide us in our dealings with the dying and bereaved.

BETTY KORNDORFFER, RN
Nurse Consultant
Texas State Department of Health

Preface

I often hear parents of children with terminal illnesses say, "If only someone had prepared us—if only we had known." Nurses and other health-care professionals have expressed the same uncertainty. Death is a subject which is rarely discussed, either in public or in private, yet it is the most singular binding event that we experience. Death transcends roles, occupations, social status, and ethnic distinctions; it touches all of us and confounds most of us. Because most people are unprepared to deal with the needs of the dying person or with their own needs, they can only grope for an appropriate response to the experience.

DEATH AND DYING: PRINCIPLES AND PRACTICES IN PATIENT CARE informs both professionals and nonprofessionals about the essentials of life in its terminal stages. It presents the practical, theoretical, social, and psychological aspects of death and dying to promote a healthy, accepting attitude toward a subject clouded by fear, confusion, and misconception.

The book may be used as a core text for the undergraduate nursing curriculum course called "Death and Dying" or as a supplementary text in other nursing courses and in community and public health education.

Chapter 1, *Termination of Life: Who Draws the Line and Why* and Chapter 2, *To Live or Die: Professional Issues and Concerns,* examine the question of who has the right (or obligation) to dispense with life-sustaining conditions. To make a logical decision, we need to know the medical, legal, and philosophical issues involved, all of which are discussed.

Almost everyone—the patient, the family, the medical personnel—has extreme difficulty coping with the anxieties of death. Guilt, rejection, isolation, and fear are some of the factors that influence the human response to death. Chapter 3, *Responses to Death and Stages of Grieving* focuses on the reactions of a person attempting to cope with finality.

Chapter 4, *The Context of Death: Implications for Patient and Family Care,* presents situations in which death occurs and the sociological and cultural factors pertinent to the terminal process.

Chapter 5, *Funerals, Death Rituals, and Religious Influences,* deals with our changing perceptions of death. When faced with the death of a family member or friend, survivors usually go through the rituals of grieving and disposing of the remains in accordance with the advice of the nurse, funeral director, physician, or pastor. That these rituals are rooted in ancient traditions is not widely known. A discussion of death and dying within a historical context will help bring into focus the meanings of our rituals.

Medical advances have made possible cures that were once undreamed. Many of these are only partial cures. Although physical therapy, plastic surgery, and comestic procedures help improve the individual's physical defects, disfigurement is a major problem for both the rehabilitant and the dying patient. Chapter 6, *Nursing Intervention for the Dying and Bereaved,* explores how we react to disfigurements that are conceived as forerunners of death.

Chapter 7, *Case Studies: Professional and Personal Reports,* is presented to share intimate experiences which will help personalize abstract concepts and enhance the learning process. Such information will allow those who are struggling with the problems of death and dying to recognize that their feelings are experienced by many.

Almost everyone in the health-care field will have the opportunity of dealing with a dying patient and surviving family. Chapter 8, *Getting in Touch: The Nurse's Response to Death and Dying* addresses the practical approaches of care giving. The forms to be filled out are discussed and several, such as a death certificate and The Living Bank, are given.

I wish to address my acknowledgment and deep thanks to all those who have contributed to this book. I am especially indebted and grateful to Sally Karioth, RN; Mary C. Thiell, RN; Betty Korndorffer, RN; Jan van Eys, Ph.D., M.D.; M.K. Chudleigh, RN; M.J. Dresser, RN, MA; Bill Korndorffer, M.D.; and Mike Thorne, LLD, each of whom shared their experiences and knowledge. Their articles and contributions give the book a unique quality of personal concern. I wish also to thank those who shall remain anonymous but who gave immeasurably to this effort. Of no less importance was the assistance of Karen Hauser, Ginny Patton, Annie Morris, and the people at D. Van Nostrand Company, in particular Harriet Serenkin.

Contents

4 **THE CONTEXT OF DEATH: IMPLICATIONS FOR PATIENT AND FAMILY CARE**   118

5 **FUNERALS, DEATH RITUALS, AND RELIGIOUS INFLUENCES**   151

DEATH AND DYING:
Principles and Practices
In Patient Care

Termination of Life: Who Draws the Line and Why?

When is death? Philosophers, physicians, theologians, and farmers alike ponder this simple phrase. How do you measure that entity, that aspect or quality called life? It seems we can more easily tell when it is, than when it is not. Man is an inquiring being and seeks continually to measure. In many fields we now have measuring devices that tell us unequivocally "how much," "when," even "yes or no." But agreement on measuring "life" is still as difficult as measuring what the perfume mixer or tea taster or chicken sexer does. This chapter will present and review the various medical, philosophical, and legal aspects of death that must be considered in the termination of a human life.

No one has ever understood death. Its full meaning has always been a mystery. But not too many years ago, most people seemed satisfied to let the responsibility for defining death rest with doctors, lawyers, and religious or philosophical leaders. While those professionals could not solve the problem of death, they at least provided both practical and theoretical definitions.

The definitions had different emphases. Medical definitions dealt with man's physical body. Legal definitions dealt with the interlocking responsibilities of the individual, the family, and society. Religious and philosophical definitions helped place the fact of death in a cosmic pattern of one kind or another. The doctor presided over the patient and pronounced the moment of death. The lawyer helped prepare a will and presided over its reading; or if there was no will, the lawyer helped the family settle the estate. The minister, priest, or rabbi offered emotional support for both the dying patient and the family, and also presided over the funeral. Philosophy books offered deeper, wider theories of death to all who sought them. There was even a time in the not too distant past when the family in rural America had full responsibility for medical, legal, and religious aspects of death.

1

For the most part, the medical, legal, and religious-philosophical realms have had clear-cut provinces. Each shared equally in formulating what understanding man had of death. Recently, however, the medical definition of death has been dominating understanding. The tilting of the triumvirate of responsibility has brought the problem of defining death to everyone's attention. People today seek to define death, partly for their own peace of mind and partly for practical reasons of controlling an overwhelming technology and clarifying public policy and legal responsibility. Numerous committees have met and published criteria for physicians. Thanatologists—people who specialize in studying death in all its aspects—have made careers of interpreting, challenging, and amending the medical criteria for death.

Advances in medical science make it possible to sustain some "vital signs," such as breathing and heartbeat, while other signs, such as brain waves, are absent. Doctors in charge of such cases must make decisions that have severe legal and philosophical repercussions. Is a person whose heart beats and whose lungs draw breath alive if the brain is dead? Doctors do not have the leisure to debate their decisions; they must act decisively during the crisis period—either pronounce the patient dead or continue life-support systems. The legal consequences of withdrawing a life-support system such as a respirator are only now being explored in the courts.

IN SEARCH OF THE DEFINITION OF DEATH: MEDICAL, LEGAL, AND PHILOSOPHICAL CONSIDERATIONS

Most Americans have heard of the Karen Ann Quinlan case and of her parents' struggle with the courts to obtain the authority to turn off her life-support systems. That famous case has brought some of the problems of defining death to popular attention. In mid-December of 1976, months after her full-time life-support systems had been detached, Quinlan appeared to be in an irreversible coma; she no longer communicated with anyone; for all practical purposes she was a "vegetable." Still, she could breathe for short periods without the respirator. Thus controversy raged over the question whether patients such as Quinlan should be considered dead because they are incapable of social intercourse or alive because they have some reflex action.

The controversy is generally known as the whole-brain theory of death vs. the neocortical theory of death. Under the former theory, and by the criteria established by the Harvard Ad Hoc Committee to Define Brain Death, Quinlan remained alive in mid-December. She was also alive according to the traditional tests of breath and heartbeat. The neocortical theory of death, however, would pronounce her dead because the higher brain functions were irreversibly damaged. The higher brain functions control man's ability to be conscious, communicate, think, experience, and feel.

Another case, while not in the public eye to the extent that Quinlan's was, appeared equally important to the search for definitions of death. Bruce Tucker, a 56-year-old laborer, fell and sustained massive brain injury on May 24, 1968. The next day he was taken to the Medical College of Virginia where he was operated on in an attempt to relieve the pressure on his brain. After the operation, he was fed intravenously, given medication, and kept breathing with a respirator. His heartbeat was satisfactory, but he was expected to die at any moment. A neurologist tested for brain waves and found virtually nothing but flat lines. The respirator was cut off in the afternoon and five minutes later he was pronounced dead and the respirator was turned back on to preserve his organs.

Not quite an hour later his heart was removed and implanted in the chest of a heart-transplant patient. The incision to remove the recipient's defective heart was made two minutes before Mr. Tucker was pronounced dead. Mr. Tucker's kidneys were also removed. Bruce Tucker's brother subsequently sued the doctors who performed the operation, accusing them of a "systematic and nefarious scheme to use Bruce Tucker's heart and hasten his death by shutting off the mechanical means of support" (Veatch, 1975, p. 233).

In 1972, a Richmond, Virginia, jury ruled in favor of the transplant team. Newspapers hailed the decision as a new legal definition of death—when the brain is dead the patient is dead. Of course, the Virginia jury's decision was not universally binding, but it set a precedent. The head of the defending transplant team remarked that the decision brought "the law up to date with what medicine has known all along—that the only death is brain death" (Veatch, 1975, p. 234).

Interestingly, the physicians in charge of Bruce Tucker felt obliged to turn the respirator off and then on again, indicating that they were far from certain that the death of the brain meant that their patient had died. Both the physicians, who were pressured by the need for a heart to transplant, and the court were faced with the same awesome task of defining death. The brother who charged the doctors with murdering the patient was faced with the task of coping with medical and legal decisions that in no way satisfied him.

The Tucker case brought to light several problems: the physicians themselves were unsure of which definition of death to use—heart death or brain death. They did not have firmly fixed scientific analyses to determine whether death had taken place: they did not then and they do not yet. They had to make a moral decision with standards quite apart from any medical criteria that will ever be available. They decided that the most essential thing to Bruce Tucker was his brain— or rather the functions that his brain performed. They disregarded his heart's ability to keep beating. The physicians also took all the responsibility for that decision upon their own shoulders. No attempt was made to contact the brother, even though the brother's address was in Bruce Tucker's pocket. The brother obviously disagreed about the patient's status. The entire controversy raised the question of who should draw the line between life and death. Can one proceed in happy-go-lucky, democratic fashion and let everyone decide for himself or herself? Should there be one law that everyone must obey in diagnosing death? Should the decision be left to the physician?

The consideration of authority brings up purely legal definitions of death. Three states of the Union—Kansas, Maryland, and Virginia— had laws defining death by the end of 1976; more such legislation was on the way. The question was: Is legislation desirable and what forms should it take?

All of these problems require investigation, particularly in light of the irony of modern scientific achievements that enable a whole Frankenstein's laboratory full of machinery to sustain life where there may be no life at all. Clearly, the problems—whether theoretical, factual, or practical—of thinking about death are magnified. It is impossible to conceive of nothing; therefore it is impossible to conceive of not being. The fear of one's not being, along with sorrow at the thought of losing a friend or relative, charge rational analysis with emotion. The definition of death—with particular reference to the issue of who has the authority to draw the line—is far from being resolved in the medical, legal, or philosophical spheres.

The Biological Event

One can approach the question of a medical definition of death through the time-honored riddle about the biological beginning of life: Which came first, the chicken or the egg? An equally puzzling riddle can be posed about the biological end of life: Which dies first, the cells or the whole person? On the one hand, extensive experiments have shown that death does not seem to be a necessary function of individual cells. On the other hand, dying seems to be part of the natural history of human beings. People normally go through stages of growth, as a somewhat cynical Shakespearean character relates in the famous "All the world's a stage" speech; there the " . . . Last scene of all, / That ends this strange eventful history, / Is second childishness and mere oblivion, / Sans teeth, sans eyes, sans taste, sans everything" (Shakespeare, *As You Like It,* 1952, pp. 163–166).

Looking more closely at the curious fact that the script for the "last scene of all" does not seem to be firmly programmed in human cells, one finds a history of biological research that extends back to the turn of the century. Oft-cited studies on one-celled protozoa and paramecia were published in 1902 by G. N. Calkins and in 1914 by L. L. Woodruff and R. Erdman (Ferrater Mora, 1965). Protozoa are those endlessly busy creatures that every beginning biology student has seen through a microscope focused on stagnant pond water. These organisms reproduce by fission: they divide themselves in two; the resulting two divide into two more and so on indefinitely. If leaving behind a corpse is a prerequisite for death, these one-celled, primitive organisms do not die. Most of the early experiments consisted in seeing how long such creatures could live in a controlled culture that removed the usual external causes of death. It appeared that they could go on and on.

Experiments with the same end in mind—to see whether living cells carry within themselves the cause of their own death—have been conducted with cells belonging to more complicated creatures. Tissue from the heart of a chicken embryo was kept alive in a nutrient medium for fifteen years. Muscle cells, nerve cells, kidney cells, connective tissue, and many other kinds of cells have been kept alive for sustained periods in nutritive solutions (in vitro) (*Encyclopaedia Britannica,* 1974, s.v. "Death"). But even these experiments do not solve the initial riddle; they only raise the same problem on a cellular level. To put the riddle another way, "Of course, we observe the close association between youth and the capacity [for a cell] to divide, but the relation of cause and effect has not been adequately investigated: Does the cell age because it does not divide or does it fail to divide because it ages?" (Hammerling, 1965, p. 126).

Human beings are made up of many cells and many types of cells. Some human cells can rejuvenate themselves, some cannot; some cellular systems can function even when other cellular systems have failed. For instance, the heart can beat while the nerve cells in the brain are dead. Since man is composed of cells, and it is doubtful that cells carry the cause of death within them, why do people die?

No one knows. "As of now, no one has been able to discover any factor, processes, or principles inherent in an organism and leading inevitably to aging and death" (Ferrater Mora, 1965, p. 127).

The biological event of death thus remains a mystery. Do persons age because their "parts" wear out, or do "parts" wear out because people age? Is death part of an inevitable process or is it accidental, caused by injuries and diseases that obtrude from the external environment? These questions are important to keep in mind as one studies the definitions of death that influence medical diagnoses of death as these are pronounced every day in hospitals around the country.

If death were clearly understood as a biological event, and if scientists were able to construct a model of something like "the death function in cells or integrated cellular systems," today's massive conflict among theories and practices would not exist. A doctor could simply look to see whether the death function was operative. The law would confine itself to squabbles over who inherits what, and to cases of foul play.

However, the moment of death is not caused by a simple mechanical flick of a "death switch," nor is it triggered by a preset time mechanism. Humankind cannot be reduced to a mechanical model any more than it can be considered completely spiritual. The problem of defining death, even as a biological event, leads to consideration of how closely knit together is human physical and nonphysical being.

As the situation now stands, a person may be considered alive in one hospital and considered dead according to another definition employed in a hospital across town. The contemporary quandary about death stems from two major problems in defining the biological event of death. First, death has no positive characteristics that can be recognized and written down on a hospital chart to pinpoint the moment of death. Death is always recorded as the *absence* of some function—the patient no longer breathes, the heart no longer beats, the electroencephalograph registers no electrical activity in the brain. Second, the whole body does not die at once. Individual cells die at a slower rate than the systems that make up a human being's vital functions: heartbeat and breath. Those vital functions, also known as the somatic structure, may cease to operate, but the individual cells can live on. The whole recently devised practice of organ transplanting depends on that biological fact. An individual may be pronounced dead and his or her heart will still be alive and able to function when placed in a living person. The practice of organ transplanting also makes establishment of the precise moment of death more important since the viability of an organ is limited once the vital functions have ceased.

The curious fact that the whole person dies before the constituent parts die was formally recorded as far back as 1836. "Individuals who are apparently destroyed in a sudden manner, by certain wounds, diseases or even decapitation, are not really dead, but are only in conditions incompatible with the persistence of life" (Ryan, 1976, p. 499). Of course, that was not the first notice taken of a body's ability to function while "in conditions incompatible with the persistence of life." Any youngster on a farm could confirm that observation—chop off a chicken's head and the body will run around wildly without the head.

Other phenomena may be noted. Muscles will contract in response to an electrical current for up to two hours after somatic death. In 1811, a French physician-researcher used the electric current test to diagnose death: when muscles failed to contract when the current was applied, the person was dead (Mant, 1976, p. 225). Checking for reflexes has been a common way to determine whether death had taken place. All of the traditional ways of defining death in medical practice, in fact, consisted in looking for vital signs—or their absence. Since tissues die at differential rates, various tests could be carried out as the different tissues ceased to function. The earliest tests were simple, visual observations of vital signs. Is the person breathing? Hold a feather to the lips, a mirror to the nostrils. With more sophisticated medical knowledge, pulse could be checked as a sign of heartbeat; later, the reflexes of the eye could be checked.

More primitive methods were hardly trustworthy, as the story of *Romeo and Juliet* poignantly dramatized. Medical literature is full of gruesome tales of people buried alive—or almost buried alive. "John Bruhier, a Paris physician of the 18th century, collected histories of persons alleged to have been buried alive. He gave 52 alleged examples of premature burial and 12 mistaken certificates of death, and recommended that burial should not take place until early putrefaction had occurred" (Mant, 1976, p. 221). Equating the state of death with putrefaction certainly provides the safest medical definition of death.

The fear of premature burial drove people to demand more precise medical definitions and prompted some bizarre requests such as decapitation and surgical incisions (Mant, 1976, p. 227). The traditional signs of recent death that are still useful in diagnosing death include absence of heartbeat, which is indicated by lack of pulse; absence of breathing, which is indicated by blueing of the extremities, mouth, and lips; and lack of reflexes in the pupil of the eye (*Encyclopaedia Britannica*, 1974, s.v. "Death").

In addition, as the whole body dies the skeletal muscles of the head, neck, and lower extremities stiffen in *rigor mortis*. The body temperature falls to that of the environment (*algor mortis*), and a purple-red discoloration of body parts results from the setting of the blood (*livor mortis*). Since *algor mortis, rigor mortis,* and *livor mortis* appear at somewhat predictable intervals after death, they are useful in pinpointing the moment of death. *Algor mortis* is especially useful. Since bodily temperature decreases at a rate depending on the temperature of the external environment, the time elapsing between death and the discovery of the body can be calculated if the external temperature is known and has been consistent (*Encyclopaedia Britannica*, 1974, s.v. "Death").

The traditional signs of death are not mere excerpts from ancient history. They appear in medico-legal books today. They also have significance that goes beyond empirical evidence for the state of death. The absence of heartbeat and breathing are particularly hallowed means of specifying death. Since primitive times, breathing as an activity and breath itself have been associated with the spirit—*pneuma* or *anima*—and considered part of an individual's nonmaterial existence. "Medicine men, in anticipation of modern mouth-to-mouth resuscitation techniques, often tried to blow the spirit back into the body, with occasional success" (Lasagna, 1968, p. 225). One materialistic philosopher, the Greek atomist Democritus, is reported to have held off death for days by inhaling the aroma of freshly baked bread (Freeman, 1947, p. 38). Some medieval pictures show dying people literally breathing out their final breath.

The heartbeat, like the functioning of the lungs, keeps the vital fluids pumping through the body. One contemporary thanatologist points out that "What the traditional concept of death centered on was not the heart and lungs as such, but the flow of the vital fluids, that is, the breath and the blood" (Veatch, 1976b, p. 30).

A 1972 medical dictionary defined death as "The apparent extinction of life, as manifested by the absence of heartbeat and respiration" (*Encyclopaedia and Dictionary of Medicine and Nursing*, 1972, s.v. "Death"). Lack of heartbeat and breathing is also part of the definition of death in the 1976 editions of *Steadman's Medical Dictionary* and *Blackston's Gould Medical Dictionary*, as well as the most recent, *Lawyer's Edition* of *Steadman's Medical Dictionary* (1972). But mention of the traditional signs of death comprises only part of the definitions of death that appear in these standard reference works. An additional part of the definition indicates an entirely new era in the understanding of death and an entirely new era in medicine. The addition refers to the cessation of activity in the brain—or brain death.

Brain Death

In lay terms, the brain functions to integrate the activities of the central nervous system. When blood ceases to flow to the brain's cells, supplying them with oxygen, they die in a relatively short time. Obviously, the flow of vital fluids—breath and blood—represents a crucial factor in the life of the brain. In the ordinary sequence of events, the heart and lungs cease functioning and then the brain cells die. As one commentator observed, "under normal circumstances a person is as dead today as he was a thousand years ago if his heart does not beat for five minutes" (Mant, 1976, p. 231).

Marvels of medical technology have extended the body's ability to survive. The new machines include the artificial respirator, cardiac resuscitation units, heart and lung machines, and machines for cleansing the blood. Cardiac massage and electric shock can start a heart beating again, even after the five minutes it takes for a brain to be irreversibly damaged. The ordinary sequence of events is no longer the necessary sequence of events. The vital flow of fluids can be maintained mechanically after the brain has ceased to function.

It is worthwhile to examine the organ that is now the focus of so much controversy regarding the definitions of death—legal definitions and religious/philosophical definitions as well as medical definitions.

The brain, as the chief coordinating center of the body and of the personality as a whole, is divided into three parts. The cerebrum, or cerebral hemisphere, forms the largest and topmost section of the brain. The cerebellum is located at the lower back of the cranial area. The brain stem, extending from underneath the cerebellum to the spinal cord, contains three sections, the midbrain, the pons, and the medulla. Commonly, the "grey matter" we think of as our brain is really the cerebrum; it also contains white matter and nerve ganglia that coordinate all the ingoing and outgoing impulses (Heifetz, 1975, p. 192). The smaller cerebellum is in charge of balance and coordination, while the brain stem conducts messages from the intricate "switchboard" of cerebral ganglia down through the spinal cord. The brain stem has an important controlling function in addition to its role as "message conveyor"; it also controls breathing. Since the heart's controlling centers lie mostly within itself, it is possible for someone to sustain an injury that destroys the cerebrum and still continue to have breath and heartbeat without the aid of machinery (Heifetz, 1975, p. 193). The term "brain death" thus refers usually to the absence of activity in all three parts of the brain, not just in one part. Some physicians and thanatologists think that the "whole-brain" definition of death is too conservative and results in ministering to dead bodies as though they were alive.

The EEG Test

Electroencephalograph (EEG) translates roughly as "electric-brain-writer." This machine is the one most often mentioned in accounts of tests for brain death. The EEG is an apparatus with amplifiers and a write-out system for recording the electric activity generated by the brain and derived from leads placed on the scalp (*Steadman's Medical Dictionary, Lawyer's Edition,* 1972, s.v. "Electroencephalograph"). Normally, people generate four different kinds of brain waves, depending on their emotional states, what activities they are engaged in, and whether or not they are asleep. These four kinds of impulses register on the EEG write-out system as various kinds of squiggly lines. A flat (isoelectric) line indicates no brain activity.

Once the brain registers a straight EEG line, there are only two circumstances in which recovery is believed possible. One circumstance occurs in the case of a drug overdose; the other occurs when the body temperature has been lowered to the point where the body is effectively in hibernation. Chilling the body to induce a flat EEG reading is a procedure used in modern heart surgery. When the patient is warmed up after the operation, the vital functions spontaneously begin pulsating the vital fluids again and the patient is restored, even though the brain registered a "brain death" and the heart registered a "heart death" (Mant, 1976, p. 229).

The EEG machine that everyone has heard so much about is not an infallible indicator of death. Indeed, a supposed brain death may not be death at all. There are remarkable cases on record of people recovering their senses after prolonged periods of oxygen deprivation.

Traditionally, scientific dogma has maintained that the brain can survive only three to five minutes without blood flow, but recently a young California woman who had sustained a ruptured heart in an auto accident recovered rapidly and completely following emergency surgery, despite the fact that twenty-one minutes of complete circulatory arrest had elapsed. (Lasagna, 1968, p. 226.)

A similar case involved a Norwegian youngster who was nearly drowned, having been submerged in a freezing river for twenty-two minutes. After touch-and-go emergency measures such as heart massage, drug injections, and blood transfusions, his vital functions started to work spontaneously. Later, "he relapsed into total unconsciousness for five weeks and during part of this time had no measurable brain function at all: in the jargon he was 'decerebrate.' However . . . , six months later he was back at home, a normal child again" (Leach, 1970, pp. 269–270).

Severe barbiturate poisoning has also produced cases of flat EEG readings in which the patients recovered. In spite of the evidence that a flat EEG does not always indicate death, " . . . some biologists accept one minute as incontrovertible proof of death" (Mant, 1976, p. 230).

Supporting the use of the EEG in diagnosing death is the 1970 case of 2,642 comatose patients whose brains were dead—all registered flat EEGs. Only three recovered. Those three had taken drugs and could be excluded from consideration with the overwhelming empirical data that a brain-dead person does not return to the world of consciousness (Veatch, 1975, pp. 27–28).

Besides the EEG machine, other laboratory equipment that is used in determining death includes the angiograph and isotope scanner. The angiograph produces a radiography of the vascular system of the brain once a contrasting material has been injected into the bloodstream (Dorland's Illustrated Medical Dictionary, 1972, s.v. "Angiography"). The contrasting material shows up on the X-ray plate if the blood is flowing to the brain; otherwise, the blood stops at the base of the skull: no blood flow, no oxygen, no life in the brain. This technique of diagnosing death had a turn-of-the-century forerunner. A French doctor recommended the injection of a dye into the bloodstream and pointed out that if the person were alive, the whole body would turn a different color shortly after the injection (Mant, 1976, p. 227).

Isotope scanning works on the same principle: the objective is to ascertain whether the blood is supplying oxygen to the brain. Isotopes are shot into the bloodstream and the rate at which they enter and pass through the brain is recorded by a radioactive measuring device (Heifetz, 1975, pp. 198–199).

Such are the tools now available to the physician faced with the task of determining brain death. The physician's judgment that the brain has died may also be influenced by observations of five important reflexes that indicate that the brain stem is not functioning. If the brain stem is not functioning, it is unlikely that the cerebrum is functioning, though, conversely, some parts of the brain stem may be alive while the cerebral cortex is not functioning. The five key reflexes, starting from the midbrain section, are, according to Heifetz (1975):

1. The pupil of the eye, usually dilated in death, will not contract when exposed to light.
2. The eye will not blink when the cornea is touched.
3. There is no proper reaction in the semicircular canals of the ear to such stimulations as ice water flushed against the eardrum, or turning the head quickly from side to side. "When the brain stem is functioning, if the head is rapidly turned from side to side, the eyes will momentarily hold the same position that they were in. . . . When this important reflex disappears, the eyes turn with the head" (p. 196).
4. The throat or trachea does not respond by gagging when stimulated.
5. There is no spontaneous respiration. Dr. Heifetz (1975) qualifies the last criterion by noting that four minutes without breathing must elapse and the carbon dioxide concentration in the blood must be normal (pp. 196–197).

The criteria for brain death are clearly connected with the traditional kinds of observations of the lack of various kinds of reflexes. The main objection to continuing to use such traditional tests of death is that someone may be considered alive who is really dead. Many today contend that it is better to be morally safe than sorry. Others say it is an affront to the dignity of individuals to treat them as though they were alive when they are dead. Still others cite the priorities of the living who may need the organs of the "dead" person, or who could be benefiting from the attention and equipment "wasted" on a person who is kept alive by machines. On the one side stands the physician who is committed to doing all that is possible for the patient; on the other side is the physician who cannot continue to treat a corpse without being accused of trying to hide the time of death for some nefarious political or financial reasons.

It is equally true that physicians cannot stop treating a patient whom they consider dead because the brain is no longer functioning—

or they risk legal charges of "killing" the patient by stopping the heart-lung machine or whatever life-support systems are being employed.

Two main controversies may be isolated from the arguments centering on identification of the whole brain with the death of an individual. The overarching controversy focuses on the statement that the death of the brain is the same as the death of the individual. The second, and equally important, controversy turns on the question whether the whole brain should be considered the location where death takes place, or whether "we are really interested only in man's consciousness: in his ability to think, reason, feel, experience, interact with others . . ." (Veatch, 1976a, p. 235). Human consciousness does not take form in the brain stem, but in the cerebrum; therefore, the reasoning goes, it is only necessary for the cerebrum to die; then death has occurred. It is possible, however, that the cerebrum can be destroyed and the heart and lungs still function.

Identifying the brain as the essence of the individual, so that when the brain dies it can be said that the person dies, represents another highly controversial judgment. An important difference exists between the statement that the brain no longer functions and the pronouncement that a person has died. The first statement is based on empirical observations of the type detailed earlier—EEG tests or observations of reflexes. The second statement is not an empirical criterion of death; it is a judgment about what is vital to the nature of a human being—a value judgment on what constitutes the *sine qua non* of human existence.

Holding that brain death means final, irreducible death attributes the essence of human life to the functions of the brain. On the practical level of hospital procedures, affirmation or denial of both the criterion of brain death and the judgment of death of the person are important. The physician must know whether to treat a patient as alive or dead. Family and friends need to know whether to go into mourning or not. Heirs of the estate need to know their legal rights.

If the brain has died, the physician can continue respirators, intravenous feeding, and medication—in other words, continue mechanically and chemically to integrate the bodily functions normally carried on by the brain. After all, as has been pointed out, it is not merely the physical brain tissue that is important in the definition of brain death, but the brain functions that are so crucial to human nature: " . . . consciousness; motor control; sensory feeling; ability to reason; control over bodily functions including respiration and circulation; major integrating reflexes controlling blood pressure; ion levels, and pupil size; and so forth" (Veatch, 1976b, pp. 36–37). The same author calls all those mechanisms and functions "the capacity for bodily integration" (Veatch, 1976b, p. 37). He feels that "Terms such as *brain death* or *heart death* should be avoided because they tend to obscure the fact that we are searching for the meaning of the death of the person as a whole" (Veatch, 1976b, p. 37).

The debate seems endless. The counterargument to the claim that life must be sustained under any circumstances runs: Where breath is artificially maintained, there is only artificial hope.

But what if an individual has retained the lower brain functions and is able to breathe without an artificial respirator after the higher brain functions have ceased? The controversy over what portions of the brain are to be considered important in brain death is the second key point of contention in the brain-death thesis. The possible but rather rare situation of a breathing but otherwise vegetating individual has led some to reject the "whole-brain" definition of brain death. These want to refine the concept of whole-brain death—not because there might occur a few rare cases of breathing people who were pronounced dead, but because those persons might *not* be pronounced dead.

The possibility of mistaking a dead person for a live person is thus a major concern. The whole-brain death concept has been rejected on the basis of two interlocking points. First, those who want to redefine the brain-death concept assume that the presence of some of the reflex action controlled by the lower brain stem does not necessarily indicate any additional functioning in the cerebrum. "If we can make this assumption, it seems very doubtful that the ability to contract and dilate the pupils and to execute any other reflex arc which happens to pass through the brain stem is in any way a significant sign of human living" (Veatch, 1975, p. 24). Secondly, the redefiners hold that a person's inability to interact socially is as important, if not more important, than the ability to integrate bodily functions. "The ability to maintain nerve circuitry to carry out . . . reflexes does not really add significantly to man's integrating capacity. Certainly it does not directly measure capacity to experience or interact socially" (Veatch, 1975, p. 24).

One school of thought, in consequence, distinguishes between brain death and cerebral death, holding that heart and lung machines should be shut off when the patient is cerebrally dead (Maguire, 1973, p. 17). Veatch maintains in turn that the EEG test would be the definitive test for determining death if the "experiential and social interaction concept of death is held or a related one oriented to more narrow brain functions . . ." (Veatch, 1975, p. 28). Accordingly, once a flat line appeared on the EEG machine, and if drugs or lowered body temperature could be ruled out as causes of the isoelectric reading, then the patient could be ruled dead and the decision to keep the blood purified and the heart and lungs pumping would depend on considerations and situations external to the individual. In particular, the need for organ transplants, or the patient's own express desire to donate his or her organs, would supersede the medical purpose of keeping the individual alive in some meaningful sense.

The notion of a "meaningful sense" of life is an important addition in the search for the medical definition of death. As physicians move from the empirical observation that brain death has occurred to action based on the judgment that the patient is no longer alive, the notion of man as a social animal comes to the fore.

Ethical and philosophical factors impinge on medical definitions no matter how one looks at the problem of finding a medical definition of death. That curious fact itself draws attention to the unusual status of human beings, and some would say, of sublunar life in general. Human beings cannot be reduced to the level of machines. Though medical criteria, legal judgments, and philosophical concepts operate on different levels, they have to be coordinated if modern man is to be successful in the search for a definition of death.

The question now to be raised is: What kind of brain activities are crucial to man as a social animal? Obviously the emotional and rational activities of human beings are the ones that are part of daily life. The very ability to live together, to communicate, to participate in some way in the general "hum" of human society all represent important humanness. Aristotle made a similar observation when he defined man as a political animal. But Aristotle was not establishing a medical definition that was intended to be functional in medical practice.

Consciousness and the capacity for social action can be absent, but some physical reactions may still persist in a patient. Brierly and his colleagues reported cases in which the "neocortex was dead while certain brainstems and spinal centers remained intact" (Brierly, 1971, p. 49).

If death is defined as "the irreversible loss of consciousness or the capacity for social intercourse" (Veatch, 1976b, p. 53), and if that situation can be established by giving the EEG test to the neocortex, then physicians may use the EEG test as the major criterion in diagnosing death. Yet some vital functions may be spontaneously present. Veatch (1975) has claimed that "one who would see the experiential and social function of man as essential to his nature would not find spontaneous respiration a sufficient indicator of human life" (p. 25). In response, one might well ask, "Would you bury a breathing body?" There is something viscerally repugnant about the thought of behaving toward a breathing body as though it were dead. It may be far better to err by treating a dead person as though alive, rather than mistake a living person for a dead one (Veatch, 1975, p. 14).

The purpose of settling on a medical definition of death was once primarily the prevention of the burial of someone who was still alive. Fear of pronouncing someone dead who is still alive remains the primary restraint on those who must decide whether or not to pronounce a person dead. The advent of organ transplants has heightened the need for publicly stated medical definitions of death— or at least has caused several major medical organizations to grapple with the definition of death and offer guidelines for medical usage.

Formal Guidelines

Definitions and guidelines have been published by the World Health Organization, by the French Academy of Medicine, by the World Medical Association, and by various committees (Lasagna, 1968). Probably the best known guidelines for diagnosing death came in 1968 from the Harvard Ad Hoc Committee to Examine the Definition of Brain Death.

The World Health Organization defined death as the permanent disappearance of life, with no possibility of resuscitation (Lasagna, 1968, p. 226). The United Nations Vital Statistics office has defined death as the permanent disappearance of every sign of life. At least one physician would like to rephrase that statement to read: "Death has occurred when every spontaneous vital function has ceased permanently" (Voigt, 1976, p. 227). But even that refinement has critics. What, some ask, happens if we apply that definition to someone who has met a violent death—someone beheaded or hanged? Spontaneous vital functions may still be present after decapitation or hanging (Mant, 1976, p. 228).

The general medical definitions are unsatisfactory because it has become necessary to know when, exactly, death occurred, especially if organ transplanting is involved. Thus, the World Health Organization's definition and that of the United Nations Vital Statistics office appear unsatisfactory as *medical* definitions. But even though those definitions do not deal with the precise moment of death or cover all possible cases of brain death, they articulate a traditional concern relating to the physician's duty to the patient. That concern has appeared in formal statements on medical ethics from the Oath of Hippocrates and the Oath of Maimonides to the World Medical Association's 1948 Declaration and the American Medical Association's 1973 Principles of Medical Ethics (Heifetz, 1975). No matter how urgently another patient needs the organ of a patient who is adjudged to be dying, it has been considered unethical to hasten death.

Some thanatologists have advocated establishment of new guidelines on death so that what formerly would have been considered unethical might be considered ethical in the future. "While the potential for use of human organs for therapeutic transplantation should never justify the adoption of a new understanding of what is essentially significant to human life and death, it may require a philosophically responsible clarification of imprecise use of these terms adequate only in a time when little morally critical was at stake" (Veatch, 1975, p. 13).

In plain English, what that amounts to is calling a patient dead who would have been considered alive according to older standards. Thus one neatly avoids the issue of mercy killing and the problem of preferential treatment of a patient in need of an organ of a dying patient.

In response to the twentieth-century dilemma centering on two alternatives—keeping a "vegetable" alive or withdrawing medical attention—Ramsey (1975), a Princeton theologian, qualified the physician's duties this way:

> Never abandon care of the dying except when they are irretrievably inaccessible to human care. Never hasten the dying process except when it is entirely indifferent to the patient whether his dying is accomplished by an intravenous bubble of air or by the withdrawal of useless ordinary natural remedies such as nourishment. (p. 63.)

Such "guidelines" inevitably raise questions. How is the physician to know when the patient is "indifferent" to being alive or dead? One way may be to establish brain death. The rest of the medical definitions that came out of the 1960s and the subsequent laws that some states adopted in the 1970s are concerned primarily with criteria for establishing brain death.

In response to today's deepening controversy over guidelines, the French Academy of Medicine in 1968 accepted the death of the brain as an indication of the "irrevocable loss of function of an indispensable organ" (Lasagna, 1968, p. 226). In 1968, the twenty-second World Medical Assembly published further detailed guidelines for physicians seeking to diagnose death (Heifetz, 1975, pp. 190–191). The Assembly listed these main points:

1. Total lack of response to external stimuli.
2. No muscular movements, especially breathing. "If the patient is on a mechanical respirator, this may be turned off for three minutes in order to establish that he is capable of breathing himself" (Heifetz, 1975, p. 191).
3. No reflexes.
4. Flat electroencephalogram.

The most often cited criteria for defining death were also published in 1968. The Ad Hoc Committee of the Harvard Medical School to Examine the Definition of Brain Death (s.v. Harvard Medical School, 1968) covered essentially the same points as the World Medical Assembly:

1. Unreceptivity and unresponsivity.
2. No movements or breathing.
3. No reflexes.
4. Flat electroencephalogram.

The Harvard committee noted that the EEG is "of great confirmatory value . . ." and went on to detail the best way to take EEG readings. The committee also recommended that the EEG test should be repeated at least twenty-four hours later, adding that EEG data are invalid in cases of lowered body temperature and drug poisoning (s.v. Harvard Medical School, 1968, pp. 205–337).

Some confusion has arisen out of interpretations of what the Harvard Committee was doing when it established its criteria. While the committee's title indicated that it sought to define brain death, the actual criteria refer specifically to "irreversible coma." The committee hedged on the issue of identifying irreversible coma with death, or brain death with irreversible coma. The committee may have been justified in sidestepping the issue: suggesting guidelines for physicians and establishing either legal definitions or ethical recommendations fall in different realms.

A 1972 proposal by Capron and Kass tried to establish a more compact set of guidelines. Part of the authors' short proposal read: "In the event that artificial means of support preclude a determination that these functions have ceased, a person will be considered dead if in the announced opinion of a physician, based on ordinary standards of medical practice, he has experienced an irreversible cessation of spontaneous brain functions" (Capron & Kass, 1972, p. 121).

That definition not only throws the problem back to the physician but brings up a question of medical ethics. Just how much authority should the physician have in determining death? Does the patient have any authority? What role in the determination of death should the family have? Do religious leaders—priest, rabbi, or pastor—have any authority in the matter?

The same conference of the World Medical Association that published criteria for brain death was clear about what it thought the physician's role should be. The conference said: "No single technological criterion is entirely satisfactory in the present state of medicine, nor can any one technological procedure be substituted for the overall judgment of the physician" (Veatch, 1976b, p. 57). What the World Medical Association was particularly worried about was legislation that would lock on one set of standards that might quickly become out of date as new medical discoveries were made.

Medical authority is clearly sovereign when it comes to establishing criteria for the death of certain organs. But once medical authority extends beyond the realm of empirically verifiable data and into the realm of "overall judgment," the physician's authority can be challenged from many sides. One commentator enumerates no fewer than seven reasons why the physician should not be the one to decide who should live and who should die (Maguire, 1975, p. 178 ff). Starting with the reason that doctors have no special wisdom and certainly no superhuman wisdom, the list continues with the view that such authority would compromise the medical profession.

Margaret Mead, the noted anthropologist, agrees with the latter point. She has also declared that society should go out of its way to protect the medical profession against being the final authority. She focuses the issue with stark clarity by noting, "The real issue that we are talking about . . . is the issue of whether the physician should ever be asked to perform, on a patient who still has any life in him at all, an operation which means certain death" (Mead, 1970, p. 14).

Maguire's reasons (1975) for limiting the physician's authority represent a cogent summation of such arguments. The author points to the advent of the specialist who is not qualified to counsel the patient or the patient's family in problems involving moral decisions— even though the specialist's expertise may be outstanding in his or her area (Maguire, 1975, pp. 180–181). Yet another reason is the increasing tendency to see the patient "as datum among data" (Maguire, 1975, p. 181). This tendency has been generated by the trend toward experimentation, which creates a conflict of interest between what is good for the patient and what is good for the "experiment." Some commentators have been even more critical of the experimental tendencies of medical technology. "We can, through misuse of ability and knowledge, unwittingly indulge in a bestial form of cruelty hidden under an arrogance of technical flexing of muscles" (Heifetz, 1975, p. 124).

Maguire (1975) makes still other points. "In consigning the decision over death to a physician," he notes, "you are actually adopting his particular religion or philosophical bias as determinative of wisdom and morality . . ." (p. 181). He also stresses that doctors have no special training in moral decisions and that some doctors are not even competent as physicians (Maguire, 1975, p. 181).

The nurse may be more personally involved with the patient than the doctor. Yet the same set of objections could logically apply to the nurse in cases where the decision to prolong treatment has to be made.

Two related issues are actually involved in the emotionally charged problem of who can assign authority to draw the line between life and death. First, there is the issue of who has the right to define death. Secondly, one faces the issue of who has the right to allow death to happen—also known as the issue of euthanasia, as the right-to-die issue, or as the death-with-dignity issue. Resolution of that issue depends on the definition of death and specification of those who have the authority to make definitions of death.

Some authorities have suggested that organizations of physicians should have the power to define death. Suggestions regarding such organizations range from state medical societies (Veatch, 1976b) to hospital staff committees (Maguire, 1975). But, though professional consensus or committee-made definitions may avoid the problems of individual prejudice or medical incompetence, other problems involving "special wisdom" and the compromise of the medical profession would remain. As Veatch (1976b) puts it, "Why should I have to be pronounced dead or alive because there is a consensus of those trained in biology and medicine in favor of the philosophical concept of life which focuses upon fluid flow or integrating capacities or consciousness?" (p. 61).

Clearly, different levels of responsibility are involved in the definition of death. One may turn to the seminal ideas in Western thought to distinguish those levels. Everyone has heard of Aristotle's "four causes" (Aristotle, 1957, p. 7), but not everyone realizes that the word used for cause includes the notion of responsibility (literally, answering back). Pursuing the etymologically older meaning of cause, namely responsibility, one can distinguish four levels of responsibility in the definition of death. (The word "responsibility" appears preferable because it avoids the misconception of thinking of the four "causes" as sequential, which they are not.)

The *material* responsibility could be defined as the various particular tests, such as those mentioned earlier in determining brain death—EEG and others—or tests to check heartbeat or lung function. The *efficient* responsibility would be what has been called the "operational criteria" (Capron & Kass, 1972, p. 104) that are used to carry out the general physiological criteria. At present there are two operational criteria: the traditional criteria of the flow of vital fluids and the recently proposed criteria of irreversible cessation of spontaneous brain functions, as specified by the Harvard Committee. The *formal* responsibility could be assigned as the definition of the area of the body whose functioning is critical. Veatch calls this level of definition the "locus" of death (Veatch, 1976b, pp. 42–45, 53, 68). The *final* responsibility consists of the philosophical concept of death itself.

Obviously, the individual physician is in charge of the material responsibility, for the physician administers the tests. Just as obviously, the medical profession must bear the efficient responsibility of deciding which tests best determine the material criteria. The formal responsibility is not entirely a matter for the medical profession since it involves choosing which portion of the human being is the most vital to the whole person—is it the brain alone or the cardiopulmonary system? Legal authority may have its place at this level.

The final responsibility belongs neither to the individual physician nor to the medical profession. "The basic concept of death is fundamentally a philosophical matter. Examples of possible definitions of death . . . include 'permanent cessation of the integrated functioning of the organism as a whole,' departure of the animating or vital principle, or 'irreversible loss of personhood'" (Capron & Kass, 1972, p. 103). The choice of basic concept will determine to a great extent the formal general standards; the general standards will limit the efficient operational criteria; the operational criteria will determine the material tests. Thus all the levels of the definition of death are linked to the final responsibility for the definition.

Society itself, along with religious leaders, has traditionally borne the responsibility for the final definition of death. More recently, remarkable advances in medical science, social consensus, and religious tradition contributed to the formal definition of death as well.

Individuals in a democracy have always had the right to their own religious beliefs. As long as an individual's beliefs do not require practices that run contrary to society's prevailing norms, everything runs smoothly. Some groups, such as Jehovah's Witnesses, who refuse medical treatment, fly in the face of accepted medical practice, and thus come in conflict with the opinions of the majority of people.

Because it is fundamental to American democracy to preserve the rights of the individual, it seems that some flexibility must be allowed in both the final and formal definitions of death. That means that medical practice on the efficient and formal levels of criteria would not be everywhere and always consistent. Nonetheless, individuals—the patient and the family—have the right to their beliefs and the right to expect treatment in a hospital that is consistent with those beliefs. Affirmation of that right may well require legislation.

Legal Definitions

A county probate judge, Hon. Michael T. Sullivan, thinks that the individual alone "should decide whether he will employ the Harvard criteria or some other definition for his death" (Sullivan, 1973, p. 216). He has extended this line of thinking into a general statement about a patient's authority over his or her own death: "The polestar of any legislation must be the dying person's right to make decisions concerning all his interrelationships. This is because death decisions as well as life decisions belong to him" (p. 210). Problems attending that point of view arise where the person has no views on the subject or has not made them known.

Unfortunately, the literature of thanatology is replete with cases where patient's "rights" are subjugated to such factors as standard hospital procedures (Kübler-Ross, 1970, p. 65), and cases in which the patient's beliefs are not questioned before medical procedures are instigated. The Tucker case revealed a classic conflict between individual authority and medical authority. It resulted in a court decision that broke with the traditional legal definition of death. By rights, it was maintained, the physician should have obtained permission from Tucker's brother before removing his heart. Further legal complications could have arisen from application of the new brain-death criteria. What if Tucker's brother had had designs on Tucker's estate and wanted the moment of his brother's death to be postponed as long as possible? That is, in short: If the authority for defining death is left solely in the hands of the individual patient or members of the patient's family, how can the sincerity and justness of their wishes be judged? Who can even sit in judgment?

From a legal point of view, allowing each individual to formulate his or her own definition is not entirely satisfactory. A need exists for some kind of limiting rules or guidelines that would satisfactorily preserve the individual's rights and control medical practice without forcing doctors to risk a lawsuit every time they make a decision.

Legal statutes and court decisions provide the vehicles by which most public opinion turns into public policy. Increasingly, as conflicts between the patient and the medical profession arise, legal definitions are desired. The law has always had much to say about the circumstances of death. But until recently, the major legal distinctions have been between the causes of death: accidental death, suicide, homicide, natural causes. There are also laws covering the presumption of death.

The first legislative action establishing a definition of death other than the traditional cessation of all vital functions came in 1968 in Kansas. Most strikingly, the Kansas statute was prepared specifically to permit organs to be procured for transplantation. The law asserted that "Death is to be pronounced before artificial means of supporting respiratory and circulatory functions are terminated and before any vital organ is removed for purpose of transplantation." Another unusual feature was that the statute seemed to offer two definitions of death that can be used in different situations. Since the Kansas statute has been the model for other states—Maryland, Alaska, California, Georgia, Illinois, Michigan, New York, Oregon, and Virginia—it is worth examining in its entirety.

A person will be considered medically and legally dead if, in the opinion of a physician, based on ordinary standards of medical practice, there is the absence of spontaneous respiratory and cardiac function and, because of the disease or condition which caused, directly or indirectly, these functions to cease, or because of the passage of time since these functions ceased, attempts at resuscitation are considered hopeless; and, in this event, death will have occurred at the time these functions ceased; or

A person will be considered medically and legally dead if, in the opinion of a physician, based on ordinary standards of medical practice, there is the absence of spontaneous brain function; and if, based on ordinary standards of medical practice, during reasonable attempts to either maintain or restore spontaneous circulatory or respiratory function in the absence of aforesaid brain function, it appears that further attempts at resuscitation or supportive maintenance will not succeed, death will have occurred at the time when these conditions coincide. Death is to be pronounced before artificial means of supporting respiratory and circulatory function are terminated and before any vital organ is removed for purpose of transplantation. (Veatch, 1976b, pp. 63–64.)

The most trenchant criticisms of this statute seize on the law's purpose—facilitating organ transplants—and on the specification of alternate definitions. "To draft a statute on death inspired apparently by the desire to facilitate what must still be considered experimental surgical procedures must serve to disturb the man on the street" (Kennedy, 1971, p. 968).

Though the Kansas statute has alternative definitions, the law does not allow the patient to choose. The alternative definitions in the statute may lead to some awkward situations: the same patient might be considered dead if a doctor wanted to transplant organs, but alive if no organs were needed. That situation clearly reduces the individual to the status of an object to be used as the circumstances require.

The awkwardness involved in having two definitions of death has encouraged two critics to present this hypothetical dilemma:

. . . suppose that Mr. Smith, a dying patient . . . is found to be immunologically well matched with Mr. Jones . . . a patient awaiting a heart transplant. Under the special transplantation "definition" Smith is then declared dead, but just as the surgeons are about to remove Smith's heart, Jones suddenly dies. The doctors then decide that Smith is no longer needed as an organ donor. His condition does not meet the standards for declaring death in non-donors. Is Smith "dead" or "alive?" (Capron & Kass, 1972, p. 197.)

Attempts at legal definitions of death thus encounter serious problems. If the statute is too general, or too much concerned with "final responsibility," it mitigates against freedom of belief. If it is too specific, or too much concerned with material responsibility, it confines doctors to criteria that may soon be outmoded. One commentator has flatly stated that "There is no need for a specific legislative definition of death" because "a flexible definition is required for differing circumstances. . . . What is needed is legislative recognition that, if done without negligence, physicians may apply criteria other than cessation of respiration and circulation in death determination without fear of adverse legal consequences" (Ward, 1970, p. 156). Such reasoning reasserts the position of the physician as the authority for defining legal death.

Some unavoidable circularity results as the medical profession appears to await for the courts or legislature to define death—and the courts and legislature seem to wait for the medical profession to provide them with the pertinent facts. Decisions emanating from the courtroom are more dependent on medical testimony than on legislative statutes. "A judge's decision may be merely rubberstamping of the opinions expressed by the medical experts that appear before them . . . [and that is so] because of the adversary nature of the judicial process; testimony is usually restricted to 'twosides' on an issue and may not fairly represent the spectrum of opinion held by authorities in the field" (Capron & Kass, 1972, p. 97).

The lawyer-physician critics, Capron and Kass (1972), have offered five principles to govern the formulation of a statute on death. Since more statutes are on the way, it is important that they be phrased as accurately as possible to avoid confusing the levels of responsibility in the definition of death. Capron and Kass's (1972) five points provide excellent starting points for the critique of any pending or future legislation.

1. "The statute should concern the death of the human being, not the death of his cells, tissues, or organs, and not the death or cessation of his role as a fully functioning member of his family or community" (Capron & Kass, 1972, pp. 102–103). This first principle leaves the *final* responsibility for defining death to the individual.

2. A statute should preserve continuity with tradition. That is, a statute should supplement the standards now in practice, since they are adequate in most instances.

3. The statute should give voice to a change in method, not a new meaning to life and death.

4. The standards of determining death should apply uniformly to all people, without regard to an individual's possible status as an organ donor.

5. The statute should leave room for medical advances (Capron & Kass, 1972, pp. 104–105).

To that list Veatch (1976b) would add that "the physicians pronouncing death should be free of significant conflict of interest—whether the interest focuses on "a respiring patient, research, continued treatment fees, or transplantation" (p. 70).

While many observers have noted the different levels of discussion involved in efforts to define death, the interlocking of those levels needs emphasis. The basic philosophical concept of death will have a bearing on the other levels of definition. In the Kansas statute, as in any statue developed according to the five principles of Capron and Kass, the brain-death criteria of death and the concomitant concept of what is essential to human life must be accepted. On the one hand, some thanatologists may object that the whole-brain concept is too conservative, and suggest that cerebral death is all that is required to conform to their concept of what is essential to mankind. On the other hand, there are those who prefer the older "whole body" definition of death because that concurs with their concept of the equal importance of body and soul in the identity of a person.

Another legislative alternative has been proposed: to amend the already existing Uniform Anatomical Gift Act. This act does not define death, but it gives an individual, next of kin, or legal guardian the authority to donate the body or organs to specified legitimate purposes. The act thus represents an unusual example of uniform judicial opinion. The Commissioners on Uniform State Laws drew up the act in 1968 and by 1971 it had been passed by all the states (Capron & Kass, 1972, p. 101). The act changes the common law concept that a will or other document indicating disposition of one's body is legally invalid.

The idea that an individual does not "own" his or her own body originated about A.D. 650, when fear of the dead impelled authorities to assign the chore of cadaver disposal to the church. The belief, followed by practice, was that the ecclesiastical courts had complete control of dead bodies; the secular courts took no interest in them. "There could therefore be no property rights in the body since the law did not recognize the corpse as a valuable entity" (Ward, 1970, p. 138).

The Uniform Anatomical Gift Act provides that the next of kin may make a gift of the patient's body immediately before death (Heifetz, 1975). Since the act does not define death, it does not define what it means by "immediately." Presumably, the decision on timing is left to the physician. But where brain death has occurred, and the heart and lungs are kept functioning, the question remains open: Is it better, perhaps, to avoid the dual definitions of brain death and cardiopulmonary death? By leaving the question undecided—by having no general medical definition or legal statute defining death—legal authority falls to the individual who can decide to be considered dead when the whole brain dies, when the upper brain functions cease, or when the whole body dies. The individual who disagrees with the concept of death properly embodied in the whole-brain or partial-brain medical criteria would have a specific right to halt any organ transplant.

One suggestion for amending the Uniform Anatomical Gift Act would involve legislative recognition of brain death. Physicians would not then risk legal action in attempting an organ transplant. The amendment would, perhaps, read: "If cadaver organs or parts are to be used for transplantation, and if death is to be determined by criteria other than irreversible cessation of heartbeat and respiration, such determination must be made by two concurring physicians, neither of whom shall participate in the transplant procedures" (Ward, 1970, p. 156).

Another proposal regarding a shift of the legal authority to define death from the physician to the individual was offered by Sullivan (1973). Essentially, the proposal suggests a "statutory" declaration that "the constitutional right securative of life encompasses the individual's right within lawful means to choose his path of death" (Sullivan, 1973, p. 216). It would be further specified that people have the right to prescribe their death style, "particularly statutory creation of a proctorship to insure enforcement" of:

1. Relationship with physicians, clergy, hospitals, nurses, paraprofessionals, and family;
2. Death definition and organ donations;
3. Funeral directions (Sullivan, 1973, p. 216).

Along similar lines Veatch (1976b) has suggested a provision for individuals who have not recorded their definitions of death. He has suggested that the authority to make death decisions be transferred to the next of kin or legal guardian. The same authority has suggested setting up a general legal standard that would be separate from the Uniform Anatomical Gift Act and would be followed unless specifically contradicted by the individual or the individual's next of kin or legal guardian. He words his proposal for a "freedom of choice statute" as follows:

> It is provided . . . that no person shall be considered dead even with the announced opinion of a physician solely on the basis of an irreversible cessation of spontaneous cerebral functions if he, while competent to make such a decision, has explicitly rejected the use of this standard, or, if he has not expressed himself on the matter while competent, his legal guardian or next of kin explicitly expresses such rejection.
>
> It is further provided that no physician shall pronounce the death of any individual in any case where there is significant conflict of interest with his obligation to serve the patient (including commitment to any

other patients, research, or teaching programs which might directly benefit from pronouncing the patient dead). (Veatch, 1976b, p. 76.)

The major criticism that can be leveled against such a statute is that it requires an individual to object specifically to organ removal. Such a law would also appear to be too aggressively in favor of the brain-death criteria: "It eliminates informed consent" (Heifetz, 1975, p. 120). It would be more in keeping with the current trend of American ethics to propose a statute which specifies that no organ "harvesting" may be made unless the patient has consented or unless the next of kin or legal guardian so specifies. Such permission places the authority for the definition of death in the hands of the individual and assures that any medical procedures performed on the patient would be consistent with that patient's definition of death. In its eagerness to drive ahead in the organ transplant program, the medical profession "has given the public the erroneous impression that the harvesting of human organs is more important than the absolute assurance that the donor of an organ is dead" (Heifetz, 1975, p. 121).

Philosophical Considerations

One can assume that a statute such as Veatch (1976b) has proposed has become law. What kinds of philosophical conceptions of death would lead to acceptance of the whole-brain or neocortical "partial" brain criteria of death and what kinds of philosophical considerations could lead one to rejection of them?

Philosophical considerations of death generally flow from larger conceptualizations that try to articulate mankind's purpose, goals, and role in a created universe, in an accidental universe, or in a mechanical universe.

Traditional religious concerns, by contrast, have always been occupied with the afterlife, drawing on or prescribing specific sacred texts, rituals, and religious experience. The Judeo-Christian religions that have predominated in the West also draw on the great Greek and Roman philosophies for insight, vocabulary, and structure. Body and soul are seen as the two significant parts of every individual. The resurrection of the body is a key tenet in traditional Christianity. The more conservative the religion, the more literal, usually, are the interpretations of Scriptures. Orthodox Judaism generally forbids autopsy and Jehovah's Witnesses have fought bitter battles to prevent such medical procedures as blood transfusions.

In opposition to the traditional Western religious views of the body as somehow sacred are contemporary philosophical methods and systems. Modern secular philosophy stands opposed to the major religious traditions as regards both the concept of the afterlife and the sanctity of the corpse. For the purposes of a brief discussion of current trends in philosophical thought, it is profitable thus to examine two schools that dominate recent thinking—or that at least dominate the proverbial "groves of academe." One is the school of linguistic analysis, whose roots extend back through David Hume and the empirical tradition. The other is existentialism, which sees itself as unique to the twentieth-century human predicament.

Just as no major modern philosopher has dealt systematically with death, neither of the two major philosophical schools, including their squabbling offspring, has had anything positive to say about an afterlife or the sanctity of the corpse.

Linguistic analysts, such as A. J. Ayer (1946), have dismissed the concept of an afterlife as an unfortunate aberration of muddleheaded metaphysics. The philosopher defined "personal identity in terms of bodily identity, and bodily identity is to be defined in terms of the resemblance and continuity of sense-contents . . ." (Ayer, 1946, p. 128). When an electroencephalogram is hooked up to a person's head it can be said to be measuring the presence or lack of presence of "sense-contents." For those holding a materialistic view such as Ayer's, death of the sense-contents would be indicative of the death of the individual.

The linguistic analysis school has also asked how beliefs could be found to be true or false. "If there can be no evidence either way, there is a suspicion that the belief is vacuous or meaningless" (Smart, 1968, p. 25). In short, if one is inclined to a philosophical method that requires empirical verification for nonmaterial things, then one is not going to be concerned with traditional religious values, other than as scratching posts for sharpening one's analytical claws.

Existentialism has generally treated death as the total end of man: a resolution into nothing. Existentialism has thus treated death as entry into a complete void or an unknowable phenomenon—as nonexistence. The existentialist emphasizes coming to terms with one's inevitable nonexistence. For Heidegger (1962), the great German existentialist, coming to terms with death meant accepting one's "authentic" life. He spoke of one's "ownmost Being-toward-death" as a way to heighten everyday life (Heidegger, 1962, p. 296).

The type of philosophy toward which any individual inclines may have practical implications. A person with traditional religious beliefs would tend to follow the burial customs of his or her church. An empiricist espousing linguistic analysis might easily be a pragmatist as well. A pragmatic materialist would probably make sure that his or her organ donor card and will are up to date, and probably would not reflect on the emotional or spiritual import of impending death. People influenced by existentialism might reflect on death in order to heighten their awareness of their present life.

Few people, it should be added, subscribe wholeheartedly or exclusively to any one system of philosophy. Many factors in human experience and society influence one's personal philosophy. Among those factors are the legal systems that inform or bespeak societies' attitudes toward death—in particular legal systems that mandate certain procedures subsequent to death.

LEGAL PROCEDURES SUBSEQUENT TO DEATH

Two major legal spheres govern the procedures to be followed subsequent to death. There are, first, laws concerning burial, including laws pertaining to the types of death, the death certificate, autopsy, and inhumation. Second, there are laws concerning inheritance, including wills and probate.

The laws governing burial cover a wide variety of practices and vary from area to area, country to country. Public health laws usually specify the procedure to be followed immediately after death. Laws governing funerals, the transportation of dead bodies, and the establishment and care of cemeteries come into operation to control the next steps after death. The funeral industry is also subject to regulatory trade-practice laws as well as to laws concerning funeral directors, embalmers, undertakers, morticians, licensing, and so forth.

Coincidentally, the funeral industry has its own rules and regulations that are sometimes confused in the public mind with state or local laws. For instance, most crematoria require a body to be embalmed and placed in a casket before cremation. However, in many areas there are no actual laws stating that embalming must take place.

The most traditional of the laws governing the procedures subsequent to death have to do with the coroner. The history of official death investigations goes back to at least 1149, when coroners were appointed by the King of England to determine the causes of death. They also collected taxes from property forfeited by murderers. The coroner system was brought to the United States by the English Pilgrims.

From its earliest days, the coroner's office has been a natural locus for bribery and scandal (Mant, 1972, p. 87). At the end of the nineteenth century, Massachusetts became the first state to renounce the system under which coroners who were neither medical practitioners nor lawyers were elected. Massachusetts instituted the medical examiner system. Most areas in the United States have since adopted the same system: instead of electing a coroner, a medicolegal pathologist is appointed to the post of Chief Medical Examiner. Medical examiners' legal obligations cover cases of sudden death. They must take charge of the dead body and make a complete examination of it clothed and unclothed. They must also make inquiries concerning the death with the goal of declaring the death to be from natural causes or from causes unknown. Medical examiners do not have to "improve the accuracy of the Registrar's statistical returns" (Mant, 1972, p. 94). If they are uncertain whether a death has natural causes, they may order a postmortem and send an official report to the Chief Medical Examiner. If unsatisfied, the Chief Medical Examiner may require an autopsy.

In the state of Virginia, medical examiners are paid for each death they investigate while pathologists are paid for each autopsy. The medical examiner's department in Virginia must issue all certificates for cremation. Cremation, of course, destroys any evidence of foul play. In most states using the medical examiner system, permission from the next of kin is not necessary prior to an autopsy.

The medical examiner, unlike the early English coroner, does not have any legal authority over the disposition of the decedent's property. In many states probate court, sometimes called surrogate court or orphan's court, has exclusive jurisdiction over the disposition of property (Encyclopedia Americana, 1970, s.v. "Death: Legal Aspects," p. 565).

Five legally recognized types of death are generally listed; each has special laws governing it. The five are accidental death, suicide, homicide, "legal" death, and death from natural causes. Accidental death may entail a survival statute which, in cases of death from the negligent or intentional acts of another individual, allows the decedent's estate to sue the wrongdoer just as if the decedent had not died. Next of kin may also bring suit against the wrongdoer; damages normally equal what the victim would have received if he had lived. Double indemnity provisions, accidental death insurance, and workmen's compensation benefits may also be activated when accidental death occurs (Encyclopedia Americana, 1970, s.v. "Death: Legal Aspects," p. 565).

Suicide, of course, suspends many laws and customs. Once the medical examiner or coroner has decided that a death is a case of suicide, accidental death benefits are barred and life insurance may be voided.

Homicide usually involves the law enforcement branch at once: the killer must be sought. "The medical decision is paramount here . . . for the victim and his estate have rights as defined by accidental death rules, while the murderer loses all rights to any property he might inherit from the victim" (*Encyclopedia Americana,* 1970, s.v. "Death: Legal Aspects," p. 565). If homicide is suspected after burial, exhumation may be allowed.

Death from natural causes first entails the legal procedure of a death certificate. "The death certificate—literally the passkey that unlocks the legal processes at death—becomes routine proof, or, if needed, evidence in court for such diverse activities as probate administration, homicide prosecution and payment of life insurance" (*Encyclopedia Americana,* 1970, s.v., Death: "Legal Aspects," p. 565). The World Health Organization is sponsoring a Uniform Death Certificate; but in the United States each state handles the death certificate through the vital statistics division of its health department. The death certificate is filled out by a physician. If the body is to be transported a permit is usually required (Morgan, 1975, p. 60).

Death by natural causes also entails the probate court or other administration of the estate.

Finally, death by natural causes places in operation laws regarding burial.

Historically, no one can "own" a body, yet the right of possession is recognized for purposes of disposition. That right usually falls to the surviving spouse, children, or next of kin unless the will specifies otherwise. If a member of the family objects to the way the body is disposed of, the usual procedure is to "claim damages for loss and suffering caused by unauthorized disposition" (Neilson & Watkins, 1973, p. 14). With enactment of the Uniform Anatomical Gift Act, the peculiar situation exists in which a person can donate part or all of his or her body to specific purposes, but cannot order that the remains be disposed of in a certain way. The preferences of the survivors take precedence over those of the deceased.

The only North American area to grant an individual ownership rights over the body is Quebec. Quebec went to the French legal tradition in establishing as part of its civil law that "a person may during his life dispose of his remains in whole or in part, so long as the disposition does not offend against public policy or police regulation . . . [But] in the absence of personal direction, the remains are the property of the family" (Neilson & Watkins, 1973, p. 15).

Some precedents in the United States also favor the right of self-disposition. The California Health and Safety Code declares that an individual's written or oral wishes for disposition shall be carried out unless they conflict with the duties of the coroner (Neilson & Watkins, 1973, p. 16). The code also specifies that even if the rest of a written will is declared invalid, the instructions given for disposition of the remains are to be carried out. However, if a funeral home does not carry out the instructions left it by a decedent, no laws prescribe penalties (Neilson & Watkins, 1973, p. 11).

A checklist of important legal procedures that should be given attention immediately after the death of a relative or friend would include:

1. See that a death certificate is filled out by a physician and filed with the proper authorities.
2. Arrange for burial with a mortuary, if interment is desired.
3. Arrange for cremation with a cremation certificate.
4. Arrange for donation to a medical school, if that is desired.
5. Notify insurance companies.
6. Notify the lawyer and executor.
7. Check all insurance benefits, including social security, credit union, trade union, fraternal or military benefits.
8. Check on the income for survivors from various insurance sources.
9. Check on debts and installment payments.

Obviously, the more thoughtful the planning that goes into these procedures, the easier they will be during a time of grief.

Inheritance

The legal systems that have developed from the tradition of inheritance can be traced back to the early history of ancestor worship and the emergence of the concept of real and reasonable ownership. Laws governing succession, wills, and probate are all part of the tradition of inheritance, which is the official articulation of social policy.

The circle of rights and duties originally included proper ancestor worship. A concept of individual rights to nonmaterial things can also be traced. The right to perform certain songs or dances is considered family property among some Eskimo tribes; medicine chants, magical powers, and war honors are also part of family property in some Indian tribes (Diamond, 1971, p. 190); a name is sometimes seen as belonging to a kinship group, though held by an individual.

In Jewish law, there are also references to the family rights to such incorporeal things as patents; copyrights; literary, musical, and dramatic products; trademarks; tradenames, and "anything tending to the benefit or advantage of the person who is subject to it" (Herzog, 1965, vol. 1, p. 12). Family guild secrets have been referred to in the *Talmudim*—including secret arts of bread making, compounding herbs, singing, and writing holy scrolls (Herzog, 1965, vol. 1, p. 23). There was, of course, no private family worship among the monotheistic Jews. Though honoring one's parents was always important, ancestor worship would have gone against the First Commandment as expressed in Deuteronomy XXVI, verse 14: "I had not transgressed the commandments, I have not eaten thereof in my mournings; nor given ought thereof to the dead."

The English common law of inheritance draws heavily on feudal canons of descent. The English common law pertained to real property and favored the accumulation of lands in the hands of a few people; personal property laws were modeled after the Roman law and were based generally on blood relationships. "All children as well as ancestors were capable of inheriting under civil (Roman) law" (Wypyski, 1953, pp. 7–8). The laws of inheritance in the United States draw on both the English common law and Roman law. The distinction between real property and personal property remains in American law; the debts of the deceased and any expenses are usually paid from the proceeds from the sale of personal property.

Collectors of curious wills agree that those documents belong among the most revealing of all human documents. "How the egotism or miserliness, or conceit, or self-satisfaction can shine out in a will!" (Harris, 1911, p. 1). Wills have specified that an heir shall never grow a mustache, that menial servitude must be performed for a specified period, that the deceased's horses be shot "lest after his death they come to be ill-treated by any person who might buy them" (Harris, 1911, p. 93). There are many wills on record that bequeath estates to pets. However, just as in life, willing does not make it so. A will has to be "proved" and "freedom of testation has never been absolutely limited. Nowhere is a testamentary provision valid if its enforcement would be shocking to public morals" (*Encyclopaedia Britannica*, 1970, s.v. "Inheritance," p. 587).

Similarly, there have always been provisions against some kinds of disinheritance: a spouse cannot be completely disinherited. Where community property systems exist, the surviving spouse is usually

entitled to one-half of the community property. The rules and traditions governing probate in the United States had come to be such an
expensive muddle by the mid-1960s that a book entitled "How to Avoid
Probate" was a runaway best-seller.

A clearly drawn will should be presented to the court. The court
determines its legality and accepts it for probate. A court-ordered legal
notice inserted in a local newspaper informs creditors of the death and
informs interested parties who may object to the disposition of the
estate. Claims by anyone objecting to a will are heard in probate court,
which will rule on their validity. If the will is unclear, the court will interpret its meaning. If there has been no will—the individual dying
intestate—the court will handle the estate, distributing it according to
the laws of the state in which the deceased lived (Darcy, 1964, p. 5).
The great variations in intestate laws and the confusion confounding the probate procedure in general have prompted the National
Conference of Commissioners on Uniform State Laws—the same
commission that prepared the Uniform Anatomical Gift Act—to draw
up the Uniform Probate Code. Most states have not adopted the code,
however. It provides alternate systems of intestate inheritance depending on whether community property laws are in effect or not. The
code also specifies the intestate share of the surviving spouse and
other kin according to degrees of kinship. Under the Uniform Probate
Code no executor is needed in simple cases, and these fall under a different system of administration than more complicated cases (*Encyclopaedia Britannica*, 1970, s.v. "Inheritance," p. 594).

SUMMARY

The search for a definition of death in the medical profession and
in the courts is a testament to mankind's desire to know and control all
the facets of life. Social history underlies the present-day legal systems
that come into action subsequent to death, reiterating the same story
of people's constant struggle to control their life—and their own death.

No ultimate definition of death exists. None may ever achieve
consensus status. But modern man has moved far in recent years
toward clarification of the issues surrounding death. At the same time
medical and legal issues have multiplied as a result of such relatively
new processes as organ transplants.

The procedures to be followed following a human death are
generally specified by law. The procedures fall into specific categories
and become more manageable for surviving spouses or relatives where
planning has been undertaken in advance.

REFERENCES

Aristotle. *Metaphysica.* ed. W. Jaeger. Oxford, England: Clarendon Press, 1957.

Ayer, A. J. *Language, Truth, and Logic.* London: Gollancz, 1946.

Ayer, A. J. *Language, Truth, and Logic.* New York: Dover Publications, 1952.

Blackston's Gould Medical Dictionary. 1976 edition.

Brierly, J. B. et al. Quoted in R.M. Veatch, *Death, Dying and the Biological Revolution.* New Haven: Yale University Press, 1976, p. 49.

Capron, A. M., and Kass, L. R. "A Statutory Definition of the Standards for Determining Human Death: An Appraisal and a Proposal." *University of Pennsylvania Law Review,* 121 (November 1972), 87–118.

Coulion, N. J. *Succession in the Muslim Family.* Cambridge, England: Cambridge University Press, 1971.

Darcy, N. *How To Avoid Probate.* New York: Crown, 1964.

Diamond, A. S. *Primitive Law Past and Present.* London: Methuen & Co., 1971.

Dorland's Illustrated Medical Dictionary. Philadelphia: W. B. Saunders Co., 1974.

Encyclopaedia Britannica. 1970 and 1974 editions. Chicago: Encyclopaedia Britannica Corp.

Encyclopaedia and Dictionary of Medicine and Nursing. 1972 edition.

Encyclopedia Americana. New York: Americana Corp., 1975.

Ferrater Mora, J. *Being and Death.* Berkeley: University of California Press, 1965.

Freeman, K. *Ancilla to the Presocratic Philosophers.* Cambridge: Harvard University Press, 1947.

Hammerling, J. Quoted in J. Ferrater Mora, *Being and Death.* Berkeley: University of California Press, 1965, p. 126.

Harris, V. M. *Ancient, Curious and Famous Wills.* Boston: Little, Brown & Co., 1911.

Harrison, G. B., ed. *Shakespeare, The Complete Works.* New York: Harcourt, Brace, 1952.

Hartland, S. E. *Primitive Law.* Kennikot Press, 1970.

Harvard Medical School, Ad Hoc Committee of the Harvard Medical School

To Examine the Definition of Brain Death. "A Definition of Irreversible Coma." *Journal of the American Medical Association* 205 (1968), 337–340.

Heidegger, M. *Being and Time*. New York: Harper & Row, 1962.

Heifetz, M. D., and Mangel, C. *The Right To Die*. New York: G. P. Putnam's Sons, 1975.

Herzog, I. R. *The Main Institutions of Jewish Law: The Home and Property*. Vol. 1. London: Socino Press, 1965.

Kennedy, J. M. "The Kansas Statute on Death—An Appraisal." *New England Journal of Medicine,* 285 (1971), 946–50.

Kübler-Ross, E. *On Death and Dying*. New York: Macmillan Paperbacks, 1976.

Lasagna, L. *Life, Death and the Doctor*. New York: Alfred A. Knopf, 1968.

Leach, G. *The Biocrats*. New York: McGraw-Hill Book Co., 1970.

Maguire, D. C. *Death by Choice*. New York: Schocken Books, 1975.

Maine, H. S. *Early Law and Customs*. New York: Henry Holt Co., 1886.

Mannes, M. *Last Rights, a Case for the Good Death*. New York: Signet Div. of NAL, 1973.

Mant, A. K. "Medical-Legal Systems in the U.S.A.," in N. Morland, *The Criminologist*. New York: The Library Press, 1972, pp. 87–94.

Mant, A. K. "The Medical Definition of Death," in E. Shneidman, ed., *Death: Current Perspectives*. Palo Alto: Mayfield Pub. Co., 1976, pp. 218–223.

Mead, M. "The Cultural Shaping of the Ethical Situation," in K. Vaux, ed., *Who Shall Live?* Philadelphia: Fortress Press, 1970, pp. 3–25.

Miller, B. F., and Keene, C. B., eds. *Encyclopaedia and Dictionary of Medicine and Nursing*. Philadelphia: W. B. Saunders Co., 1972.

Mitford, J. *The American Way of Death*. New York: Fawcett Crest Book Division of Simon and Schuster, 1963.

Morgan, E. *A Manual of Death Education and Simple Burial*. Burnsville: N. C.: The Celo Press, 1975.

Morland, N. *The Criminologist*. New York: The Library Press, 1972.

National Conference of Commissioners on Uniform State Laws. *Uniform Probate Code*. St. Paul, Minn.: West Publishing Co., 1969.

Neilson, A. W. W., and Watkins, C. G. *Proposals for Legislative Reform Aiding the Consumer of Funeral Industry Products and Services*. Burnsville, N.C.: The Celo Press, 1973.

Ramsey, P. Quoted in D. C. Maguire, *Death by Choice*. New York: Schocken Books, 1975, p. 63.

Russell, O. R. *Freedom To Die: Moral and Legal Aspects of Euthanasia*. New York: Laurel Edition, Dell Pub. Co., 1975.

Ryan, M. Quoted in E. Shneidman, ed., *Death: Current Perspectives*. Palo Alto: Mayfield Pub. Co., 1976, p. 499.

Shakespeare, W. *As You Like It*. In G. B. Harrison, ed., *Shakespeare, The Complete Works*. New York: Harcourt, Brace, 1952, pp. 163–166.

Shneidman, E., ed. *Death: Current Perspectives*. Palo Alto: Mayfield Pub. Co., 1976.

Smart, N. "Philosophical Concepts of Death," in A. Toynbee et al., eds., *A Man's Concern with Death*. New York: McGraw-Hill Book Co., 1968.

Steadman's Medical Dictionary, Lawyer's Edition. Baltimore, Md.: William & Wilkins, 1972.

Steadman's Medical Dictionary. 1976 edition.

Sullivan, M. T. "The Dying Person—His Plight and His Right." *New England Law Review*, 8 (1973), 197–216.

Toynbee, A. et al. *Man's Concern with Death*. New York: McGraw-Hill Book Co., 1968.

Van de Brink, H. *The Charm of Legal History*. Amsterdam: Adolf M. Hakert, 1974.

Vaux, K., ed. *Who Shall Live?* Philadelphia: Fortress Press, 1970.

Veatch, R. M. "The Whole-Brain Concept of Death: An Outmoded Philosophical Formulation," *Journal of Thanatology*, 3 (1975) 15–29.

Veatch, R. M. "Brain Death," in E. Shneidman, ed., *Death: Current Perspectives*. Palo Alto: Mayfield Pub. Co., 1976 (a), p. 235.

Veatch, R. M. *Death, Dying and the Biological Revolution*. New Haven, Conn.: Yale University Press, 1976 (b), pp. 30–68.

Voight, J. Quoted in E. Shneidman, ed., *Death: Current Perspectives*. Palo Alto: Mayfield Pub. Co., 1976, p. 227.

Ward, W. C. "Human Organ Transplantation." *University of Florida Law Review*, 23 (1970), 136–156.

Wypyski, E. *The Law of Inheritance*. New York: Oceana, 1953.

2

To Live or Die: Professional Issues and Concerns

Who shall have the authority in determining the point at which life has quality and sufficient "humanness"? How shall he, she, or they acquire such license? Should an individual have the right to determine his or her own end? At what point does medical cost outweigh sustaining life? How is the price of a life determined? If there is life after death should this make a difference in our life goals and earthbound behavior?

Literally volumes have been devoted to dealing with some of these questions. As yet, there appear to be no simple answers. *To Live or Die* is a chapter that deals with the heart of issues posed by these confounding questions.

To live or die? People have faced the question since they first became rationally aware of their mortality. They wrestle with the problem more than ever today because of increased knowledge of the processes of death, the meaning of death, and the various roads to death. The reality of "finitude," or mortality, arouses antipodal reactions even in healthy persons—or perhaps primarily in healthy persons. The aged and infirm face the problem squarely. "Here we have acceptance, familiarity with death, tranquility and resignation on the one hand, and fear of death, terror and disregard of death as expressions of escapism on the other" (Munnichs, 1966, p. 8).

Technological advances that make it possible to maintain life long after life has no practical significance have sharpened the problem. Machines and medication enable doctors to extend life until it becomes "an artificial 'vegetable' existence" (Langone, 1972, p. 57). A report of an actual case tells what may happen:

> The body [of a patient suffering from acute heart disease] . . . recovered sufficiently to linger for three more weeks, but in a decerebrate [unconscious] state. . . . Intravenous nourishment was carefully combined

39

with blood transfusions and measures necessary to maintain electrolyte and fluid balance. In addition, antibacterial and antifungal antibiotics were given as a prophylaxis against infection, particularly pneumonia. . . . On the last day of the illness preparations were being made for the work of the failing respiratory center to be given over to an artificial respirator but the heart finally stopped. (Dempsey, 1975, p. 65.)

The armamentarium of other drugs and devices for sustaining life, beyond those mentioned, is extensive; it illustrates well how technology has given the medical profession what amounts to control over life.

But people still die. *When* they are to die, once they have reached a terminal stage, whether decerebrate or not, has leapt to prominence as a question requiring hard answers. Light has been shed on the definitions of death—medical, legal, and philosophical. Can light also be shed on the question whether life should be sustained beyond a given point? In a moral or practical sense, is there a point at which life becomes an intolerable burden and not a gift? "In the Judeo-Christian tradition—and especially in the Christian phase—life, for the individual, is defined in the first instance as a *gift*, directly or indirectly, from God" (Parsons, Fox, & Lidz, 1973, p. 5). Can that gift be returned, or thrown away, or voluntarily surrendered?

The questions summarize modern man's dilemma, particularly in cases of terminal illness. Man has attempted to resolve the questions in various ways: by promulgating the concept of euthanasia, for example. Man has also sought to soften the harsh reality of death by searching for keys to perpetual life, or eternal youth, and by—in a sense—extending life by positing the reality of life and experience after death. An examination of the writings on such subjects indicates how far man has progressed in the quest for acceptable answers.

EUTHANASIA, ANTIDYESTHANIA, AND STEWARDSHIP

Two cases illustrate the depth of feeling that colors discussions of cases involving euthanasia, antidyesthania, and stewardship. In one case George Zygmaniak, 26, had been paralyzed from the neck down as a result of injuries sustained in a motorcycle accident. The victim's brother Lester, unable to bear the knowledge of his brother's probably permanent incapacitation, went to the hospital and killed George in his hospital bed (Maguire, 1974). George had stated that he would "kill himself if he could" (Maguire, 1974, p. 72).

In the second case Dr. Herman Sander was charged with the murder of a cancer-stricken patient by intravenous injection of air. Some evidence indicated that the patient had asked the doctor to "put her out of her misery." The doctor made no attempt to conceal his action: he even noted on the patient's chart that the injections of air had been given.

The cases involved antidyesthania—opposition to a painful death—as well as euthanasia. The latter has been defined as meaning "good death"; but in recent years it has come specifically to mean "mercy killing," or "the willful putting to death of an individual with an intent to prevent suffering" (Heifetz & Mangel, 1975, p. 96).

Neither case turned specifically on the issue of stewardship. Yet both, in a sense, contained suggestions that stewardship and its implied hegemony over questions of life or death for a terminally ill or permanently disabled person might some day be primarily at issue. The Sander murder case was tried in 1950, the Zygmaniak case in 1973. In 1975 and 1976, the Karen Ann Quinlan case made repeated headlines as the victim's parents strove to retrieve from a hospital and its staff the right to decide whether their daughter should be kept alive through extraordinary means. Quinlan was eventually placed by court order in the guardianship, or stewardship, of her parents. The "extraordinary" life-support systems that had kept her alive were detached and the 22-year-old woman was removed to a nursing home to be "allowed to die in peace" (Colen, 1976, p. 53).

The problems posed by such cases have made it necessary for many hospitals to establish "human resources" committees to evaluate patient candidates for certain immediately required medical procedures. Many such procedures involve the heart, kidney, or other areas; cancer may be involved. The basic function of the committee is to recommend patient treatment priorities where there are more candidates than available facilities. In some instances it may be recommended that the treatment or service be withheld for given patients. The criteria of selection are complex, but the issue often remains: stewardship or euthanasia?

Far-reaching side effects may be encountered where such decisions are made. In personal communication with several patients the author has found residual resentment among those whose cancer operation had to be postponed because no operating facility was immediately available or because of a scheduling mixup. In one case, the patient felt his life span had been shortened by months or years.

At least to some extent the principle that committee decisions may be required is thus underscored. So—in cases involving permissive death—is the principle that life need not be supported for undue periods by extraordinary measures. Permissive death became a legally sanctioned reality; but whether any of the issues involved in the question of stewardship had been resolved remained open to debate.

Stewardship as a concept has raised extraordinarily difficult questions. The concept has been interpreted in general and specific ways. From a general point of view, stewardship represents in the Judeo-Christian dispensation a "cultivation that must bear fruit. God will hold us accountable for not merely preserving His gifts [including that of human life], but for adding to them by our own intelligence, imagination, and effort" (Ashley, 1976, p. 37). In a restricted sense stewardship becomes a question of who, under what circumstances, has the right to decide whether a person whose life is being prolonged without hope of recovery may be allowed to die. The Quinlan case, as it unfolded, became a contemporary paradigm of the latter issue.

Religious and Philosophic Positions

The religious and philosophic positions on euthanasia, and on the closely related questions of antidyesthania and stewardship, have their roots in history and tradition. Those roots have been traced to Hippocrates, the Father of Medicine, who lived some 24 centuries ago.

> When Hippocrates . . . sat under his giant plane tree on the Aegean island of Kos, euthanasia . . . was widely practiced and took many different forms. But from beneath that plane tree came words that have been immortalized in the physician's Hippocratic oath, part of which reads: "I will neither give a deadly drug to anybody, if asked for, nor will I make a suggestion to this effect." (Cant, 1973, p. 36.)

Down the centuries the words of the Hippocratic Oath have been variously interpreted. Usually they were taken to mean that the physician was not to administer a fatal overdose. The stricture was to apply "no matter how terrible [the patient's] pain or how hopeless his prospects" (Cant, 1973, p. 36). The more common contention today is that such an interpretation ignores the possibility that the words of the oath were "designed to keep the physician from becoming an accomplice of palace poisoners or of a man seeking to get rid of a wife" (Cant, 1973, p. 36).

Judeo-Christian philosophy provides a starting point for modern theses on the taking of life. Euthanasia and related issues naturally came to be regarded under that rubric, though many generalizations have been questioned in recent years. "The starting point for medical ethics," it was widely acknowledged, "is proper respect for the human person" (Weber, 1973, p. 1229). The implication may be stated explicitly: "This implies the moral obligation to preserve and prolong life" (Weber, 1973, p. 1229). Thus the classic definition of euthanasia as a form of killing became the religious and philosophical, if not always the practical, rule.

Opponents of euthanasia cite the commandment, "Thou shalt not kill." They also maintain that mercy killing is only a

> euphemism for murder and only God, not man, has absolute control over life. God, in effect, is the property-owner, man only the housekeeper. . . . For some Christians, suffering is not an absolute evil and may have its redeeming side. This argument likens the torment of the sufferer to the white heat of a forge, and the elevation of spirit and closeness to God it can bring to the fine steel that emerges. (Langone, 1972, pp. 60–61.)

Many other arguments have been adduced to support the basic religious-philosophical denial of the right to take life under any circumstances. Opponents of euthanasia have maintained that selfish, not humanitarian, motives may too often motivate the individual who decides that another should die. Granting the right to terminate life under any circumstances, it is further contended, may obliterate the line dividing man and animals. "The physician who performs euthanasia, with or without the patient's consent, may have erred in his diagnosis, and the patient might not have been as hopelessly ill as assumed" (Langone, 1972, p. 62).

Beyond that, to discuss euthanasia seriously is to speak of surrender, or defeat; science could at any time arrive at the medical answer to an individual's physical problems. "And what of the sufferer who begs for death today and changes his mind tomorrow or a week later? What of the conniving relative who might inherit the wealth of the dying patient?" (Langone, 1972, p. 62).

Perhaps most crucially, the opponents of euthanasia ask to what extent might euthanasia be carried. Twentieth-century man already lives with the specter of the Nazi death camps. The Hitlerian "final solution" hangs like an emotional cloud over discussions of mercy killing; the millions put to death in the gas chambers present their own silent argument against delegation to the individual or the state—any state—by legal fiat the right to terminate life.

The debate has nonetheless raged without surcease. To a degree it has been fueled by the stress placed in recent years on the avoidance of pain and the pursuit of comfort at any cost. Underlying that approach may be modern hedonism; but the net result is the same as if philosophical considerations were cited exclusively. Modern man has, simply, come to the realization that pain and suffering may not have a valid purpose once all hope of recalling the sufferer to a more normal state is gone.

The churches have made their particular adjustments to the veering currents of thought on euthanasia. The new approaches stop short of approval of active intervention to bring about death. But they do indicate agreement with the principle that the physician and the hospital need not continue to support life by all available artificial means after hope of recovery has ended. "Whatever its application in practice, the right to die, under certain circumstances, finds a substantial theoretical sanction in present-day religion. In 1957, Pope Pius XII, in an allocution to physicians, expressed the view that doctors are not bound to use extraordinary treatment to prolong life in cases where the patient cannot be consulted" (Dempsey, 1975, p. 111).

Jewish law contains a parallel thesis. The doctor is, essentially, permitted to withdraw any factor, whether extraneous to the patient or not, that could artificially delay death in the terminal phase. "However, [Jewish law] continues to condemn any form of active intervention" to terminate life (Dempsey, 1975, p. 111).

Protestant churches have moved toward even more liberal views while endorsing passive euthanasia in theory. Discussion of the problem has been encouraged under the rubric, "Death with Dignity." "It is hard to find a city parish today that has not staged at least one conference on death and dying, and the movement is filtering down to smaller communities" (Dempsey, 1975, pp. 111–112). A more inquisitive attitude has developed; and the weight of popular opinion has made itself felt. The consensus, as reported in various studies, has tended toward acceptance of passive euthanasia (Dempsey, 1975; Mannes, 1973; Mead, 1973).

The Case for Euthanasia

American ambivalence on euthanasia is reflected in court decisions. The law as written continues to prohibit mercy killing under most circumstances. In practice, the law functions unevenly. Those whose humanitarian motives for terminating another's life can be proved may or may not be acquitted in court trials for murder. Dr. Sander, the physician who injected air into his patient's veins to bring about death, was acquitted. Others have been convicted. Many more have found themselves the beneficiaries of curiously ambivalent sentences: the verdict is guilty, but the defense of insanity at the time of the murder is upheld.

Religious and philosophical thinking in recent years has generally supported—and perhaps, in a sense, caused—such ambiguity by acknowledging the need and propriety of a form of passive euthanasia. The phenomenon may be already occurring: Dr. Jan van Eys (1976) has coined the term "psychological euthanasia" to describe the situation when a hospital staff feels a patient is hopeless and dying and becomes less responsive, available, and supportive toward that patient. But the proponents of euthanasia have gone further. Theologian Joseph Fletcher, for one, has called for "active or positive euthanasia, which helps the patient to die" (Fletcher, 1973, p. 82). Thus an ethical question has evolved, one among many that "were once abstract or speculative" and that "have become practical and immediate" (Mothner, 1973, p. 58).

Fletcher and others advance powerful arguments. Contending, accurately, that passive euthanasia is no longer an issue, these supporters of active euthanasia deny that "biological survival is the first-order value and that all other considerations, such as personality, dignity, well-being and self-possession, necessarily take second place" (Fletcher, 1973, p. 82). The attack on traditional ethics continues in similarly humanitarian terminology:

> The traditional ethics based on the sanctity of life—which was the classic doctrine of medical idealism in its prescientific phases—must give way to a code of ethics based on the quality of life. This new ethics comes about for humane reasons. It is a result of modern medicine's successes, not failures. . . .
>
> Many of us look upon living and dying as we do upon health and medical care—as person centered. This is not solely or basically a biological understanding of what it means to be "alive" or "dead." It asserts that a so-called vegetable, a brain-damaged victim of an auto accident or a microencephalic newborn or a case of massive neurologic deficit and lost cerebral capacity, is no longer a human being, no longer really alive. It is *personal* function that counts, not biological function. Humanness is understood as primarily rational, not physiological. This doctrine of man puts man and reason before life. It holds that being human is more "valuable" than being alive. (Fletcher, 1973, p. 82.)

The ways in which euthanasia may be accomplished have been detailed in equally specific terms. The patient may terminate his or her own life in what is described as *voluntary and direct* euthanasia. In the most common case of this type, an overdose of a drug or medication is made available to the patient. In a second form, *voluntary but indirect* euthanasia, the patient has given prior, specific consent to termination of life under given circumstances *by another person*. In *direct but involuntary* mercy killing, death is accomplished by direct intervention "on a patient's behalf without his present or past request" (Fletcher, 1973, p. 82). A fourth form of euthanasia is both *indirect and involuntary*: "This is the 'letting-the-patient-go' tactic that is taking place every day in our hospitals. . . . What is done negatively is decided *for* the patient rather than in response to his request" (Fletcher, 1973, p. 83).

Such arguments, stressing the humane and humanitarian in preference to the religious and philosophical considerations that underlie most debates on euthanasia, point up the dilemma facing so many today. Not only doctors are involved. Ultimately the legal profession, legislatures, theologians, philosophers, and others must be concerned as well. Even though few of these, in all likelihood, will agree that "acts of deliberate omission are morally not different from acts of commission" (Fletcher, 1973, p. 83), the debate will undoubtedly continue.

Unquestionably doctors and other members of the helping professions are primarily involved. These individuals see death at close range. Many of them who espouse euthanasia in one form or another are motivated by compassion. But there may be other motivating forces: "Do we ever as physicians feel that the patient by . . . dying, has turned traitor . . . , challenging our omnipotence . . . ? Apropos of this, the arguments adduced in favor of euthanasia often appear to be in the service of the doctor, relieving him of his hostility, care, and guilt, rather than in the service of the recipient" (Wahl, 1969, p. 761).

The law may never overtake public or medical opinion. It may be that the sense of the 1970s, stressing humanitarianism impregnated deeply with compassionate morality, will remain the ideal. Heifetz's (1975) dictum may find continually wider acceptance:

> I approve of euthanasia. There is no doubt in my mind that euthanasia for the seriously deformed and retarded newborn or, for that matter, in a rare case of the adult, is at times humane and correct, moral and right. I believe that at times euthanasia should be done at both the newborn and the adult level. *But*, to kill—regardless of circumstances—must remain a crime so that the taking of life can never leave the scrutiny of our courts. (Heifetz & Mangel, 1975, pp. 114–115.)

Such a dictum may accurately reflect the *Zeitgeist*. Yet some will nonetheless subscribe to other concepts of euthanasia. The controversial view that death is a form of energy transformation and that the goal should always be survival without compromise will undoubtedly continue to be promulgated.

The Living Will

The "scrutiny of our courts" may under certain circumstances have predictable results. The reason is that public opinion increasingly tends to view euthanasia as acceptable and even desirable under certain conditions. To an imponderable but definite extent, such opinion influences court decisions, particularly where juries are involved.

A Gallup poll suggests how far-reaching have been the shifts in popular attitudes on euthanasia.

> The question asked both in 1950 and in 1973 was: "When a person has a disease that cannot be cured, do you think doctors should be allowed by law to end the patient's life by some painless means if the patient and his family request it?" In 1950 only 36 percent said yes to this question. In 1973, 53 percent replied in the affirmative. (Maguire, 1974, p. 77.)

Just as startling were the statistical breakdowns among groups of respondents. "Among adults under thirty years of age, the approval figure is 67 percent. It is noteworthy too that only 46 percent of the Catholics interviewed said they disapproved. . . . Not even a majority of Catholics voice disapprobation of mercy killing" (Maguire, 1974, p. 77).

In this climate the notion that people may in advance ameliorate at least some of the details of their passing has become widespread. An example of how the effort to order such details is carried through is provided by the "living will." This document in essence expresses the subject's desire to die when artificial means offer the only hope of sustaining life—when the subject has crossed into the gray zone between functional living and death proper.

The living will indicates mature acceptance of death at that point where life is no longer tenable. Nothing suggests denial of the kind that "prevents us from adjusting to death . . . , and . . . fills us with dread when the thought of our own future crosses our minds"

(Langone, 1972, p. 51). The wording of such a document may vary, as does the wording of any final testament; but a typical form is as follows:

TO MY FAMILY, MY PHYSICIAN, MY LAWYER, MY CLERGYMAN, TO ANY MEDICAL FACILITY IN WHOSE CARE I HAPPEN TO BE, TO ANY INDIVIDUAL WHO MAY BECOME RESPONSIBLE FOR MY HEALTH, WELFARE OR AFFAIRS:

Death is as much a reality as birth, growth, maturity and old age—it is the one certainty of life. If the time comes when I, _____, can no longer take part in decisions for my own future, let this statement stand as an expression of my wishes, while I am of sound mind.

If the situation should arise in which there is no reasonable expectation of my recovery from physical or mental disability, I request that I be allowed to die and not be kept alive by artificial means or "heroic measures." I do not fear death as much as the indignities of deterioration, dependence, and hopeless pain. I therefore ask that medication be mercifully administered to me to alleviate suffering even though this may hasten the moment of death.

This request is made after careful consideration. I hope you who care for me will feel morally bound to follow its mandate. I recognize that this appears to place a heavy responsibility upon you, but it is with the intention of relieving you of such responsibility and of placing it upon myself in accordance with my strong convictions, that this statement is made. (Heifetz & Mangel, 1975, pp. 33–34.)

The individual's signature, the date, and the signature of a witness are appended in the normal case.

Clearly, the living will ranks as a request for passive euthanasia—from the very person whose life is at stake. As a practice before death, completion of such a document can unquestionably be described as an effect of the growing public awareness of medical technology and its immense powers. The living will must also be considered an expression of a new openness about death:

Death is in vogue as a topic of books, seminars, scholarly articles, and classes at every level from college down to elementary school. There are two professional journals devoted to the study of death, dozens of volunteer groups working with the dying, and one or two medical centers geared solely to helping people die with dignity. (Goleman, 1976, p. 44.)

The form that the will takes remains a subject for debate. Heifetz has criticized the model already cited, a sample prepared by the Euthanasia Education Council of the Society for the Right to Die. "The instructions of the 'Living Will' . . . are vague. What do 'heroic measures' mean? Or 'artificial means'? Interpretations can vary from doctor to doctor and situation to situation. Besides the vagueness of terminology, the statements . . . are only requests, not demands" (Heifetz & Mangel, 1975, p. 34). The author goes on to compose a living will that would be acceptable to both the medical and legal professions:

DIRECTIVE TO MY PHYSICIAN
This directive is written while I am of sound mind and fully competent.
I insist that I have complete right of self-determination. That includes complete right of refusal of any medical or surgical treatment unless a court order affirms that my decision would bring undue or unexpected hardship on my family or society.
Therefore:
If I become incompetent, in consideration of my legal rights to refuse medical or surgical treatment regardless of the consequences to my health and life, I thereby order and direct my physician, or any physician in charge of my care, to cease and refrain from any medical or surgical treatment which would prolong my life if I am in a condition of:

1. unconsciousness from which I cannot recover,
2. unconsciousness over a period of six months,
3. mental incompetency which is irreversible.

However, although mentally incompetent, I must be informed of the situation, and if I wish to be treated, I am to be treated in spite of my original request made while competent.
If there is any reasonable doubt of the diagnosis of my illness and prognosis, then consultation with available specialists is suggested but need not be considered mandatory.
This directive to my physician also applies to any hospital or sanitarium in which I may be at the time of my illness and relieves them of any and all responsibility in the action or lack of action of any physician acting in accordance with my demands.
If any action is taken contrary to these expressed demands, I hereby request my next of kin or legal representative to consider—and if necessary, to take—legal action against those involved.
If any of my next of kin oppose this directive, their opposition is to be considered without legal grounds since I remove any right of my next of kin who oppose me in this directive to speak for me.
I hereby absolve my physician or any physician taking care of me from any legal liability pertaining to the fulfillment of my demands. (Heifetz & Mangel, 1975, pp. 36–38.)

Whether such a document serves the purpose of a living will better than its simpler counterpart may be questioned. Whatever the wording of such a document, passive euthanasia will remain a question of medical ethics and practice, of the physician's own beliefs and attitudes, and of prevailing medical trends. Active euthanasia may remain illegal, a process mired in unavoidable uncertainties. Fundamental questions will continue to plague the medical personnel faced with the actual decision, and the questions will in the future as in the past be both humane and legal. The cooperation of others will remain necessary "if he/she is to be able to die in dignity and not be kept 'alive' with extraordinary measures which prevent 'nature taking its course' " (Morgan, 1973, p. 14).

"Doctor, Let Me Die"

Euthanasia, antidyesthania, and stewardship have become pressing issues for a number of reasons. One has been noted: "Using new technologies, the physical existence of more and more bodies can be extended—heart beating, lungs functioning—long after the brain is irrevocably dead" (Etzioni, 1973, p. 109). Another important reason might be cited: Americans are increasingly dying in institutions, not at home. In an institution neither the patient nor the patient's family, and sometimes not even the patient's physician, has total control of the situation. As the Karen Ann Quinlan case showed, the institution itself may play a controlling part in the decision for or against even passive euthanasia.

The question of euthanasia appears in intensive form in societies employing advanced technological innovations in the care of the sick or aged. In cultures that emphasize equal technological modes of treatment less intensively, the issue seems to be less prominent. Yet even in such societies there appear to be well-established guidelines determining living priorities when food, shelter, or security are threatened.

Mundane realities underlie the shift of the locus of death from home to hospital, geriatric center, or nursing home. Most simply, the hospital has facilities that make possible expert technical care when life is most threatened. Thus, today, "no dicta from ancient Greece," such as the Hippocratic Oath, "can neatly fit the modern logistics of death" (Cant, 1973, p. 36). The death at home has become more and more the exception:

> Until this century, death was a relatively common event in the household, particularly among farm families. Today more than 70% of deaths in American cities occur in hospitals or nursing homes. Both medical care and death have been institutionalized, made remote and impersonal. In major medical centers the family is elbowed out by specialists and house physicians who have their elaborate and expensive gadgets. The tendency is to use them. (Cant, 1973, pp. 35–36.)

Alternatives to hospitals and formal nursing homes have been devised. In particular, the hospice has been held up as a possible answer to the need for terminal care. The prototype of such an institution may be St. Christopher's Hospice, in the London suburb of Sydenham. "The hospice opened in 1966 and, in its few years of existence, has become a model for care of the dying the world over" (Dempsey, 1975, p. 234). Factors that differentiate St. Christopher's from hospitals and other institutions include the policy of admitting children; personalization of care, even to the point where patients can bring some of their own furniture; little patient-staff protocol; informal social life, including garden parties in pleasant weather; freedom to issue drugs and even liquor, and similar provisions.

Other hospices have been opened, all of them basically modeled after St. Christopher's:

> Special emphasis is put on the alleviation of pain. It has been found that success depends not only on providing the right drugs at the right time but also on developing an attitude of understanding, confidence and hope. . . . The patient feels surrounded by ongoing normal life. (Morison, 1973, p. 42.)

In general, such new departures have not yet affected the basic— and somewhat altered—role of the hospital. Where this institution once served as a refuge for the poor and for pilgrims, it changed over the years to become a true medical center. But it healed people, and assisted in the struggle against death. Many individuals still returned to their homes to die. The hospital "still has that curative function, but people are also beginning to consider a certain type of hospital as the designated spot for dying. One dies in the hospital because the doctor did not succeed in healing" (Aries, 1974, pp. 87–88). Worse, death has become a matter of passage through invisible, undetectable phases that in the last analysis make it almost impossible "to know which step was the real death, the one in which consciousness was lost, or the one in which breathing stopped" (Aries, 1974, pp. 88–89).

The new dispensation has altered the role of the hospital or institution for the elderly and infirm. Hundreds of people are maintained in such institutions in vegetative states, strapped in beds and chairs and unable to talk or voluntarily to move. The numbers of such persons are growing steadily, raising fundamental questions concerning death with dignity. Family visits may even become difficult because of institutional rules specifying visiting hours. Children under 14 are not normally allowed on hospital wards, partly because of fears of disturbances or emotional difficulties. On the whole the situation reflects the growing impersonality of institutions where the seriously ill, aged, or dying are concerned.

A corollary situation places the doctor, the family of the patient, relatives, and others outside the circle of decision makers. The hospital team has taken over, or the institution's staff. A decision on passive euthanasia or continued therapy may be made by a group, meaning that it may never be made. And patients who say to their physician, "Doctor, let me die," may be asking more than the doctor can deliver.

Events of the quarter-century ending about the mid-1970s both clarified issues for professionals and students and rendered uncertain some old, established practices and approaches. The physician who in 1968 could "pull the plug" on a terminally ill patient would have hesitated to do the same thing in 1976. The threat of lawsuit might have stayed the doctor's hand in the latter year; but in fact the basic issues had become more clouded:

> Until recently the question of how much effort to invest in sustaining a dying patient or a severely malformed newly born infant was left largely in the hands of physicians. Most patients' families and society as a whole gave the problem no more complicated thought than the simplistic dictum that one did "all" one could for the loved one. (Etzioni, 1973, p. 109.)

Today everything has changed. "The initiative has passed from the family. . . . The doctor and the hospital team . . . are the masters of death—of the moment as well as of the circumstances of death" (Aries, 1974, p. 89). The public has become involved and concerned. "The very increase in the number of persons for whom an explicit decision, to 'turn off' the body-maintaining machines, must be made, has called the public attention to the question: 'Who should decide? Using which criteria?' " (Etzioni, 1973, p. 109).

The question is no longer a legal or philosophical one, at least insofar as the patient's family is concerned. The question is, rather, one that demands practical answers so that decisions can be made on the basis of available information. If a patient has made out a living will, and if the physician and members of the patient's family agree that the terms of the will should be carried out—even that the moment for death has arrived—how is the decision to be obtained?

The question cannot be answered simply. Nor, any longer, can the doctor in most cases simply order that the plug be pulled. A committee may be involved if the suggestions of Etzioni (1973) and others become common practice:

> Institutions will have to adapt to these new technologies and new demands for participation by resting such decisions not in an individual physician bu in committees made up of several health professionals who will have to base their ruling on publicly stated criteria; or, much better, in committees that include clergy, humanists, community leaders, citizens-at-large, who review these matters and set guidelines within which individuals could come to their decision. (p. 111.)

Committees, it should be stated, have never been noted for rapid decision formulation. Is it possible that days or weeks might pass before a hopelessly terminal patient might be released from his or her final agonies? If one reads "committees" as meaning that individual cases must be decided on the basis of committee decisions, that untoward possibility exists.

Legal decisions that have become background for the current situation are now history. They include the Quinlan and Tucker decisions. At the level of the hospital ward, because of those judgments, things can never be the same. While stressing the need for indirect and involuntary—passive—euthanasia, the courts have also hedged their decisions in such a way as to give pause to the individual physician faced with a life-or-death decision:

> Upon the concurrence of the guardian and family of Karen [Quinlan], should the responsible attending physicians conclude that there is no reasonable possibility of Karen's ever emerging from her present comatose condition to a cognitive, sapient state and that the life-support apparatus now being administered . . . should be discontinued, they shall consult with the hospital "Ethics Committee" or like body of the institution in which Karen is then hospitalized. If that consultative body agrees that there is no reasonable possibility of Karen's ever emerging from her present comatose condition to a cognitive, sapient state, the present life-support system may be withdrawn. (Highlights of New Jersey Court's Ruling, p. 14.)

Such wording suggests that physicians not only cannot, but probably *will* not, ever again, be the repository of the power over life

and death that they once were. Doctors' fears are justified: the right
to decide has been taken out of their hands. Perhaps the alternative offers a solution, if a somewhat uncertain one:

> Society, as it has already begun to do, will have to invest some time for a
> grand debate on all these matters. It is only in this way—through talk
> shows, symposiums, dialogues in coffee houses, places of worship, over
> dinner tables, even cocktail parties—that we slowly come to terms with a
> new issue, overcome our old-fashioned sentiments and form new ethical
> criteria. (Etzioni, 1973, p. 111.)

A start toward that kind of dialogue has been made. The American
Medical Association offered a key contribution in November 1973
when it passed what was called the "Death with Dignity" Resolution.
Designed to help the patient who has made out a living will, or the sufferer who asks the physician to let him or her die, the resolution
specifically "cleared the way for such statements as . . . [the living
will] . . . to be used in providing 'death with dignity' to terminally ill
patients" (AMA Passes "Death with Dignity" Resolution, p. 375). Beyond such developments, several states, including California and Virginia, were in late 1976 considering "Death with Dignity" legislation
(Cohen, 1976).

Prior to consideration of its resolution, the AMA had canvassed a
number of churches regarding their feelings on passive euthanasia.
The churches indicated strong support for such a statement. But "the
convention . . . turned away from a controversial motion by some of
its own members urging a legislative definition of death" (AMA Passes
"Death with Dignity" Resolution, p. 375). The issue again centered on
the question whether life-prolonging machines should be kept in
operation after the brain has died. Once again the dilemma facing doctors was stressed:

> Many doctors are eager to have some legislative protection so they cannot
> be sued for taking an organ for transplant out of a person whose brain has
> ceased to function but whose heart did not stop until the machines were
> turned off. The current AMA position is that any legalistic definition of
> death . . . is "inflexible" and that individual doctors should remain free
> to define death using "currently accepted criteria." (AMA Passes "Death
> with Dignity" Resolution, p. 375.)

Thus, again, the issue was evaded. The patient seeking to die
quickly and without pain may still be forced to await the decision of a
committee. Hope may be drawn, however, from the fact that "there is

now much discussion of the relative merits of assigning ultimate authority to the next-of-kin, to an ombudsman, or to a committee of social scientists, philosophers and theologians" (Morison, 1973, p. 45).

THE SEARCH FOR PERPETUAL LIFE

The perverse threat of death has driven people to suicide, to theories assertive of reincarnation, to immersion in strange philosophies, and to religious, philosophical, and social aberrations of many kinds. The reality of death has also spurred a quest for perpetual life on earth. Evidence abounds that this quest has been pursued for many centuries.

The quest may take a number of forms. Where one individual follows a strict dietary regimen in the hope of prolonging health and life, another finds promise of longevity in sex or liquor or exercise. Old people, including centenarians, offer little help because their formulae differ so widely. A New York woman, 112 years of age, said: "I don't have rules" for living to an advanced age; a Russian who died at 160 in 1966 noted that his longevity derived from "Allah and the Soviet power" as well as "lots of children and a good nature" (Langone, 1972, pp. 181, 183).

Religions have provided paradigms of immortal life that have inspired generations of the faithful to hope. Millions through the ages have conducted themselves in ways that would entitle them to the perfection of Heaven. In Buddhism, the ideal state has another name: Nirvana.

> The answer to death is Nirvana, the state of deathlessness. According to Buddhist thought most people, after suffering death, are reborn according to their Karma in one of the six destinies: in a hell-body, demon-body, ghost-body, animal-body, human-body, or heavenly-body. . . . Life in these six destinies is only temporary and death will follow, and so on endlessly. (Amore, 1974, p. 127.)

Where some persons are reborn on earth, others such as evil-doers go to hell. Good-doers enter Heaven. Those who are free from the causes of rebirth achieve the state of Nirvana: "the going out of the consciousness-that-is-reborn" that is likened to the extinction of an oil lamp (Amore, 1974, pp. 127–128).

Immortality has been sought in every other conceivable guise. Perpetuation of life on earth, of the life of the organism, has belonged among man's consuming passions: a road to physical immortality.

Some have seen human beings as pursuing their quest out of a haunting fear of death. People repress that fear; the quest for immortality may become, simply, a frenetic pursuit of life.

> On the one hand, we see a human animal who is partly dead to the world, who is most "dignified" when he shows a certain obliviousness to his fate, when he allows himself to be driven through life; who is most "free" when he lives in secure dependency on powers around him, when he is least in possession of himself. On the other hand, we get an image of a human animal who is overly sensitive to the world, who cannot shut it out, who is thrown back on his own meagre powers, and who seems least free to move and act, least in possession of himself, and most undignified. (Becker, 1973, p. 24.)

The Historical Quest

The Babylonian *Epic of Gilgamesh* may be the oldest recorded tale of a superhuman search for a lost Eden in which man could not die. The story concerns the hero Gilgamesh, who first builds the Sumerian city of Uruk on the Euphrates River, then goes in search of the key to immortality. All Gilgamesh's adventures end in failure, and eventually the wanderer returns to Uruk to live out his life as happily as he can.

> The tale in its most complete form comes from Babylonian clay tablets dating from about 650 B.C., but there are Hittite, Assyrian, and Sumerian fragments and versions. It is evident that the story goes back at least to the original Sumerian civilization of 5,000 years ago, and no one knows how far back into oral history the various elements reach. (Segerberg, 1974, p. 15.)

By extension Gilgamesh's lost Eden is the immortality that man enjoyed in Paradise. "Already visible in the Gilgamesh epic and Ecclesiastes are seedlings of 'philosophy,' that brave attempt to conduct a reasonable life before an unreasonable death: hedonism—'eat, drink and be merry, for tomorrow we die'—pessimism, stoicism" (Segerberg, 1974, p. 18). But over time the search for perpetual life on earth took many more concrete forms. For example, the alchemists sought a basic substance that would, ingested or otherwise taken, assure man of eternal life on earth. The alchemists, forerunners of today's chemists and scientists, worked with actual elements.

> The Chinese Taoist alchemists . . . thought the red cinnabar is restored so that the process is a permanent and stable shifting from a red powder to

a fluid mercuric metal and back again. It was regarded as an immortal chemical. "Immortal" as it is used here . . . [means] only "stable" or "permanent" relative to other changing things, yet it seems to have been taken as metaphorically meaning "eternal" or "longevity producing." (Shibles, 1974, pp. 475–476.)

The alchemists, of course, also became noted for "mystical, spiritual and symbolic alchemy" (Shibles, 1974, p. 476). Emphasis was placed on purification of the soul to achieve a kind of metamorphosis or transformation: *eine Verklaerung*. Man could in this way become immortal. "Pure substances could purify the body. . . . Everything is made of breath of varying degrees of purity and so if the breath is kept one would live longer" (Shibles, 1974, p. 476). Yet foods and medicines could also contribute to longevity. The more effective ones were identifiable by their "signatures"—characteristics or appearances. "In this way qualities thought to be especially powerful were shiny (mercury), translucent, fluid, wet, slippery, root-shaped like man," and so on (Shibles, 1974, p. 477). Among the metals, gold and silver were held to be longevity producing, whether ingested, used in utensils, or otherwise incorporated into everyday human life.

The traditions underlying such medieval and Renaissance efforts to find the magic elixir of life stem from far earlier periods. Even mythology offers examples of gods who renewed their youth or warded off senescence by magical means. Jupiter's Fountain of Youth survived, in one form or another, down the centuries in both literature and the popular imagination. "The gods themselves were not too proud to make use of this rejuvenating water cure: Juno regularly took the waters at the fountain of Canathos, which helped to preserve her charms" (Guillerme, 1963, p. 13).

Other evidence of man's longing for immortality—physical or spiritual—comes from graves, from literature, from studies of ancient customs and rites. The quest, it appears,

is as nearly universal as anything we know pertaining to the inner wishes of human beings; but some men, from time to time, have renounced any interest in the subject. . . . They are lost, however, in the vastness of the general quest. So much so that we can strengthen our earlier definition . . . by saying that the quest for immortality may actually reflect the inherent desire in man for the indefinite perpetuation of the self. (Cousins, 1974, p. 4.)

Certainly the keys to eternal youth or life that man sought reveal a deep spiritual hunger. In diversity they have few parallels in human history. Aside from the fountain with special properties, a theme that "did not cease with the end of paganism, but passed into the immense fund of medieval superstition" (Guillerme, 1963, p. 13), a catalogue of other objects, elements, animals, and formulae might be drawn up. The magic fountain itself may survive as a superstition today, as one writer notes, since "a hot spring in the Andes can attract rich Americans of both sexes driven to despair by the sight of their wrinkles" (Guillerme, 1963, p. 13). But in antiquity it represented only one of many potent items, among them pearls, other precious gems, amber and bezoars, the heartbone of a deer—"otherwise called the hardened root of the aorta of an old deer"—brews, plasters, baths, exotic drugs, skinned vipers and coral, amber, and rubies, "and last but not least, the famous theriac, which may be found in every druggist's cupboard" (Guillerme, 1963, p. 15).

Traceable to the second chapter of Genesis, in Judeo-Christian lore, the fountain theme probably remains paramount as evidence of man's hunger for immortality. Psalm 36 refers to a "fountain of life," the waters of which could renew the bather's youth. By the sixteenth century Ponce de Leon had become the apostle of a new search for the magic fountain. The conquistador's quest, like the alchemist's of his time, had a somewhat blurred double goal: to find gold, the magic restorer, and the fountain as well.

Naturally, Ponce de Leon never found his fountain. He did, however, create excitement at the Spanish court of the early 1500s. Perhaps more importantly in history,

> in his search he discovered Florida where the aged still go hoping to regain their vigor. For himself, the legendary seeker of eternal life found death. Returning to Florida in a later expedition, the Spanish party was resisted by hostile Indians and Ponce de Leon suffered an arrow wound which proved fatal. He lived sixty-one years. (Segerberg, 1974, p. 79.)

Modern Medicine: Fountain of Youth?

With the advent of modern medicine the search for the transforming alembic or elixir that would ensure eternal youth took new forms. Some extraordinarily outré experiments took place. For example, in June of 1878 Charles Edouard Brown-Sequard announced that he had "cut the testicle of a young dog into small pieces, mashed it with water, filtered the juice, and injected the extract into his leg. He repeated the process using a guinea pig testes, then administered still a third injection" (Segerberg, 1974, p. 84). The transformation was, reportedly, remarkable.

A procession of "youth doctors" of greater or lesser renown and professional competence moved across the public stage. Serge Voronoff, a Russian émigré, is reputed to have earned more than $10 million during his career by grafting human and anthropoid testicles onto human recipients. "A conference of 1,000 surgeons in Austria in January 1928 agreed that 'the gland transplantation operation devised by Dr. Serge Voronoff could provide 'transient regeneration' " (Segerberg, 1974, p. 86). Voronoff's earnings, it was estimated, were matched by the American John Brinkley "who 'operated' in rural areas of the United States and favored billy-goat testicles" (Segerberg, 1974, p. 86). Paul Niehans's cellular therapy; Dr. Anna Aslan of Romania with her procaine, or novocain, injections; and Elie Metchnikoff, discoverer of the phagocytes, or white blood cells that fought disease, followed. All contributed something to medicine while also furthering the quest for a key to longevity.

The search continues. Psychosomatic medicine has encouraged mind control, sound reasoning, the subjugation of "negative emotions that seem to cause stress, heart attacks, fast aging, and death" (Shibles, 1974, p. 483). Various remedies for the deterioration of old age have been developed, among them Dr. Aslan's Gerovital H3, used mainly with arthritic patients. But the shortcomings of some modern medicines have been criticized roundly:

> They ignore practically everything which has been learned since the turn of the century about the functioning of living matter and about the processes of aging. In fact, all the contemporary therapies for old age apply nothing better than the out-dated approaches and methods of the nineteenth century. The amount of knowledge on which any of these contemporary therapies of old age is based is so small that it does not scratch the surface of what we already know, which in turn is still very little compared to what we have yet to know. Using these out-dated weapons is like fighting the enemy with stone-age weapons. (Hrachovec, 1972, p. 21.)

It has also been asserted that the funds available for research on aging and on means of prolonging useful active life are insufficient. Grants have been "too little and too late" (Hrachovec, 1972, p. 22). Efforts to transplant the life habits of regions noted for the longevity of their citizens have been criticized because social and other conditions cannot be transplanted. One can drink yogurt, the goat's milk drink popular in the Balkans; but one cannot duplicate the social and psychological climate of that part of the world. Nor can one transplant values and attitudes. Exercise seems to be important and may be among the most important remedies for aging: "Many Soviet physicians believe that regular exercise, such as walking up and down slopes in mountain regions, helps develop resistance to diseases and consequently is a factor in longevity" (Benet, 1976, p. 159).

Psychotherapy has begun to make a contribution to gerontology. "Physicians find that one must have a will to live to survive operations or illness. Self-suggestion or hypnosis may also be relevant here. The body is seen to adapt or adjust to the direction given it" (Shibles, 1974, p. 483).

To die or not to die? More precisely, to prolong life by one means or another or not to do so? The entire subject has become a science whose name, gerontology, refers specifically to the pursuit of the elusive secret of remaining young. Of necessity, various theories have come under consideration. From the psychological and environmental, scientists have moved on to the biological and chemical aspects. These occupy researchers today to an increasing degree. If, as speculation holds, aging takes place at the minutest level of life, the cell, might not regeneration be accomplished in advance—by preventing cellular degeneration? Can this be accomplished by creating an environment in which the cell can live without undergoing the changes that aging brings?

Research has raised the possibility that life may be prolonged by creating mutations and permutations of basic life forms. Experiments reported in 1976 appeared to indicate a step in that direction: "A Florida Atlantic University research team has successfully fused a tobacco plant cell to a chicken blood cell in a development that eventually might lead to animals sustaining themselves on fertilizer and sunshine" (*Houston Chronicle*, August 18, 1976, p. 26, sec. 1). The next phase of such research could well be cells, animal or human, that can successfully reproduce themselves.

The questions range still more widely. Scientists, pursuing the problem of aging from other aspects, have speculated that

> there is a structural change in the genes with aging, and that the aging process might be controlled by transplanting DNA (the stuff of life in the cell) from a young person to an older person. Genes undergoing structural changes causing aging could be stopped immediately. (Langone, 1972, p. 184.)

Whether modern medicine and science will ever prove to be

man's fountain of eternal youth remains an open question. But as theories proliferate the chances that man will be able to enjoy more years on earth—that life expectancy will increase—become better. The secret will not necessarily lie in Bjorksten's cross-linkage, which holds that more and more molecules of the human body, the smallest units of any element or compound, including the human body, become cross-linked as life goes on. "The accumulation slows down or stops the activity of essential molecules and interferes with normal biochemical activity" (Langone, 1972, p. 184). The secret may not lie in collagen chemistry, which concentrates on studies of the protein collagen "that makes up about 40 percent of all the protein in the body," and that "fills the space between the muscle fibers and between the cells, thus serving as the stabilizing fiber of collective tissue" (Langone, 1972, pp. 184–185).

The secret may not lie in Dr. Alex Comfort's drug research. The purpose of such research is to locate man's biological clock, tamper with it, slow it down, and thus postpone "all the deteriorative changes that affect individuals" (Langone, 1972, p. 185):

> The aging process . . . may be like a phonograph record that, once played, cannot be replayed; the performance can only be prolonged by running the record more slowly, but not so much slower that the music is spoiled. Or if the aging process is one of "noise accumulation"—like the noise that accumulates in a record with years of playing—maybe all that is necessary is that the needle be kept clean. (pp. 185–186.)

Certainly some answers will be forthcoming. Recent research has suggested that the thymus, which is important to the body's immunological defense system, may control aging. Some evidence has been found to indicate that thymus stimulation in young animals results in a prolonged life span. Within the next several years investigators will very likely test such procedures with human beings.

Other answers may be found. Antioxidants, the preservatives that keep rubber tires from aging or spoiling, may affect man as they have affected mice: by prolonging life by some 40 percent. The antioxidants BHT and vitamin E have already been added to foods, including cereals, in small amounts. Such efforts have shifted attention to man's diet, with the result that a kind of diet cult has grown up. The point at which charlatanry and exploitation of the gullible leave off and where scientific fact begins can hardly be determined in many publications on the subject. The lengths to which the faddists go can, however, be specified. One such notes that he takes the following food supplements: 500 mg of vitamin C, 400 I.U. of vitamin E, 500 mg of Ginseng, 300 mg RNA, 25 mg of another preparation, 1200 mg of a second, and so on through the typical day (Braswell, 1976, p. 4).

Laboratory research has advanced into still other fields. In one case, "Several investigators, taking a cue from the process of hibernation in which certain animals pass the cold months in a sleeplike state, have been able to retard aging and boost the life spans of several kinds of animals by dropping the normal body temperature" (Langone, 1972, p. 187).

Enter cryonics. The controversial technique of deep-freezing has the goal of preserving the entire human organism until science has discovered the cure for the disease that threatened it. At that point the body would be thawed out, treated medically, and restored to active life.

Immortality at 196 Degrees below Zero

Cryonics, more properly termed cryogenics, has aroused controversy for a number of reasons. Scientists have denounced the deep-freeze technique because, they maintain, freezing has a violently adverse effect on cellular structure. "The delicate chemical and physical makeup of the cells would be so damaged," it is contended, "that it would be exceedingly difficult, if not impossible, to restore life. Thus far, no one has been able to revive a single frozen organ, let alone anything so complex as a man" (Langone, 1972, p. 188).

Other reasons for decrying the "cryogenics movement," as it has been called, are less specific and perhaps more pertinent. What would a person do on returning to life, Rip Van Winkle style, after a sleep of 50 or 100 or 1,000 years? Would not the process of reintegration occupy the wanderer returning from the frozen Purgatory to the point where coping would be difficult or impossible? Even more mundanely: Where would the thawee live and with whom? What changes would have taken place in the social, political, economic, and psychological climate between the time of entering sleep and emerging from it?

Science fiction and professional qualms aside, cryogenics requires a complex technological base from the start. That base now exists in the United States.

> Blood is drained from the veins; arteries and lungs are perfused with a glycerol fluid to retard cellular damage; and the patient is then wrapped in aluminum foil and stored, like frozen food, at a temperature of −79

degrees Celsius. The process, however, does not end there. A sealed capsule becomes what is hoped the temporary home of the "deceased." Temperature is further reduced to −196 degrees Celsius through the use of liquid nitrogen; this ensures that no further cellular deterioration takes place. And here, in cryonic suspension, the patient awaits ultimate resurrection. All this costs about $10,000, plus $1,200 a year in storage costs. To cover these initial expenses, individuals who contemplate going the cryonic route are encouraged to take out an insurance policy naming the Cryonic Suspension Society as beneficiary. (Dempsey, 1975, p. 189.)

If "monkey gland transplants" represented the end means of the prolongation of life's basic powers in a simpler society, cryogenics may constitute the ultimate denial of death in a much more advanced technological age. But movement it is not, at least not yet; despite sometimes heroic efforts to proselytize, the devotees of cryogenics have remained a select "sodality in which the here-and-now seems to have taken precedence over the hereafter" (Dempsey, 1975, p. 190). Yet the public has been given ample opportunity to join:

AN INVITATION TO HELP ATTAIN
PHYSICAL IMMORTALITY
We invite you to join the Cryonics Society of New York. As a member of the first and largest Cryonics Society in the world you will have a unique opportunity to work for the attainment of the most profound objective imaginable—the indefinite suspension of *your* life.

How many persons have joined the "cryonics underground" in response to such blandishments? Estimates vary. Around the world, as many as 2,000 were said to belong in 1974 (Kovrer, 1974, p. 23). But even at that time, when the movement was less than a decade old, enthusiasm for the idea of joining a cryonics group had waned. Dropouts were reported in "chapters" in major cities across the country. One chapter had even lost a member who lay, unsuspecting, in deep freeze.

The wife agreed to have her husband frozen, using his insurance policy and some other investments to finance the cost of maintaining him. . . . One year later she decided she wanted him back to support her. She got her contract broken and took the money. We just took him out of the capsule and buried him, still frozen. (Kovrer, 1974, p. 20.)

Equally elusive are figures on how many Americans have been frozen cryogenically. A 1974 estimate put the total at 20 (Kovrer, 1974, p. 20) while a later statement indicated that four bodies were in cryonic suspension (Berman, 1976, p. 76). The disparities pointed up the dubious nature of the cryonics movement's basic promise: to assure immortality.

Not that the movement has uniformly gone on record as guaranteeing that cryonics would fulfill the most sanguine expectations. On the contrary, it has taken the statements of legitimate cryobiologists and restrained its own extrapolations. Where the scientists have stopped short of claiming that "such a complex freezing job (of the entire body) is possible," the movement's leaders have simply stated their willingness "to take their chances anyway and be frozen instead of being cremated or buried" (Berman, 1976, p. 76).

Cryonics, it has been said, could lead to a brave new world in which man would enjoy the potential for limitless life. But first, clearly, the movement must "have its Resurrection. When the first cryonaut comes back through the icicles, after having been frozen for a number of hours or days, only then will the world be changed" (Harrington, 1969, p. 256). At that point, it should be added, recruitment will probably become simpler. The proof that freezing works, and that on return a person can resume fully conscious, sapient functioning will have been proved.

Millions will undoubtedly be watching when the effort is made. Until the day arrives, the movement will, in Harrington's words, "remain pre-revolutionary" (Harrington, 1969, p. 256). Once the feat has been accomplished the returnee may be disappointed. A growing body of opinion inclines to the view that prolongation of life cryogenically or by any other means hardly seems worthwhile unless man takes steps to make life more livable. "There's no question in my mind that we have the technology to prolong life," as Gaitz noted. "But prolong life for what? If we're just going to warehouse them in some nursing home, then why bother?" (Galvan, *Houston Chronicle,* October 8, 1976, p. 10, sec. 1).

The argument will undoubtedly continue, proving that, for most persons, life under almost any circumstances will remain preferable to the dusty death of which Shakespeare wrote.

AFTER-DEATH EXPERIENCES

Accounts of after-death experiences have proliferated in the United States in the mid-1970s. Television shows feature participants who relate how, while "dead," they saw colored lights, walked Elysian fields, sensed one or another form of ineffable peace and well-being.

The speakers are serious; they do not seem to be the victims of exploitation; and they use the simple, straightforward language of the street and the dinner table.

Whether brain or biological death has actually taken place in many of these cases represents a question that may be unanswerable. In some cases doctors have testified that the subject had, to all intents and purposes, died. But the cases and the experiences they involve illuminate a far broader question: Does man, or a part of man, survive the death of the flesh, and if so, in what form?

The ways in which survival *could* take place are numerous. In Christian theology, and particularly in Roman Catholic theology, man's soul survives the body and lives eternally. At death the soul "goes" to Heaven, Purgatory, or Hell. The afterlife becomes a fellowship with God whose exact dimensions are left to silence:

> Unlike other religious systems, with the often elaborate descriptions of the abode of the dead and the pleasures or punishments there awaiting us, Judeo-Christianity contains surprisingly little detailed information about the afterlife. Such speculation is avoided, lest it become misleading escapism. . . . Instead there is a strong (and healthy) this-worldly or "existential" bias in authentic Judeo-Christianity: The God of Israel reveals only what is needful for a full and complete life . . . on earth. (Cleary, 1975, p. 43.)

At the other end of the spectrum of possible modes of survival, perhaps, lies the theory that personality may continue to exist after death as "a kind of field or system of associations around the objects with which the person was in physical contact when he was alive" (Roll, 1974, p. 2). The theory goes on to draw a physical parallel: "In the same way as the gravitational field of a material object is part of the gravitational field of the earth, the consciousness of a person seems to be part of wider consciousness of which he may or may not be aware . . ." (Roll, 1974, p. 2).

There may also, of course, be some middle-ground; obviously, views more extreme than those indicated might be cited. The fact is that the question haunts human beings today as it has haunted them down the centuries.

What the Evidence Suggests

Religious persons have found evidence for the survival of the soul in man's nature, in history, and in literature. In the view of such believers, man enjoys "the uniqueness of being human," a state that essentially "transcends biological conditions" and "cries out for continuation" (Schoville, 1975, p. 8). History or, more specifically, anthropological research, suggests the possibility of human survival beyond death because "From what we are able to ascertain . . . man has buried his dead . . . in ways that have signified, to almost a universal degree, the existence of the concept of life beyond death" (Schoville, 1975, p. 8). Over the centuries man's literature has reflected—and supported—such beliefs; but particular reference must be made to "Biblical literature, which records ideas about man and life and death that should not be ignored nor rejected out of hand . . . for they were forged in the crucible of human experience" (Schoville, 1975, p. 8).

More scientific, or at least less partisan, inquiry has reached opposite conclusions. For example, Murphy has gone on record as noting that " . . . there is, so far as I know, no survival evidence which is completely unambiguous, complete in itself, and free of all competing or alternative explanations" (Murphy, 1959, p. 272). The same author admitted that there might be a dualism "between normal and paranormal processes" (Murphy, 1959, p. 272). But "the paranormal phenomena, like the normal, might best be described as an expression of certain conscious or unconscious needs of the individual" (Dempsey, 1975, p. 229).

Empirical research that would settle the question remains elusive. One comes full circle, repeatedly, on the truism that the meanings that men and women assign to death stem from the meanings they assign to their own lives. The research thus partakes, usually, of the taint of partisanship. Those who believe in survival find evidence to prove that there is an afterlife. One encounters case histories that "prove" the speaker's view:

> At the point of injury there was a momentary flash of pain, but then all the pain vanished. I had the feeling of floating in a dark space. The day was bitterly cold, yet while I was in that blackness all I felt was warmth and the most extreme comfort I have ever experienced. . . . I remember thinking, "I must be dead." (Moody, 1976, pp. 28–29.)

Such accounts, it must be noted, constitute evidence but not proof. One cannot judge what was occurring in the speaker's mind even if one grants the reality of the experience and the speaker's good will. The author of *Life after Life* (Moody, 1976) admits the existence of the quandary: "I am not trying to prove that there is life after death. Nor do I think that a 'proof' of this is presently possible"—and yet: ". . . it is my firm conviction that this phenomenon of after-death experience has great significance, not only for many academic and practical fields—especially psychology, psychiatry, medicine, philosophy, theology and the ministry—but also for the way in which we lead our daily lives" (Moody, 1976, p. 5).

That many thinkers have believed in an afterlife constitutes additional evidence. Philosophers from Plato and Aristotle to Kant had notions of an ethical basis for the immortality of the soul or spirit (Laird, 1970). "Mystics and sages have said for centuries that consciousness is the fundamental fact of the universe and that death is only a change of consciousness" (Mitchell, 1975, p. 63). William Godwin (1736–1836) is said to have believed not only that one could gain immortality but also that one could prolong life by achieving voluntary control over the emotions (Shibles, 1974). If such contentions have any validity, an afterlife may be a necessity, and not merely a possibility.

Laird (1970) has examined in succession the arguments for immortality. These range from the belief that man, in dying, enters into a preordained union with a Godhead to the argument that man represents values—abstractions—and therefore cannot totally die. In between one encounters the thesis that the partnership between soul and body is only temporary and must end with death: but not the death of the soul.

> . . . it is hard to imagine a conclusive general reason why the mental partner should cease to exist when its bodily companion falls a prey to corruption. This cessation is possible; but it is certainly not a necessity; and on general grounds it may even seem very unlikely. A discarnate self . . . must be supposed to be very different indeed from an incarnate one. . . . (Laird, 1970, p. 180.)

The arguments do not all rest on empirical evidence, clearly. But they do represent important strains of thought. To an increasing degree, in recent years, the belief in a life beyond death has also become socially acceptable. The proliferation of philosophic arguments and experiential accounts that appear to support the basic contention bear part of the credit—or responsibility—for this gradual change. Scientifically oriented researchers have contributed by conducting investigations purporting to prove or disprove the existence of persons in incorporeal forms.

The trend toward acceptance is incipient. The evidence has already grown quantitatively and qualitatively. However, the materials for conducting rigorous scientific experiments designed to reach "final" conclusions—as if conclusions in this area could ever be final for all people in all times—are still lacking: " . . . we lack the proper instrumentation. However, there is work going on which seems promising. I refer to the fields called paraphysics and radionics" (Mitchell, 1975, p. 63). In essence the extraordinary fact can already be stated: "that science—or, at least, some scientists—is approaching the same position" held by the traditional religionists in viewing death as no more than a change of consciousness (Mitchell, 1975, p. 63).

Man is a "time-ridden being confronted by the task of identifying himself with eternity" (Feifel, 1969, p. 673). The search for evidence of an afterlife will undoubtedly be continued. But some basic verities have not, and never will, change: "The obligations of morality . . . do not stand or fall with the fact of immortality or of any other such thing" (Laird, 1970, p. 188). Even so, some evidence begs for acceptance. A key portion of that evidence touches on the experiences that so many men and women have reported on their return from what they believed was death.

Those Who Came Back

The ones who came back to provide evidence of an afterlife represent many different areas of life and specialization. They come from professional ranks—doctors, dentists, and others; they are also housewives, truck-drivers, students, secretaries. Not surprisingly, they form one small cadre in a great army of persons who, through the centuries, have reported afterlife experiences. But the modern voyagers into the world beyond life, if indeed they reached that world, enjoy an advantage that their predecessors missed: the moderns, in many cases, are both believed and made the subjects of formal or informal research efforts.

Religion has played a role in the lives of many of these voyagers of today. But religious sense and inspiration were incidental; religion did not direct or dictate the transition to and through the after-death state. Rather, the religious content of the experience appears to have been generally less important than the purely mystical. Rarely does one encounter the kind of Greco-Roman, religion-specific protocols requiring successive passages through experience until some elevated state is reached:

> The human soul was believed to remain in the after-death state during a period of three thousand years. Its human-plane body of the moment of death disintegrating, the constituents went to form the bodies of animals and plants, transmigrating from one to another during the 3,000 years. At

the end of that period the soul gathers together the identical particles of matter . . . , and from them rebuilds . . . , as a bird its nest, a body and is reborn in its state as a human being. (Evans-Wentz, 1973, p. 45.)

Much different are the experiences reported in the mid-1970s:

I knew I was dying and that there was nothing I could do about it, because no one could hear me. . . . I was out of my body, there's no doubt about it, because I could see my own body there on the operating room table. . . . Then this really bright light came. It . . . was a little dim at first, but then it was this huge beam. . . . And it gave off heat to me; I felt a warm sensation.

I wasn't sure what was happening, but then, it asked . . . me if I was ready to die. It was like talking to a person, but a person wasn't there. The light's what was talking to me, but in a voice. (Moody, 1976, pp. 63–64.)

And: "I heard a voice, not man's voice, but like a hearing beyond the physical senses, telling me what I had to do—go back—and I felt no fear of getting back into my physical body" (Moody, 1976, p. 57).

To what extent the innate need to believe in the possibility of a return to familiar Earth plays a role in such experiences is difficult to assess. All human beings share the belief to an extent. ". . . The heroes of the epics—Babylonian, Sumerian, Greek, Roman, Alexandrian, and medieval European—are linked to each other and to us by their central quest: the search for immortality" (Harmer, 1963, p. 32). But the "out-of-body" experience has become so common that "Virtually every doctor or nurse who works with the dying has witnessed a 'miraculous' recovery [and heard the account] of someone who has been pronounced dead" (Woodward, 1976, p. 97). But is the out-of-body experience merely the reflection of that universal ambition—a psychological construct without validity outside the mind of the subject?

No one can say. If it is true, as Stuart (1956) wrote, that "No man really begins to live until he has come close to dying," it may be equally true that people do not really live until they have died. Appreciation of life does not end for those who came back. Rather, such persons have gained a new awareness of life.

No one that I interviewed has reported coming out of this experience [of dying and returning] feeling morally "purified" or perfected. No one with whom I have talked in any way evinces a "holier-than-thou" attitude. In fact, most have specifically brought up the point that they are still trying, still searching. Their vision has left them with new goals, new moral principles, and a renewed determination to try to live in accordance with them, but with no feelings of instantaneous salvation or of moral infallibility. (Moody, 1976, p. 93.)

Thus the reported brushes with immortality have inculcated in the subjects a sense of the need to cultivate "love for others, a love of a unique and profound kind" (Moody, 1976, p. 92).

Despite such accounts, the school of thought that denies the possibility of an afterlife remains a powerful influence. Existentialism has had an influence, especially in countries such as France. In that country, "where Existentialism was an important influence during the twenty-year period 1948–1968, there was a violent swing of the pendulum" (Segerberg, 1974, p. 22) toward denial of life after death. The defenders of this view appear to remain proof against the winds of popular opinion. They believe, simply, that death must be regarded as "real, not just apparent, involving the total destruction of the person, body and spirit" (Ammerman, 1976, p. 10).

Stories of returns from the other world persist nonetheless, and will undoubtedly continue to multiply. Reincarnation, the ultimate mode of repetitive return to life, will continue to attract attention—and scorn. The Bridey Murphys will report on events with which they could not, in all likelihood, have had knowledge unless they had come back. The Welsh housewife who "saw Roman Emperor Constantine learning swordsmanship in the year 286" (*Houston Chronicle*, November 14, 1976, p. 14, sec. 1) will continue to make news:

> She reportedly remembered being an American nun who died in 1920, an 18th-century sewing girl in the London of Queen Anne and a Jewess in 12th-century York.
>
> Her other previous lives happened to brush those of Constantine the Great, Henry VIII, Ferdinand and Isabella of Spain, Catherine of Aragon and a 15th-century French merchant named Jacques Coeur. (*Houston Chronicle*, November 14, 1976, p. 14, sec. 1)

The shadow world of occultism, spiritualism, extrasensory perception, clairvoyance, telepathy and similar phenomena begins here to impinge on the more or less straightforward "return" phenomena.

The Borderline Beliefs

At this frontier at which accounts of visits to a life beyond become the stuff of parareligious belief, some admissions have to be made. Evidence has accumulated, for example, that "there is something outside sensory perception as we normally perceive it" (Dempsey, 1975, p. 229). Is that "something" a psi factor "that seems to link communication among the living through ESP" and that also "binds human beings in an ethereal and dematerialized afterlife of pure energy and disembodied consciousness?" (Dempsey, 1975, p. 229). Or has man returned, in espousing such beliefs, to a primitive view in which "the structure . . . is that of a dialogue [between the living and the dead] . . . ?" (Bastide, 1968, p. 104.)

Whatever the answer, in crossing this frontier one enters a new dimension. Witchcraft, precognition, astral travel, devil worship, demonic possession, and many other phenomena become the stuff of afterlife—or beyond—life—lore. Communication with the dead may take the form of ghost walks, mediumism, hauntings.

> The supernatural—a vast area within which man's accepted knowledge and beliefs no longer hold true. It is a world of terrifying powers and nightmares; of voices from nowhere, footsteps in empty rooms; of demons and curses and apparitions; a world where fear reigns! But it can also be an area of gentleness and charm, of helpful entities attempting to aid those of the physical world. (Sawyer, 1973, p. 9.)

The underlying explanation for such outré beliefs may lie in man's fear of the unknown: the occultists may be attempting to come to grips with death and the concept of an afterlife in their own ways. They may be banishing, at least to a degree, the seven fears of which Murphy spoke: the fear that death is the end; the fears of losing consciousness, of loneliness, of the unknown, of punishment, of what may happen to one's dependents, of failure (Murphy, 1959). They may, most basically, be making an "outward reach for a spiritual world of some sort" (Graves, 1973, p. 141). But the popular literature on this subject has nonetheless produced no clear indication "that any poltergeist has been run to earth" (Dempsey, 1975, p. 226). Rather,

> . . . the most that can be said is that some strange cases remain unexplained. Swaying chandeliers, mysterious knocking, falling dishes, gyrating furniture—these are the familiar signs. . . . The Psychical Research Foundation's investigators have looked into dozens of these reported occurrences without much success. They conclude that most such hauntings appear to be caused by a living person. . . . Other cases appear to be explained by psychokinetic energy of which the agents are unaware. The poltergeist activity . . . is an involuntary outlet for aggression. (Dempsey, 1975, pp. 226–227.)

Efforts to investigate the factual or scientific bases of after-death experiences and of related psychic phenomena have been undertaken in plethora. Dr. J. B. Rhine has gained fame for his research in the field of extrasensory perception. Whately Carington has investigated telepathy in depth. Gustave Geley has become noted for his work in the field of materialization. In his down-to-earth study of "the unknown," Anspacher (1947) suggests that "where every other science stops, psychical research begins" (p. 25). What has this research uncovered?

In essence, the research has produced "scientific proof for the survival of personality" (Anspacher, 1947, p. 67). Thus death becomes ". . . a leaping of the gap" that "would provide us with an entirely new and august sense of human destiny" (Anspacher, 1947, p. 67). Human beings gain in stature because they no longer represent a mechanistic equation whose resolution in death is the total end. Physical science, which has been accused of reducing man's "sense of his high destiny" (Anspacher, 1947, p. 67), falls into perspective as another study of mundane phenomena.

Acceptance of the premise that man survives in some form does not necessarily or even probably render credible the more unusual beliefs associated with an afterlife. An element of partisanship colors the accounts based in such beliefs to the point where one suspects charlatanry. Tales of the strange and uncanny, of supernormal occurrences, of experiences beyond the grave have been so often unmasked as frauds that healthy doubt is mandatory. The search for acceptable answers must continue no matter where it leads. One may or may not accept Freud's (1963) dictum that ". . . the uncanny in connection with . . . secret power to do harm and the return of the dead" (pp. 53–54) represent vestiges of older, more primitive beliefs; but it can no longer be doubted that "the world beyond reason," including that of experience beyond life, has begun "to reassert itself, becoming more and more visible in the closing decades of our century" (Editors of *Playboy*, 1973, p. 6).

Modern science has in a sense been forced to stand back and watch while knowledge of the afterlife has expanded. Some scoffing has taken place, certainly. But in general a spirit of acceptance or at least of agnosticism has set in. Psychology, a science for less than 100 years, has moved on to a Fourth Force level at which all paranormal phenomena may be considered as legitimate subjects for study. The question thus becomes: Are survival after death and returns to life—in ghostly, electric field, psi, or completely human form—paranormal?

Perspectives on Postmortem Life

One can place a period after such speculations, but only with difficulty. Man has learned to classify most of the facts of human existence, to bring them into some kind of acceptable or understandable order. Where the afterlife is concerned, an element of disorder, or of incomprehensibility, prevails. Man in the modern context sees medicine and the machine technology advancing at a dizzying pace while, on the other hand, the evidence mounts that technology and medicine and related arts do not explain everything.

In particular, they cannot explain the multitudinous reports of afterlife experiences—many brought back by individuals who were clinically dead at the time when they had the experiences. Even discounting the more borderline evidence, the possibility that a *Geisteswissenschaft* must be allowed to exist and function arises; the field of study would be related to that of theosophy, whose "basic idea . . . is perhaps reducible to the aim of exploring and developing all unexplained laws of Nature and all the latent powers in [and characteristics of] human beings" (Tabori, 1968, p. 23).

> The religious mind can probably accept such an interpretation. One can see both positions [stress on the importance of life and on the importance of the afterlife] within religion itself. . . . For the Jew the crux of his being is the way life is lived—the ethics, morals and values by which he lives. . . . For the Christian, the "good life" is a preparation through sacrifice for salvation, the reward of the afterlife. We can see the essence of these two arguments presented over and over again in the history of ideas. (Alexander & Adlerstein, 1959, pp. 281–282.)

It can be noted too that the great classics of religious literature contain accounts of afterlife experiences and of returns from the dead. Christ Himself, according to the New Testament, resumed human form after three days—even if that form appeared to be somewhat insubstantial. Thus "life . . . actually has no significance except as a preparation for the ultimate goal of death. In both the greatest living religions, Christianity and Buddhism, the meaning of existence is consummated in its end" (Jung, 1959, p. 8).

The scientific perspective has for years been moving toward an open-minded approach to the study of postmortem life and experience. "Today there is a wide measure of agreement, which on the physical side of science approaches almost to unanimity, that the stream of knowledge is heading toward a non–mechanical reality; the universe begins to look more like a great thought than a great machine" (Jeans, 1937, p. 122, n. 14). *Thought* here can encompass the notion of a spiritual, immortal essence of life: the concept of a soul, whether so rationalized or not. Kübler-Ross, enunciating her belief based in personal experience that death does not really exist, is only making specific what science has long suspected: that after-life experiences occur and may be believed. Kübler-Ross's 1976 updating of a growing conviction in scientific circles constitutes a reasoned judgment based on years of observation. Insofar as the death situation permitted, the observation and subsequent analysis shared the rigors of scientific research methodologies, including tapings, group analysis, and other approaches.

Nonetheless, it must be noted, the jury must stay out. Doubt adheres to rationalizations. No matter how extensive the evidence, death is a fact of life.

SUMMARY

Increased awareness of the processes of death and dying has led to a modern dilemma of major proportions. That dilemma centers on the question whether life should be sustained beyond the point at which man ceases, irrevocably, to be rationally functional—and on *when* that point is reached. Euthanasia, antidyesthania, and stewardship all involve threads of argument, pro and con, whose social significance is far reaching.

The arguments may be summarized. In opposition to euthanasia, whether permissive or direct, one finds religious and philosophic positions asserting the sacredness of life. Positive support for these positions may be found in pronouncements from the Ten Commandments to modern elucidations of Judeo-Christian philosophy. Negative support, if it may be termed that, has been found in abuses of the power to command and control life. The Nazi "final solution" that resulted in the deaths of millions of Jews in the 1930s and 1940s provides the apt—and frightening—modern paradigm of such abuse. By contrast, the advocates of "death with dignity" stress man's need to die while shreds of humanity remain. To provide assistance toward death after all hope of recovery is gone represents, in this view, a humanitarian gesture.

The search for perpetual life constitutes yet another aspect of the question: To live or die? The search has increased and waned in intensity over the centuries. Philosophers, alchemists, early scientists, writers, and many others have given expression to the basic and primitive need to deny the reality of death and affirm the possibility of eternal life. In modern times medicine has been seen as the ultimate answer. In a bizarre extension of the basic human drive, a "cryonics" movement has come into being: by technical means, an individual can be frozen at the moment of death, to be "thawed out" and returned to life when the contemporary cause of death has fallen victim to medical advances.

A particularly sensitive facet of the live-or-die debate involves after-death experiences. The debate holds practical significance because it influences modern man's entire orientation toward death—and thus toward life. Much philosophical and other evidence suggests the possibility of life and experience after death; but more direct evidence comes from those who have been "clinically dead" and who have nonetheless revived to tell their stories of bright lights and Elysian prospects. Confusing the debate to an immeasurable degree are multitudinous studies, reports, investigations, and scientific or pseudoscientific experiments involving not only after-death appearances and experiences but "stranger-than-fiction" phenomena such as witchcraft, prerecognition, and mediumism. Legitimate doubt concerning the validity of such reports and studies has, to some extent, subverted the case for an afterlife.

REFERENCES

Alexander, I. E., and Adlerstein, A. M. "Death and Religion," in H. Feifel, ed., *The Meaning of Death*. New York: McGraw-Hill Book Co., 1959, pp. 281–282.

"AMA Passes 'Death with Dignity' Resolution." *Science News*, December 15, 1973, p. 375.

Ammerman, R. R. "A Logical Incoherence." *Wisconsin Alumnus*, 44(1) (1976), 10–11.

Amore, R. C. "The Heterodox Philosophical Systems, in F. H. Holck, ed., *Death and Eastern Thought*. New York: Abingdon Press, 1974, pp. 127–128.

Anspacher, L. K. *Challenge of the Unknown: Exploring the Psychic World*. New York: Current Books, 1947.

Aries, P. *Death in America*. Philadelphia: University of Pennsylvania Press, 1974.

Ashley, B. "Perspective of a Moralist," in D. G. McCarthy, ed., *Responsible Stewardship of Human Life*. St. Louis: The Catholic Hospital Association, 1976, p. 37.

Bastide, R. "Réligions africaines et structures des civilisations." *Présence Africaine*, 66 (1968), 104.

Battelle, P. "Let Me Sleep: The Story of Karen Ann Quinlan." *Ladies' Home Journal*, September 1976, pp. 69–76, 172.

Becker, E. *The Denial of Death*. New York: The Free Press, 1973.

Benet, S. *How To Live To Be 100: The Life–Style of the People of the Caucasus*. New York: The Dial Press, 1976.

Berman, S. "Frozen Immortality: An Idea Whose Time Has Gone." *Science Digest*, July 1976, pp. 73–77.

Braswell, A. G. "Letter from the Publisher." *The Body Forum 1* (6) (1976), 4.

Cant, G. "Deciding When Death Is Better than Life." *Time,* July 26, 1973, pp. 36–37.

Cleary, F. X. "On Death and Afterlife: A Biblical and Theological Interpretation." *Hospital Progress*, December 1975, pp. 40–44.

Cohen, R. Personal communication, November 4, 1976.

Colen, B. D. "The Long Dying of Karen Ann Quinlan." *McCall's*, September 1976, pp. 50f.

Cousins, N. *The Celebration of Life: A Dialogue on Immortality and Infinity*. New York: Harper & Row, 1974.

Dempsey, D. *The Way We Die: An Investigation of Death and Dying in America Today*. New York: Macmillan Co., 1975.

Editors of *Playboy*. Preface to *Beyond Reason: Playboy's Book of Psychic Phenomena*. Chicago: Playboy Press, 1973.

Etzioni, A. *Genetic Fix*. New York: Macmillan Co., 1974.

Evans-Wentz, W. Y. *The Tibetan Book of the Dead*. New York: Causeway Books, 1973.

Feifel, H. "Perception of Death," in M. Krauss, ed., *Care of Patients with Fatal Illnesses. Annals of the New York Academy of Sciences,* 164 (1969), 671–677.

Fletcher, J. "The Control of Death: An Argument for the Dignity of Dying Well Instead of the Inhumanity of Enforced Living," in R. H. Williams, ed., *To Live and To Die*. New York: Springer Verlag, 1973, pp. 82–83.

Freud, S. *Studies in Parapsychology*. New York: Collier Books, 1963. (Originally published, 1919–23).

Galvan, R. "Why Prolong Life If We Can't Make It More Worthwhile? Psychiatrist Asks." Interview with Dr. Charles Gaitz. *Houston Chronicle*, October 8, 1976, sec. 1, p. 10.

Goleman, D. "We Are Breaking the Silence about Death." *Psychology Today*, September 1976, pp. 44-48; 50; 52.

Graves, R. "Reincarnation," in *Beyond Reason: Playboy's Book of Psychic Phenomena*. Chicago: Playboy Press, 1973.

Guillerme, J. *Longevity*. New York: Walker & Co., 1963.

Harmer, R. M. *The High Cost of Dying*. New York: Collier Books, 1963.

Harrington, A. *The Immortalist: An Approach to the Engineering of Divinity*. New York: Random House, 1969.

Heifetz, M. D., and Mangel, C. *The Right To Die*. New York: Berkeley Publishing Corp., 1975.

"Highlights of New Jersey Court's Ruling." *American Medical News*, April 12, 1976, pp. 13–14.

Hrachovec, J. P. *Keeping Young and Living Longer: How To Stay Active and Healthy Past 100*. Los Angeles: Sherbourne Press, 1972.

Jeans, J. *The Mysterious Universe*. Cambridge, England: Cambridge University Press, 1937.

Jung, C. G. "The Soul and Death," in H. Feifel, ed., *The Meaning of Death*. New York: McGraw-Hill Book Co., 1959, p. 8.

Kovrer, D. "Never Say Die!" *Today's Health*, July 1974, pp. 20–23; 67–68.

Laird, J. *The Idea of the Soul*. New York: Books for Libraries Press, 1970.

Langone, J. *Death Is a Noun: A View of the End of Life*. Boston: Little, Brown & Co., 1972.

Maguire, D. C. "Death, Legal and Illegal." *Atlantic*, February 1974, pp. 72–85.

Mannes, M. *Last Rights*. New York: New American Library, 1973.

Mead, M. "Margaret Mead Answers: Are You in Favor of Mercy Deaths?" *Redbook*, July 1973, pp. 33–34.

Mitchell, E. D. "Death and Consciousness: New Concepts in the Space Age." *Journal of Thanatology*, 1975, 59–65.

Moody, R. A. *Life after Life*. New York: Bantam Books, 1976.

Morgan, E., ed. *A Manual of Death Education and Simple Burial*. Burnsville, N.C.: Celo Press, 1973.

Morison, R. S. "Dying." *Scientific American*, 229 (1973), 1–10.

Mothner, I. "Who's Asking Life-and-Death Questions Today?" *Saturday Review/World*, September 25, 1973, pp. 58–59.

Munnichs, J. M. A. *Old Age and Finitude: A Contribution to Psycho-gerontology.* New York: Karger, 1966.

Murphy, G. "Discussion," in H. Feifel, ed., *The Meaning of Death.* New York: McGraw-Hill Book Co., 1959.

Parsons, T., Fox, R. C., and Lidz, V. M. "The 'Gift of Life' and Its Reciproca-tion," in A. Mack, ed., *Death in American Experience.* New York: Schocken Books, 1973, p. 5.

"Plant, Animal Cells Are Fused; Could Be Important Food Source." *Houston Chronicle,* August 18, 1976, sec. 1, p. 26.

"Reincarnation: Maybe You Don't Live Only Once." *Houston Chronicle,* November 14, 1976, sec. 1, p. 14.

Roll, W. "Survival Research: Problems and Possibilities." *Theta* 39–40, 1974, 1–13.

Sawyer, J. *Deliver Us from Evil.* Westfield, Mass.:.Phillips, 1973.

Schoville, K. N. "Two Views on Death." *Wisconsin Alummus,* 77 (1) (1975), 7–9, 27.

Segerberg, O., Jr. *The Immortality Factor.* New York: E. P. Dutton & Co., 1974.

Shibles, W. *Death: An Interdisciplinary Analysis.* Whitewater, Wis.: The Language Press, 1974.

Stuart. J. *The Year of My Rebirth.* New York: McGraw-Hill Book Co., 1956.

Tabori, P. *Companions of the Unseen.* New Hyde Park, N.Y.: University Books, 1968.

Van Eys, J. Personal communication, November 1976.

Wahl, C. W. "The Physician's Treatment of the Dying Patient," in M. Krauss, ed., *Care of Patients with Fatal Illnesses. Annals of the New York Academy of Sciences,* 164 (1969), 759–767.

Weber, L. J. "Ethics and Euthanasia: Another View." *The American Journal of Nursing,* 73 (7) (1973), 1228–1231.

Woodward, K. L. "There Is Life after Death." *McCall's,* August 1976, p. 97.

Responses to Death and Stages of Grieving

3

Darwin wrote that man was the only animal that could frown. For a period of time it was thought that man was the only animal to show grief with tears. However, some researchers have found that the Stellar seal, and even some alligators, "weep" in times of acute stress. What is this propensity in man that caused Balinese women to jump into the pyre with their burning spouse—American Indian women to lop off fingers when their warrior husband or son did not return?

Often we talk of our "emotional attachments" but rarely if ever speak of "detachments." If human beings somehow have the propensity to form attachments, then it is likely they also have a means of "detaching." This process is perhaps witnessed in the "stages of reacting to death."

It has been my pleasure and fortune to know Dr. Bz Cobb who has indicated that some of her thinking on the matter of death was influenced by the writings of Viktor E. Frankl. Her lectures and writing likewise influenced Carl Nighswonger, one of her students in Houston. Later, Mr. Nighswonger moved North and began an association with Dr. Kübler-Ross. This chapter explores the cultural influences on man's expression of grief as well as the underlying commonality of reactions to perceived loss.

Loss of a loved one through death invokes various responses. The specific responses may depend on the age of the bereaved, his or her sociocultural background, and other factors. In many individuals "the emotional impact of the loss of someone important . . . can cause a major life crisis" (Jackson, 1970, p. 1). In others, grief can call forth mental aberration, sickness, and even, in extreme cases, a second death as a kind of sympathetic reaction.

Grief may be cued by events other than the death of a loved one. But loss of some kind is usually experienced: "significant losses of persons may take place . . . through . . . divorce, extended separation related to business or military assignment, children growing up and leaving home, etc." (Switzer, 1970, p. 12). In children, forms of grief have been observed after the death of a pet, the loss of a parent through the departure of one parent for an extended period, and in other situations.

A definition of grief has been attempted by Switzer (1970). The definition emphasizes loss through death as a common cause of grief: "grief has as its core experience an acute attack of anxiety, precipitated by the external event of the death of a person with whom one is emotionally involved, and . . . other behavioral responses are dynamically related to the anxiety" (pp. 12–13). Death in such cases has taken someone unique; a relationship has been destroyed and cannot be restored. "When an animal dies, there is the loss of an 'it'. . . . When a human being dies, an 'I' is lost to the world and a 'thou' to the survivors" (Burghardt, 1973, p. 366).

For the dying, grief and other emotions present a challenge of almost incalculable magnitude. The fact of impending death, once recognized, stirs emotions that appear to be relatively parallel from one person to another. Because America has become a "gerontocracy," a nation "ruled" by the elderly and old, the questions surrounding the fact of grief—and relating to ways of mediating its relief or moderation—have come increasingly under study. Like thanatology, gerontology has become a separate field of study with the subject of death and responses to death as one of its subbranches.

PSYCHOLOGICAL COPING PATTERN OF THE DYING AND BEREAVED

In the context of the 1970s it has become virtually impossible to discuss death, dying, and emotional responses to them without reference to Elisabeth Kübler-Ross, the eminent psychiatrist. Kübler-Ross has charted the stages of emotional response through which dying patients pass; in the process she has contributed materially to today's new awareness of the individual's need for compassion and attention in the final phases of life.

Kübler-Ross has been widely credited with bringing to both public and scholarly attention the most basic details involved in psychological coping patterns employed in the face of death. But others had researched the same field extensively before Kübler-Ross. Charles Darwin (1899), for example, examined the relationship between weeping and mental suffering. Bain (1875) and Borgquist (1906), both early psychologists, attempted to formulate conclusions regarding the sources of grief and coping patterns. Bain (1875) found that the intensity of the emotion appeared to be directly proportioned to the depth of the attachment of the bereaved to the dead person. Borgquist (1906) found linkages among the state of despair, the desire not to live, the general feeling of helplessness and hopelessness, and the individual's physiological responses.

During the first half of the twentieth century others examined the subject of grief and coping patterns or related subjects. A relationship between sorrow and fear was established by Shand (1914) while Troland (1928), observing bereaved persons, concluded that the pattern of interaction between the bereaved and the deceased tended to continue after the latter's death under the influence of stimuli appearing in the immediate postdeath situation. Later investigators saw that a death might tear away part of one's self, at least in an applied sense; that negative self-feeling constitutes a part of the emotion of grief; and that grief as a psychosocial phenomenon deserved deeper study and analysis. Eliot (1948) attempted a definition of bereavement:

> Psychologically, bereavement is a major type in the general class of traumatic frustration-situations. Arrested impulse or thwarted habit is at the root of all sorrow. Bereavement is one's own blocked wish for response following death of the loved object. The loved one is gone, but the associated memories and habits and needs remain alive as a real complex in the mind of the bereaved. (p. 643.)

Still other factors in the coping patterns of the dying and bereaved were isolated in the early literature. The findings were not always in conformity with later conclusions. For example, where earlier investigators saw a direct correlation between the intensity of the in-life relationship of the bereaved and the deceased and the intensity of the bereaved's response, later researchers seemed to indicate otherwise: "a high initial vulnerability to the problems of bereavement is produced when the emotions of the bereaved person (sense of loss, hostility, guilt) are maximal and complex. Problems are avoided and intensity of emotional reaction is reduced" (Switzer, 1970, p. 28) where some congruence exists between the self and the social role of the bereaved.

The Dying: Six Stages to Death

Five basic stages of response have been identified by Kübler-Ross (1969, 1974) as common to those facing death. The five have been described as denial, anger or the "Why me?" stage, bargaining, depression, and, finally, acceptance. Many students of thanatology include a sixth stage: the act of dying itself.

In the first of the five stages, the patient first senses shock and numbness, then enters a distinct phase of the dying process: denial. This stage has been described as adaptive; the patient requires it as a "buffer after the unexpected shocking news, [it] allows the patient to collect himself and, with time, mobilize other, less radical, defenses" (Kübler-Ross, 1969, p. 39).

Anger, as the second stage in Kübler-Ross's model, occurs because the patient feels his or her plans and activities have been interrupted. The patient envies those who can still enjoy life. From the point of view of the staff of the hospital, geriatric center, or other institution, the anger stage is usually more troublesome than the previous stage: the patient's anger, in a natural reaction, may be directed almost randomly at anyone in the environment.

The bargaining stage preceding inevitable death is, in general, relatively short. The patient in this stage may still believe that he or she "can succeed in entering some sort of agreement which may postpone the inevitable" (Kübler-Ross, 1969, p. 83). In most cases the patient offers good behavior, in the form of prayer or some other action, in exchange for a postponement of death. Yet when a specific deadline arrives and passes, the patient begins bargaining again in an effort to gain more time.

The fourth stage observed by Kübler-Ross is depression. The stage may be precipitated by the realization on the part of the patient that he or she has developed new symptoms or has grown weaker and thinner. "Surgical procedures such as the removal of a breast or part of the face often result in deep depression" (Schulz & Aderman, 1976, p. 47).

In the fifth stage the patient has accepted his or her fate. "If a patient has had enough time . . . and has been given some help in working through the previously described stages, he will reach a state during which he is neither depressed nor angry about fate" (Kübler-Ross, 1969, pp. 112–113).

The findings of Kübler-Ross have been both acclaimed and criticized. Researchers have noted, for example, that the observational research methods Kübler-Ross used were essentially subjective, even if permeated by deep regard and compassion for the dying. Others have expressed the fear that the five key stages would be regarded as both descriptive and prescriptive, that those charged with caring for the dying might seek to force patients into a mold according to their knowledge of the responses in impending death. It has been suggested that the various stages be accepted as different *types* of response, or different *forms* of coping, where death is imminent. The forms need not occur in sequence.

Some studies have reached conclusions that appear to conflict directly with those of Kübler-Ross. Hinton (1963), for example, assessed anxiety as a separate emotional dimension. Where Kübler-Ross felt that anxiety afflicted many patients through the early stages and then disappeared before the final stage, Hinton found it to be present all through the final phases of life. In a separate study by Weisman and Kastenbaum (1968), patients whose final weeks and days were reconstructed *post hoc* appeared to adopt individual coping patterns and remain in them without great variation until death.

Such findings may be regarded as extending the basic area of Kübler-Ross's conclusions, or as modifying to conform with variant considerations. Many patients in hospital situations undoubtedly do pass through stages in their passage toward death. In her second book, Kübler-Ross (1974) herself appeared to moderate her stand regarding the stages of dying. For example, she noted that denial may persist until the final hour of life and may in some instances appear to work a kind of miracle of recovery:

> It is not your role, whether you are a member of a helping profession or a family member, to break down a defense [such as denial]. It is your role to help the patient, and if he needs to believe that he is cured, it is cruel and untherapeutic to tell him there are no such things as miracles. . . . He may even end up convincing you. Over the last eight years we have had several patients who had been given up, and from a medical point of view had no practical chance of recovery, but who are still alive several years after the predicted date of their death. (Kübler-Ross, 1974, p. 20.)

Peak Experience or Final Trauma?

Analyses of psychological coping patterns have not uniformly stressed negative factors. On the contrary, where those facing impending death could still function with relative normalcy, it has been remarked that a substantial proportion continues to engage in daily activities. Many such persons were even able to "initiate new activities and interpersonal relationships" (Schulz & Aderman, 1976, p. 48).

A still more unconventional stance has been assumed by those who maintain that death, as the end of life, is also life's goal. The contention is that man should work toward death as a mystical experience, that one should then embrace it without fear or hesitation. The principle underlying such a thesis appears to be that "all life is a terminal illness." Those proclaiming belief in the position have belonged among society's most creative personages. Albert Einstein is said to have believed that it meant little that a friend died a few weeks ahead of his own demise: past, present, and future were man-created illusions in any case. Mozart has been quoted as writing: "Since death (properly understood) is the true ultimate purpose of our life, I have for several years past made myself acquainted with this truest and best friend of mankind so that he has for me nothing terrifying any more but much that is tranquillizing and consoling" (Mannes, 1973, p. 124).

Other statements echo the faith that death holds more than mere extinction. Eleanor Roosevelt is said to have welcomed imminent death and to have believed in an afterlife of some kind. Artists such as Beethoven and Michelangelo not only had no fear of death; they felt, in a sense, that they had conquered it by achieving the level of the "universal spirit" of art that defied time and death. Unquestionably a quasi-religious sense of man's permanence in spiritual or other form colors such views and informs the psychological coping mechanisms that they can foster. As Murphy (1959) wrote of Marcuse:

> For Herbert Marcuse, the primary fact in the experience of thoughtful men of the West relative to death seems to be the capacity to make death a fulfillment or consummation, a biological reality involving more than the sheer termination of life; the establishment of a dualism in which death both terminates and fulfills life. Conceptions of immortality, such as those derived from Plato, are, however, compared with more shadowy conceptions in which existence beyond death is left in uncertainty. (Murphy, 1959, p. 321.)

The question whether death must represent a peak experience or a final trauma clearly places the debate in too harsh and categorical a light. Between each extreme individuals inevitably must and will find their own different ways of going to death. Some ambivalence will have to be admitted: where most persons can acknowledge death as a mark of man's finitude, most would also find it difficult to face death as merely a biological counterpart to birth.

Death, in this view, can be met in accord with the individual's characteristic manner of meeting life—barring extremely crippling or disfiguring physiological symptoms. Death *can* be a peak experience or a final trauma as individuals seek their own level of coping: the patient "wants to be a human, to play a role consistent with his identity, his individuality" (Aronson, 1959, p. 252). As Hinton also notes, the helping professional or the relative seeking a *modus* by which to speak to a dying person about death can be guided generally by the dying individual's approach to life. "Their habitual manner of dealing with life can be a useful guide, [as can be] their style of facing former difficulties or attaining their social position" (Hinton, 1976, p. 312). Experiments designed to test the validity of such a theory have generally produced positive findings.

> In order to evaluate more reliably the effect of telling patients that they have a mortal illness, a careful and courageous investigation was carried [out]. . . . Some patients with an incurable illness were told and others were not. . . . A psychiatrist made a preliminary assessment of the patients to see if there were any indications of emotional instability in the past to see if there were any indications of emotional instability in the past or present to contraindicate telling. In the overwhelming majority of those he thought it suitable to tell, [and] the patients maintained their emotional balance and did not regret being told. (Hinton, 1976, p. 313.)

A danger resides in such experimentation despite its surface usefulness: that a patient's apparent social status or value will influence the attitudes of those charged with helping him or her in the coping process. That the danger exists in real terms has been noted by professionals: "Variations in patient care based on social loss also hinder the professional ideal of treating all patients in accordance with their medical needs. The morale of a dying patient needs to be maintained irrespective of . . . his social class or 'personality' " (Glaser & Strauss, 1964, p. 121).

The question whether death represents a victorious, peak experience or a final trauma will, of course, never be conclusively answered. For most, death will remain the latter: a consummation to be avoided at all costs and as long as possible. For others, even though these may not go consciously and purposefully toward death, it will represent a culmination and a triumph.

"We Who Mourn"

The increased attention paid to the coping patterns of the dying has been accompanied by, or has spawned, new and more intense study of the ways in which the survivors of a deceased cope with bereavement. The reason has become obvious: grief as "the hidden illness" may account "for many of the physical symptoms that doctors see in the course of their daily practice" (Dempsey, 1975, p. 149).

The "broken heart syndrome" can hardly be questioned today. Statistics have shown that 12 percent of surviving spouses die within a year after their wives or husbands had died. Mortality in a nonbereaved control group was only 1.2 percent for the same period (Rees & Lutkins, 1967).

What do these and many confirmatory statistics mean? They must be interpreted cautiously:

> More bereaved people live than die; they become reconciled to their loss, in one way or another. And for those who do not, death or illness may be only indirectly grief related. In many cases, the stricken person goes to pieces: he neglects himself, turns to alcohol, doesn't eat properly and becomes vulnerable to physical disease. But in seemingly far more cases, the illness is literally a reaction—a protest—to an emotional loss. . . . (Dempsey, 1975, pp. 150–151.)

Modern statistics on the physical or psychosomatic effects of bereavement and grief are difficult to interpret for other reasons. The reduced influence of religion in individual lives may be reflected in a greater incidence of physical problems at or after crisis periods of life. The trend toward simpler funerals and streamlined rituals connected with death and burial has been cited as a possible contributory cause in cases of poor adjustment to bereavement. The applicable theory is that rituals involving religious custom and protocol and formal or traditional funerals reduce the bereaved's guilt-sense: the survivor has the opportunity to adjust to the death with others whose participation is important (Figure 3.1).

Under any circumstances, "We who now mourn and weep" have become the subject of intense study. The process of investigating the anatomy of grief began decades ago and has become, increasingly, a preoccupation. At least four stages of grief have been identified:

> The Immediate Stage, up to several hours following the death, included the Stoic, Dazed, Collapse, and Incrimose responses. The Post-Immediate Stage, to the end of the funeral, included the Acquiescent, Excited, Protestive, Detached, and Despondent responses. Categories of Alternating, Enforced, and Attention-Getting described the behavior in the Transitional Stage, from the funeral to reentry into active life. The final stage was that of the Repatterning of behavior categorized as Projective,

Participative, Identification, Memory-Phantasy, and Repressive-Seclusive. (Fulcomer, 1942, p. 101.)

Such analysis advances modern man's knowledge of grief without telling us precisely what are its components. Nor can brief and simple answers be provided. In the main, authorities appear to agree that melancholy resides in grief; but the psychoanalytic element of *melancholia* does not. The latter represents a failure of self where the former refers to the deficiencies of the world: in grief the world has become empty whereas in melancholia, the individual sees his or her own ego as impoverished, defeated.

Coping patterns may be conspicuously lacking in contemporary analyses. But these patterns clearly depend on the degree to which the individual responds and on the form that response takes. That, in turn, depends on a number of factors, including at least those listed by Flesch (1975). The factors include the intensity of affective response

Figure 3.1 Members of a bereaved family comfort each other.

in connection with the loss; the hostility engendered in connection with the loss; the religious orientation of the bereaved, including the view of death; the time orientation of the bereaved individual—whether extreme disorientation occurs; the memories that the bereaved has of the deceased; the adhesion to the deceased on the part of the bereaved—the extent to which the bereaved seeks to retain intact parts of the former life; the changed self-image of the bereaved as a result of the loss; and the bereaved person's capacity for reinvestment in new sources of satisfaction (Flesch, 1975).

Grief has also been found to contain elements of anxiety and guilt. Some analysts have gone so far as to identify grief and anxiety. "Adult mourning is seen as the reproduction of a separation experience which is analogous to the separation experiences of the infant . . ." (Klein, 1940, p. 126). More usually, severe anxiety is regarded as a neurotic response. "The loss of an emotionally significant person, being a reproduction of the original anxiety producing situation—separation from the mother—would simply increase his anxiety to a level where the neurotic mechanisms were no longer adequate . . ." (Switzer, 1970, p. 35).

The Management of Acute Grief

The management of acute grief involves an agent of some kind, recognition of certain realities, and direct action. The agent should, preferably, be the bereaved; but members of the bereaved's family, the clergy, and others may also help as occasion demands. In extreme cases psychological or psychiatric assistance and therapy may be required. But such cases go beyond the normal to the pathological, and are considered as outside the competence of either the bereaved or others without professional competence.

Realities that must be acknowledged by both the bereaved and others close to him or her before management can become effective include the fact that anxiety can be used constructively. In anxiety, in short, inheres a motivational force that can be used for positive ends: "The anxiety which is always experienced when one is confronted with his own potentiality, the outcome of which is uncertain and is thus a threat to the level of security which one has already attained, becomes the stimulus to move from one's present internal situation" (Switzer, 1970, p. 192). Anxiety becomes, in a sense, the source of knowledge and inspiration or motivation in one's life, "searches it thoroughly" (Kierkegaard, 1944, p. 142), and creates the drive to eliminate the trivial and restore balance.

The effectiveness of talking and listening has also been held up by authorities as a factor to be recognized in the management of grief. Talking as a therapeutic or pastoral methodology has, of course, long been accepted. In the management of grief, talking serves the purpose of reestablishing security patterns:

> The concept of the development of the self and the integral affective relation of the learning of language . . . show how language in the infant and small child takes shape as essentially a security measure: first, as a necessary means of communicating basic survival and physical comfort needs; second, as a means of winning and maintaining parental approval; and third, even when the child is alone, as a means of holding the parents emotionally near. (Switzer, 1970, p. 195.)

Talking serves as a direct action approach in the management of grief. In that role it can serve at least six purposes.

1. *Release of negative emotions.* A key function of talking while in the grief state is to work through negative emotions such as hate and guilt. The aid of another person, whether friend, relative, or the clergy, may be required, both as listener and as interpreter of such emotions; but the end effect to be sought is that catharsis in which "speech becomes a substitute form of the emotionally charged acts that need to be performed, understood, and accepted" (Switzer, 1970, p. 196).

2. *Affirmation of one's self.* A reduced image of one's self has been noted by many authorities as an accompaniment of grief. Talking as a mode of strengthening the self-image has been found to have therapeutic effect. Care is required to ensure that the bereaved, in depression, does not indulge in self-accusation.

3. *Breaking libidinal ties.* The purpose of talking through former experiences involving both bereaved and the deceased is to make a necessary emotional break: to "free one's self from bondage to the deceased" (Switzer, 1970, p. 198). As Weiss (1950) has noted, grief represents the conflict between uncontrollable desire for the loved person and recognition that the person no longer exists. Thus verbalization that helps the bereaved to relive earlier experiences also aids in the process of breaking libidinal ties. The inner world of needs and the outer world of reality also come increasingly into healthy alignment as such verbalization proceeds.

4. *The resurrection of the deceased within the self of the bereaved.*
   Verbal communication also serves to "reaffirm the life of the
   deceased within one's own self" (Switzer, 1970, p. 200). Thus the
   loved person becomes a permanent, active force in the life of the
   bereaved.

   > One's self has certain aspects of the significant other as a living com-
   > ponet of it. When the other dies, the self is perceived as threatened with
   > death by the loss. . . . But the external event of the death of an emo-
   > tionally significant other need not annihilate the self. Rather, the other
   > which is within one can be reaffirmed as living as a part of one's self.
   > (Switzer, 1970, p. 200.)

5. *Renewal of relationship.* The need to cultivate old friendships and
   acquaintanceships, and to reestablish new relations with other
   persons, has also been emphasized. The bereaved is seen as being
   strengthened by such ties against the threat to his inner life that
   the loss poses: "The restoration of the harmony of his inner world
   is promoted, his fears and distress are more quickly reduced"
   (Klein, 1940, p. 145). Since separation anxiety has been found to
   be a main ingredient of grief, the use of communication to extend
   or establish personal relationships ranks as an important process.

6. *The rediscovery of meaning.* Communication that seeks to recover
   a sense of meaning in the life of the bereaved actually serves as a
   kind of summing-up; the success of other efforts to meet basic
   needs of the bereaved receives a kind of confirmation. But if the
   other needs have not been, or cannot be, met, rediscovery of
   meaning in the bereaved's life cannot take place.

Meaning, of course, ranks as a primary source of motivation in the
life of man (Frankl, 1962). "We cannot really exist as fully human
without a sense of coherence, purpose, values, and an understanding
of our own roles in the larger life about us" (Switzer, 1970, p. 203).
The death of a loved one often destroys that sense. Its restoration in
verbalization, if only by gradual degrees, reconstitutes the motivational
power of the sense of meaning in life and enables the bereaved more
quickly to put aside grief. The process takes place, according to
Switzer (1970), on two levels—the emotional-relational and that
involving conceptualization and verbalization, "which itself is reinforcing to the entire process" (p. 204).

Finally, it should be noted that grief is endemic to the human condition. At some time or another, it challenges the life and powers of ad-

justment of nearly every individual. Thus the management of acute grief has importance for every individual. For the bereaved, "death does not conclude the matter" even though there is "the pain, and the ache of separation, and the long, dark hours of the night when sleep is absent and time is a deep loneliness" (Rudin, 1969, p. 44).

OUR CAPACITY FOR GRIEF

It can probably be stated as fact that no one has an infinite capacity for grief. Many persons would in all likelihood succumb under repetitive losses of loved ones. Yet, depending on the individual, on the relationship of the bereaved to the deceased, and on other factors, the human capacity for grief is enormous. Individuality and individual tolerance are the key elements here.

> There is almost an infinite gamut of emotional reactions which divergent human personalities may manifest in the presence of death. Occasionally no real grief is felt; sometimes grief is felt and expressed, but is mastered by a strong, well-integrated personality. Sometimes grief is felt and remains unexpressed and comes to master and dominate the whole personality. . . . (Liebman, 1946, p. 107.)

Such comments underscore the need to express oneself on matters of importance when grief strikes. The same writer makes the need for expression explicit: "express as much grief as you actually feel" (Liebman, 1962, p. 108). But whether every person can accept such advice remains a question. Each individual lives under the influence of cultural and other forces that, in a sense, predetermine that person's capacity for grief. The forces, or determinants, also in many cases dictate the extent to which grief can be expressed.

Evolutionary and Sociocultural Determinants of Grief

Evolutionary and sociocultural factors must rank among the primary determinants of the individual's capacity for grief. People come to maturity with evolutionary capabilities and limitations imposed on them by family, relatives, special traditions unique to their racial or social group, and other persons and factors. "Because we are human and grow up in the same society, we are more similar to one another than to an Arapesh tribesman. However, within that broad similarity lies tremendous diversity" (Peretz, 1969, p. 140).

Evolution thus becomes prescriptive insofar as the capacity for grief is concerned: it prepares the individual as the inheritor of group attitudes toward death, bereavement, and one's fellows to behave in patterned ways when a loss occurs. The patterns vary necessarily because of other influences. But a surprising degree of uniformity may be achieved, to be violated only when temperamental characteristics, interacting with hereditary and evolutional ones, effect a variation.

Sociocultural determinants are both explicit and implicit in the surrounding society. Because "each society has a prevailing system of values" (Peretz, 1969, p. 141), including guides to human conduct, the individual absorbs attitudes and, by implication, tolerances for grief, anxiety, sorrow, and related emotions. Attitudes toward death are, to an extent, preprogrammed. "Different patterns of family life produce variable emotional levels of self-involvement with other persons, and this is a major factor in the behavioral reactions of bereavement" (Switzer, 1970, p. 26). The effects of sociocultural influences may be even more pronounced:

> The bereaved person has a social role to perform. So problems may arise not just because of the loss [but also because] . . . experiences in the relationship may have tended to contradict the role and emotions [which were appropriate] to it. . . . In bereavement, society says to feel the loss and express the sadness. But this is not always possible with one's self-feelings, and our society has not provided for sanctioned channels of expression for hostility and guilt in the context of bereavement. (Switzer, 1970, p. 27.)

Even ethics comes under the dominance of sociocultural determinants in the mythology of death. All known human societies lay down prescriptions according to which death can take place "morally" or "ethically" or "unethically." The grandmother in Eskimo cultures who decides that her time has come will not meet resistance from her sons and daughters. The same was true of many Indian tribes. Thus the phenomenon of choice regarding the hour of death has social and cultural underpinnings. In modern technological societies the issue has become far more complex; but different determinants still work to place the individual's attitudes within the approved framework.

Darwin's (1899) study of emotional expression in man and animals constitutes one of the few sociocultural or other analyses of the ways in which sorrow or grief is expressed by animals, young children, and adult human beings. Darwin noted that man and animals exhibit many of the same reactions to loss; an exception was man's capacity to frown. In Darwinian theory the use of the "grief muscles" in frowning—the corrugator muscle—was to protect the eyeballs from popping out during intense emotion.

Whatever the ways in which grief is expressed, human beings clearly condition themselves to meet grief according to social or tribal standards. In some modern European societies crying is not only permitted, the bereaved are encouraged to cry; and the act of crying is believed to effect relief from the stresses that accompany grief and anxiety. Social mores suggest the degree to which the bereaved can feel grief: "Where a person grows up in a tribe where the life of the tribe is the highest value and where emotional ties are diffused among many persons rather than a few, the individual is less vulnerable to intense feeling of loss at the death of another individual" (Switzer, 1970, p. 26).

Much of one's capacity for grief appears to stem from one's view of death. That view is inevitably formed, at least partly, by prevailing social attitudes. In contemporary American society, one encounters in the midst of great diversity a cosmology that denies both the fact of death and concomitants such as growing old, being sick, and finiteness. The result, insofar as the capacity for grief is concerned, is predictable: the bereaved is expected to mourn quickly and then put aside sorrow. "America, conjured into its superficial stereotype, is a country of the eternal now, of the young, face lifting, good teeth into the seventies, old ladies in Bermuda shorts, hair coloured at will, endless euphemisms for chronic disease, affliction and death" (Rakoff, 1973, p. 150). Death and grief, one might add, become all but impermissible in such circumstances.

Many historic influences have combined to produce the modern situation. As Rakoff also notes, "every American family begins with leaving the old people behind" (p. 151) so that the new generation can start a new life in the New World. With the past safely placed in distant escrow, as it were, one could move on to new things, new problems. Death did not necessarily rank immediately as one of those problems. A new society was coming into being, and who had time to spend with the dying or the dead?

The interrelationships between attitudinal patterns regarding death and such sociocultural institutions as family and kinship, socioeconomic and religiocultural systems require more elucidation before conclusions can be drawn. But the interrelationships exist, and certainly affect the individual's capacity for grief. In preindustrial Europe and North America, for example, the bereaved, living under conditions that included the "noncontrol" of mortality, were exposed to sociocultural determinants that would be unrecognizable today: "Life under extreme conditions of the noncontrol of mortality is precariously short, death is ever-present, shrouded in mystery and uncertainty, and is concentrated among the very young" (Goldscheider, 1976, p. 182). By contrast, in the America of the 1970s, in which death is "controlled," an entirely different situation obtains:

> The level of mortality is low—crude death rates are below 10 per 1,000; life expectancy is over seventy years, and only about 1 percent of all babies born die in their first year. Death rarely interrupts the daily activities of societies, and when it occurs it is largely to older persons dying in institutions from degenerative diseases. The quality of life is discussed not in terms of uncertainties but as "probabilities," and death is explained largely in rational, scientific vocabularies. (Goldscheider, 1976, p. 182.)

The problem may be that grief, like death, comes under a form of control, even if the control is informal. The expression of grief is restricted, making the role of psychophysiological mechanisms in the expression and management of grief more fundamentally important.

Psychophysiological Mechanisms

Grief has uniformly been seen as an interpersonal phenomenon: part of the definition of grief indicates a focus on another who has died. Physical or physiological effects may be observed at once. Where the act of dying is protracted, the "aftereffects" of the loss may even begin before death takes place. Physiological effects may include constriction of the throat muscles, weariness, loss of appetite, hyperactivity.

Switzer (1970) has found three forms or categories of illness that may be precipitated by grief and that appear to be amenable to control through operation of basic psychophysiological mechanisms.

> One of these is neurotic in nature and the second is psychosomatic. The former is the result of the mechanism of identification, in which the dynamics of this mechanism, already operating in the relationship, are intensified by the increased anxiety brought about by the separation of death, and the bereaved begins to exhibit symptoms related to the final illness of the deceased. (Switzer, 1970, p. 113.)

The second form of illness "which can be seen . . . rising out of grief-anxiety is psychosomatic, or psychophysiological" (Switzer, 1970, p. 114). In such cases medical practitioners encounter actual organ pathology, including forms of colitis; the belief is that the grief-anxiety seeks to be converted into what the organism senses as more tolerable physical symptoms.

In the third category of grief-related illnesses, physiogenic or organic, the grief is believed to play at least a preconditioning role (Switzer, 1970): the grief lowers the body's resistance to germs and viruses. More serious somatic changes may take place.

Such reactions to the death of another, whether that death has occurred or is awaited, suggest parallelisms between the situations of the dying and the bereaved. For one thing, as Neale has noted, "the individual who knows or senses that he is dying is also himself bereaved" (Neale, 1971, p. 83). Thus individuals must accustom themselves to the thought of loss—of life, of the love object, of all that they wanted to accomplish—and endure physiological reactions that may exacerbate their initially poor physical condition. For a second thing, both the survivors and the dying face the challenge of "transforming the No to death and the No to life into affirmations" (Neale, 1971, p. 83).

Are there psychophysiological mechanisms that extend the capacity for grief: that actually enable the sufferer to rise to the fact of death and accept it? Many students of death and dying are convinced that such mechanisms exist. Clearly, they have an opportunity to function and become apparent in the survivor, the bereaved, more than in the dying, who under any circumstances stands under a sentence of death.

The view that "life is a terminal illness," or that all human beings, whatever their station or health situation, stand under a death sentence, may underlie and direct the basic mechanisms. Such a view implies acceptance of an inevitable fact of life: one's own death. The fact of death, if accepted rather than rejected, becomes an integral part of one's world-view; it is integrated into the character without becoming a morbid preoccupation. Death is simply *there*, where such a foundation for other mechanisms is present.

It has already been noted that strength of ego or of personality may function as another mechanism making possible acceptance of death. The rubric applies to the bereaved as to the dying. A positive, constructive approach to living appears to carry the survivor forward in the face of death; the bereaved seems to remain "in character" and to emerge from grief with his or her approach intact. Even earlier, the relationship of the bereaved to the dying person may continue to flower: "When a relationship grows and develops, . . . the destructive elements of living and dying do not get in the way of either" (Neale, 1971, p. 85).

An elemental life-force appears to be at work where such an effect is produced. The bereaved finds it possible to die vicariously and then to live again: "So what is the task of the bereaved? *It is to die* and be reborn" (Neale, 1971, p. 88). Grief becomes the healthy mechanism making rebirth possible, extending the capacity for life, moving one "from the old and banal to new life" (Neale, 1971, p. 89). A principle of psychotherapy comes into play: "A common . . . assumption of psychotherapy is that the psychotherapist works with a patient to increase the value of his long-term productivity and his long-term relationships with others, and, perhaps, to better his adjustment to his environment" (LeShan & LeShan, 1973, p. 109).

Such evidence suggests that other psychophysiological mechanisms may help to determine the individual's capacity for grief. In the bereaved, the ancient triad of faith, hope, and love may be functional: one's capacity for all three may extend the boundaries of tolerance for grief. The faith indicated involves belief in the ultimate meaningfulness of life; hope rests on the ability of the life instinct to persevere. Love, of course, posits a capacity to relate to others in deep, significant ways (Switzer, 1970). The faith, hope, and love may or may not have religious roots: the effects, both psychological and physiological, may be the same. The will to live receives confirmation: "Our analysis has shown that when disconnected from other influences [grief's] varieties seem to be reducible to two, the depressed and the excited, and that these are conditioned by the degree of the sorrow-producing stimulus on the one hand and the amount of energy present to resist sorrow on the other—by the strength of the *will-to-live*, which seeks the continuance of stimuli affording to the organism a sense of the furtherance of life" (Becker, 1973, p. 100).

Once strengthened, the "sense of the furtherance of life" produces positive physiological effects that, in their turn, further the process of emergence from grief. Will or will power may enter in; the bereaved must help him- or herself to be helped by others. By drawing parallels to the basic propositions concerning sorrow as evolved by Becker (1973), one can arrive at some corollaries for the grief state. For example, the degree to which the bereaved can positively take part in his or her attack on grief may determine (1) the extent to which the impulses of attraction and restoration of grief are furthered, impeded, or frustrated and, in turn, the degree to which the emotion itself is reduced, heightened, or pushed toward maximum levels; (2) the effect of the remembrance is accepted as a means of diminishing the dimensions of the present sorrow; (3) the degree to which the bereaved can draw comfort from the knowledge that others grieve sympathetically; (4) the bereaved's ultimate ability to share grief and thus to mitigate it; (5) the degree to which the bereaved can *control* grief in a pure sense (Becker, 1973, pp. 200-210).

The latter two phases of psychophysiological adjustment suggest, finally, the lines of Shakespeare: "Give sorrow words. The grief that does not speak / Whispers the o'erfraught heart, and bids it break" (*Macbeth*, act IV, scene 3, lines 209–210).

THE EMOTIVE DISPLAY TO DEATH AND DYING

Displays of emotion in situations where grief is natural and inevitable have been difficult to study. The reason is obvious: researchers who appear too clinical may seem inconsiderate and even ruthless in their pursuit of data for analysis. As the head of a research team noted,

> We may say that initially we came to [the bereaved] with great hesitation. We realized only too well that we came as total strangers, even as intruders during a time of sorrow and crisis, asking that they share with us their most intimate feelings. Our own fearfulness was itself severely inhibiting, initially almost to the point of persuading us that the task could not be carried out. However, through trial and error we learned how to approach these families. (Flesch, 1975, p. 95.)

The importance of permitting the expression of grief, and even of grief's various moods or stages, has been underlined by many authorities. As Switzer (1970) noted regarding the expression of grief by bereaved persons, unless grief is given expression directly and openly, "there is the strong likelihood that its form of expression will be in ways destructive to the happiness of the bereaved" (p. 186). "Unmanifested" grief has also been described as, in effect, uncontrollable: it will, in one way or another, be expressed to the full (Deutsch, 1973). In her relatively extensive writings, Kübler-Ross has underscored a similar point. Two groups in particular, widows and widowers, "present themselves with somatic symptoms as a result of the failure to work through their grief and guilt" (Kübler-Ross, 1969, p. 162).

The positive side of the question of emotional displays of grief has also been explored in depth. Grief itself has been defined at least tentatively as a response of emotional pain. Included in such a definition, necessarily, is the factor of physiological symptoms or accompaniments. Excluded are those specific manners and means by which emotive display is effected: the signs, movements, moods, expressions, and other physical signals that are visible to the eye.

Grief is Sharing, Caring

Kübler-Ross has, with many others, stressed the intimate character of death and the necessity of the emotive displays that normally accompany or follow it. Grief in this context becomes a matter of caring and sharing, particularly in its more obvious manifestations. But the focus may shift to the professional who arrives to help the dying patient through the final hours. The family may not help at all: "The family of such [dying] patients may share their feelings of sorrow and uselessness, hopelessness and despair, and add little to the patient's well-being. They may spend the short remaining time in a morbid depression . . ." (Kübler-Ross, 1969, p. 36).

The facts of death that find the dying person in a hospital or other institution at the final hour—and often much before that—obviously make outsiders more important as intermediaries and helpers. The physician, the social worker, the nurse, and others in the helping professions may be the only ones who can be present when the patient dies. But in many other cases grief may be shared constructively by the dying person and members of the family. In such cases "grief work," an unusual sense of remorse, or of guilt stemming from a feeling that not all had been done for the patient before death may be reduced or eliminated. The absence of grief work "means no . . . feeling of, 'Oh God, if I had only done this or that,' and no guilt" (Kübler-Ross, 1974, p. 98).

Granting the importance of the roles played by members of the family or by members of the helping professions, what are the emotions commonly displayed by the dying? Do affective displays, in particular negative ones, indicate a sense of isolation that negates the element of sharing? The emotions run a surprisingly broad gamut:

> What I . . . see is a complicated clustering of intellectual and affective states, some fleeting, lasting for a moment or a day or a week . . . , set . . . against the backdrop of that person's total personality . . . , a hive of affect, in which there is a constant coming and going. The emotional stages seem to include a constant interplay between disbelief and hope and, against these as background, a waxing and waning of anguish, terror, acquiescence and surrender, rage and envy, disinterest and ennui, pretense, taunting and daring and even yearning for death—all these in the context of bewilderment and pain. (Shneidman, 1976, pp. 446–447.)

The question whether such waves of affect negate the element of sharing cannot be answered simply. Certainly both loved ones and helping professionals may sometimes sense rejection. But even when it appears total and irrevocable, rejection may constitute a passing stage or phase. A professional consensus would agree that the stages are not only natural but expectable. In the words of Kübler-Ross (1972), "We find . . . [it] to be true among many patients who developed strong positive feelings toward us and were still able to pass through a stage of rage and anger often displaced onto others in the environment who reminded them of their own failing strength, vitality and functioning" (p. 57).

The process of terminating life's ties and relationships when death is near has been called *decathexis*. The extent to which the process advances before death varies from individual to individual. In many persons it may never take place at all. The dying person may cling until the final moment to those whom he or she has loved, or learned to love during a final illness. Yet *some* decathexis probably occurs in all who become aware of impending death and move toward it consciously: sharing probably ends at that moment when no additional emotive display is possible. The patient simply subsides into death. Decathexis, like earlier denial, may not even imply rejection; it may suggest weakness, or weariness, or an inability to relate socially or otherwise to those around one.

Earlier, verbal and other communication may prove the need and the efficacy of the process of sharing grief emotionally. Holding hands may constitute a symbolic act that brings the dying person through periods of great stress. Other, and equally simple, gestures may accomplish the same purpose. Often, not even verbal language is required. "Sometimes it just takes companionship and care. You do not desert people who are not ready to talk. If you simply sit with them and continue to show your care . . . , they will occasionally open up without a word spoken . . . (Kübler-Ross, 1974, p. 42). Within such communication, whether it takes place in words, through nods of the head, in handwritten notes, or in other ways, resides an emotional content whose release may be crucial to the patient's well-being.

For the bereaved the emotive display of grief serves the same basic purpose as for the dying. In a real sense the bereaved must pass through the same stages as the dying person with the difference, of course, that the bereaved lives on. Except in cases of sudden death, grief normally begins before loss, and will occasion emotive displays: "Anticipatory grief may range from quiet periods of sadness and tears to those symptoms usually associated with . . . actual loss" (Peretz, 1970, pp. 25-26).

The control of grief that may be required before a loved person dies has been found to have effects subsequent to the person's death. Some intensification of emotive display may result, for example. But "normal" grief among the bereaved after a loss is accompanied by recognized signs of deep emotion.

> In addition to mental pain, the bereaved will usually exhibit physical reactions—dyspnea and deep sighing, "lumps" or tight sensations in the throat, weakness, feelings of emptiness, exhaustion, decreased appetite, and insomnia. . . . There may be agitation and restlessness, hand-wringing and an appearance of confusion and puzzlement. (Peretz, 1970, p. 22.)

Emotional stress may lead to grief symptoms that are not apparent or visible: the bereaved may imagine that he or she hears the footsteps of the dead person, or other people may appear smaller than usual. With time, such effects normally dwindle in number and intensity, and the need to express grief affectively also gradually disappears. One cannot assume that the sense of loss grows less intense; rather, the bereaved by degrees builds a new web of life that, hopefully, provides protection and distraction and genuine new meaning.

In those cases where grief work is successful, and they are unquestionably the majority of instances, grief may recur at times and produce new affective signals. For several weeks and even sometimes after many months, depressive symptoms of a transitory nature may include restlessness, weeping, and hypersensitivity. But public displays of emotion usually cease in a few weeks except under unusual circumstances: for example, where the bereaved is suddenly reminded of the loved one. "It should be expected that when faced with reminders of the deceased (such as by pictures, songs, and old haunts) temporary upsurges of grief will occur even in later months" (Peretz, 1970, p. 25). Where the emotional aftereffects of a loss continue to be felt and exhibited six months to a year after the death, the individual may be in need of psychiatric help.

Emotion: A Cultural Response

As one of the most common modes of expressing grief for a person with whom one has shared part of life, crying has presented a subject of interest to poets and dramatists as well as scientists. Darwin's (1899) study presents a key scientific view—that "we are the only weeping primate of any kind. . . . If you want to find the only weeping carnivorous animals, you have to go into the sea again, and meet the weeping seals, and the weeping sea otters" (Morgan, 1972, p. 43).

Human beings have been represented, thus, as those animals that distinguish themselves from other animals by more than their rational nature. They can express grief uniquely through the use of the corrugator muscles. But they also distinguish themselves by developing or adopting uniquely variant ways of expressing emotion, particularly in the face of death. These ways are largely determined by cultural factors. In other words, man's diverse cultures employ particular methods of expressing emotion (Saucier, 1967).

Parallels have been drawn between culture-determined responses to pain and those responses called forth by the facts of death and dying. The latter, in fact, inflict psychological pain as real as the physical pain of an injury. Thus the acceptance of death among the American Indians had its counterpart in Sun Dance self-torture ceremonies. The young man taking part in the Sun Dance first had two incisions made, one on each side of his chest, by a sharp knife. Skewers were inserted through the incisions, running across the chest under the skin, and lariats were attached to the skewers at one end and the sacred pole at the other. Then each young man danced around the pole, hurling himself away from it until the skin of his chest tore and he fell to the ground.

Other parallels relating grief over a loss through death and the physical pain inflicted in formal or routine life situations might be cited. In the hook-hanging ritual practiced into modern times in India, steel hooks attached by strong ropes to the top of a special cart are inserted under the skin of a specially chosen man. The celebrant, chosen to represent the power of the gods, then travels on the cart from village to village. At the height of the ritual, he swings free, supported only by the hooks.

One could assume that societies in which such rites are accepted would look on death realistically, or even with indifference. To a large extent, such is the case. But "socially acceptable affect," or expression of emotion, can still be permitted and may take many forms. One recalls that suttee, the practice in which wives in India threw themselves, in grief, on the funeral pyres of their dead spouses, was not outlawed until the nineteenth century (Figure 3.2).

Socially acceptable affect of any kind has a purpose, of course, even though that purpose may not always be obvious. Among Italy's Lucanian peasants, the highly dramatic reevocation of memories of the deceased through wild funeral laments has been seen as a mechanism for "isolating the participant from the destructive potentialities of the immediate and most poignant grief reaction; the

Figure 3.2 The Suttee. The burning of a Hindu widow with the body of her husband. Woodcut. (The Bettmann Archive)

repetition stereotypes the affect so that it is depersonalized and mastered and given meaning in a wider cultural framework" (Parsons, 1969, pp. 235–236). Needless to say, the laments would be regarded by the more reserved Anglo-Saxon as excessively demonstrative.

The witchcraft beliefs of primitive societies may entail unusual expressions of grief that also have the purpose of exorcizing the survivors. The witch in most cases represents an outside, evil force; fear becomes a driving energy behind rituals of exorcism and incantations. Sometimes "acts of vengeance against real agents supposed to be witches" (Parsons, 1969, p. 188) are prescribed, though not necessarily as part of the grief syndrome. The practice of chanting incantations gives the mourner and the mourner's family a culturally approved means of control of evil where death has not taken place and prevention is the goal.

Status-related expressions of grief are also common in primitive societies. Such expressions have usually been ritualized over centuries. At least four levels of burial formality, including the public display of grief, have been noted: "The burial of common people at Saa is a simple affair; an ordinary man is buried the day after death, a very inferior person at once. . . . Men of some rank and consideration are not buried for two days. . . . If a very great man dies . . . , the body is hung up in the son's house" (Codrington, 1969, p. 261). Where a man of substance has died, the grief forms are highly stylized: "Women sit around the corpse and wail, *i'o pe'i rae*, and people assemble to see the dead man for the last time and to eat the funeral feast" (Codrington, 1969, p. 261).

Some researchers have seen such expressions of grief and, indeed, *all* expressions of grief as semantic, or as a form of language. Undoubtedly a semantic element is present. That means that all emotive reactions to grief, whatever the culture, have some form of universal human meaning.

> The winter which makes possible spring, the dark of night followed by the light of day, the suffering which prepares the way for the deepest insight and the greatest ecstasy—these are images of death and rebirth that find universal cultural expression. They suggest a human quest for forms of integrity, movement, and connection that affirm life in the face of death. (Lifton & Olson, 1975, p. 121.)

Guilt, Loss, and Aftereffects

Guilt has been cited as an element of the grief resulting from the loss of a loved person. But the roots of a guilt sense reach into complexities of the earlier relationship that may not be fathomable. To an extent, clearly, the bereaved may ask why he or she did not "do more" for the deceased during the latter's lifetime; or the bereaved experiences remorse over genuine wrongs done to the deceased.

> The roots lie deeper than such more or less conscious attitudes. Guilt is probably due to the ambivalent quality of the love relationship where there is self-giving and self-satisfying, a craving for mutuality between loved and lover, as well as the resentment of loss of freedom. When the love object dies, the feelings are set free and there is guilt. The guilt may be expressed in excessive idealizing of the deceased. . . . Self-condemnation is a normal part of emotional withdrawal. (Jackson, 1959, p.223.)

In such a context grief becomes one part of a triad of psychological processes clustering around the fact of bereavement and the bereaved's responses to it. The other two elements are incorporation and substitution. Incorporation has been defined as the process whereby individuals turn their feelings in upon themselves and in effect become part of the deceased person; in substitution the grief-stricken individual, "in order to protect himself from the intolerable stress of his emotion, attaches it to somebody or something outside himself and resolves his feeling by such an external attachment" (Jackson, 1959, p. 223).

Guilt as an element of grief may draw the bereaved into forms of evasion. One person experiencing a loss may hide grief in public and experience release only in the privacy of home or room. Such persons "may be ashamed of feeling as deeply as they do about the dead loved person" (Peretz, 1970, p. 27), and in consequence may limit the degree to which they can either express grief or obtain support.

Those who neither show grief nor sense any awareness of feeling deeply grieved may be undergoing a somewhat different form of guilt reaction. Essentially, such a person can usually be seen as experiencing intensely ambivalent feelings—an admixture of love and hate, but in exaggerated form—and "in his grief . . . will reveal strong hostility as well as love" (Peretz, 1970, p. 27). Accusations that the bereaved is unfeeling may exacerbate the situation; the individual may isolate him- or herself and may engage in some form of compulsive busywork. "Apprehensions may be expressed about what should have been done for the deceased" (Peretz, 1970, p. 27).

Grief tinged with guilt may delay or extend normal mourning patterns or eliminate them completely. "Anniversary reactions" involving poignantly intensified feelings of loss annually on the date of the loved one's death may become habitual. Other dates of importance in the shared life that once bound the two persons together may be marked by similar accesses of emotion.

No imputation of fault should be inferred from such analyses. The grief that any person experiences runs its course according to patterns established by the bereaved's past life, personality, mode of looking at life, love, and death, and other factors. The danger is that depression, a persistently withdrawn and pessimistic state in which "sadness, tension, and a sense of depletion are prominent" (Peretz, 1970, p. 29), will sooner or later develop out of grief. In depression, symptoms indicating rather pronounced pathology may appear: suicidal feelings or ideas, negative self-preoccupation, lack of responsiveness to stimuli, facial expressions indicating despair, and so on.

Emotive displays of grief among human beings have been likened to forms of regression. In this theory, the adult who has been bereaved becomes like a child who has lost a precious object. "This approach helps explain much of the childlike [if natural] behavior that we see in grief-stricken people—the uninhibited weeping and even wailing, the rage at fate that such a thing could happen. They protest vehemently, through tears and screams" (Dempsey, 1975, pp. 154-155). In some cases the bereaved even hallucinate concerning the lost person. A man who lost his daughter in a tragic fire saw her calling him from a telephone booth. In another case a man who had lost his wife sixteen years earlier told a doctor, "I find hearing her breathing disturbing, but I like the feeling that she is in the house" (Dempsey, 1975, p. 155).

The aftereffects of loss and grief can be minimized, according to some authorities, through intense expression of the normal grief reactions as and when they are experienced. "Screaming rooms" have been recommended for hospitals: rooms for bereaved persons "so overwhelmed by grief that conventional outlets are insufficient" (Dempsey, 1975, p. 164).

> Let the relative talk, cry, or scream if necessary. Let them share and venti-
> late, but be available. The relative has a long time of mourning ahead of
> him, when the problems for the dead are solved. He needs help and
> assistance . . . until months after the death of a member of the family.
> (Kübler-Ross, 1969, p. 179.)

The purpose of emotive expression, in whatever place or circumstances, is to make possible rebirth. Basic needs have to be redirected constructively to minimize feelings of guilt, shame, or fear of retribution (Kübler-Ross, 1969). The cry of grief may or may not be likened to the *lost call* that is common among monkeys; human beings have their own special meanings for emotional reactions to loss. But grief, the available research suggests, *requires* expression if healthy adjustment is to be made. Grief must in this context be regarded as a coping mechanism, and its expression stands as the essential factor making possible a return to some form of more normal existence.

Clearly, some never return to anything resembling normal existence. Guilt survives and in extreme cases may indicate suicidal tendencies. The pain of loss remains too fresh to be dealt with or even materially reduced. The aftereffects endure for months and sometimes throughout the bereaved's remaining years. Yet for most there is hope. "The ancient principle of death and rebirth affects all our enterprises; every significant step in human experience involves some inner sense of death. The image of rebirth is inseparable from hope itself" (Lifton & Olson, 1975, p. 136). One can, with authors Lifton and Olson (1975), recall profitably the poet's words:

> In a dark time,
> The eye begins to see.

DEALING WITH DEATH: THE CHILD, THE ADOLESCENT, THE ADULT

That man perceives death in different ways at different ages of life has long been recognized. A companion reality is that the process of dealing with death must take account of such differential perceptions.

Authoritative writings on death and means of dealing with it reflect an abiding concern with the various ways in which people meet death depending on their ages and other factors. In her seminal book *On Death and Dying* (1969), in the midst of a chapter on "The Patient's Family" Kübler-Ross discussed the challenge of helping children to meet death. Jackson (1965) addressed directly the question of telling children about the death of a loved one. Many other such writings exist. An even larger body of writing deals with ways of dealing with death, or the resolutions of problems accompanying death, among the mature and older groups. A branch of the relatively new science of gerontology is concerned with the ways in which older persons adjust to the loss of a spouse or loved "other."

Responses to death and ways of dealing with it may be considered in relation to three basic age groupings: the child, the adolescent, and the adult. Within those groups some special subgroupings should also be considered.

Different Ages, Different Approaches

As in other areas of life, age-group classifications may generalize too freely. They may obliterate the reality that "each child is an individual shaped by the experience of his life" (Jackson, 1965, p. 58). Yet within the age groups certain basic elements have been identified; these help to establish the parameters within which grief is normally met at given ages.

Change keynotes the responses of the child. Because the young person's intellectual and emotional makeup is changing so rapidly, his or her behavior may also change from period to period during early life and sometimes from year to year. But patterns in the way in which the child deals with death have become apparent:

> A child from birth to three or four can sense loss but cannot conceptualize death. His feelings invite love, reassurance, and emotional support. From four through seven, biological interests will take the center of the stage and will have to be met with simple, direct biological answers. From eight

through twelve the meaning of death will acquire a social dimension, and the concern for the consequences of death on the lives of the living will be paramount. (Jackson, 1965, p. 59.)

Recognition of such stages helps those who would seek to aid the child facing the task of dealing with the death of a parent or other loved person. "These young personalities can [thus] be helped to face the crises of life caused by death, so that they will grow through them to become more competent persons" (Jackson, 1965, p. 58). It should also be remembered that the process of dealing with death, no matter what the bereaved's age, can never be static. "It is . . . characterized by stages of development and resolution, degrees of intensity, and variable external manifestations" (Schwab, 1968, p. 110).

For the child dealing with death, such factors are fundamentally aspects of the change process. They work with other factors to produce an overall effect: the net result of the grief work. Other variables, besides age, that must be considered include the following:

Who died?

How and when and where?

What this death means to the child.

How important adults react to the death.

The child's physical and emotional condition.

The child's prior experiences in the area of loss or death.

The ultimate effects of this death on the child. (Lamers, 1965, p. 16.)

In light of such differentiating factors, a child's response to death, his or her way of dealing with it, becomes more understandable. It can be seen that "death . . . is not a permanent fact for the three-to-five-year-old. . . . After the age of five death is often regarded as a man, a bogey-man who comes to take people away" (Kübler-Ross, 1969, pp. 178-179). By the ages of nine or ten death has begun to represent a biological fact. But even at this age the child may expect to see the parent or other loved one return: "They may . . . utter such statements as 'She will come back for the spring vacation,' or secretly put an apple out for her" (Kübler-Ross, 1969, p. 179).

For the adolescent, approaching maturity alters the situation in fundamental ways. The task of dealing with death is usually handled more as an adult would handle it: even though the death of a parent may constitute an irreparable loss, the adolescent seeks ways through his or her grief. The adolescent may depend heavily on adults close to him or her to serve as models; but "from thirteen through the years of adolescence the main effort will be to seek a psychological, spiritual, or religious meaning for death, which is part of the teen-age quest for the meaning of life" (Jackson, 1965, p. 59). Once successfully faced, the grief experience hastens maturity and cumulatively develops the ability to express grief in socially acceptable ways.

Researchers and members of the helping professions generally agree that neither children nor adolescents should be spared the task of facing and dealing with death. But basic needs must be considered. The child, for example, may fear abandonment when a parent dies. His or her need for security may then focus more strongly on the surviving parent, and require special attention. The child who displays anger following a death is probably expressing grief based in a sense of deprivation.

Middle-aged and older people are generally seen as dealing with death in similar ways. Yet some research has indicated differences between the middle-aged reaction and that of the older person. The difference lies basically in the manner in which the grief emotion is integrated into the bereaved's life. "A person in his middle years tends to show his grief through emotional reactions. He is normally in his vigorous years physically and is well organized and competent in meeting the demands of daily life" (Jackson, 1965, p. 67). The older person, by contrast, tends to develop physical symptoms. Aches and pains become more common; the bereaved may contract diseases that reflect a loss of interest in life (Jackson, 1965).

Among the elderly, the challenge of waiting for a loved one to die may also produce irreparable effects. "Aged surviving spouses of a chronic illness death lasting more than six months had poorer medical adjustment than survivors of a shorter-term fatal illness" (Gerber, 1975, p. 34). Middle-aged persons presumably fare better; they have not been stripped by age of physical and emotional defenses and, as noted, they remain in the midst of life and can usually absorb the pain of loss better. The weakness of age, earlier losses of loved ones or of friends, increased dependency on the former love object, and many other factors also have a bearing on the older person's mode of dealing with death.

Similarities That Cross Age Barriers

Just as all people fear death, all respond to it in one way or another. Grief itself provides the element of commonality that spans family, religious, cultural, and other differences. Within a given society there remains diversity: the task of dealing with death through grief may endure for months or years or for hours or days. The manner of expressing grief may vary from person to person. The intensity of the felt emotion of grief obviously differs from case to case. As noted, age differences provide a measure against which to assess responses to grief and a basis for predicting them as well.

For all men and women of any age, bafflement may underlie grief. The bafflement is of the kind whose roots are buried in fear and wonder. "We are all baffled children before the scythe of the grim reaper, and the themes which can be played to express our emotions or to articulate our thoughts are extremely limited in number" (Liebman, 1946, p. 103). From one period of history to the next, thus, man appears to employ the same death themes over and over, at least in literature. Advances in scientific knowledge of death do not change that basic fact: "there is little essential difference between what the writers of twenty centuries ago said on this ultimate problem and what the writers say about it today" (Liebman, 1946, p. 103).

Whatever the individual's or the group's specific responses to death, and whatever the means of dealing with it, the mystery of man's final fate remains a conundrum without solution. Societies and individuals appear, or claim, to have every answer, but the mystery nonetheless leaves a shadow in the mind. The details concerning death and what follows it—whether it is absolute end, a passage into a new sphere and a new life, or something not yet conceived by man—remain unexplicated. The verdict of Hindu philosophers and of the mystics of many countries—that death constitutes a remerger with an Ultimate Spiritual Reality—remains as valid on the surface as the concepts of heaven and hell. As a Greek playwright wrote, "Who knows if to be alive is not really to die, and if dying does not count in the nether world as being alive?" (Euripides, from his lost play, *Polyidus*.)

Some students of death have seen guilt as yet another common factor in the efforts of man to deal with death. Kübler-Ross notes, for example: "I think all of us who have lost someone we loved have moments when we torture ourselves and wonder if we could not have done a better job" (Kübler-Ross, 1969, p. 93). Guilt may take variant forms: "The focus of guilt on small, inconsequential facts of the relationship may serve as a screen for more profound guilt for being the survivor" (Peretz, 1970, p. 23).

While it may be questioned whether bereaved persons pass through clearly defined stages of grief any more than the dying inevitably go through Kübler-Ross's five stages of death, some authorities have asserted that a virtually universal grief pattern exists. Edgar (1972) found five stages including (1) "numbness of the whole being" (p. 105); (2) the hard struggle with dreams concerning the loved person; (3) psychological reactions that "are natural but sometimes repulsive to those who listen" (pp. 106-107); (4) a phase involving a flood of grief accompanied where possible by weeping and tears; and (5) a return to normalcy as quickly as possible including reoccupation of former premises if the bereaved shared them with the deceased.

These stages subsume such universals in grief patterns as feelings of desertion and rejection. "At a time like this, without realizing it, in this process of healing through grief we . . . find ourselves saying, 'In the middle of everything he just lay down and died. We have so much to do together and look, he's gone off and left me' " (Edgar, 1972, p. 107). Those in contact with the bereaved are advised to accept such statements so that the survivor can work through the feelings behind them.

Other similarities in modes of dealing with death through grief have been isolated by psychologists and psychiatrists. Anger, for example, appears to inhere in grief and to be directed normally toward the fate that took away the loved one or toward others who have survived. The anger component may not, however, be always recognizable. Introjection, the process by which the bereaved integrates into his or her own personality some or many of the characteristics of the deceased, constitutes another basic element. Introjection is usually accompanied by idealization, in which the dead person's image undergoes revision that seeks to produce perfection. Finally, the bereaved may undergo a process of "image-splitting." "This splitting of the ego is a reflection of the actual psychic state of affairs in that the ego is faced on the one hand with a highly cathected mental representation of the love object, and on the other with an absence of perceptions of the object" (Lipson, 1973, p. 274).

As noted, some universal characteristics of grief reproduce from one stage of life to the next the emotions encountered by the child who is bereaved. "Just as the young child passing through the depressive position is struggling, in his unconscious mind, with the task of establishing and integrating his inner world, so the mourner goes through the pain of re-establishing and reintegrating it" (Klein, 1973, p. 247). The purpose of grief and mourning, from this point of view, is to test reality. By degrees, in this testing, the ego becomes acclimatized to the knowledge of loss. The fact that "there is a close connection between the testing of reality in normal mourning and early processes of the mind" (Klein, 1973, p. 237) thus receives new emphasis.

The similarities among ways of dealing with death are found in some measure where a normally healthy person is the bereaved and where death arrives after a period of illness and preparation. In cases of untimely death, the various basic elements may appear in more or less intensified form. "Grief reactions are actually much more normal when death occurs in an aged person and has been expected. Under such circumstances the work of mourning is done quickly, because a certain amount of this work (detaching the libido from the object) has already preceded the event of death" (Lehrman, 1973, p. 223). Where untimely death occurs, pathological reactions are much more common than where the bereaved has been able to prepare for the death.

In Memoriam

Dealing with death successfully requires, finally, that the bereaved *relate* to the deceased. While "the dead seem less real and powerful . . . than in bygone cultures" (Kastenbaum & Aisenberg, 1972, p. 481), the need to find a niche for the dead person in one's life and thoughts remains imperative. The search for that basic, healthy relationship with and to the deceased represents the reverse of the modern tendency to seek a total forgetfulness that obliterates all thought, all remembrance of both death and the dead.

Eradication of the dead not only rules out erection of any kind of psychological memorial to the dead; it may also lead to the untoward mental consequences whose dimensions have already been described: "The dead, expelled from our conscious and social lives," might now "return as dream figures, as ghosts, or in other, unprecedented forms" (Kastenbaum & Aisenberg, 1972, p. 481). The survivor may find it impossible even to talk of the deceased. A "generation gap" rises deceptively between living and dead, forcing the survivors—they are no longer the bereaved because they do not *sense* bereavement—into extremes of existentialist pursuits. Past and future disappear into the mists of a manic search for the present, the Now.

One can ask, with Kastenbaum and Aisenberg (1972), "What exchanges will take place between the living and the dead" (p. 481) once a healthy relationship has been established out of grief? Certainly other mundane relationships will be formed, and in these the bereaved who has come to grips with the facts of death and loss will be able normally to speak of the dead. Unnatural preoccupation with the severed relationship will not obtrude abnormally; rather, a web of daily interests and tasks will occupy the bereaved to an acceptable degree. Resumption of old friendships will not be abhorrent; nor will visits to places that deceased and bereaved once built into common memories.

No one can prescribe for another. No one can say to a bereaved person, "This is what you must do; once it is done you will have developed the relationship with the dead that you must have." Each person must go his or her own way. Under any circumstances prescription is impossible because "We know little enough about the subtle dynamics of interchange between the living and the dead . . ." (Kastenbaum & Aisenberg, 1972, p. 482). As the authors add regarding this facet of dealing with death:

> It seems likely that this relationship will continue to change as a function of our system for disposing of the dead. Whatever we do with respect to the dead must have some impact on our own feelings. Is it possible that potential transformations of our behavior toward the dead will exceed our capacity for adaptation? Can we truly banish the dead without offending an important part of our nature? (Kastenbaum & Aisenberg, 1972, p. 482.)

These are questions without answers—today. But today it appears from the available evidence that a successful effort to deal with the dead requires integration of the memory of the deceased into the thought processes of the bereaved. If the deceased achieves a kind of rebirth, an attenuated, spiritual form of immortality thereby, the bereaved achieves functionality, the right to go on living, the capacity to enjoy life again. Serenity comes within reach: "Perhaps we can eventually become serene because we feel that in facing the separation of death we have undergone life's ultimate test, and in the testing found our strength sufficient" (Bartlett, 1972, p. 125).

In memoriam. The bereaved becomes acclimatized, at least insofar as acclimatization is possible. One makes peace with death, and thus copes in the most perfect way. The death of one individual, while neither forgotten nor brushed aside, is acknowledged as being "really no more nor less than a punctuation mark in the endlessly fascinating conversation amongst all living things" (Trombley, 1976, p. 507). Death is not circumvented; it is met face to face. Burial of the loved person in the "long, long night" of which poets have written prepares the sufferer for both life and eventual death. The cycle of one relationship is completed; grief has done its purgative work and life goes forward, burdened only by commemorative love.

SUMMARY

Somewhat parallel coping patterns have been identified in the dying and in bereaved persons. The pattern followed as death approaches has been shown by Kübler-Ross to have, generally, five stages, with a sixth—the act of dying—sometimes added. The question whether death represents a peak experience or a final trauma of overwhelming proportions has never been answered fully, and probably cannot be; but evidence points to positive answers on both sides. The bereaved, in passing through the grief stages, experiences emotions whose intensity is dependent on the intensity of affective response in connection with the loss, the hostility engendered in connection with the loss, and other factors. But grief in the normal case is cathartic, and methods of managing it, including conversation, are crucially important.

Even if not unbounded, man's capacity for grief is immense. But that capacity is always influenced, and to an extent determined, by evolutionary and sociocultural factors and psychophysiological mechanisms. The former suggest social forces regulating methods of dealing with grief while the latter involve man's deepest impulses, including the interconnections between the mind and emotions on the one hand and physical health on the other.

Emotive displays vis-à-vis death and dying take many forms, from crying and screaming to expressions of weariness and obvious loss of interest. Grief has been viewed as caring and sharing for at least two reasons: first, the degree of attachment to the love object helps determine the intensity of the grief reaction, and, second, where possible grief should be worked through with the aid of loved others. Emotional expressions of grief take variant forms depending on the bereaved's family and cultural inheritance and on many other factors. As components of grief, the sense of guilt and feelings of loss can produce aftereffects with serious somatic consequences.

Ways of dealing with death differ from one period of life to the next as well as from culture to culture. At least three different phases may be identified in children, while adolescents, facing the onset of physical and emotional maturity, tend to model their reactions after those of adults around them. Despite such differences, similarities cross age barriers; anger, a sense of guilt, and other elements are among those universals characterizing normal grief processes.

While no one can prescribe for another, authorities generally agree that the bereaved will normally take out of the grief state a relationship to the deceased. In that relationship the memory of the dead is integrated into normal thought patterns. The bereaved achieves a kind of rebirth in which normal life functions and new friendships become possible.

REFERENCES

Aronson, G. J. "Treatment of the Dying Person," in H. Feifel, ed., *The Meaning of Death*. New York: McGraw-Hill Book Co., 1959, p. 252.

Bain, A. *The Emotions and the Will*. London: Longmans, Green & Co., 1875.

Bartlett, G. E. "Grief and Humanity," in A. H. Kutscher and L. G. Kutscher, eds., *Religion and Bereavement: Counsel for the Physician–Advice for the Bereaved–Thoughts for the Clergyman*. New York: Health Sciences, 1972, p.125.

Becker, H. "The Sorrow of Bereavement," in H. M. Ruitenbeek, ed., *The Interpretation of Death*. New York: Jason Aronson, Inc., 1973.

Borgquist, A. "Crying." *American Journal of Psychology*, 17, 1906, 104–110.

Burghardt, W. J. "The Life and Death Question." *America*, April 21, 1973, pp. 366–367.

Codrington, R. H. *The Melanesians: Studies in Their Anthropology and Folklore*. Oxford, England: Clarendon Press, 1969.

Darwin, C. *The Expression of the Emotions in Man and Animals*. New York: D. Appleton, 1899. (Originally published, 1872.)

Dempsey, D. *The Way We Die: An Investigation of Death and Dying in America Today*. New York: Macmillan Co., 1975.

Deutsch, H. "Absence of Grief." *The Psychoanalytic Quarterly*, 6, 1973, 11–21.

Edgar, R. A. "How To Understand Grief," in A. H. Kutscher and L. G. Kutscher, eds., *Religion and Bereavement: Counsel for the Physician–Advice for the Bereaved–Thoughts for the Clergyman*. New York: Health Sciences, 1972, pp. 105–107.

Eliot, T. D. "Bereavement: Inevitable but Not Insurmountable," in H. Becker and R. Hill, eds., *Family, Marriage, and Parenthood*. Boston: D. C. Heath & Co., 1948, p. 643.

Euripides. *Polyidus*. Quoted in A. Toynbee et al., eds., *Man's Concern with Death*. New York: McGraw-Hill Book Co., 1968, p. 214.

Flesch, R. "A Guide to Interviewing the Bereaved." *Journal of Thanatology*, 3, 1975, 95-103.

Frankl, V. *The Search for Meaning*. Boston: Beacon Press, 1962.

Fulcomer, D. "The Adjustive Behavior of Some Recently Bereaved Spouses: A Psycho-Sociological Study." Unpublished doctoral dissertation, Northwestern University, 1942.

Gerber, I. "Sequelae of Anticipation of Bereavement on the Elderly Survivor." *Journal of Thanatology*, 3, 1975, 31–34.

Glaser, B. G., and Strauss, A. L. "The Social Loss of Dying Patients." *American Journal of Nursing*, 64(6), 1964, 119–121.

Goldscheider, G. "The Mortality Revolution," in E. Shneidman, ed., *Death's Current Perspectives*. Palo Alto: Mayfield Pub. Co., 1976, p. 182.

Hinton, J. M. "The Physical and Mental Distress of Dying." *Quarterly Journal of Medicine*, 32, 1963, 1–24.

Hinton, J. "Speaking of Death with the Dying," in E. Shneidman, ed., *Death: Current Perspectives*. Palo Alto: Mayfield Pub. Co., 1976, pp. 312–313.

Jackson, E. N. "Grief and Religion," in H. Feifel, ed., *The Meaning of Death*. New York: McGraw-Hill Book Co., 1959.

Jackson, E. N. *Telling a Child about Death*. New York: Channel Press, 1965.

Jackson, E. N. "The Law and the Right to Grieve." *International Journal of Law and Science*, 7(1), 1970, 1–10.

Kastenbaum, R., and Aisenberg, R. *The Psychology of Death*. New York: Springer Verlag, 1972.

Kierkegaard, S. *Concept of Dread*. Princeton: Princeton University Press, 1944.

Klein, M. "Mourning and Its Relation to Manic-Depressive States," in H. M. Ruitenbeek, ed., *The Interpretation of Death*. New York: Jason Aronson, Inc., 1973. (Originally published in *International Journal of Psychoanalysis*, 21, [1940], 120–129.)

Kübler-Ross, E. *On Death and Dying*. New York: Macmillan Co., 1969.

Kübler-Ross, E. Review of *Dying* by J. Hinton, in *Life-Threatening Behavior* 2, 1972, 56–58.

Kübler-Ross, E. *Questions and Answers on Death and Dying*. New York: Macmillan Co., 1974.

Lamers, W. M. *Death, Grief, Mourning, the Funeral and the Child*. Illustrated presentation given at the 84th Annual Convention of the National Funeral Directors Association, November 1, 1965. (Pamphlet.)

Lehrman, S. R. "Reactions to Untimely Death," in H. M. Ruitenbeek, ed., *The Interpretation of Death*. New York: Jason Aronson, Inc., 1973, p. 223.

LeShan, L., and LeShan, E. "Psychotherapy and the Patient with a Limited Life-Span," in H. M. Ruitenbeek, ed., *The Interpretation of Death*. New York: Jason Aronson, Inc., 1973.

Liebman, J. L. *Peace of Mind*. New York: Simon & Schuster, 1946.

Lifton, R. J., and Olson, E. *Living and Dying*. New York: Bantam Books, 1975.

Lipson, C. T. "Denial and Mourning," in H. M. Ruitenbeek, ed., *The Interpretation of Death*. New York: Jason Aronson, Inc., 1973, p. 247.

Mannes, M. *Last Rights: A Case for the Good Death*. New York: New American Library, 1973.

Morgan, E. *The Descent of Woman*. New York: Stein & Day, 1972.

Murphy, G. "Discussion," in H. Feifel, ed., *The Meaning of Death*. New York: McGraw-Hill Book Co., 1959, p. 321.

Neale, R. E. *The Art of Dying*. New York: Harper & Row, 1971.

Parsons, A. *Belief, Magic, and Anomie: Essays in Psychological Anthropology*. New York: The Free Press, 1969, p. 141.

Peretz, D. "Understanding Your Mourning: A Psychiatrist's View," in A. H. Kutscher, ed., *But Not To Lose: A Book of Comfort for Those Bereaved*. New York: Frederick Fell, 1969.

Peretz, D. "Reaction to Loss," in B. Schoenberg, A. C. Carr, D. Peretz, and A. H. Kutscher, eds., *Loss and Grief: Psychological Management in Medical Practice*. New York: Columbia University Press, 1970, pp. 22–26.

Rakoff, V. M. "Psychiatric Aspects of Death in America," in A. Mack, ed., *Death in American Experience*. New York: Schocken Books, 1973, pp. 150-155.

Rees, W. D., and Lutkins, S "Morality of Bereavement." *British Medical Journal*, No. 5570, October 7, 1967, pp. 23-31.

Rudin, J. R. "Thoughts on My Wife's Death," in A. H. Kutscher, ed., *But Not To Lose: A Book of Comfort for Those Bereaved*. New York: Frederick Fell, 1969, p. 44.

Saucier, Jean, "Anthropology and Psychodynamics of Nursing," *Canadian Psychiatric Association Journal*, 12(5) 1967, pp. 477–496.

Schulz, R., and Aderman, D. "Clinical Research and the Stages of Dying." *Nursing Digest,* January-February 1976, pp. 47–48.

Schwab, M. L. "The Nurse's Role in Assisting Families of Dying Geriatric Patients to Manage Grief and Guilt," in *American Nursing Association Clinical Sessions, 1968*. Chicago: American Nursing Association, 1968.

Shand, A. *The Foundations of Character*. London: Macmillan Co., 1914.

Shneidman, E. S. "Work and Stages of Dying," in E. Shneidman, ed., *Death: Current Perspectives*. Palo Alto: Mayfield Pub. Co., 1976, pp. 446–447.

Switzer, D. K. *The Dynamics of Grief*. New York: Abingdon Press, 1970.

Toynbee, A. "Perspectives from Time, Space, and Nature," in A. Toynbee et al., eds., *Man's Concern with Death*. New York: McGraw-Hill Book Co., 1968.

Troland, L. *The Fundamentals of Human Behavior*. New York: D. Van Nostrand Co., 1928.

Trombley, L. E. "A Psychiatrist's Response to a Life-Threatening Illness," in E. Shneidman, ed., *Death: Current Perspectives*. Palo Alto: Mayfield Pub. Co., 1976, p. 507.

Weisman, A. D., and Kastenbaum, R. "The Psychological Autopsy: A Study of the Terminal Phase of Life." *Community Mental Health Journal*, 1968, Monograph No. 4.

Weiss, E. *Principles of Psychodynamics*. New York: Grune & Stratton, 1950.

The Context of Death: Implications for Patient and Family Care

The material of this chapter will attempt to focus on the context in which human death occurs. Thus the material of the chapter has been divided into categories which are somewhat arbitrary. Clearly, in some instances there are multiple and simultaneous processes, any one of which would be singly sufficient to render death. Nevertheless, the diversity of the material of this chapter dictates some type of subgroup organizations. Thus the discussion will address the contexts of death in the following order: *diseases; accidental death; wars; homicides/suicides; sacrificial and religious ceremonies; execution, banishment, and incarceration; torture; aging; medicocultural methods; mental aberrations.*

DISEASES

At times a society that is afflicted with enormous numbers of deaths may begin to break up. This is even more likely to occur when other elements in the society are either in disorder or are undergoing a significant change. Sometimes the nature of the death system itself will aid in the destruction of the society because the prevailing approach cannot accommodate the presence of large numbers of people dying. This is what happened during the Middle Ages, especially during the fourteenth century, with the advent of the Black Death (Kastenbaum & Aisenberg, 1972, p.195).

The fourteenth century in Europe was a world under siege of plague and war. We know that Europe was just emerging from the era of the Crusades in which a great many young, healthy people were killed. Perhaps contact with new cultures and strange germs was responsible for the outbreak of the bubonic plague that hit Europe before it could recover from the losses suffered during those religious wars. As the dread disease spread, the weakened population became increasingly unable to deal with other natural disasters: earthquakes, fires, or floods (Kastenbaum & Aisenberg, 1972, p. 196; Shneidman, 1976, p. 69).

The bubonic plague held special terror for medieval people. Never before in human memory had a society been victim of a disease which dealt so harshly with the population. The illness itself was particularly ugly. The symptoms have been described as follows: "Headache, dizziness, and fever, followed by nosebleed or spitting of blood, swelling of glands in the armpit, groin, or neck, severe inflammation of lungs and throat, intense thirst, violent chest pains, delirium, and dark spots on the skin which gave the disease its familiar name, the Black Death" (Kastenbaum & Aisenberg, 1972, p. 196). Only about ten percent of those that contracted the disease survived its course, and figures indicate that approximately one-quarter of the total population of the Western world died from this disease. In some cases, entire towns were completely devastated.

Medieval societies were not properly equipped to handle the prolonged stress resulting from the massive numbers of fatalities that occurred with the coming of the plague. Not only was the cultural system unable to alleviate any appreciable fear of death, but it was also unable to prevent an almost perpetual preoccupation with the subject. With this preoccupation, the workings of nearly all other social institutions came to a halt, with the inevitable result that society began to break up. Some scholars have argued that the very nature of the medieval concept of death encouraged the spread of terror, panic, and actually increased the effects of the disease and other natural disasters (Kastenbaum & Aisenberg, 1972, p. 197).

The Black Death held a special terror for people during the Middle Ages because it appeared that all previous methods of combatting disease had little or no effect: religion, medicine, magic—nothing helped. People who were not themselves victims of the disease were soon affected by the resulting food shortages and widespread terror of seeing an incredible number of people dying all around them. Most people believed that it was only a matter of time before they, too, would succumb and perish. The plague changed European society permanently. We may assume that some of our present-day methods of dealing with death are directly related to systems developed to deal with the possibility of mass destruction by disease (Kastenbaum & Aisenberg, 1972, p. 201).

The interaction between the realities of the Black Death and the religious attitudes of the Middle Ages caused the development of many new philosophical and theological ideologies in an attempt to explain that holocaust. A noted literary critic, exploring the topic of *Death and Elizabethan Tragedy*, writes,

> The philosophy of Plato, which taught that true reality lay outside the shadowy world of the senses, the metaphysical hierarchy of the neo-Platonists, which virtually identified evil with matter, the teaching of the Stoics, who were compelled to face the worldly ills they did their best to deny, the visions of the Near-Eastern ascetics, who elaborated with increasing fervency of detail the tortures or delights of the next world—all these things made men look forward to death, and had prepared the way for a scorn of man's natural abilities and an emphasis on the next world which should be the only satisfactory attitude for serious minds to maintain. But Christianity added one remarkable doctrine which pagan disillusionment and transcendental philosophy had never mentioned. *It taught that death was a punishment for man's sin.* (Spencer, 1960.)

There was widespread belief that man's sinfulness was responsible for the plague, that God was punishing man for evil deeds. The preoccupation with death was thus partly an attempt to deal with the guilt and anxiety that these beliefs fostered.

In the Christian view there were only three basic causes of death: *disease, sin, and preordained experience.* In many non-Christian cultures death is brought by deities, or some form of evil spirit. Until the advent of the germ theory most Christian societies and industrial societies were strong adherents of the sin and preordained causes explanations for death. The invention of the microscope, inoculation, and rational purification practices (aseptic procedures)* greatly alleviated man's anxiety about foreboding death. Nevertheless, there are still numerous sects and groups that will not submit to certain medical procedures lest they infringe upon the preordained process.

It is generally agreed that the intensity and pervasiveness of man's thought about "the end" permeated the intellectual and lay thought of the entire fourteenth century. Spencer notes that:

---

*In May 1977, *The New York Times* reported a dread conclusion: a deadly virus had been transmitted through surgery. The virus, difficult to detect, apparently resists the usual sterilization techniques (boiling, exposure to ultraviolet rays and chemical disinfectants). The resultant Creutzfeld-Jakob disease causes brain degeneration with loss of memory and muscle coordination, and senility.

More than any other period in history, the late Middle Ages were preoccupied with the thought of death. In Northern Europe for two hundred years—from the middle of the fourteenth century to the middle of the sixteenth—death was the favorite topic of preachers and moralistic writers, it was one of the most common subjects for popular art, and if a man of the period followed the prevailing doctrine, there was no object so frequently or so vividly before his mind's eye as the skeleton he would one day become. (Spencer, 1960.)

In addition to artistic representation, death became an integral part of other areas of society. The children's game "Ring around the Rosy" ended with the cry, "Ashes, ashes, we all fall down." This game, among others, originated during the plague-ridden fourteenth century and is still popular with children today. Although modern children probably do not attach the same meaning to the last phrase, few adults may understand it all. In the fourteenth century, "magical thinking flourished among adults as well as children. No proposed prophylactic or cure for the Black Death was too arcane, repulsive, or foolish to find a ready market" (Kastenbaum & Aisenberg, 1972, p. 200). In modern times people reacted to the 1920 "Swine flu" pandemic and more recently to polio with similar perturbation.

Fear is not always a prominent reaction to death. Aries (1974) has reported that non-Christians as well as Christians have faced impending death with no sign of fear. He has traced the changing attitudes of Western cultures toward death from medieval times to the present. He writes that in many old chivalric romances the warriors knew that they were going to die; death was not a sudden, unexpected occurrence. In one old story an ancient king had fallen in battle. When he saw blood pouring from his mouth, nose, and ears, "He looked up to heaven and uttered as best he could . . . 'Ah, Lord God, help me, for I see and I know that my end has come' " (Aries, 1974, p. 3).

Aries adds, "Let us note that the warning came through natural signs or, even more frequently, through an inner conviction rather than through a supernatural, magical premonition" (Aries, 1974, p. 4). Some rebelled against the awareness of death, but it was usually generally accepted with equanimity eventually (Pine, 1976).

This sense of the naturalness of death was observed by Jean Guitton, who, in 1941, recorded a view of a French family.

We can see how the Pougets in those bygone days passed on from this world into the next, as simple and practical persons, observers of signs and above all of themselves. They were in no hurry to die, but when they saw that their hour had come, then without haste or delay, but with a proper sense of timing, they died as Christians. (Aries, 1974, p. 7.)

The cause of death and the "how and why" of dying influence one's approach. Sometimes people dread disfigurement or pain more than the actual loss of life, or fear becoming a burden to their relatives during the final phases of the process (Koenig, 1973).

Outwardly modern attitudes toward death may appear to be unchanging; Aries reminds us that this is not so. Not too many years ago death was not feared, but accepted as a familiar aspect of life. Today death is spoken of with awe and fear, with respect for the enormous power of fate. Aries calls the old form of demise "tamed death." "I do not mean that death had once been wild and that it had ceased to be so. I mean, on the contrary, that today it has become wild" (Aries, 1974, p. 14).

Before proceeding to the next topic, *accident,* it is useful to note that concepts of disease and accident stem from different historical roots: doctors treated ailments in which causative agents could be ameliorated or reversed. In accidents only the aftermath can be treated. Disease incorporated "process" qualities. The concept of accident seems to have evolved partially as a mechanism whereby a state of blamelessness existed. Thus the victim of an accident was not considered to be the object of the wrath of deities; his or her relatives and friends could not be held responsible for the occurrence. To be without blame was to be without guilt (of sin). On a practical level it is clear that one could induce a state of illhealth by erroneously ingesting poisons, and therefore negligence could result in a disease process. Perhaps this circumstance contributed to the legal definitions of responsibility of negligence.

ACCIDENTAL DEATH

Some deaths are clearly caused by external agents that can be called accidental. It is rather difficult to differentiate "individual" accidents from those events that appear to come under the same heading but involve a number of victims. Is an avalanche that kills two mountaineers an individual accident? How many victims must there be to cause a mass disaster? Train wrecks may involve dozens, even hundreds of deaths, while floods and earthquakes sometimes affect thousands of victims who cannot escape in time. (Pine, 1976).

The distinction among the various categories of accidents is sometimes clear, occasionally blurred, and at times impossible to define.

Besides old age, disease, and war, there are other circumstances that can end human life. Sociologists provide the following generally accepted definition of an accident: "Accident: (1) Something that did not have to happen, but did; (2) Something that had to happen because it did happen" (Kastenbaum & Aisenberg, 1972, p. 354). Both of these definitions state that an accident is beyond the control of the individual. The definitions include the concept of luck and the role of "bad luck" in determining at least some of the events that affect our lives. The second part of the citation implies an underlying cause to the accident—a feeling that the accident is the manifestation of another purpose, hard to define. Some see the accident as a punishment from God meted out for sins either consciously or unconsciously committed. Both segments of the definition also indicate a sudden occurrence for which preparation is impossible and intervention useless (Pine, 1976).

The possibility of perishing and/or sustaining a severe injury from an accident is an integral part of American culture. Apart from the obvious example of the automobile, there are an incredible number of implements that may cause accidental death or injury: water, boats, knives, poison, toys, ropes, bicycles, motorcycles, skateboards, and airplanes all add to the fatality statistics which make dying by accident the leading cause of death in the United States (Kastenbaum & Aisenberg, 1972, p. 356). Apart from the enormous number of people who lose their lives in accidents, an even larger group are severely injured accidentally. In 1965, more than 108,000 people died in accidents and approximately 45.1 million people suffered injuries serious enough to require medical attention (Kastenbaum & Aisenberg, 1972, p. 355).

Kastenbaum and Aisenberg believe that ". . . most accidents have identifiable causes and are preventable." They define an accident as ". . . simply a disastrous event that occurs suddenly, unexpectedly, without (conscious) planning or intention." For example: The probability of being wounded or killed by a gunshot wound is greatly increased by entering certain occupations such as police work, or by taking up certain hobbies, such as hunting. Without the presence of a gun, such an accident would be virtually impossible. They add: "In many other ways, some obvious and some subtle, we act upon our environments either in the direction of increasing or reducing the probabilities of 'accidental' death" (Kastenbaum & Aisenberg, 1972, p. 357).

Alexander, the author of *The Psychology of Death,* questions the generally accepted theory that some people are accident-prone. He acknowledges, however, that many scholars agree that some people's personalities predispose them toward accidents:

> The contention of modern psychiatry that most accidents are not accidents at all but are caused largely by the victim's own disposition is but a confirmation of common observation. . . . The sufferer from the accident has some active part in its causation. It is popularly assumed that he was clumsy, tired, or absentminded; otherwise, he might have avoided the accident. Scientific accidents are not due to such simply human qualities. Certain people are prone to have more accidents than others, not because they are clumsy or absentminded, but because of the total structure of their personalities. (Alexander, 1950, p. 209.)

Another medical expert agrees with this theory and adds that the manifest behavior of accident-prone individuals can be compared to the behavior of juvenile delinquents and adult criminals. Dunbar calls it: "The behavior characteristic of the persistent breaker of bones right up to the point where one commits a crime and the other has an accident" (Kastenbaum & Aisenberg, 1972, p. 357).

One of the authorities that questions the belief in accident-proneness is M. Schulzinger, in his book *The Accident Syndrome*. Schulzinger carefully studied 35,000 cases of accidental injury over twenty years. Some of the conclusions that he drew include: "Most accidents are due to infrequent solitary experiences of large numbers of individuals." He adds: "The tendency to have repeated accidents is a phenomenon that usually passes with age and is not a fixed trait of the individual." And, "The frequently reported observation that most accidents are due to a small fixed group of accident repeaters holds true only when the period of observation is relatively short or when the numerical strength of the observed population greatly exceeds the numerical strength of the accidents" (Schulzinger, 1956, p. 13).

The element of negligence in regard to accidental deaths cannot be overlooked, although it would be difficult to determine exactly how many so-called accidental deaths are actually due to negligence. John Langone writes of an incident when two little boys in Boston, ages six and seven, made a raft and decided to float down the Charles River. Not surprisingly, they both fell off the raft and subsequently drowned. Langone went to interview the parents for his newspaper and, to convince the parents to talk to him in the midst of their grief, he used the argument that their story might prevent other children from making the same mistake. Yet the question of negligence was certainly in his mind regarding the accident when he wrote:

> I explained frankly what we were after, and this was after I gave some weak sympathy. Something like, I'm terribly sorry about the loss of your sons. My experience has been that generally close relatives of the dead,

especially mothers and fathers of young children, aren't very talkative to reporters as a rule. This was no exception. . . . I told him, we'll be running a story on this tomorrow, and we're going to warn other young-sters. If I had said that we're going to warn parents, as should have been the case here because the kids should have been in school and the parents knew it, they knew they were lax . . . if I had said that, it would have been a serious mistake and I would have been cut off fast. . . . (Langone, 1974.)

The question of negligence again comes up with regard to the feelings of guilt often felt by survivors. Kavenaugh in *Facing Death,* (1972, p. 12) claims that it is very common for survivors of almost any sort of accident to feel guilty. They frequently ask themselves why they were spared while others died, and usually wonder whether or not they did enough to try to help those that were eventually lost. Such feelings are not, apparently, as common when death follows a more normal course, Elisabeth Kübler-Ross writes, "In our death-denying society we are ill-prepared to handle the loss of a member of our family when there is no illness preparing us slowly for this eventual outcome" (Kübler-Ross, 1974, pp. 15, 25). Even though people are shocked at the death of someone close to them, a long illness from which there is little chance of recovery gives friends and relatives time to adjust to the expected loss so that when death actually does occur, guilt feelings are minimal.

It is considered particularly tragic when the dying patient is a child. Should the nurse or doctor tell him or her the truth? Should the parents perform this sad task? What language should be used in giv-ing such information? Interesting aspects of these problems are dis-cussed by two physicians with many years of experience in this field, who highlight the issue from various angles (Tietz & Powers, 1975).

Many natural disasters are also probably the result of negligence, especially in our modern age, although so-called natural disasters have, of course, plagued mankind since earliest times (Nash, 1977; Cornell, 1977). The apparently uncontrollable aspects of such oc-currences as fires, floods, hurricanes, tornadoes, diseases, etc., have led us to question why they happen to the particular people that are affected. There is a general belief that these occurrences are indeed natural disasters, and not until fairly recently have scholars theorized whether some of these so-called natural disasters are, perhaps, the result of the actions of man. Martha Wolfenstein (1958), for example, suggests in *Disaster: A Psychological Essay,* that perhaps so many people perish in a natural disaster because they pay little or no attention to obvious warning signals. Kastenbaum and Aisenberg cite the following example which supports Wolfenstein's theory:

> On October 21, 1966, the village of Aberfan, South Wales became the scene of "an act of God," a natural disaster, or whatever euphemism you choose to adopt. A slag tip (heap of coal-mine debris) slipped and, in a veritable avalanche, crashed down upon the village school and eight houses. One hundred and sixteen children, most of the village's younger generation, and 28 adults were killed. Some might regard this as an act of God or Nature but Wendy Danforth echoes the words of many realists who called it instead "an act of unquestioned negligence." (Kastenbaum & Aisenberg, 1972, p. 387).

There appears to be a consensus that many natural disasters could be partially, if not completely, avoided by simply using common sense and implementing methods of prevention. It is a well-known fact that cigarette smoking can lead to such health problems as heart disease and lung cancer, and yet many people continue smoking and then wonder why they are stricken with a fatal illness that is directly attributed to their smoking. They have been warned but fail to heed the warning (Brinkmann, 1977).

WARS

It could be held that war can be viewed as an extension of capital punishment on a grand scale (Becker, 1967). During a period of war, killing is elevated to a national directive, and social controls such as patriotism are encouraged and fed in order to keep the bellicose policy supplied with enough people to carry out the governmental intentions. During a period of war,

> A large proportion of the nation's resources is mobilized for the related purposes of self-defense and other-destruction. The build-up in weaponry and supportive systems provides financial rewards to some people. Financial gain often leads to increase in social and political power. It is not easy to withdraw from a situation which offers both money and power. The system thus generates pressure for its own perpetuation and expansion, independently to some extent, of the objective need for military strength. (Kastenbaum & Aisenberg, 1972, p. 330.)

Thousands of people die in wars every year, mostly from violence but also from sickness and poor nutrition. It has been estimated that at one time during the Vietnam War, 59 percent of American casualties were the result of venereal disease. Yet,

> it is difficult to avoid recognizing that, during wartime, a more general cause of death finds multiple pathways to achieve its objective: People die in time of war because human life becomes a low priority item in the prevailing value system. The life of a civilian may count for even less than that of a combatant. How often would nations wage war if the preservation of human life were truly a strong and secure fixture in the individual and group value system. (Kastenbaum & Aisenberg, 1972, p. 333.)

In order to enhance the war effort, most governments use various systems of propaganda to indicate to the population that to fight and perhaps to die while defending their country is an honorable and esteemed act. Propaganda is also used to dehumanize the enemy—to deprive them of most of their human characteristics and to insinuate that they are animallike in their daily lives. The propaganda policies allow feelings of fear and distrust to further enrage the general population as well as the people trained to kill.

The changes that war brings to a society can have devastating effects. Sociologists hold that war has a " . . . tendency to disorganize both the individual family and the social mores. The literature on juvenile delinquency and mental illness has demonstrated a relationship between family disorganization and anti-social behavior" (Kastenbaum & Aisenberg, 1972, p. 334). It also appears that "Death in war is death utilized in an effort to achieve a temporal goal. Whether the goal is to protect one's homeland from aggression or to achieve a homeland, death or the threat of death is involved" (Vernon, 1970, p. 46).

Obviously there are potential problems that can result when people who are physically and emotionally trained to kill return to a peacetime society. That most of these people return to their families and occupations with little or no difficulty is a source of considerable amazement to Freud, who wrote during World War I:

> When the frenzied conflict of this war shall have been decided, everyone of the victorious warriors will joyfully return to his home, his wife and his children, undelayed and undisturbed by any thought of the enemy he has slain either at close quarters or by distant weapons of destruction. It is worthy of note that such primitive races as still inhabit the earth, who are undoubtedly closer than we to primitive man, act differently in this respect, or did so act until they came under the influence of our civilizations. The savage—Australian Bushman, Tierra del Fuegan—is by no

means a remorseless murderer; when he returns victorious from the war-path he may not set foot in his village nor touch his wife until he has atoned for the murders committed in war by penances which are often prolonged and toilsome. . . . Behind this superstition lurks a vein of ethical sensitiveness which has been lost by us civilized men. (Vernon, 1970, p. 46.)

Vernon feels that Freud's analysis is somewhat simplistic. He believes that "human behavior is relative to the situation, and given the right situations man can be taught or can learn to kill; whereas given other situations quite different behavior patterns are followed" (Vernon, 1970, p. 47). In other words, Vernon holds that killing during wartime is a value that is sanctioned by society and temporarily takes precedent over other values that people may hold, such as the religious belief that "Thou shalt not kill." But when the war is ended the values of the society revert to those that were held sacred before the outbreak of fighting, and people are able to make the transition because the old values are reinstated as soon as the war is over (Becker, 1967).

HOMICIDES/SUICIDES

A person is much more likely to die a violent death in the United States than in most other countries in the Western world. One authority writes that:

In 1967, more than 5,600 persons died of gunshot wounds in America as compared to fewer than 30 in Great Britain, less than 20 in France and fewer than 12 in Belgium. In 1968, there were 13,650 murders in the United States, a 13 percent increase over 1967. Between 1960 and 1970, murder incidence increased nationally by 62 percent, according to the FBI's Uniform Crime Reports. And in 1969, 86 law enforcement officers alone were "feloniously murdered," compared to the national average of 53 policeman killings per year in the 1960's. (Langone, 1974.)

During the twentieth century in the United States, more Americans have been killed by their fellow citizens with guns than have died in all of the wars that the United States has been involved in (Langone, 1974). There is no single reason that has been identified by physicians, psychologists, sociologists, or criminologists that would account adequately for the incredible number of homicides in the U.S. It has been suggested that the real reason is probably a complex combination of a variety of factors, including genetic predisposition to violence, childhood upbringing, and cultural environment.

There are three basic legal kinds of homicide in the U.S. The first is first-degree murder, which consists of a carefully planned, premeditated killing. Then comes second-degree murder, which includes cases of killing in the heat of passion, without deliberate planning. Finally, there is manslaughter, killing without intent to harm, as in an automobile accident. Langone states:

> Generally, murders are angry, spur-of-the-moment acts by ordinary, law-abiding citizens who strike out only in moments of blind fury. Or they are committed by those with some deep subconscious compulsion to kill. It has been said, in fact, that murder is not in general a crime of the so-called criminal class but of the non-professionals, our relatives and friends. (Langone, 1974.)

The crime of suicide, according to Kavanaugh, in *Facing Death,* " . . . remains among the stickiest problems for Americans to face. Official statistics count some twenty thousand suicides annually while unofficial estimates put the total at thirty thousand Americans" (Kavanaugh, 1972, p. 153). Despite the seemingly large number of occurrences of intentional self-destructors in the United States, Kavanaugh is surprised, given our violent environment and the ease with which weapons can be obtained, that the number of deaths by suicide is so low.

He rejects the popular notion that people who commit suicide are either insane or severely disturbed. He writes that in some cases,

> . . . suicide demands commitment and courage. . . . Suicide can be the fruit of a tortuous ethical decision made by a moral and sane individual, surely more sensitive than most. We pay to see racing-car heroes risk their lives for cash and fame and even thrills—and inevitably a substantial number wind up in flaming wrecks. Men in war put life on the line for patriotism or for fear of resisting the draft or letting their buddies down. Martyrs risk their lives for causes and creeds that seem illusory to nonbelievers. Our narrow sense of national morality is only now widening to admit that many suicide victims are heroes, too, within their own world view, and they are more deserving of our plaudits than our shame. (Kavanaugh, 1972, p. 155.)

Basically, suicide is ending one's own life in a culturally non-endorsed manner. There are endorsed forms of self-sacrifice not viewed as suicide, hara-kiri among them.

Vernon considers that a person's own death can be used as a way of punishing various people in his or her life. "An individual may permit or facilitate his own death in an effort to get even with certain others or as a means of vengeance or maybe to inflict pain upon others" (Vernon, 1970, p. 291). Certainly the person who commits suicide because of being jilted in a love affair is using death to make the former lover feel guilty and miserable. Vernon sees the "revenge suicide" as another way in which death can be used for punishment of others.

> . . . interpretations of suicide have been changing from an old interpretation which placed major responsibility for the suicide upon the suicide himself to an interpretation which recognizes the involvement of others and of situational factors as causative factors. It is not uncommon today to speak of the suicide as the victim rather than the evil doer. The moral denunciation of external factors has been increasing. (Vernon, 1970, p. 301.)

Vernon adds that suicide can also be viewed as a way of obtaining a reward in some cases. He uses for an example the Japanese suicide pilots during World War II, as seen in the following letter from a pilot to his parents:

> Please congratulate me. I have been given a splendid opportunity to die. . . . I shall fall like a blossom from a radiant cherry tree. . . . How I appreciate this chance to die like a man. . . . Thank you, my parents, for the 23 years during which you have cared for me and inspired me. I hope that my present deed will in some small way repay what you have done for me. (Vernon, 1970, p. 40.)

SACRIFICIAL AND RELIGIOUS CEREMONIES

A translation of the sixteenth-century work of Diego Duran, a Dominican friar, gives a vivid account of some of the sacrifices used by the Indians of ancient Mexico. Human sacrifices were very common then and Father Duran writes, "While I am reluctant to give inexact information, I believe I was told that more than a thousand men died in this land on that day, all to be carried off by the devil" (Duran, 1971). Father Duran states that the Indians honored many different gods, nearly all of whom demanded human sacrifices. During the ceremonies honoring the god Huitzilopochtli, six priests, or sacrificers, carried out the bloody work demanded of them. These details have been confirmed by various eminent researchers (Frazer, 1957).

Duran writes of the scene just before the sacrifice occurred:

Seeing them come out with their ghastly aspect filled all the people with dread and terrible fear! The high priest carried in one hand a large stone knife, sharp and wide. Another carried a wooden yoke carved in the form of a snake. They humbled themselves before the idol and then stood in order next to a pointed stone, which stood in front of the door of the idol's chamber. The stone was so high that it reached one's waist. And it was so sharp that when the sacrificial victim had been stretched across it on his back he was bent in such a way that if the knife was dropped upon his chest it split open with the ease of a pomegranate. . . . All the prisoners of war who were to be sacrificed upon this feast were then brought forth. . . . Surrounded by guards . . . the victims were forced to ascend to the long platform at the foot of the skull rack—all of them totally nude. . . . They seized the victims one by one, one by one foot, another by the other, one priest by one hand, and another by the other hand. The victim was thrown on his back, upon the pointed stone, yoke upon his throat. The high priest then opened the chest and with amazing swiftness tore out the heart, ripping it out with his own hands. Thus steaming, the heart was lifted toward the sun, and the fumes were offered up to the sun. The priest then turned toward the idol and cast the heart in its face. After the heart had been extracted, the body was allowed to roll down the steps of the pyramid. (Duran, 1971.)

Duran writes that these sacrifices were ways of eliminating all of the prisoners of war that the Indians had captured. After the ceremonies, the owners of the prisoners, that is, those men who had actually captured them, claimed their bodies. They were taken joyfully away and eaten during the feast that immediately followed the rites. Duran describes the universality of the practice among the Indians of Central America:

The same feast, the same rites, were performed in front of their god, just as was done in Mexico. All the provinces of the land practiced the same ceremonies. It was a universal festival and was named Coailhuitl, which means Feast Which Belonged to One and All. Every town sacrificed the prisoners taken by their own captains and soldiers. Thus it is possible for us to calculate the number of men sacrificed on that day in the entire land. (Duran, 1971.)

Duran believes that the Indians waged these wars solely to obtain new victims to feed the hungry gods. Some Indian gods demanded female virgins, while others demanded the blood of young children. The Indians tried not to kill their enemies, but rather to capture them for sacrificial use. The soldiers that captured the most victims were accorded much honor and became wealthy and famous among their people.

The foregoing example concerns the new world and may be of particular interest to the American reader. However, human sacrifices were common all over the world; in remote areas they still exist, and occult sects have recently taken up this habit again, even in the United States (Frazer, 1957).

As far as anthropologists can determine, most early civilizations followed such practices, and human sacrifices were common in virtually all parts of the world. The Old Testament ascribes such rites to all the nations that surrounded the Israelites, and it can be assumed that the Hebrews themselves followed similar practices before becoming more civilized. Traces of such barbaric customs probably prevailed longer in the rural areas than in Jerusalem and in other major centers. The episode in which Abraham is ordered to sacrifice his son, and appears willing to do so, supports such an assumption. Jewish tradition holds that this passage, which reports the substitution of an animal for a human being, could be considered the beginning of a new chapter in biblical history (Baron, 1952).

Cannibalism was not always connected with these rites, and it appears that economic factors, combined with religious beliefs, determined the exact nature of the human sacrifice ritual. Although considered cruel by modern standards, such sacrifices were sincerely believed by their practitioners to be necessary; undoubtedly the conquerors were just as cruel, but probably less sincere.

EXECUTION, BANISHMENT, AND INCARCERATION

Vernon believes that dying is an integral part of any society's development and that death-related behavior is culturally determined:

> The social process involved in dying is clearly illustrated by the process of capital punishment where the social behavior which terminates in death is institutionalized or spelled out in the norm-role definitions, the laws of the state. . . . Capital punishment involves a whole series of decisions which are interrelated, each of which influences subsequent behavior and decisions. The method of death, or possibly alternative methods, are specified, and may be related in specific ways to the past behavior of the individual who is to die. The validation of death by a specially designated functionary is incorporated in the system. A motive language is provided whereby the behavior is defined as morally acceptable. Capital punishment, then, is planned, timed dying. The factors involved are usually seen *not* as somehow being provided by mother nature or God the Father, but rather as being provided by man himself. (Vernon, 1970, p. 95.)

Some civil rights groups have suggested that once a legal decree of death has been made and punishment has been meted out, the condemned person should be given an option of how he or she is to die. These arguments are raised against the factors related to depriving the convicted of control over his or her destiny: the decisions as to time and manner of death.

The arguments in favor of and against capital punishment have raged on during most periods of history. At the present time in the United States, many states that had banned capital punishment not too long ago are enacting laws to reinstate the practice. Most people who favor capital punishment feel that it protects the public by acting as a deterrent to violent crime, that it is more economical than long periods of imprisonment, and that the old adage of "an eye for an eye" is still a valid moral precept in today's society.

Those opposed to legalized executions claim that capital punishment may result in the death of an innocent person, that it precludes any effort at rehabilitation of criminals, that it is ethically wrong, and that it is unevenly applied with regard to race, sex, class, etc. (Becker, 1967). These abolitionists cite statistics to show that capital punishment in reality does not serve as an effective deterrent to violent crime. MacNamera clearly feels that "punishment, no matter how severe or sadistic, has had little effect on crime rates" (Kastenbaum & Aisenberg, 1972, p. 328).

It is interesting to note that Texas and Oklahoma passed a "humane execution" act in 1977. Basically, the new laws provide for the substitution of lethal injections in lieu of electrocution. In ancient times the condemned were sometimes offered hemlock tea to sip. Opposition has been expressed to the new humane way of execution by the American Civil Liberties Union. The San Antonio chapter suggests injecting watermelons to kill minorities even more painlessly since statistically it is principally minority ethnics who are executed.

In *The Psychology of Death* Kastenbaum and Aisenberg claim that there is a basic inconsistency in a society that attempts to stop murder by legalizing murder for some people. They believe that a society that advocates capital punishment is implying that killing is an acceptable answer to seemingly unsolvable problems.

Execution contributes to the atmosphere of violence simply by being one more example of a life destroyed. . . . Individual life may have become devalued in our minds. The very existence of the state-supported occupation of executioner helps to legitimize killing and to dehumanize both executioner and victim: Killing is just another job; the dead product becomes an object, not a person with feelings like our own. (Kastenbaum & Aisenberg, 1972, p. 329.)

A horrifying account about "authorized" killings of entire populations can be found in a study of extermination camps that describes the gory details of executions of inmates. It is difficult to comprehend the base motivation for such actions (Des Pres, 1976).

Langone finds evidence that capital punishment might be considered a stimulus to other violent forms of crime. He tells of "an Ohio man who killed his wife shortly after a neighbor had been executed for murder, as a case of 'suggestive influence' " (Langone, 1974). Langone goes on to write that "In 1929, Dr. Alfred Adler theorized that capital punishment was a stimulant to crime because the more severe the punishment the more attraction there was to commit crime" (Langone, 1974). A more recent example is the case of James French, who in 1966, just before being executed for murder, told his psychiatrist that he had been disappointed at not getting the death sentence the first time he had been in prison, so when he got out he killed another person in order to make sure the state would recognize his qualifications for execution (Langone, 1974).

The beliefs of nearly all of those people who are against legalized executions was summed up by Clarence Darrow in 1924:

Do I need to argue to Your Honor that cruelty only breeds cruelty, that hatred only causes hatred? That if there is any way to soften the human heart, which is hard enough at its best, if there is any way to kill evil and hatred and cruelty, it is through charity and love and understanding. I am pleading for the future; I am pleading for a time when hatred and cruelty will not control the hearts of men, when we can learn by reason and judgement and understanding and faith that all life is worth saving, and that mercy is the highest attribute of man. (Langone, 1974.)

At present, the Supreme Court has basically reconfirmed the legality of capital punishment for the United States, but the individual states are still confused as to the equitable manner in which each case must be handled so as to avoid "arbitrary" application of the law.

Death by banishment was sometimes symbolic and sometimes real in bygone eras. Criminals were reportedly the first inhabitants of Japan—banished from China. Similar practices of banishment have been noted throughout history as a way of dealing with the undesirable. Incarceration is a form of banishment where symbolic as well as biological death occurs.

Figure 4.1   The planton. (Ginny Patton)

TORTURE

It seems, contrary to general awareness, that authorized torture is still an element of incarceration (*Time* magazine, August 16, 1976). Amnesty International, a human rights organization with headquarters in London, has estimated that sixty countries were officially practicing torture tactics in 1976. The United Nations Commission on Human Rights has said torture "is a phenomenon of our times."

Evaluating the nature and prevalence of torture is a very difficult task. In regions where it has official sanction, it is often impossible to verify because the ruling power can thwart detection. On the other hand, aspiring political groups often try to dominate public sentiment by accusing the ruling powers of torture tactics. Still, independent human rights organizations have compiled a credible account of torture throughout the world. It was not invented with the Inquisition and did not end with Hitler, despite the United Nations Human Rights Declaration of 1948.

While torture techniques reflect the miscarriage of human creativity, they are limited by prevailing technology. Some modern companies manufacture electronic torture instruments. However, sophisticated equipment is not always necessary. Some of the more common torture methods reported by *Time* (1976) include the "Planton," by which victims must hold weights at arm's length (Figure 4.1); the "Horsemen," by which the person must sit astride a rail for long periods; the "Dry Submarine," in which the victim's head is enveloped with an airtight plastic bag that results in suffocation (Figure 4.3); the "Magnifier Helmet," which amplifies the victim's screams (Figure 4.4); the "Parrot's Perch (Figure 4.2)," genital snap, and on and on.

Figure 4.2   The parrot's perch. (Ginny Patton)

Figure 4.3   The dry submarine. (Ginny Patton)

It is said that the torturers, as a group, are apt to refer to themselves by nicknames, and often insist that prisoners address them as "doctors."

Dr. Anthony Storr, a psychiatrist at Oxford University, believes that torture is motivated more by an overpowering will to obey than by sadism (*Time,* 1976). In any event, torture, unlike capital punishment, generally prolongs suffering. It may be used to extract information or seek a recanting of stated beliefs. It may result in eventual death of the victim.

Nurses and health care givers are not often in contact with persons who have experienced torture. However, it is an important area of care. In the United States the most frequent occasion which arises for the care giver is in child abuse cases. Abused children are often tortured in premeditated ways not just in violent, spontaneous moments of uncontrolled anger. Also, sometimes children are held captive.

Figure 4.4   Magnifier helment. (Ginny Patton)

A pioneering medical study recently conducted concluded that *mental disturbance* is the most important consequence of torture. Amnesty International reported that a Danish medical team found three-quarters of the study group suffered from anxiety, depression, loss of memory, nightmares, lethargy, and inability to concentrate. This may be the first scientific study of consequences of torture techniques. Although this study focused on adults, the implications for child abuse cases are obvious.

AGING

Sociologists feel that the most pressing problem concerning the aged in today's society is that "vastly increased numbers of people survive middle age and face the prospect of living for a long time in a society that as yet has found no ways to use the qualities, talents, and skills of its aging citizens" (Becher, 1967). "Since most of us view life as an ultimate value, we hail any act or artifact that extends it as a boon to humanity. Perhaps some day that will be true. For the present, however, I question the wisdom of a society that allocates considerable resources and talent to prolonging human life but fails to provide meaningful social roles for older people" (Blau, 1973).

Old age has become a problem in the modern world mostly because of the enormous technological advances made in the field of medicine since the turn of the century. The average life span during Roman times and up until the Middle Ages was about twenty-five years. In the United States around 1850, the average life span had increased to approximately forty years. But by 1964, the average life span in the United States had increased at an incredibly rapid rate to seventy years:

> Between 1900 and 1960 the American population was multiplied two and a half times. In that same period, however, the proportion of the population sixty-five years and older increased five times. Thus in 1900 there were only 3.1 million people in this age group. By 1960 there were 16.7 million older people in the United States, and by 1990 the figure is expected to reach 20.7 million. In short, within twenty years, older people will constitute at least 10 percent of the American population. (Blau, 1973.)

It appears that old age in the United States is a time of enforced detachment from most of the functioning institutions of the society. This was recognized by the late 1940s, when Parsons wrote:

> By comparison with other societies the United States assumes the extreme position in the isolation of old age from participation in the most important social structures and interests. Structurally speaking, there seem to be two primary bases of this situation: In the first place . . . the isolation of the individual conjugal family. . . . When the children of a couple have become independent through marriage and occupational status the parental couple is left without attachment to any continuous kinship group. . . . The second basis of the situation lies in the occupational structure. So far . . . as an individual's occupational status centers in a specific "job"; he either holds the job or does not and the tendency is to maintain the full level of functions up to a given point, and then abruptly to retire. (Parsons, 1949.)

He adds, "In view of the very great significance of occupational status . . . retirement leaves the older man in a peculiarly functionless situation . . ." (Parsons, 1949).

Blau theorizes that because old age results in a severe diminution of former roles, many of the elderly become sick since the role of a sick person is more clearly defined and accepted in our society. She writes that "The sick role, in short, provides an individual with a defense against the shame engendered by desertion and banishment, and a form of restitution for the roles he is forced to relinquish" (Blau, 1973). But because the burden of caring for the elderly sick is often unacceptable to their children and relatives, the old people are frequently placed in nursing homes or hospitals where their role becomes one of waiting to die.

Thus, while Americans are too tenderhearted to openly consider banishment or outright execution for the elderly (as the Eskimos used to), the actual treatment given to many old people today has nearly the same effect as legal measures might. In our society where achievement is believed to be an essential ingredient in measuring the quality or existence of life, old people who are unable to work either because of illness or because of compulsory retirement, are more or less told to go off by themselves and wait to die. Much research is needed in the area of old age to determine some useful functions for men and women who are presently being shunted aside. It is likely that many among our "senior citizens" die every year who really have nothing physiologically wrong with them, but who simply have nothing else left to do. There is a definite pressure within our society for people who cannot perform certain social and economic functions to abdicate their positions. These people are thus virtually dead even before their biological processes cease.

MEDICOCULTURAL METHODS

Various culturally sanctioned methods of causing death have been used at different times in different societies. These include the practices of abortion, genocide, and infanticide. These practices are distinguished from banishment and execution in that the victim has not been adjudged as having willfully broken a law, taboo, or societal code. Environmental and economic factors are often cited as germane to the issue of who shall die. The issue of abortion is a popular one in the United States today. But before one can adequately discuss ending a life, one must first decide on a definition of life itself. In the United States, for example, a fetus is not legally declared alive unless it can live outside of the mother's womb, or, in other words, until it is at least twenty or twenty-eight weeks old (Vernon, 1970). This follows the ancient definition of Roman law where the fetus was not considered alive until twenty-eight weeks old, but was rather defined as a part of the mother.

Even in the Catholic religion, different definitions of life have been applied at varying times in history:

> For eighteen centuries Catholic dogma generally specified that it was at the time of "quickening" when a rational soul first develops, and no serious attempt was made to punish those who sought abortions during the first trimester of pregnancy. The current dogma is only a hundred years old, dating from 1869 when Pope Pius IX changed the definition to the moment of conception. For only one century out of the past nineteen has abortion in the early months of pregnancy been considered by Catholics to be against the precept of God or the law of nature. (Vernon, 1970, p. 311.)

Because of the fact that there is no single definition of what constitutes life with regard to an unborn baby, one could conclude that:

> Most, if not all norm definitions are situationally relevant, in that in some situations certain aspects are given precedence over others. Rules of relevance and irrelevance are developed, so that decisions which take the situation into account can be made. Value definitions are themselves evaluated into some hierarchical structure so that the group can identify its high-intensity values and its low-intensity values—its first commandment and those of lesser salience. (Vernon, 1970, p. 309.)

The issue of abortion often becomes confused with the problem of infanticide, such as during the thalidomide scandal during the early 1960s. One mother in Belgium, with help from her physician and several other people, killed her deformed eighty-eight-day-old baby. A magazine article of that period discussed the case:

> The prosecution demanded conviction but recommended leniency. The defense asked acquittal, blamed 'a poisoned gift from modern science.' The court admitted as evidence stacks of letters supporting the defendants, and a public opinion poll promoted by Radio Luxembourg ran 10–1 in their favor. At week's end, the jury of twelve men took just 105 minutes to reach its verdict: Not guilty. (*Time* magazine, 1962.)

The fact that infanticide has been practiced to some degree since ancient times has been noted earlier (Frazer, 1958). But the problems of its legality still exist in most countries today, and the ethical position of infanticide is constantly being debated. Heifetz, writing about babies born with deformities from either hereditary or congenital defects, observes:

> Congenital defects are due to something that happened to the child during pregnancy. Science knows some but not all reasons for congenital defects—for example, exposure to excessive radiation, to German measles, or to the well-known drug Thalidomide. Hereditary defects are problems caused by characteristics of the genes . . . transmitted to the child by the parents. (Heifetz, 1975.)

Despite much recent work in the field of genetic study and counselling, children are still being born with severe deformities that will prevent them from ever becoming normal, functioning members of society. Heifetz divides these defective infants into three classes. Infants in the first two he considers outside the realm of this discussion. For those in the third class, however, he believes numerous variables must be considered before deciding whether medical care should be administered.

1. Those who are so damaged that nothing can keep them alive.
2. Those damaged infants who will live without need of medical care.
3. Those newborns who could not live without medical care and, even with medical care, would live only a subhuman existence. (Heifetz, 1975, p. 50.)

When considering the third class, he presents his rationale: "When evaluating the tragic newborn, we must balance its present and future condition against its effect on parents and siblings" (Heifetz, 1975.) Heifetz apparently agrees with Vernon's hypothesis that there can be no absolute meaning placed on the value of life or death but that the issues of life and death must be considered in relationship to the culture in which they exist. Heifetz is not alone in his concern over the fate of the tragically deformed newborn and its parents.

> Two physicians—Yale University pediatrician Raymond S. Duff and pediatrician A. G. M. Campbell of the University of Aberdeen, Scotland . . . reported in 1973 that forty-three infants were permitted to die during a thirty-month period at Yale-New Haven Hospital, New Haven, Connecticut, because parents and staff members there felt those children had "little or no hope" of achieving . . . meaningful humanhood. The children, who had a variety of profound defects, died because essential medical treatment was withheld from them. (Heifetz, 1975.)

It can be assumed from the available data that similar situations exist in hospitals throughout the United States and Europe. Newborn babies who are so deformed that it is unlikely that they will live for long even with the finest medical care, are usually allowed to die in as comfortable a manner as possible. Any guilt that might be felt by the medical personnel is apparently fairly easily dealt with. Guilt feelings on the part of the parents are more difficult to judge, but it is assumed that they are considerably less disruptive to normal social functioning than caring over the years for a hopeless child.

The governmental policy of genocide has been employed since the beginning of history. The most notorious example, of course, in modern times is the destruction of millions of Jews by the Nazi government in Germany during World War II. Des Pres writes,

> We live in an age of genocide, a time of willingness to remove humanity in chunks from the path of this or that policy. Hitler set out to eliminate, among others, the Jews, the Poles, the Communists. Stalin began by crushing the Old Bolsheviks, the intellectuals, the recalcitrant peasantry, and then went on to spread a web of random death through the very fabric of social interdependence. In Hiroshima it was to the population at large, and in Indochina all life—plant, human, animal—in the countryside. Genocide is a "crime against humanity" because it negates human values as such. Its victims are the innocent occupants of a certain amount of human space which henceforth will be empty. . . . But when the administration of death becomes a bureaucratic procedure, when killing is computerized and efficiency is the only value left, then clearly we behold something more than the age-old disregard for life. In our time the outcome of power is hostility to life itself. (Des Pres, 1976.)

Des Pres reminds us that even though the horrors of Nazi Germany (Figures 4.5, 4.6) are remembered by all, other pogroms that have called for the annihilation of large numbers of people have taken place, even within our own country. He writes, "In Turkey in 1915, for example, a million people were massacred as part of a deliberate policy to rid the country of its Armenian population. There were pogroms in the cities; villages were burned; men, women and children were driven into the desert to starve and be cut down" (Des Pres, 1976). Because so few people knew or cared about the fate of those million Armenians, Hitler thought that his policies to eliminate the Jews and other "undesirables" from Germany would also be overlooked by history.

According to sociologists, the old argument that the German people were unaware of the atrocities being conducted within their

Figure 4.5 Dachau concentration camps. Attendants dragging body using prong device on head. (The Bettmann Archive)

country must be questioned. They feel that people actually choose not to be informed of news events that threaten their well-being.

> . . . most people have been exposed to the facts . . . blinders are not applied from without. They are developed from within, and utilized defensively by the individual to serve his own needs. Often one of these needs is to avoid facing unpleasant truths and the guilt and discomfort attendant

Figure 4.6 Starved bodies of prisoners held by the Germans, who were transported to the Dachau concentration camp, where atrocities were carried on the the fullest extent, from another camp, lie grotesquely as they died in route. Here are the contents of one of the fifty similar freight cars. Clenched fists of several are evidence of the agony in which they died. (The Bettmann Archive)

thereupon. Frequently, *we don't know because we don't want to know.* (Kastenbaum & Aisenberg, 1972, p. 337.)

Obviously this statement refers to other analogous situations as well.

MENTAL ABERRATIONS

Many people with mental health problems in our society are treated like the elderly. We seem to believe that if a person is unable to provide some evidence of being able to cope intellectually, socially, and economically, he or she might as well be dead. Failure to "make it" is today strongly equated with death—they are both unproductive roles. Just as old people's lives are consistently devalued, so are the lives of chronic mental patients. Since we are unable to cure many of these people, we prefer to ignore them and tend to avoid or shun them.

There is a stratum of links characterized in the following words:

> . . . an individual may be considered to be symbolically dead when he ceases to be aware of, or able to define, his own existence. Such a condition may apply to a comatose or heavily drugged individual. He does not know who he is or, for that matter, what he is. Such a condition could occur sometime before biological death. (Vernon, 1970.)

As Kalish wrote in 1966,

> Many people react to psychological death, when apparently irreversible, by suggesting that the patient be allowed to die physically as well; some encourage euthanasia, even though the person is not necessarily suffering discomfort. In our pragmatic, achievement-oriented nation, a man who does not behave like a human being is not a human being, and, therefore might as well be dead, and therefore, is dead. (Vernon, 1970, p. 53.)

Under Hitler (and possibly other dictators) thousands of feeble-minded persons were simply put to death, allegedly because of food shortages.

Symbolic death can occur whenever people believe that they might as well be dead. Such feelings can be seen among the elderly, among prisoners serving life sentences, among dying people, and among people in mental hospitals. There are advantages in thinking of a relative as dead, Vernon writes, because then " . . . his survivors . . . are able to attend to other matters with a minimum of interference and a reduction of affective involvement" (Vernon, 1970, p. 53).

Kalish claims that relatives

> . . . may settle the "dead" person's affairs, give away his belongings, talk of him in hushed tones, refuse to speak ill of him, and think in terms of how they will take care of his body and spend his bequest. In some instances, if the biological death does not occur as anticipated, the family may become impatient and have difficulty in accommodating themselves to an individual whose role was to have ceased. (Vernon, 1970, p. 53.)

In some countries people jailed under a life sentence, with no chance for parole, or those hopelessly affected by terminal illness, are declared civilly, i.e., legally dead, and their spouses may remarry. It is difficult to judge what is right and what is wrong when problems of this nature are involved.

Not only do people with mental differences often get treated as if they are dead but mental aberrations are associated with numerous bizarre and wanton deaths. Although one may argue that mental problems accompany many fatal circumstances, the murderer is more likely to be called a mental case if the death in question has bizarre and/or sexual qualities. Although Lombroso's notions of "Born criminals" has largely been discarded, there are vestiges of such a doctrine in the resentment expressed toward the individual who kills for bizarre and self-gratifying purposes. In contemporary history the crimes of the Charles Manson "family" received nationwide notoriety. There have been others that commanded society's attention; Peter Kürten of Düsseldorf killed more than forty people during a thirty-year period. He experienced sexual pleasure at seeing flowing blood. Harmann killed young boys and sold their flesh during the famine in Germany following World War I. Gilles de Rais—a companion of Joan of Arc—killed more than 200 young boys. Charles Whitman killed a number of people from the University of Texas "Tower." John Carona committed mass murder in California.

It was England that first passed a law dealing with moral insanity (Prichard's Law) holding that the morally insane individual could work but was constitutionally unable to behave in a moral and responsible way. In the United States the McNaughton rule usually applies to cases where insanity is tested. Although sanity and insanity are generally viewed as legal terms that those in the mental health profession have little cause to use, the terms are of considerable import in many cases of homicide.

SUMMARY

Nine categories of circumstances in which human death typically occurs have been outlined. Although the categories are arbitrary they provide a reasonable framework in which clusters of deaths occur. In *diseases,* the first circumstantial category of death discussed, it is pointed out how unremitting epidemics and pandemics can devastate a whole society—as in fourteenth-century Europe. Some estimates suggest that one-fourth of the total Western world population died from the "Black Death." The medieval concept of death did not equip people to deal with such massive deaths and may have encouraged panic. Mankind's sinfulness was thought to be somehow responsible for the plague. In the Christian view there were only three basic causes of death: *disease, sin,* and *preordained experience.* The advent of the microscope, inoculation, and sterilization practices begins to alter people's views of the causes of death.

Accidental death has sometimes been categorized death by "an act of God," or "act of misadventure." Accidental death also raises the difficult question of negligence. It appears relatively common for survivors of almost any sort of accident to feel guilty even when there is no objective way in which they could have contributed to the mishap.

Wars are by no means "natural" disasters, but may be accidentally started. Becker (1967) has called wars capital punishment on a grand scale. In any event, during war every effort is mounted to heighten patriotism and loyalty. Thousands of people die each year in wars not only from combat, but from disease and poor nutrition. Sociologists have suggested that war disorganizes the individual family unit as well as altering social mores.

Homicides/suicides are categories that occupy prominent news coverage in the United States perhaps more than in any other nation. While American citizenry may disdain politically motivated death in other countries, other countries may similarly wonder about the high American homicide/suicide rates for which there are no political reasons. There are three kinds of homicide recognized by U.S. law: first-degree murder, second-degree murder, and manslaughter. Manslaughter is the legal term for "no-fault" death.

Sacrificial and religious ceremonies. From the earliest times it seems that man has practiced widespread human sacrifice. Cannibalism was not always connected with such sacrifice. Economic and religious ritual often dictated the form of the sacrifice.

Execution, banishment, and incarceration are forms of death-related behavior thought to be culturally determined. In present times there has been persistent controversy concerning the justification of capital punishment. Its proponents feel it acts as a deterrent to violent crime and its opponents argue that no such evidence exists. Death by banishment was sometimes real and sometimes symbolic in bygone eras. Incarceration may be thought of as a form of banishment in the sense that freedom of access to the society is lost. Two of the most common causes of death during incarceration are illness and torture. While relatively little attention is given torture in modern times, it is clearly prevalent.

Aging. Sociologists contend that a major current social problem concerns the vast numbers of people surviving into old age with their talents and skills devalued and rendered useless. Old age has become an enforced detachment from most functioning institutions of the society. While outright banishment is not practiced, retirement often constitutes symbolic banishment.

Medicocultural methods of inducing death have been used at different times in history by different societies. These include hara-kiri, abortion, genocide, and infanticide. The victim has generally not broken a law or flouted a taboo or social custom. Genocide was practiced on an enormous scale in the concentration camps of World War II.

Mental aberrations cause their victims to become devalued as being unable to maintain socially defined roles of productivity. Symbolic death can occur whenever a person sees himself or herself as dead. This may happen to ill or retired persons whose work ethic dictates that they must be productive to be of value. Persons with mental "differences" may be treated like the dead. Mental aberrations have come to be associated with numerous bizarre deaths. England passed the first law dealing with insanity. In the United States insanity is primarily viewed as a legal term by mental health professionals, but it is nonetheless of considerable importance in many homicide cases.

REFERENCES

Alexander, F. *Psychosomatic Medicine*. New York: W. W. Norton & Co., 1950.

Aries, P. *Western Attitudes toward Death*. Baltimore, Maryland: The Johns Hopkins University Press, 1974.

Baron, S. W. *A Social and Religious History of the Jews*. 2nd ed. Philadelphia: The Jewish Publication Society of America, 1952.

Becker, H. S., ed. *Social Problems: A Modern Approach*. New York: John Wiley & Sons, Inc., 1967.

Blau, Z. S. *Old Age in a Changing Society*. New York: New Viewpoints, 1973.

Brinkmann, W. "Clinatologist Finds Many Can't Face Up to Natural Disasters." *Houston Chronicle,* January 2, 1977.

Cornell, J. *The Great International Disaster Book*. New York: Charles Scribner's Sons, 1977.

Des Pres, T. *The Survivor*. New York: Oxford University Press, 1976.

Duran, F. D. *Book of the Gods and Rites and the Ancient Calendar*. Norman, Oklahoma: University of Oklahoma Press, 1971.

Ellis, A., and Aberbanel, A., eds. *Encyclopedia of Sexual Behavior*. New York: Hawthorn Books, 1961.

Frazer, J. G. *The Golden Bough*. New York: Macmillan Co., 1958.

Heifetz, M. D., and Mangel, C. *The Right To Die*. New York: G. P. Putnam's Sons, 1975.

Kastenbaum, R., and Aisenberg, R. *The Psychology of Death*. New York: Springer Verlag, 1972.

Kavenaugh, R. E. *Facing Death*. Baltimore, Maryland: Penguin Books, Inc., 1972.

Koenig, R. "Dying vs. Well-Being." *Omega*, 4(3), 1973.

Kübler-Ross, E. *Questions and Answers on Death and Dying*. New York: Collier Books, 1974.

Langone, J. *Death Is a Noun*. New York: Dell Publishing Co., 1972.

Langone, J. *Vital Signs*. Boston: Little, Brown & Co., 1974.

Nash, J. R. *Darkest Hours*. Chicago: Nelson-Hall Publishers, 1977.

Parsons, T. "Age and Sex in the Social Structure of the United States," *Essays in Sociological Theory, Pure and Applied*. Glencoe, Illinois: Free Press, 1949.

Pine, V. R., ed. *Acute Grief and the Funeral*. Springfield, Illinois: Charles C. Thomas, Publisher, 1976.

Schulzinger, M. *The Accident*. Springfield, Illinois: Charles C. Thomas, Publisher, 1956.

Shneidman, E. S., ed. *Death: Current Perspectives*. Palo Alto: Jason Aronson, Inc., 1976.

Spencer, A. *Death and Elizabethan Tragedy*. New York: Pageant Books, 1960.

Tietz, W., and Powers. "The Pediatrician and the Dying Child." *Clinical Pediatrics,* June 1975.

"Torture as Policy: The Network of Evil." *Time* magazine, August 1976, pp. 31–34.

Vernon, G. M. *Sociology of Death*. New York: Ronald Press Co., 1970.

Wolfenstein, M. *Disaster: A Psychological Essay*. New York: The Free Press, 1958.

Funerals, Death Rituals, and Religious Influences

Funerals are services which are emulated in the context of a dead or dying person and appear to have been present in the majority of societies and cultures around the world. Some groups—like the Tasaday Indians of whom the rest of the world has only recently become aware—appear to have no elaborate rituals. Other groups of people have very elaborate and extensive death rituals. Is man the only animal to recognize death with ritual? The answer remains uncertain. Elephants reportedly have covered the head and tusk area of their dead. Other animals—the Steller Sea Lion and some species of birds and primates likewise appear to demonstrate emotional reactions in the context of stress, danger, and death of their respective kind. Although these appear to be analogous emotional reactions and stereotypic behavior patterns, we do not think of other animals having ceremonies. Human beings are clearly set apart by the elaborate and varied ways in which they observe the final rite of passage.

In present times, when death comes to one who is significant in our lives, we typically feel a crushing pang of emotional hurt. The foci of "hurt" may have anatomical definition. For a period of time, we are clumsy and groping and may turn over the management of funeral proceedings to a funeral director. By doing this we make tacit assumptions about this person and his or her skill. Necessarily, we make an alliance with the funeral director somewhat as we do with the surgeon who momentarily will be in charge of affairs dear to our life or in charge of our life. Our knowledge of funeralry and other accompaniments of death is typically ahistorical and naïve. This chapter will therefore attempt to highlight historical threads of continuity relating to funerals and death rituals.

Ancient Customs

Extend wide thine arms, O Earth, to embrace the dead.
With tender pressure and with welcome sheet

151

wrap him tenderly, even as the mother
wraps her soft roll about the beloved child.

From an ancient Indian burial rite

Those words, dating from India's Vedic period, probably between 1500 and 1000 B.C., were sung by Aryans during funeral rites. Although not part of the Vedas themselves, the quatrain suggests poignantly how ancient peoples viewed death and separation. A mystic quality expressive of deep religious feeling pervades the leave-taking; Earth is enjoined to accept the dead person as a mother would. The parallel between chants calling on Earth to "Extend wide thine arms . . ." and the Christian "Dust thou art . . ." indicates enduring philosophic-religious continuities.

The continuities are real. Through the ages, and today in most societies, people have observed death customs and rites the deepest meanings of which are shrouded in speculation. People feared death: so much is known. The customs and rituals surrounding final disposition have as their purpose, at least in part, the exorcism of fear through acclimatization to the fact of death. But funerals and death rituals have wider meaning, a social significance deriving from the importance accorded the rituals and, often, from their elaborate nature.

Overarching continuities of meaning have not ruled out enormous diversity. From age to age and country to country, death rites and customs have evolved along such unique, yet related, paths as to provide the subject matter for endless study. The variations do not relate exclusively to tribal, clan, or other forms of rites and rituals. Within any given group, they may vary also depending on the age of the deceased, the manner of death, and the dead person's relationship to family and society. As Hertz (1960) notes of various Australian tribes: "The type of death also causes numerous exceptions to the normal ritual. All those who die a violent death or by accident, women dying in childbirth, people killed by drowning or by lightning and suicides, are often the objects of special rites" (p. 85).

Other factors may call for still greater departures from a society's norms or customs. The manner of disposing of the body, for example, dictates variations in funeral customs. Rituals will vary depending on whether the body is cremated, inhumed, or disposed of in some other way.

In the face of such rich multiplicity of forms and approaches to death and funerals, the task of characterizing the funeral and death rituals of even a single human group assumes gigantic proportions.

Certain aspects can, however, be highlighted as, for example, in the case of African customs and beliefs:

> Varied peoples, races and cultures, and a confusion of tongues. . . . Animism, a world of spirits. . . . Tribalism, exclusive. . . . Tribal man, a living personification of the ancestral dead. . . . Fantastically varied funeral folkways. . . . The contravening forces of Christianity. . . . And an archipelago of whites in a sea of blacks and coloured. (Habenstein & Lamers, 1960, p. 215.)

Such a method offers the greatest promise of treating the subject effectively.

FUNERALS IN HISTORY

The funeral, as a ceremony associated with the act of disposing of the dead, has existed since the early centuries of recorded history. Modern man's knowledge of such ceremonies or rites has been derived from records found in tombs or—in the cases of the more advanced cultures of antiquity—in both literature and monuments. The evidence is so complete, in some instances, that some ancient funeral customs can be described almost as fully as the ceremonies of today. Indeed, a good part of our knowledge of some cultures derives solely from funerary artifacts.

Contributing to current understanding of the funerals of older societies and peoples are the rites of more modern primitive groups such as the American Indian. These rites, archeologists believe, derive from older ceremonies and thus aid in the task of interpretation. Students of the subject have for years heeded the strictures laid down by Madden in 1851:

> The modes of treating the dead, and the rites of sepulture that prevail in different nations, are deserving of more attention. . . . The analogies that exist, or existed, between those of civilized countries . . . would afford information of the highest value: those, for example, of the natives of Africa and Australia with those of the Indians of Mexico and Peru; the funeral customs of the people of China with those of the Malays and South Sea Islands; and, finally, the funeral ceremonies and customs of those nations considered in relation with the same usages in the ancient nations of Egypt and Judea, which have influenced so materially the modes, customs, and opinions of all the people of the earth. (Madden, 1851, p. 53.)

Comparative studies of funeral customs have led to efforts to classify such rites in such a way as to illuminate ancient beliefs concerning death. Classification has also exposed early man's fears, hopes, and attitudes toward the dead person or persons, and even the survivors' attitudes and beliefs concerning the living. Deeper understanding of old cultures has resulted. In some cases the historic roots of modern practices have been revealed, with consequent benefit to today's anthropologist, sociologist, archeologist, and those representing still other disciplines.

An early attempt to classify customs isolated eight principal ideas underlying ancient funeral rites:

1. The pollution or taboo attaching to the corpse
2. Mourning
3. The continued life of the dead as evinced in the housing and equipment of the dead, in the furnishing of food for them, and in the orientation and posture of the body
4. Communion of the dead in a funeral feast and otherwise
5. Sacrifice for the dead and expiation of their sins
6. Death witchery
7. Protection of the dead from ghouls
8. Fear of ghosts (*Encyclopaedia Britannica,* 11th ed., 1911, Vol. 11, p. 329.)

Such common threads in burial rites and customs are often more readily specified than explained. Why, for example, a corpse should be regarded as unclean, and why such uncleanness may extend to persons or things touching the dead, is uncertain. Decomposition and the accompanying sense of a loss of purity (or the religious notion that sin causes death) may have suggested that interpretation. But the taboo has a long history: in Old Testament times, a high priest might not for any reason "go into any dead body" (Leviticus 21:11). In like fashion the ancient Persians built dakmas or "towers of silence," far from human habitation, into which the dead were thrown. Birds of prey and dogs soon picked the bones clean, removing the unclean flesh.

Other ideas central to the custom of holding funerals for the dead suggest the existence of beliefs and superstitions that survive today. Some of them, as might be expected, continue in attenuated form. Wearing mourning, in modern times an outward sign of grief, apparently served in an earlier epoch to warn people that unclean death was present. Mourning, too, took many forms: where, in ancient Rome, funeral mourners wore black, or *lugubria,* among the Aruntas of Australia the wives of the deceased smeared themselves with white pipe clay. The tombs of ancient times, including the *tumuli* of northern Europe, represented the houses of the dead. Often, as among the ancient Egyptians, the Vikings, and other peoples, the deceased were laid to rest with everyday tools, artifacts, weapons, and clothing so that they might be prepared for the afterlife, or reincarnation, at some future time.

The funeral feast for the survivors of a dead person has been seen as yet another means of assuring peace in death. Held at the tomb or grave in ancient ritual, the feast became "the pledge and witness of the unity of the kin, the chief means, if not of making, at least of repairing and renewing it" (Hartland, 1895, Vol. 2, p. 278). In cannibalistic societies, human victims might be sacrificed and eaten while other groups included expiatory totem sacrifices of animals during burial rituals. Human sacrifices might take place at the tomb or grave—a way of giving the deceased company on the journey to the next world, or of appeasing the departing spirit (Davey, 1890). Feasting off the remains of the dead seems to have had the purpose of effecting a sacramental union of the living and the deceased in some societies.

Among primitive groups the feast was an essential feature of the final rites. In the Irish "wake" it still survives. In older times "a dead man's soul or double had to be fed at the tomb itself" (*Encyclopaedia Britannica,* 11th ed., 1911, Vol. 11, p. 331). Sometimes the corpse was required to sit in attendance at the feast. Often food was buried with the remains, whereupon the living enjoyed a banquet separate from the funeral. Animals might be slaughtered to provide food for such meals.

Death witchery, the practice of placing a curse or of employing sorcery to take another's life, survives today only in the most primitive societies. By contrast, inhumation as a means of protecting the body from ghosts or evil spirits—and conversely of insuring against the return of the dead person's soul or spirit—still represents the most common climax to funeral ceremonies. The body was placed in a tomb or directly into the earth or was cremated. Protection of the deceased against the ravishes of vampires or ghouls seems similarly to have inspired prayers in Christian burials and the construction of tombs by many ancient races.

Superstition that peopled the world of ancient man with terrible demons that might violate tombs gave rise in later centuries to the practice of burying the dead under the floors of churches. Thus the evil spirits were kept at bay. The Code of Justinian (about 850 A.D.) banned the practice.

That fear of ghosts inspired many funeral customs appears to be established fact. To make sure that the living would not be haunted, a corpse was "buried or burned, or scaffolded on a tree, a tower or a house-top" (*Encyclopaedia Britannica*, 11th ed., 1911, Vol. 11, p. 332) (Figure 5.1). All such rites "afford ample evidence that death, as the most solemn and mysterious fact of our existence, has exercised the thoughts of men from the remotest ages. When they arose, the idea of a soul or spirit, as distinct from its corporeal tenement, had hardly yet been evolved" (*ibid.*).

ANCIENT FORMS OF FUNERAL RITES

Where literature does not supply details on ancient funerals, friezes, carvings, or drawings do; or deductions may be made from the mute evidence found in graves and tombs. In the period following the Babylonian captivity, the Jews, for example, adhered to relatively strict forms or customs.

> The custom was to bury the dead the same day. . . . The poor were borne to the grave lying on an open bier, as the Arabs are to this day. . . . People of rank and station were carried on costly biers, and Herod's body was borne to the grave on a wooden bier. . . . Caves and caverns served as catacombs likewise for dead bodies. . . . The funeral obsequies were attended by the friends of the deceased, both men and women, "who made loud lamentations for the dead, and some of whom were hired for the occasion. . . . The use of musical instruments at funerals by these hired mourners is alluded to by Jeremiah and by Emmaus." (Davey, 1890, p. 12.)

Few peoples of the ancient world appeared to have followed the Jewish custom of holding the funeral the same day. "The funeral in Greece took place three days after the exhibition of the remains" (*ibid.*, p. 14), much in the manner of many peoples of modern times. But the Greek funeral was held before sunrise, so as to avoid any kind of show or ostentation. The deceased was not buried in silence: "Many women surrounded the bier, weeping and howling, and not a few, being professionals, were paid for their trouble" (*ibid.*). The coffin, made of cypress wood, which is noted for its marvelous durability, was placed on a chariot. With male relatives walking behind and those of close

Figure 5.1   Burials. North American Indians depositing a corpse on a scaffold.
Lithograph 1879. (The Bettmann Archive)

kinship joining the cortege with shaved heads, the coffin was escorted to the dead person's final home. A choir of musicians accompanied the mourners. "The procession, as a rule, had not far to go, for the body of a wealthy person was usually buried in his garden—if his city house did not possess one, then that of his villa residence" (*ibid.*, p. 15).

Europe saw many other funeral customs in pre-Christian times. Scythians, the early Tartars, who inhabited southeastern Europe including the Don River steppe country until about the fifth century B.C., had especially elaborate rites for the burial of a king. On the death of the royal person, a rectangular hole was dug in the ground. The body was covered with wax, whereupon the deceased's belly was opened, cleansed, and filled with bruised cypress, incense, seeds of parsley, and anise. These preparations done, the body was carried in a chariot to another province. Here, "those who [were to] receive it . . . cut off part of one ear, shaved their heads, wounded themselves on the arms, forehead, and nose, and pierced the left hand with an arrow" (Madden, 1851, Vol. 1, p. 296). The same procedure was repeated in other provinces until the royal corpse had made a circuit of the kingdom, whereupon the body was placed in the grave that had originally been dug.

As was the custom among so many primitive tribes of peoples, the Scythian king went to the next world with company. "In the spaces that remain vacant, they place one of the king's concubines strangled, with a cup-bearer, a cook, a groom, a waiter, a messenger, certain horses, and some of all things necessary" (Madden, 1851, Vol. 1, p. 297). Other groups known to have offered human sacrifices as integral parts of the final rites for the dead included the Gauls and the Druids. The Gauls killed serfs and slaves on the death of a leader, carrying the leader then to the grave in magnificent pagan rites.

Less is known of Druidic sacrifices because the Druids committed nothing to writing. We know, however, that Druidic sacrifices took place in sacred woods or groves. The purpose was both to appease the gods at the time of death and to redeem one person's death with that of another. "In their funerals, which are very magnificent, they throw into the burning pile every thing that the deceased delighted in, even to living [human and animal] figures" (Madden, 1851, Vol. 1, p. 322).

MOURNING RITUALS IN PRE-CHRISTIAN TIMES

The rituals surrounding the act of disposing of the dead evolved and were elaborated upon as mankind progressed through ages that are identified according to the techniques of stone polishing and metalworking. Over time, funerary customs and rituals were conditioned by the beliefs of various ancient peoples concerning life after death and the relationship of the dead to the living.

Such facts suggest why much of what we know today of ancient cultures has been derived through studies of evidence found in graves and tombs. Methods of disposition and the objects deposited with the deceased have told researchers, including anthropologists, about our earlier ancestors in a variety of ways: how those people felt about an afterlife, how they regarded the deceased specifically, what religious or superstitious beliefs shaped their attitudes toward death, and so on. Extrapolating, one can deduce that early peoples, like many today, were performing a rite of passage in observing rituals of mourning. They were assuring the successful passage of the deceased to the final state of human existence.

As rites of passage, funeral or burial rites and customs have to be seen in the context of many other kinds of ceremonies with which people mark major changes in status or steps on the road through life. Religious beliefs and convictions shaped many of these ceremonies and gave them continuity. In like fashion, many religions today prescribe the forms for particular rites such as baptism, confirmation, or marriage.

Death rituals appear from archeological evidence to date from the Pleistocene or Ice Age. Some of the earliest clues to such rituals were found with Peking Man, and indicated ceremonial cannibalism. Neanderthal remains from the late Pleistocene Age—70,000 to 100,000 years ago—have been unearthed in ossuaries occupied also by the bones of mammals. In Italy a Neanderthal skull was found in a circle of stones in the inner chamber of a cave.

Other Neanderthal remains, found in France, suggest the existence in the Paleolithic period of a cult of the dead. Involving the placement of implements and food in graves, the cult gave rise to other practices such as comfortable positioning of bodies in their graves. The intention appears to have been ritualistically to provide for the dead in a life beyond the grave and, coincidentally, to insure that the dead did not return to haunt the living.

One ritual thought to be as ancient as the sun worshipers is *orientation*, the formal placement of bodies with their feet to the East and their heads to the West. The custom originated in the desire of early peoples properly to prepare a deceased person to meet the Sun God. Thus ritual interment, even then, had importance. That the custom has survived to the present in some human groups suggests how differing interpretations may be placed on the same rite.

Orientation is not primarily of Christian origin, but a relic of the rites of the early sun-worshipers. . . . To the Christian, the burial of bodies with their faces to the east is the outcome of the belief noted of the resurrection of the body, but also that from the east shall come a final summons to Judgment. Hence in Wales the east wind is known as the "wind of the dead man's feet." (Puckle, 1926, p. 149.)

Bronze Age paintings on sarcophagi left by the ancestors of the ancient Greeks in Boeotia add further evidence of ritual burial, and even of funerals. The paintings depict mourners with their hands held to their heads in schematic gestures that presage similar drawings on plaques and vases of the later Archaic and Classical periods of Greek history (Kurtz & Boardman, 1971). More important, perhaps, the ceremonial lament for the dead seems to occupy these ages-old figures. Certainly the lament had become a part of ritual burial in Bronze Age Greece:

The lament for the dead remains an essential part of Greek funerary procedure. A more lasting embodiment of grief for a lost loved one—a painting on a sarcophagus, or on a vase, or a clay mourner figure—accompanied the dead whose family had performed the burial with the honoured funerary lament. (Kurtz & Boardman, 1971, p. 28.)

Evidence of ceremonial burial accumulates from this point on. Reasoning human beings seemed to be developing awareness of death and the dead as they emerged from prehistoric darkness. Egypt's tombs evolved from the most simple form, the mastaba, to the elaborate royal pyramid tombs of the pharaohs at Giseh. Such changes took place primarily between the beginning of the First Dynasty—about 3200 B.C.—and the Fourth Dynasty—about 2700 B.C. All the tombs were built as residences for the dead.

Construction of these magnificent tombs may, in itself, be considered a preparation for the funeral observance even though it sometimes took place before death, over a period of many years. Yet the formal obsequies for the dead must have taxed the endurance of even the most hardy. Where, on the death of a plain citizen, "in carrying the body to the grave, both men and women made very horrid lamentations" (Muret, 1682, p. 3), the funeral rites for a deceased pharaoh boggle the imagination:

The mourning [continued] no less than 72 days, during which time all manner of rejoicings and festivals were forbidden; they all bedaubed their faces with mire and dirt; walked in troops together along the streets, without anything but a linen-cloth wrapt about them, mixing the name of their deceased Prince with their sighs and out-cries: They abstained from wine and delicate meats; deny'd themselves the use of baths and perfumes; they did not so much as make their beds, nor accompany with their wives, and express'd all the signs of an extraordinary affliction. (Muret, 1682, pp. 4–5.)

Such orgiastic observances had no place in Classical Greek and Roman funeral and death rites, even though many such rites can be traced to old Egypt. The Greeks, in addition to chanting the death lament, might variously wash the corpse clean with water or wine, or pour upon the deceased "a thousand sweet perfumes" (*ibid.*, p. 5), while still others covered the dead only with olive leaves. Some clothed the loved one in crimson, others in white, with garlands strewn about. Greek custom also, in some areas, required that a sealed letter be placed in the hands of dead persons to let residents of the next world know that the dead had been properly sped on their way. Local custom, as in Platea, also called for corteges in which a trumpeter marched first, followed by chariots loaded with bay and myrtle leaves. After the chariots came people carrying bowls of milk and wine, which they poured over the sepulchre.

In both Greece and Rome certain aspects of the basic funeral practice were prescribed by law. Thus in ancient Rome the practice of burying deceased family members in their own homes was eventually prohibited because of the danger of infection and disease. Thenceforward no dead could be buried in Rome, but had to be interred along the Via Flamminia or Latina—the Flamminian and Latin Roads—and the funerals generally followed a pattern.

As soon as they [the mourners] were arriv'd, one of the Relations standing in the midst of the company, who made a ring about him, pronounced the Funeral Oration in praise of the Deceased: Afterwards they laid him in the Grave with an ever-burning lamp, and some small vessels of several sorts of drink and meats (not forgetting to put in also a piece of money to pay Charon, for wafting them in his ferry), and some Woollen Garlands. (*Ibid.*, pp. 25–26.)

The pagan burial rites of ancient Rome were suffused with superstitious awe that contrasted strongly with the later Christian view of death. Where pagan, imperial Rome practiced ancestor-worship—the lares and penates, or household gods, were literally the ghosts of ancestors—the Christians saw death as the prelude to a glorious afterlife with the Creator.

Funerals and Death Rites in the Christian Era

*I have given unto thee one thousand breadcakes, and one thousand
vessels of beer, and one thousand oxen, and one thousand geese, and
one thousand changes of apparel . . . , and one thousand things of all
kinds, beautiful and pure, and one thousand things of all kinds, beautiful
and sweet . . . Purifications, purifications to thy Ka, O Osiris.*

Chapter of the Purification of the Altar, from The Book of Opening
of the Mouth, by E. A. W. Budge

If, as Puckle (1926) contended, the earth has become over the
centuries "one vast burial ground" (p.129), it is equally true that early
Christian and modern funerals and death rituals have grown out of the
pagan ceremonies of old. Early Christianity even inherited its
cemeteries from pagan Rome.

We have already seen that the pagan burial-places were considered as
something sacral and set apart, and how the early Christians inherited the
guardianship of the dead, and erected their first places of worship on the
actual site of the pagan temple. . . . Cemeteries and church yards were
under the immediate control of the church. (Puckle, 1926, p. 139.)

Many Christian rituals, of course, had original, if not contemporary, significance. "The custom of lighting candles around the dead
body and watching at its side all night ['waking'] was originally due to
the beliefs that a corpse, like a person asleep, is specially liable to the
assaults of demons" (*Encyclopaedia Britannica*, 11th ed., 1911, Vol.
11, p. 332). Similarly, tolling a bell when a person died was designed to
frighten off the evil demons that seek to waylay the deceased's soul. In
Catholic ritual, too, the Holy Eucharist was often placed in the grave
for like reasons.

The early Christian funeral was appropriately simple and dignified. As prelude, "The eyes were closed, the body was washed,
anointed, and wrapped in a linen sheet with spices" (*New Catholic
Encyclopedia*, 1967, Vol. 6, p. 225). Afterward, a wake or period of
watching designed to assure that death had actually taken place preceded a Mass that had death as its main theme. "The body was then
solemnly carried to the cemetery ['the sleeping place'], white torches
of eternal light and triumph preceding" (*ibid.*). Psalms and hymns
were interspersed with alleluias, and graveside prayers might be
terminated with a last "kiss of peace."

Over the centuries following the beginning of the Christian era, funerals and death rituals came to be matters of deeply ingrained tradition. Differing cultural and economic levels dictated broad variations in the degrees to which the traditions were honored. But threads of commonality linked the hugely ceremonial and pomp-filled rituals accompanying the deaths of kings and princes with the rites accorded the poorest serf.

Cremation, once an accepted method of disposing of human remains, had no place in these Christian rites. The body of the deceased would someday rise again—such was the belief then as today—and therefore Christian burial, or interment, was required. Burial might have a plural aspect: in the catacombs, where *loculi,* or shelflike graves, were dug in the clay walls of subterranean tunnels, two or three corpses might lie side by side. Following funeral rites, the individual graves were covered with tablets of slate or other material on which might be inscribed the dead person's name, age, date of death, and sometimes a blessing. An image or representation of the deceased might be affixed to the tablet.

The same periods of history witnessed a curious efflorescence of cultural activity in the Byzantine Empire, with consequent effects on death rituals. The ritual lament, essentially pagan, survived in altered form as the Byzantine rulers pursued liberal policies that made the Empire heir to an impressive variety of influences. Among the latter were not only the pagan Greek but also those of numerous mystic cults from the Middle and Far East. Against this background, the Byzantine funeral developed a character of its own. The ritual actually began before death as the soul was launched into the death struggle (Alexiou, 1974, p. 25).

THE BELIEF IN IMMORTALITY

Human beings, it appears, have always stood in awe of their own soul, or mind-soul. Many ancient races believed the soul could never die; and many more "modern" peoples, such as those scattered throughout the Pacific areas, considered man's soul incapable of death. Such beliefs probably stemmed from very ancient times. The reason underlying the belief resides in the soul's incorporeality: what is immaterial cannot die, or cannot die immediately. "At all events, the Maoris undoubtedly believed that the souls of the departed survive the death of their bodies for a longer or shorter time, and in their disembodied state can influence the living for weal or woe" (Frazer, 1924, Vol. 2, p. 24).

Among the early Christians, belief in the immortality of the soul helped shape funeral customs directly. The Mass, the Celebration of the Passion, Death, and Resurrection of Christ, became an integral part of the final rites. The simplicity that marked the death rites was undoubtedly dictated in part by the need for secrecy. A drawing of an early Christian divine service (Davey, 1890, p. 19) shows the berobed faithful gathered in a roomy chamber that looks out upon a catacomb gallery. The priest, robed like the rest, stretches forth his hands in benediction from his superior vantage point on a shelf of rock. A crude box, apparently a casket, stands to one side. Children are shown in attendance with the adults. In the far background, six young people pray at an altar made by placing a large flat rock on two smaller slabs of stone.

One can imagine the cold, damp aura that must have pervaded this scene that dates to the middle of the first century of the Christian era. More difficult to sense is the dedicated group loyalty that bound the participants together in a tiny community of faith. The deceased, whose soul had entered the afterlife, could there intercede for them. Thus the dead person could be thrice beloved.

> Among the early Christians the sincerest respect for the memory of their dead was paid; for most of them, in the early centuries of the Church, were either martyrs or near connections of such as had suffered for the faith. The Catacombs are covered with inscriptions recording the deaths of martyrs; and many of these memorials are exceedingly pathetic, testifying to the fortitude with which the first Christians endured any manner of torture rather than deny the new faith which had been imparted to them by Divine revelation. The remains of the martyrs, however mangled they might be, were gathered together with the greatest reverence, and their blood placed in little phials of glass, which were considered relics of a most precious nature. (Davey, 1890, p. 18.)

As the church moved out of the catacombs, funeral customs that had the belief in immortality as a cardinal tenet became both more public and more elaborate. Resurrection of the body remained a principle theme. Funerals such as that accorded the Empress Theodolinda in A.D. 595 became almost legendary. Funerals took place in churches.

> The Cathedral of Monza, where she [Theodolinda] was buried, was hung with costly black stuff, and the body of the Empress was exhibited under a

magnificent catafalque, surrounded with lights, and was visited by pilgrims from all parts of Lombardy. Many hundreds of Masses were said for her in all the churches, and all day the great bells of the Cathedral and of the various monastic establishments tolled dolefully. At the end of the week the body of the illustrious Empress was placed in the vault under the high altar, where it remains to this day. (*Ibid.*, p. 21.)

By 752 St. Cuthbert had obtained permission from the Pope to have churchyards established as places "suitable for the burial of the dead" (Puckle, 1926, p. 140). Earlier, most funerals had led the mourners out of the cities and into the surrounding fields for interment; burial inside a city was prohibited.

The so-called Missal of Rathold of the tenth century prescribed the basic form of the Christian funeral service that, with some variations, still survives. The obsequies are generally seen as being divisible into three parts. "The corpse is met where it has been laid out (or often, in the vestibule of the church); the priest sprinkles it with holy water . . . , *De profundis* is sung. . . . The body is taken in procession to the church. . . ." (*New Catholic Encyclopedia*, 1967, Vol. 6, p. 226). In the two final phases of the funeral the Requiem Mass is sung and Matins and Lauds may be recited, with other prayers and chants, and the body is taken to the cemetery. Here, *In paradisum* and various psalms may be sung, and a final oration, or prayer, concludes the rites.

In Anglo-Saxon England, as elsewhere, these strictures underwent modifications. The Anglo-Saxon funeral called for placement of the body on the bier or in a hearse. A book of Gospels was laid on the corpse along with a cross, symbol of hope.

A pall of linen was thrown over it [the body] 'til it reached the place of interment. The friends were summoned, and strangers deemed it a duty to join the funeral procession. The clergy walked before or on each side, bearing lighted tapers in their hands, and chanting a portion of the Psalter. If it were in the evening, the night was passed in exercises of devotion. In the morning, Mass was sung and the body deposited with solemnity in the grave, the sawlshot paid, and a liberal donation distributed to the poor. (Davey, 1890, pp. 23–24.)

The funeral of the Tudor Henry VII, while not completely typical, gives an idea of the lengths to which a king's relatives and followers might go in bidding godspeed to the deceased. The ceremonies brought out the Lord Mayor of London. Representatives of the city's guilds of craftsmen were honored in formalities at Westminster and St. Paul's cathedrals.

> The body of the King was brought from Richmond and was met at St. George's Bar, Southwark, by the Mayor and Alderman, accompanied by a body of commoners on horseback, appropriately dressed in black. The streets were lined by members of the various "companies" carrying torches. . . . On the day following the shrouded but uncoffined body of the King was taken from St. Paul's to Westminster. . . . The Mayor and Alderman proceeded to Westminster by water to attend "Masse and offering." (Puckle, 1926, p. 195.)

The guilds affected somewhat less ornate ceremonies when burying their own dead. These funerals, however, rank as public affairs. The "company" to which the deceased belonged appeared in their livery; songs were sung over the grave; and black gowns were distributed to poor men and women—apparently so they could attend the obsequies. A leading citizen who was also a guild member might be accompanied to his grave by 100 mourners, by the choir of St. Paul's, and by many others. The reader of St. Paul's is known to have preached sermons on both days on which the body lay exposed.

Embalming practices, practiced by the Egyptians and other peoples (Figure 5.2), had apparently become a lost art in Europe by the start of the Christian era. Thus, because "embalming was crude" all through the Dark and Middle Ages, "burial was quick" even for kings (Giesey, 1960, p. 19). By the thirteenth century, however, the process of evisceration had come into some vogue as a means of prolonging funeral rites—or, more practically, of providing time for transport of a royal corpse from a distant place of death to the burial place.

Embalming techniques thus influenced the ritual forms. Precedent for the display of the kingly remains through the entire period of the wake and funeral had been set before evisceration came into use. "In 1189, when the Angevin ruler Henry II died at Chinon, his body had to be carried just ten miles to its burial place, the Abbey of Fontevrault," as Giesey (1960) noted: "during these two days [needed to accomplish the burial], the body was exposed for all to see, attired in regal apparel, bearing a crown on the head and holding a sword and sceptre in the hands" (p. 22). With the almost simultaneous development of more sophisticated methods of embalming, it became possible to display royal corpses customarily.

Embalming through evisceration eventually aroused papal opposition because it deviated from the Christian practice of inhuming bodies intact. Pope Boniface III prohibited evisceration in his bull *Detestande feritatis,* issued in 1299 (Giesey, 1960). But the ban became a dead letter after exceptions began to be made for members of French royal families.

Among the more macabre funerals recorded in Renaissance Europe was that accorded Inez de Castro of Portugal in the fourteenth century. Inez, consort of Pedro, the king's son, was murdered in her apartment and buried with appropriate pomp. But Pedro had not yet

Figure 5.2 The process of embalming. Friends of the deceased go to an embalmer and choose the style of mummy. Body is filled with spices and there were different price ranges for different mummies. (The Bettmann Archive)

ascended the throne. When he did, his father having died, Pedro had Inez's body exhumed. Then the dead beauty took part in a ceremony whose like history has perhaps never known again.

> The body of Inez was . . . placed on a magnificent throne, and crowned Queen of Portugal. The clergy, the nobility, and the people did homage to her corpse, and kissed the bones of her hands. There sat the dead Queen, with her yellow hair hanging like a veil around her ghastly form. One fleshless hand held the sceptre and the other, the orb of royalty. At night, after the coronation ceremony, a procession was formed of all the clergy and nobility, the religious orders and confraternities—which extended over many miles—each person holding a flaring torch in his hand, and thus walked from Coimbra to Alcobaca, escorting the crowned corpse to that royal Abbey for interment. The dead Queen lay in her rich robes upon a chariot drawn by black mules and lighted up by hundreds of lights. (Davey, 1890, p. 28.)

The wishes of the deceased might or might not determine whether a person of high office or great social estate were to be buried with very formal or less formal death rites. Mary, Queen of Scots, is said to have requested before death that she have a simple funeral, with no public display of any kind. Contrary to her desire, a state funeral was held, an indication that some of the more vulgar aspects of great funerals are designed more to swell the egos of the living than give homage to the dead. In Mary's case, the funeral costs totaled 50,000 pounds.

Military funerals have long been known for their elaborate protocols. Symbolic usages in such military obsequies may be numerous. One recalls, for example, the riderless horse, ancient symbol of a fallen leader. The custom of including such a horse, usually with the boots of the deceased placed in the stirrups in reverse position, is believed to stem from the primitive time when a chieftain was buried with his horses (Puckle, 1926). Other symbols common to the funerals of military leaders include the use of a gun-carriage as a hearse; troops marching with reversed arms; the final bugle call—"The Last Post" in British lore, "Taps" in the United States; the use of the flag as a pall; and the practice of hoisting the national flag to half-mast.

Some of these ceremonies marked the otherwise simple funeral of Napoleon I, who died in exile on the island of St. Helena on May 5, 1821. The fallen emperor had chosen a scenic place for location of his grave in the event his body could not be returned to France. British authorities refused such permission. But burial with military honors was nonetheless permitted.

The funeral took place in the presence of a few of Napoleon's friends. British grenadiers detailed for the purpose carried Napoleon to his grave. The onetime conqueror of Europe was dressed "in the dress he had worn during his many campaigns" across the Continent—"his head covered by his historical three-cornered hat—volleys were fired over his grave, and a huge stone was afterwards placed to mark the deserted spot where the remains of the great soldier lay" (Puckle, 1926, pp. 201–202). *Sic transit gloria.* But that did not bring to an end the Napoleonic story. In 1840, the British released Napoleon's body to France. It was returned to Paris, scene of so many of the conqueror's greatest days, and buried again with a degree of pomp adequate to redress the lack of ceremony of the 1821 rites.

On a bitterly cold day—December 15, 1840—an estimated 600,000 persons gathered in the streets of Paris to pay their final respects to Napoleon. He was finally laid to rest in the Church of the Invalides, companion at last to other famous warriors.

State funerals had become huge spectacles. In Victorian times the trend increased. Wellington, conqueror of Napoleon at Waterloo, was buried in 1852 in ceremonies hardly less elaborate than those held for Napoleon. Wellington's body was trundled in a great funeral car through enormous crowds that had waited for hours for a view of the cortege. The car itself appears to have been a forerunner of the later hearse. It boasted a great superstructure on a strong wagon serving as an undercarriage and was decorated with banners and weapons. A canopy hung over the heavy car, which was pulled by a "large team of horses" (Puckle, 1926, p. 203).

In the United States, not many years later, Abraham Lincoln's funeral marked the cataclysmic high point of an outpouring of national grief seldom recorded in history. Lincoln's body lay in state in the Capitol in Washington to launch the final rites, then was transported by rail car to Springfield, Illinois, where the dead President was buried in memorable services in Oak Ridge Cemetery. Enroute to Springfield, crowds gathered at railway stations to honor the man whose tenacious leadership had saved the Union.

Such funerals partook of both civil and military protocol. No expense was spared to stage a fitting farewell for the deceased leader. But state and public funerals slowly influenced the obsequies held for the less famous and the unknown. Customs such as the display of ostrich feathers at Victorian funerals became common; that particular usage is thought to have entered England from France after the Restoration of 1660 (Morley, 1971). Funeral customs also succumbed to the economic facts of life. A list of the various "classes of funerals" was published in England in 1870. It detailed possible combinations of ceremonies that were graded by cost, with total expense charges ranging from three pounds five shillings to fifty-three pounds. Some of the elements that could be provided for: hearses, velvets (for covering carriages and horses), pairs of horses, mutes (as mourners), feathers, lead coffins, and so on, almost without end.

FUNERAL ORATIONS AND FUNERAL DRESS

From relatively dim beginnings, and perhaps as an outgrowth of the chants and special death rites prescribed for ancient Egyptian funerals, the sermon or oration evolved over the centuries to become an integral part of modern obsequies. In Europe particularly, the practice of having orations delivered—and, often, printed later—became relatively common. Many of these discourses have been lost. Originally printed in limited editions as keepsakes for the friends and relatives of the deceased, they have simply disappeared.

Hundreds of others have survived. Some, by today's more pragmatic standards, seem quaint even as regards their titles:

> A funeral oration, delivered before the City Government and citizens of Roxbury, on the occasion of paying funeral honors to Zachary Taylor, late president of the United States; July 31, 1850. . . . Together with the other services. Printed by order of the City Council. (Anderson, 1850, flyleaf.)

Or:

> Living loves betwixt Christ and dying Christians. A sermon preached at M. Magdalene Bermondsey in Southwark, near London, June 6, 1654. At the funeral of that faithful servant of Christ Mr. Jeremiah Whitaker, minister of the Gospel, and pastor of the Church there. With a narrative of his exemplary holy life and death, by divers ministers in the city of London. (Ashe, 1654, flyleaf.)

Whatever the modern ring of such tributes, they must be understood for what they were: eminently sincere and well-meant paeans of praise to men and women whose lives had special meaning for their contemporaries. Usually, that meaning was inspirational in tone. The themes chosen for elaboration in such sermons and orations may be less important than the fact that they ranked, and still to some extent rank, as funeral highlights. Today, as in older times, the words are usually spoken during church services. But wherever the sermon or oration is delivered, it serves as a means of drawing attention to eternal, and appropriate, verities.

Lincoln's funeral has been mentioned. Those ceremonies, however, are not as well known or remembered as the Gettysburg Address, an oration delivered during ceremonies held well after the battle to dedicate part of the Gettysburg battlefield. A sort of funeral oration, the Address has ever since served as a model of finely chiseled prose. It thus represents, in its own way, man's struggle to find solace, inspiration, and deeper meaning in death.

Unique in its genre because of its classic simplicity, the Address bespeaks a nation's grief at its losses in internecine conflict. It served, with words, to acclimatize the survivors to the challenges that lay ahead. Where a basic purpose of funerals, down through history and continuing into Christian times, has been to accustom people to the fact of death, Lincoln wanted not only to honor the noble dead but to inspire the survivors: "That these dead shall not have died in vain—that this nation, under God, shall have a new birth of freedom—and that government of the people, by the people, and for the people, shall not perish from the earth."

By Lincoln's time the prescribed mode of dress for funerals and the postfuneral period had passed the bounds of reason. The Empress Frederick of Germany, daughter of Queen Victoria, immediately on being widowed donned a black dress trimmed in white and a long black veil with a "widow's peak." The dress had deep "weeper cuffs" (Cunnington & Lucas, 1972, p. 267). According to other customs, the widow could show no hair at the funeral; her face might, during the ceremonies be shrouded by a heavy veil; for over two years after the death and burial the widow customarily dressed in black when appearing in public.

> The rules dictating the period during which a widow had to remain in mourning were strict and complex. Deep mourning was required for a year and a day, after which the widow "slighted her mourning"; for the next six months she might change parmatta for black silk, still trimmed with crape. After 18 months crape was omitted and after two years half mourning began, which was usually black and white. (*Ibid.*, p. 268.)

Counterinfluences were at work, however. They led finally to nearly complete abrogation of such rules. Arbiters of social mores might caution that the process of discarding mourning should be a gradual one so that the discerning observer would not be shocked; the widow was not to adopt colorful dress all at once or it might appear that she had been counting the hours to liberation from black. In strong contrast, a lady's maid in a novel of the 1870s defies any possible future husband to marry her, then to expect her—in case of his death—to wear *hideous* widow's weepers for two years.

Some relaxation of rules was clearly taking place. But the dictates governing mourning dress remained definite and largely unbreachable through the nineteenth century. Those rules specified dark suits and top hats for men even when a poor man was being interred. Needless to say, there were many exceptions, and such ceremonies were usually brief. For the funerals of the more affluent Englishmen of the nineteenth century, men might wear white crepe over the crowns of the top hats and a white drapery over the right shoulder. But the long trains and black mantles common to Elizabethan state funerals had disappeared.

World War I seems to have administered the final blow to some older rituals of dress, mourning, and burial that had developed over centuries.

> The depreciation and eventual disappearance of mourning reflected the disappearance of the values and life that we call "Victorian." The process was not sealed until the coming of the Great War. Then, mourning succumbed before the vast numbers of dead; faced with this, family mourning and its conventions were an insufficient comment. The stage had become too wide for propriety. (Morley, 1971, p. 79.)

Coincidentally, people were moving in greater numbers into cities where life became more compartmentalized and less community-oriented. Industry was spreading with a rapidity that would have astounded even the great business barons of the 1800s.

Today the choice of clothing is left largely to the discretion of the individual mourner. Final selection depends on the person's relationship to the deceased, on family and ethnic traditions, on the socioeconomic status of the dead person, and on other factors. Widows have not discarded totally the practice of wearing veils at the final rites, but such is not required by virtually universal social rubric. The dictates of common sense, "taste," and tradition have become far more authoritative as guides to appropriate mourning dress, as they are to so many other death rites and customs.

Modern Practices and the Funeral Industry

> *. . . Ye undertakers! tell us,*
> *Midst all the gorgeous figures you exhibit,*
> *Why is the principal conceal'd, for which*
> *You make this mighty stir? 'Tis wisely done;*
> *What would offend the eye in a good picture,*
> *The painter casts discreetly into shades.*
>
> *From "The Grave," by Robert Blair*

More and more in modern times death has come to be regarded in a new light. From superstitious awe before the fact of their own mortality to religious belief in death as a stage to a higher plane of life, men and women have learned to see positive and negative aspects to death: "Negative because it is the end of physical life; positive because of its great potential for the maturing and deepening of the lives of the survivors" (Morgan, 1968, p. 3).

The ancient religions have not materially altered their basic beliefs in an afterlife; nor have all the superstitions surrounding death and the disposition of the remains been shattered by the power of cold reason. Rather, modern man appears to have outgrown many of the more unreasonable attitudes that have shaped funeral customs and death rituals over the centuries. While today's practices are cast in the image of older ceremonies, and retain their symbolic significance, a trend toward simplicity—or simplification—has become evident. Contributing to the trend are many factors, some of them already indicated: the acceptance on a wider scale of the practice of cremation, one of the simpler methods of returning human remains to the elements; growing recognition that cost and the drive for ostentation can influence too heavily the form of a funeral; and, in very recent years, the publication of books critical of "the American way of death," or the British, or that of various other nations, or of specific aspects of modern-day funerals. Such criticisms focus often on the expense involved in funerals: "After buying a house and a car, the most expensive purchase a man makes in his life is, surprisingly, his funeral" ("The Consumer Newsletter," *Moneysworth,* July 12, 1971, p. 1).

As cryomedicine has evolved, and as the number of cryonics, or frozen ones, has increased slowly, other trends have appeared. Awed by the feats of modern science, a few believers have turned their eyes to a future in which people will be recalled from a kind of frozen sleep to a life of eternal good health and youth. New medical techniques combined with freezing or near-freezing temperatures have produced the cures that have spawned such beliefs (Barry, 1972). In a more general way, the tendency to "cosmeticize" the fact of death has waned. Some publicized funerals, such as that of General Charles de Gaulle, which involved the use of a casket reportedly costing $63.00, have spurred the trend.

Some cults and religions of relatively recent origin have gone so far as to deny the fact of death. "The modern sects of Spiritualism and Christian Science dogmatically deny the existence of death; and consequently convinced adherents of these sects they would be going against their tenets if they admitted mourning for those who have 'passed on' " (Gorer, 1965, p. 65). Despite such influences, a pattern of modern funeral practices and death rituals persists and can be described in brief.

MODERN PRACTICES

The form of the modern funeral hinges more than ever on whether the method of disposition is cremation or inhumation. Again, economics may influence the choice today as in recent decades and centuries. "A widow in Scotland . . . whose husband had died of a heart attack in the South of England explained that she had chosen cremation 'on account of you see his family wanted him brought back here; I thought I would keep the expense down, doing that' " (ibid., p.39). But whether cremation is actually less expensive may be open to question. "Others choose this method of disposal because they believe it will be less expensive; actually the cost of cremation is little less, because a casket is required, plus transportation to a crematory" (Christensen, 1967, p. 25).

More directly, the method of disposition is determined by the feelings and religious conviction of the survivors. Roman Catholics and members of the Jewish faith still, for the most part, believe the body should be buried, not burned. Those who disagree may see cremation as the ideal method of disposing of the remains because it appears to be quick, clean, and practical. But each person's inner sense of the proprieties, and of himself or herself, bears on the question as well; in families, such an inner sense often links brothers and sisters, parents and grandparents, and even near and distant blood relatives in a community of belief about death and the "correct" ways of taking leave of the deceased. Some, sharing such attitudes, may be "horrified at the rapid destruction of the physical remains; they consider it an interference with natural processes" (Gorer, 1965, p. 26).

> All of us have "body consciousness," or a "body image." We have many feelings about our own bodies. When we think about the death of someone dear to us, the "body image" is involved—we identify emotionally. We tend to feel sensations that the deceased is now incapable of feeling. For example, we tend to cringe a bit at the thought of a corpse being dissected, or of burning, or of intolerable injury. This is the reason why many choose the casket and vault. (Christensen, 1967, p. 26.)

The increasing use of cremation suggests that such feelings have become rarer, perhaps because the family itself has dwindled in importance as a social unit as modern, alienated man has grown more urbanized. In any case, a funeral leading to cremation has developed a form of its own. "Cremation usually takes place after the public funeral service" (Christensen, 1967, p. 26) but may precede the services. A memorial reading is held, followed by interment of the ashes. Interment in this case does not involve a journey to a cemetery, but takes place, more likely, in a columbarium—a structure providing vaults or pigeonholes—that may be provided by the municipality or a cemetery company.

As with funerals involving inhumation, committal of the deceased's ashes in a mausoleum or columbarium is carried through while a minister reads special literature. If the ashes are to be scattered at a location prescribed by the deceased, meditations may be recited.

The final ceremonies generally adhere to a particular form. The minister leads the procession of friends and relatives to the place of interment, pausing at the head of the casket. A service consisting of a few words of committal, a pastoral prayer, possibly the Lord's Prayer, and a benediction may also include a reading of other literature meaningful to the deceased. Most such ceremonies today exclude the practice of strewing the casket with flowers or dust, "and ministers are eliminating the sentence, 'Earth to earth, ashes to ashes, dust to dust' " (Christensen, 1967, p. 137). But scriptural material may commonly be intoned:

> What is sown is perishable, what is raised is imperishable. It is sown in weakness, it is raised in power. It is sown a physical body, it is raised a spiritual body. If there is a physical body, there is also a spiritual body. (I Corinthians 15:42– 44.)

The funeral leading to inhumation will originate typically in the funeral home. The funeral normally ends on the third day after death. The inhumation ceremonies are held at the graveside or in chapels provided at the cemetery for that purpose. An exception to the three-day span is provided by Orthodox Jews who believe inhumation should take place within twenty-four hours after death. Among members of the Jewish faith, however, no funerals are allowed on the Sabbath.

In the three-day period allowed for Christian funerals, much takes place. The body has, in the normal case, been prepared for viewing by a licensed embalmer. The process of restoration, requiring skills similar to "those of sculptor, artist, and plastic surgeon" (Habenstein & Lamers, 1963, p. 570), has been employed to give the deceased an appearance similar to that enjoyed in healthful life. The remains have been placed on view in the funeral home so that friends and relatives can join in the waking, or vigil, during hours or at times of day that are set aside by the funeral home for that purpose. Finally, a ceremony initiating the journey to the church and the cemetery is held at the funeral parlor, usually in the morning and with the immediate family and relatives and friends present.

Nine centuries have changed only slightly the next stage of the burial ceremony in the Catholic church ritual. The three-part, formal ceremonial prescribed by the Missal of Rathold still obtains. The corpse is greeted at the entrance of the church by the priest, who says to the mourners, "The grace and peace of God our Father and of the Lord Jesus Christ be with you"—to which comes the answer, "And also with you" (*The Catholic Burial Rite*, 1971, p. 3). The Requiem Mass is celebrated, then the body is taken to the cemetery. The funeral cortege, formed of vehicles driven by the mourners, proceeds to the cemetery in file, following the hearse and, often, a special car for members of the immediate family. A "flower car" may also be part of the cortege.

In recent years it has become common in the United States to hold the cemetery rites, not at graveside but in closed chapels on the cemetery grounds. Moving such ceremonies indoors obviates the need to expose mourners—many of whom may be elderly—to possible extremes of weather.

The modern trend toward simplicity and even informality in funeral forms and customs may be noted particularly in the funeral home. The type of casket chosen may vary considerably; a wooden box may be used in rare cases. More commonly, the half-couch style of casket, of mahogany, copper, or some other material, is used. A certain reserve may govern the funeral parlor arrangements: "An uninhibited giving way to grief, great floral display, and open mourning are frowned upon in the middle and upper socioeconomic classes" (Habenstein & Lamers, 1963, p. 567). Among lower socioeconomic groups the situation, curiously, may be reversed: "There is a feeling that a direct connection will be drawn between the money spent on the funeral and the respect judged to have been shown for the deceased" (*ibid.*).

Funeral rituals and services today may vary according to the geographic location in which a death takes place. "In villages, small towns and open country, death and burial are still events which touch many, if not most, inhabitants of the community" (*ibid.*, p. 569). Neighbors and friends may, in consequence, participate directly in the obsequies or in peripheral customs or rituals. Services may be held in a private home. Even where they are not, neighbors may assist with some of the details of the leave-taking, preparing food, taking care of children, or performing other small services designed to relieve the deceased's family of minor responsibilities. Many such contributions may be offered and accepted symbolically, in perpetuation of local tradition. They may thus have the force and meaning of more pertinent rituals and observances.

The spirit of close community that can result from such participation is generally lacking in urban funerals. "In urban America today a death touches a limited number of persons, and except for cases involving community or other leaders or, unfortunately sometimes, those who are notorious—its occurrence is made public only through the obituary columns of the daily newspapers" (*ibid.*). Where death in a small town may have personal meaning for every resident, death in the city may, thus, be far more impersonal. "With the gradual dissolution of racial and ethnic groupings in the cities, those living in fairly close proximity to the deceased may not be affected by a death since they may not share the same customs, traditions, or other personal or social relations" (*ibid.*).

Factors that militate against home funerals—once a common practice, and still, as recently as the 1940s and 1950s, a tradition in many family groups—include the architectural design and structural characteristics of residential buildings. Apartment residences, because of their narrow halls and doorways, and the inconvenience of their common lobbies and stairways, virtually rule out such funerals.

Enter the funeral director, or undertaker, who can aid the bereaved family with nearly all necessary arrangements—and with many services that lighten the burden of grief and ease the transition to life without a loved one.

THE FUNERAL INDUSTRY

As the integrating element in modern funeral practices and rituals, and as provider of professional help throughout the period of postmortem preparation of the body, mourning, and final disposal, is the funeral director or undertaker. He or she stands, too, at the focal point of an industry that has, at various stages of history, been alternately covered with contumely, ignored, and praised for its efforts to maintain the highest standards of professionalism.

The history of the funeral industry may be summarized briefly. Essentially, it should be remembered that the industry in its modern form centers on the undertaker, who emerged as a specialist in his own right—one serving a basic social function—as funerals became more complex. Such growth in complexity followed naturally as the early Christian funeral, a simple ceremony, became public; as the early Christian church came out of the catacombs. Medieval and Renaissance Europe saw extension and elaboration of early practices, virtually all of them based in Judeo-Christian concepts and customs.

By the seventeenth and eighteenth centuries the English undertaker had appeared. This forerunner of the undertaker of today had a special occupational status, although not to be ranked with the modern professional. The undertaker might have been first and foremost a cabinetmaker, a sexton, a minister, or a nurse. All such persons, it appears, had basic occupational qualifications for advertising themselves as undertakers. And advertise they did, according to Habenstein and Lamers (1963):

> For the good of the Publick, I Edward Evans, at the Four Coffins in the Strand, over against Somerset House; furnish all Necessaries for all funerals both great and small. And all sorts of set Mourning both Black and Grey and all other furniture suitable to it, fit for a person of Quality. Which I promise to perform 2s in the Pound cheaper than any other of the Undertakers in town or elsewhere. (Habenstein & Lamers, 1963, p. 170.)

The nineteenth century brought furthur rapid evolution. By the 1850s, those who offered their services as undertakers could provide for "laying out," coffining, funeral direction, and transportation. During the Civil War, embalming came into prominence as a method of preserving the remains through the use of preservative chemicals. But such embalming, an accepted practice today, was not widely used until after the turn of the century.

Development of a true funeral industry focusing on the undertaker proceeded rapidly. As sanitation became a major concern, especially in urban areas, the needs both to preserve the dead for a period of time and to protect the living assumed major import.

> With the defining of the occupation group two natural impulses developed. The first was closely associated with the sanitation movement and involved licensure to practice embalming. . . . The second such impulse, that of the associational movement, was formalized in 1882 at the first convention of the National Funeral Directors Association as a creation and federation of state associations. (Slater, 1964, p. 3.)

Undertaking had thus emerged as a true and distinct vocation by 1900. The term "undertaker" was replaced by "funeral director" as the latter was thought to be more dignified. Professionalization became assured as training and specialized education emerged as prerequisites to the successful accomplishment of tasks assigned to undertakers by law and custom. Funeral details and arrangements, and personal contact with the survivors, came within the purview of the undertaker to an increasing degree; no longer was the undertaker charged exclusively with taking care of the dead. By the 1950s and 1960s, "an emerging professional consciousness continued to take funeral operations out of the category of trade and business and into the category of professional service to people" (Slater, 1964, p. 3).

Funeral service as a career within a viable, socially significant industry had begun to draw tens of thousands of young people by the second half of the twentieth century. In the 1960s, some 65,000 men and women were engaged in serving the public in approximately 24,000 funeral homes in the United States (Slater, 1964). The typical practitioner ranked as a community conscious, home-oriented citizen with better-than-average education and cultural and other interests that set him or her apart from the average.

Figures on the industry illustrate its growth and provide an index to the degree in which people came to accept and depend on the funeral director. In 1940, according to one writer, "with a population of 131,000,000 [the United States had] 1,417,000 deaths; in 1960, with a population of almost 178,500,000, there were only 1,702,000 deaths" (Harmer, 1963, p. 163). Some $2 billion were being spent on funerals in the latter year—in contrast with about half a million dollars in 1935 (Harmer, 1963).

The figures have mounted with other costs in more recent years.

Inflation has inevitably provided the spur. Yet the cost of the average funeral has not risen proportionately. A survey taken by the National Foundation of Funeral Service in 1975 showed that the average funeral cost $1,152 while the median overall "sale" was $1,119 (see Table 5.1 at the end of this chapter). By way of confirmation of such figures, *A Statistical Abstract of Funeral Service Facts and Figures* (Pine, 1974) showed median funeral costs ranging from $920 in the Pacific Coast area to $1,184 in the East North Central region of the United States.

How does the funeral director of today work? Significantly, some of his or her services are optional.

> For instance, you might not need the limousine or the flower car. If not, ask the funeral director to eliminate them and their charge. . . . Another optional element is embalming, because it is not required by law in any state except under certain conditions (for example, if the body is kept unburied for longer than a specified period or if it has to be transported by common carrier). (*Good Housekeeping,* 1972, p. 180; Winter, 1975.)

Even more to the point of funeral directors' *modus operandi* is their approach to their calling. Generally, two schools of thought have been identified. The whole-man/total-funeral concept calls for complete person-to-person professional service to the family of the deceased, with continuous consultation provided by a single representative of the funeral home and with advice tendered on a wide range of personal problems and questions. "The whole-man/total-funeral concept makes one person licensed to practice funeral service responsible to a family to try to meet all their needs in relation to the total funeral" (Raether, 1971, p. 20). Delegation of some duties is not ruled out; but to the greatest extent possible the individual assigned to a family will be responsible for all arrangements.

The owner-manager-technician concept provides for broader distribution of duties and functions within the funeral home staff. "Unlike the previously described concept, the same licensee will not be involved in all facets of the funeral" (*ibid.*). "Rather there will be one or more persons with specialized knowledge or skills who will perform their tasks and having done so their responsibility for that 'service' ends" (*ibid.*, p. 21).

Whichever concept animates and guides any given individual in the funeral industry, that individual is faced with a code of ethics, of a formal nature, that provides the guideposts to professional practice. "It would be difficult to estimate the extent to which the present code has become an 'inner control' over the behavior of some 50,000 to 55,000 practitioners of funeral directing and embalming because a minority of indeterminate size has rejected the concept of professional morality. Yet the code, even while it may be less effective than those [guideposts] of older and more firmly established professions, [is] definitely more than a . . . set of statements of honorable intentions made for public consumption" (Habenstein & Lamers, 1963, p. 395). The code represents a step toward professionalization that the industry has sought for many years.

TABLE 5.1   The 1974 Funeral Dollar[a]

Funeral Cost	Where It Came From	Where It Went	
		Percentage	Expense
$ 200-Under	.6%	36.5%	Salaries
201-300	1.6		
301-400	2.5	18.9	Caskets
401-500	2.2		
501-600	2.9	15.9	Miscellaneous
601-700	4.0		
701-800	6.3	11.0	Building
801-900	8.1		
901-1,000	10.2	5.5	Autos
1,001-1,100	10.3		
1,101-1,200	9.5	4.9	Profit
1,201-1,300	9.4		(before taxes)
1,301-1,400	8.6		
1,401-1,500	6.7	4.5	Advertising and
1,501-1,600	5.3		promotion
1,601-1,700	3.5		
1,701-1,800	2.5	2.8	Supplies
1,801-1,900	1.6		
1,901-2,000	1.2		
2,001-Over	3.0		
	100.0%	100.0%	

Notes. Sample: 70,578 funerals; average sale: $1,152; median sale: $1,119.
[a]Adapted from table prepared by National Foundation of Funeral Service; based on National Selected Morticians Merchandising Service—Average Retail Sale.

SUMMARY

Elaborate death rituals in the form of funerals are unique to humans. History demonstrates that there are many similarities as well as differences among funeralry practices.

The ceremony that accompanies disposal of remains has apparently existed since recorded history. Comparisons have led to classification of funeral practices that seem to concern man's fears, hopes, and attitudes toward the dead. Eight principal ideas have been enumerated which are present in ancient funeral rites.

As one progresses toward modern day funeral practices, other themes may be observed such as orientation, mourning, death laments and orations, corteges, wakes, disposal and affixing remains, funeral art, sepulchers, and plaques. These physical demonstrations reflect belief systems concerning immortality, status, power, and moral values.

While some segments of ancient customs are notably present in modern funeral observances, a definite trend can be noted which attempts to preserve symbolic significance while doing away with superficial pomp. Technological advances have also contributed to this more rational approach. Increased psychological freedom to question heretofore taboo topics is a definite indication of practical changes.

The modern approach to funeralry became prominent after the 1850s. Sanitation at that time became a major concern. Embalming and a trend toward professional affiliation brought about professional status for the industry. Today funeral directors attempt to meet all family needs in relation to a total funeral. The funeral industry is not, however, without critics, and memorial societies have endeavored to offer an alternative.

REFERENCES

Alexiou, M. *The Ritual Lament in Greek Tradition*. New York: Cambridge University Press, 1974.

Anderson, T. D. *A Funeral Oration Delivered Before the City Government and Citizens of Roxbury*. Norfolk: Norfolk County Journal Press, 1850.

Ashe, S. *Living Loves Betwixt Christ and Dying Christians*. London: T. M. Smith, 1654.

Attfield, W. "Funeral and Sepulchral Honours," in *Oxford Prize Essays*. Oxford: D. A. Talboys, 1830.

Barry, B. "Immortality on the Rocks?" *Chicago Sun-Times,* Midwest Magazine, February 6, 1972, p. 8.

Bendann, E. *Death Customs: An Analytical Study of Burial Rites.* New York: Alfred A. Knopf, 1930.

Boase, T. S. R. *Death in the Middle Ages.* New York: McGraw-Hill Book Co., 1972.

Budge, E. A. W. *The Book of Opening of the Mouth.* 2 vols. London: Kegan Paul, Trench, Truebner & Co., Ltd., 1909.

Burton, A. *The True Sources of Comfort, to the Children of God.* Windsor, England: Alden Spooner, 1793.

The Catholic Burial Rite. Collegeville, Minn.: The Liturgical Press, 1971.

Christensen, J. L. *The Complete Funeral Manual.* Old Tappan, N.J.: Fleming H. Revell Co., 1967.

"The Consumer Newsletter." *Moneysworth,* July 12, 1971.

Cunnington, P., and Lucas, C. *Costume for Births, Marriages and Deaths.* New York: Barnes & Noble, 1972.

Davey, R. *A History of Mourning.* London: Jay's, Regent St., 1890.

Douglass, W. A. *Death in Murelaga.* Seattle: University of Washington Press, 1969.

Encyclopaedia Britannica, 11th ed., 1911, s. v. "Funeral Rites and Customs."

Frazer, J. G. *The Belief in Immortality and the Worship of the Dead.* 3 vols. London: Macmillan Co., 1924.

Genêt, J. *Funeral Rites.* New York: Grove Press, 1969.

Giesey, R. E. *The Royal Funeral Ceremony in Renaissance France.* Geneva: Librairie E. Droz, 1960.

Gorer, G. *Death, Grief, and Mourning.* Garden City, N.Y.: Doubleday & Co., 1965.

Graham, R. *Remembered with Love.* New York: The American Press, 1961.

Habenstein, R. W., and Lamers, W. M. *Funeral Customs the World Over.* Milwaukee: Buffin Printers, Inc., 1960.

————. *The History of American Funeral Directing.* Milwaukee: Buffin Printers, Inc., 1963.

Harmer, R. M. *The High Cost of Dying.* Garden City, N.Y.: Doubleday & Co., 1963.

Hartland, E. S. *The Legend of Perseus.* 3 vols. London: D. Nutt, 1894–1896.

Henschen, F. *The Human Skull: A Cultural History*. New York: Frederick A. Praeger, 1966.

Hertz, R. *Death and the Right Hand*. Glencoe, Ill.: The Free Press, 1960.

Krieger, W. M. *Successful Funeral Service Management*. Englewood Cliffs, N.J.: Prentice-Hall, 1951.

Kurtz, D. C., and Boardman, J. *Greek Burial Customs*. Ithaca, N.Y.: Cornell University Press, 1971.

Madden, R. R. *Shrines and Sepulchres of the Old and New World*. 2 vols. London: I. C. Newby, 1851.

Mitford, J. *The American Way of Death*. New York: Simon & Schuster, 1963.

Morgan, E. *A Manual of Simple Burial*. Burnsville, N.C.: The Celo Press, 1968.

Morley, J. *Death, Heaven and the Victorians*. Pittsburgh: University of Pittsburgh Press, 1971.

Muret, P. *Rites of Funeral, Ancient and Modern*. (A. Lorraine, trans.) London: Printed for R. Royston, 1682.

New Catholic Encyclopedia, 1967 ed., s.v. "Funeral Rites and Customs."

Pine, V. R. *A Statistical Abstract of Funeral Service Facts and Figures*. Milwaukee: National Funeral Service Directors of the United States, 1974.

Puckle, B. *Funeral Customs: Their Origin and Development*. London: T. Werner Laurie, 1926.

Raether, H. *Successful Funeral Service Practice*. Englewood Cliffs, N.J.: Prentice-Hall, 1971.

Slater, R. C., ed. *Funeral Service*. Milwaukee: National Funeral Directors Association of the United States, 1964.

Toynbee, J. M. C. *Death and Burial in the Roman World*. Ithaca, N.Y.: Cornell University Press, 1971.

"What you should know about funeral and burial costs." *Good Housekeeping*, February 1972, p. 180.

Winters, A. Director Commonwealth School of Sciences, Houston, Texas. Personal communication.

World Book Encyclopedia, 1963 ed., s.v. "Funeral Customs."

———, s.v. "Gettysburg Address."

6

Nursing Intervention for the Dying and Bereaved

With considerable regularity, persons in the health care fields are in contact with patients who are terminal and with surviving families. The health care field is principally concerned with living, and dying is an important aspect of life. Treatment protocol in virtually every other area of health care is vastly more organized. Consequently, health care staff often enter patient-contact areas with little or no preparation. This frequently results in awkward and inadequate patient/family care and staff guilt and lingering survivor resentment. This chapter will discuss some of the more common psychological facets encountered with children, family, adults, and staff. The practical level of this chapter allows the reader to gain perspective of commonalities that exist in patient as well as staff reactions. These commonalities provide a basis for developing a unified and emotionally sound approach to care for the dying, survivors, and fellow staff.

PRACTICAL APPROACHES TO TRAUMATIC SITUATIONS

The patterns of death and dying in the United States have been changing noticeably in the last seventy-five to one hundred years. These changes have not only affected the one who dies, but also those who care for him or her emotionally and physically. Persons who die today most often die in a hospital or nursing facility or on the way to one or the other. This is a relatively recent phenomenon and one which has been fostered by the attitude that advanced technology can, more frequently than not, forestall death—and forestalling death is the ultimate goal of modern medical practice.

Although the importance of forestalling death seems to be self-evident, it has not always been unequivocally the aim of Western societies. There are, even today, exceptions: the exhausted and distraught family of a comatose patient may decide that the "plugs"

185

should be pulled; a person may decide his or her time has come and go to bed to die; a grandfather may starve himself to death (Jury, 1975, p. 18).

Ironically, one of the most common fears people express is a fear of dying alone (Grollman, 1974). Unfortunately, the administration of care and the adherence to aseptic procedures necessary in a hospital sometimes intimidate patients and families and contribute to feelings of aloneness either real or imagined. These feelings may be exacerbated by the patient's and family's emotional fluctuations as they work through the various stages of coping. Patients and hospital staff alike are especially vulnerable during stages of anger and depression when expectations and blame placing may become exaggerated. At these times it may be difficult for a tired staff member to restrain from retort when an upset patient is being particularly demanding.

In earlier times, it was not uncommon for children to be present at deathbed scenes (Aries, 1974, p. 12). Most modern hospitals forbid children under fourteen to be present on the care floors. Even so it is likely that many families would not allow children to visit a relative during the terminal period—especially if the dying patient is experiencing pain and discomfort. Thus, the family may try to avoid instilling a fear of dying in the child or performing any ill-conceived act which might have a deleterious and everlasting effect on the child. Although children often perceive death and dying differently from adults, the temperament of the child should definitely be taken into account before any effort to "educate" in matters of death is undertaken.

My observation has been that many children focus on life or death and not on dying, except in fantasy play. This, of course, may not be a general phenomenon but may reflect cultural influences already present. A well-meant attempt to dispel death fears through heightened exposure might not have the desired results. Occasionally, the adult seeks to nullify fears of the child which are also, in fact, unresolved fears of his or her own. The outcome in such instances are quite often mutually disturbing for adult and child, increasing tension, mutual distrust, and disappointment. On the other hand, it is clear through various studies (Nagy, 1948; Schilder & Weschsler, 1935) that children do contemplate death and formulate ways of coping with the concept. Thus, the responsible adult may feel caught "betwixt and between." How does an adult help children without inadvertently traumatizing them? Actually, this conflict is partly fostered by our adult tendency to avoid listening to the emotional content of what children say to us with their incessant questions and stubborn affirmation of views we know to be erroneous. Adults often feel helpless when they

have no "right" answer. They may react by minimizing the significance of the question or ignoring it, admonishing the child for
demanding so much time and attention, postponing an answer or
elaborating a religious doctrine—"God loves little children and every
body and takes them into His house in heaven when they die"—which
sometimes allays fear and sometimes provokes more difficult questions—"Why does He kill us to do that?"

Rochlin (1967, p. 62) has stated that children tend to regard death
as a result of strife, as defiance of authority and retaliation, as the satisfaction of destructive, aggressive, and sexual impulses and hostility.
His thesis is that the child perceives death as an outcome of certain
relations between people and not so much as a result of natural causes.
These findings may be valid but tend to amplify parental and nursing
anxieties rather than provide basis for supportive intervention
strategies.

Kavanaugh (1974, p. 136) has suggested a way out of this conflict
by emphasizing the importance of openness and directness. He has
suggested that it is healthy for parents and adults to ventilate their
own death-related feelings and allow the child to know that sometimes
we cannot find a good or comforting answer. In other words, a "good"
answer does not mean that emotional hurt and grief must be avoided,
evaded, or minimized. The implicit teaching of the terror and agony of
emotional loss and hurt tends to suggest to the child that these conditions are devastating. Instead, allowing the child to grasp that emotional hurting is also a part of a healthy life, is intermittent, enhances
resiliency and reduces the child's likelihood of developing self-defeat-
ing attitudes when traumatic life pressures are present. It is more important that adults be aware of their own death-fears rather than try to
guide a child's concept development. Instead of evading questions, it
may be more productive if the adult attempts an answer and even tells
the child that he or she does not know the answer, further reassuring
the child that it's all right not to know answers to some questions.
Actually, sometimes the child does not even want an answer—that is,
a verbal reply. The child may want to know that he or she has the
adult's attention and affection. If the adult listens in a relaxed,
comforting, receptive fashion the child will perceive this tranquility. If
the adult is internally anxious, this will also be perceived by the child
and foster apprehension. Sometimes the child is best comforted by a
touch, or simple nearness of the adult. It takes much more than words
to communicate.

In the United States crying can invoke a multitude of feelings in
the observer. The mother who is anticipating the death of her child is

often beset with the uncontrollable urge to cry and may find herself spending hours in the bathroom, closet, or other secluded nook crying—out of view of the child. The child who is exposed to incessant parental crying may be burdened by guilt in several ways: feeling that he or she is the cause of the parent's unhappy state; feeling guilty about leaving the grieving parent(s) alone; feeling guilty about the burden of expense he or she has become; not completing school, personhood, specific expectations, etc.; not being able to respond adequately to the care provided by the parents and doctors.

The parent may be beset with guilt over not being able to control the grief which, in a circular way, creates more guilt. Yet in many ways crying may be the single emotive means available. The dying child may wonder why the parent(s) continues to be upset. Parents who are having difficulty managing their grief may well need to seek the assistance of a professional.

The health care staff of a hospital is often faced by the situation in which parents want to shield the child from knowing his or her condition. This may become increasingly awkward as when the child is placed in an intensive care ward in which other children are obviously very ill. Interestingly, the child in some such cases has a greater level of awareness than do the parents and, in fact, may feel compelled to help the parents deny the truth. Sometimes the child does not pick up even obvious cues and is then tacitly content to utilize denial as programmed by the parents. The patient may thus exhibit a long-standing pattern of parent-child interaction fostering emotional immaturity, dependency, and even the perceptual distortion of reality. When parental denial is deemed by the professional health care team as excessive and detrimental to the child's welfare, it may be necessary for them to inform the parents of their judgments and if the parents are unyielding, obtain an indemnity agreement.

I am reminded of a young patient who had received extensive chemotherapy on several occasions. His parents had steadfastly maintained silence and a "light" atmosphere. Finally, after having been home for several months the boy—about seven years of age—told his parents to take him to the hospital. They were puzzled, but did so. The boy never spoke openly of death with his parents. About two or three days later he died. He knew. A study conducted in the early 1970s in Israel indicates that children when exposed to life-threatening conditions adjust better when they are informed of the contingencies. The study showed that children will fantasize answers to their questions anyway and that providing factual information is a better alternative.

Parents obviously do assume a lot of responsibility in overseeing the treatment available to their sick child. It is essential that the health care staff assist the parents in understanding and evaluating treatment techniques available for the illness. Various associated conditions or side effects may not be touched upon because of fear that parents will overinterpret and deny a basically sound treatment procedure. Yet there is a clear indication of iatrogenic (treatment-caused) disease with some medical procedures.

Some undesirable delayed effects of treatment procedures are unknowable when new drugs or techniques are employed. Van Eys (1976, p. 85) has briefly related some of the more commonly known undesirable side effects—bone marrow depression, suppression of immunity with radiation or chemotherapy. Dr. van Eys points out that the benefits of a physical cure may be undermined if the child's self-image is impaired by the psychological reaction to disfigurement. Some children perceive certain kinds of side effects as more disturbing than others. Some female patients are more concerned about hair loss than males. There are other physical features, however, that may be equally disturbing to family and friends—swelling, bloating, skin-color change, weight gain or loss, "oozing" lesions, etc. Initial reactions are sometimes embarrassing for the patient as well as for friends and family. It is sometimes curiously difficult to assist the patient and family in dealing with phobiclike discrimination in the home community. I am reminded of two such cases. One—a boy with an unusual genetic skin disease that caused chronic scablike tissue over the entire body—did not fit the usual visual standards of esthetic beauty. Yet his feelings, awareness, and intellect were at least of average keenness. He was not allowed to attend public school because his presence was too disruptive, although his condition was easily documented as noncontagious. He grew up without a school education. Another child had a type of cancer that perpetuated large, oozing sores (lesions) on his forearm and cheek. On returning to his hometown from the hospital he was allowed to take up his schooling, but the teacher was disturbed by his wounds and would not let him use the restroom. Eventually, it was necessary for this child to seek teaching at home. This may have had some benefits, but on the negative side it deprived him of social contact with his peers.

Not all iatrogenic disease is visible. Increasingly, there are reports of possible central nervous system damage from treatment for cancer (van Eys, 1976, p. 84). Although documentation of cognitive and intellectual impairment has not been demonstrated it is my feeling that such side effects are likely to occur in some cases where extensive and repeated multiple-process treatment has occurred. In this regard I am reminded of the mother whose child was diagnosed as having cancer when he was about five years of age. At that time the mother virtually abandoned the rest of her family to turn her attention to the care of her sick child. The mother divorced and became alienated from her teenage children. Her child has now been in treatment for more than twelve years and has undergone a dozen operations, chemotherapy regimens, etc. Several times during that period her son was pronounced "cured." The mother was elated, especially the first time. Then the child went out of "remission" one of the most feared syndromes of leukemia patients. I've heard parents say that the first time their child goes out of remission (evidence that cancer is back) is worse than when they first heard that the child had cancer.

This boy's mother has scrupulously monitored his health signs and pursued treatment for twelve years. During this time she frequently found it impossible to deny him anything. Perhaps this helped alleviate her own guilt. Whatever emotional good it may have done for her, it did none for him. He became increasingly demanding and difficult to be around. He had greater difficulty dealing with people of any age in healthy give-and-take fashion.

Still the mother had high hopes; she even planned college for her son. After some psychological consultation and testing it was obvious that the child could not finish junior high school. His intellectual functioning was substantially below average. After further counseling the mother was able to adjust her expectations and goals to a more reasonable level.

Recently, a new lesion has been detected. The mother now questions whether she will allow further surgery. "The cost, the agony, and then what." In pronouncing this child "cured" the physicians were honest because no further disease could be detected. Yet, if they had outlined the statistical probability of new lesions occurring, this parent might have chosen different treatment options. Some physicians do commonly present patients and families with statistical likelihoods. Apparently some parents, even in poor prognosis categories, maintain hope that their child will be the exception.

It is increasingly important for the health care team to treat the whole person and indeed the whole family when necessary. Some diseases are not cured by three days in the hospital. Some diseases that are disfiguring and terminal disrupt the coping patterns of the entire family, not just the person in the hospital bed. Hospital staff must recognize that the patient and family do not turn on and off like switches. I recall an occasion in which a physician returned from reviewing the results of his studies and announced to his patient and the patient's family that the man had cancer and was going to die and not to fool around but get his business in order. He declared that there was no time for emotional nonsense and feelings of self-pity. Needless to add, the patient and family were appalled. I am pleased to note that such bedside manners are more and more a rarity.

The members of a family are in a vulnerable position when a life-threatening condition afflicts one of them. Health care professionals should be able to foresee and anticipate at least some of their needs. Explaining the use of local, state, and federal resources—such as welfare, rehabilitation, and visiting nurse services—is important for follow-up care. State agency contacts at the local level may be facilitated by the health care teams and may alleviate considerable pressure.

A good picture of what families cope with when they have a dying child is presented by Futterman and Hoffman (1973). They indicate that the parental task is to achieve a balance within the following basic areas of conflict:

1. Acknowledging ultimate loss of the child and maintaining hope
2. Attending to immediate situational needs and planning for the future
3. Cherishing the child while allowing the child to separate
4. Expressing disruptive feelings; maintaining daily activity
5. Delegating child care to a health team or continuing active personal care of the child
6. Trusting the physician and health care team and recognizing realistic limits of their techniques, knowledge, and capability
7. Preparing for the child's death through gradual emotional detachment while caring for the child

Groping for an emotional balance, parents go through periods of anticipatory grief—acknowledgement, grieving, and reconciling. Early in this phase the emotional fluctuation is often between despair and hope for survival. Later, parents begin to grieve over anticipated loss of the child and move toward emotional adjustment that allows them to reflect on the love and positive legacy of the parent-child relationship, bolstering the value of the child's lived years. In the United States parents are especially prone to view children as "incomplete adults" and tend to experience guilt over not having been able to provide them with a life span encompassing adulthood, freedoms, pleasures, and perspectives. Focusing on the positive features of the years the child lived and what parents interpret as the child's achievements helps counterbalance their guilt in this sphere. While this style of focusing attention on positive attitudes may in certain ways be a form of denial, it is appropriate and constructive (Leventhal & Hersh, 1975).

The second area of coping conflict outlined by Futterman and Hoffman reflects the difficulty parents have in parcelling time and emotional commitment between moment-to-moment needs and future planning. This is often a double guilt bind: the parents, being under considerable stress, are prone to react with emotional instability. When they spend too much time dealing with the sick child's needs, other things, including other family members, are neglected and this may generate guilt. Yet, as the parents turn their attention to other responsibilities and momentarily leave the sick child totally in the hands of a health care team, guilt may set in. Some parents become more distraught from guilt than others and these parents may need additional counseling and reassurance. Leventhal and Hersh (1975) report that chronic stress in leukemia patient families is more effectively handled when the family is helped from the beginning to verbalize their feelings and deal with the impact of the disease upon their lives. Parents should be provided with as much information on the disease as is available. They may be in such emotional turmoil that they have trouble assimilating the information that is being presented. Finally, the staff's willingness to take time to answer some questions reassures the parents that their child is just another number on a chart.

It is hard to predict which health care team member parents or patient will choose as their confidant. It is often not the staff physician. It may be allied health professionals or housekeeping personnel. It is important to be aware of these patterns because it provides staff with important information. Patients and parents talk to those persons who do not intimidate them, who, they feel, will not mind taking time, and who have genuine concern and can give simple answers and listen.

The conflict between cherishing the child and allowing him or her to separate may be seen in the parent's attempt to be consistent with the sick child. Again guilt is a management problem. Parents are often willing to dismiss school and anything else the child finds distasteful. The verbalized parental reply is "For God's sake, the poor child is so sick and may die, I can't see any point in putting extra burdens on him." This loosening of controls may alleviate parental burdens of pressure and guilt but may be disadvantageous to the child. It may be difficult to draw the line categorically, but a sick child may become demanding, manipulative, and generally unpleasant. Again, these conflicts are sometimes fostered by parents who are having difficulty working through their grieving and denial stages.

To delegate care of the child or to continue with active personal care can be a grim dilemma; with proper health team intervention the decision can be a positive step in parental adjustment. After assessing the family's capability for dealing with the stress of the child's illness, it may be of considerable value to train the parents in certain care functions—dressing lesions, dealing with fluids, blood counts, etc. Getting the family mobilized helps to reduce their guilt and remorse. The family feels that they aren't totally helpless and they are contributing to the effort. This may be especially helpful to those parents who are traumatized by some procedures that are dreaded by the child such as bone marrow studies. This type of training is also practical, especially when patients are required to return to home communities that may not have certain needed health care resources.

While parents' trust in the physician and health care team is essential, the parents must be helped to appraise realistically their capacities and limitations. This trust is best established and nurtured by mutual availability, openness, and honesty in communication.

A seventh dilemma for parents (Futterman & Hoffman, 1973) is preparing for the child's death, effecting emotional detachment without loss of love and caring. As parents reach resolve in this area they become more oriented in the present and no longer guard their sentences so closely about "next year we'll. . . ." There is less tension and often even moments of laughter.

Although many of our insights into death and dying coping patterns are of recent origin, Bz Cobb conducted numerous studies in the early 1950s which parallel, with remarkable depth, many of our modern writings. In one study Cobb (1954, p. 746) addressed four areas relating to the psychological impact of long illness and death of a child on the family. The areas studied and respective findings are summarized:

1. Reactions to remissions and regressions following experimental treatment: pediatricians sometimes question the desirability of promulgating remissions when eventual death is certain. A consensus of twenty parents interviewed indicated that they were grateful for the additional few weeks or days. A typical reaction was "While there is life there is hope."

2. The impact of enforced separation and the disruption of family living or marriage: the consensus suggests strong marriages survive with spouses even sometimes experiencing a closer bond. This is

not always the outcome however. Sometimes parents begin to harbor resentments toward each other that become amplified. Inability to share anger in constructive ways and the guilt and grief incurred by anticipated loss troubles marital adjustment. The effect of separation on children, having to leave the family's other children with relatives or giving them less attention, created some difficulty. The other children were described as having lost time. "They seemed to have stopped and waited for us."

3. Reaction to death: in attempting to prepare the sick child and healthy siblings for death, personal reports suggested that there was conviviality in some areas of reacting, some became talkative, some quiet and withdrawn, some cried, some (healthy children) needed considerable reassurance of their health. One parent said, "Comfort them as you can, but let them do as they want; reassure them; explain to them; answer their questions. If they want to talk about it, let them. Don't urge them to visit the cemetery."

4. The role of religion: a composite of family reactions suggested that to many religion provides comfort and capacity to accept. Cobb writes, "There seems to be a period endured by the parents when rebellion against death is paramount, but . . . once the parent was able to say 'Thy will be done,' some sort of peace and acceptance descended (p. 750)." Cobb suggested three ways of assisting the family and patient: be available, physically and emotionally; listen to what is being said but also be alert to feelings which may be expressed in nonverbal ways: body posture, tone of voice, facial expression; provide reassuring information regarding treatment, prognosis, and return home.

There is today not only disagreement on what, how, and when to tell patients but also a frequent discrepancy between what some physicians think they have conveyed and what actually has been conveyed. There seem to be three basic sources of this discrepancy: cultural or language barriers; tactful evasion on the part of the physician; and comprehension failure of the patient from denial, emotional numbness, or limited verbal fluency. Gilbertsen and Wangensteen (1961) have reported that about eighty percent of patients say they would like to be told. A study in that same period by Oken (1961) indicates that over eighty percent of attending physicians rarely tell patients when their illness is fatal.

To tell or not to tell is not necessarily the question. If the health care team is in close emotional rapport with the patient then a mutual movement toward understanding can usually be achieved. In any case one of the first priorities is to find out what the patient knows, what the patient really wants to know, and from whom does the patient want to hear the facts. For example, Glaser and Strauss (1965) reported the practice of one hospital that informed patients who had fatal illnesses in short, blunt announcements. Sociologists studying this treatment mode determined that it simply amplified depression and despair. Alvarez (1952, p. 86) warned against divulging the truth dogmatically. He suggested that the aim of granting the patient this information was to make dying easier. Even though some doctors are outspoken in their view that it does patients no good to be told they are dying (Asher, 1955, p. 373), a study in 1960 by Gerle et al. (1960, p. 1206) made a strong case for informing patients and families in supportive ways. Although they found that in some patients the initial emotional reaction was distress, subsequent adjustment and composure was marked with serenity and improved family relationships for the vast majority.

So how do you find out how much a patient knows? Basically, the same tactful way you obtain information from anyone. The first thing that blocks your attempts to ascertain the patient's emotional orientation and knowledge is inexperience and anxiety. The second difficulty usually arises much later in the professional career—the callous reaction. This latter reaction has been accounted for in many ways. Psychodynamic explanations often suggest that the professional begins to build an insulating wall which becomes emotionally necessary when his or her frustration and anger are aroused by patients who do not respond to the professional's best efforts to cure. Inability to preserve life and bring about cure is the very embodiment of failure, and personal involvement combined with too much failure may force hospital staff to reconsider their skill, occupation, and self-worth. Thus an impersonal approach is developed in self-defense.

The first sensitivity block may be easier to circumvent than the second simply because the first is usually found in students or new health care personnel. Training and guidance and proper exposure are the best remedies. The latter type of sensitivity block is more difficult because the person so afflicted is usually in a position of higher authority and autonomy and persons who might conceivably influence his or her behavior are not present in the immediate environment. Those persons present are likely to be of junior standing and unable to call attention to behavior patterns needing review. In both cases, I have found that staff groups can be of great help. Even though a certain amount of guardedness may be present at such staff meetings, they will pay off with improved staff trust and congeniality. The diminution of sensitivity barriers will give the health professional greater confidence in his or her capacity to know and correctly identify the emotional state of patients and parents. Ogilvie (1957, p. 584) has suggested intuitive judgment is a necessary ingredient in guiding one's rapport with a patient while communicating information concerning prognosis. He indicates that it is important to study the patient's habitual pattern of dealing with life as a guide to a style of communicating. In other words, some people chronically prefer to deny reality, postpone decisions, etc., while others are forthright, practical, and assertive.

THE COMMUNICATION TRANSITION: PRETENSE TO OPENNESS

The pivotal point of much staff, family, and patient behavior is the pretense-openness dimension. This single dimension rules the anxiety levels of all who become involved with a dying patient. A great deal of what is communicated to the patient is predicated on evaluative behavior stemming from this area. What and how to tell patients and families become inextricably related to the pretense-openness dimension. Glaser and Strauss (1965) have discussed this dimension clearly and in detail. Basically, they contend that health care staff and patient and family tend to engage in a pretend ritual not unlike childhood games of make-believe. They identify several essential ingredients of the make-believe ritual: either player can initiate the game; the other players must play properly; nonfictional action will destroy the illusion; behavior during the game is impromptu; and eventually the game ends.

The presence of these game behaviors can be readily recognized by anyone who has worked on a hospital ward. In the context of a dying patient the ritual comes into play as soon as both patient and staff are aware that death is imminent. There must be some detectable signal, verbal or nonverbal, intimated by staff or patient that pretense is desired. The other must agree. As Glaser and Strauss (1965) point out, the patient has more options than the staff. The patient, by rules of etiquette, has the first move. Thus the patient can choose to initiate open conversation about his or her death or initiate some level of pretense. The staff is not required to broach the topic. Usually the staff feels obligated to follow the physician's or patient's cue.

Glaser and Strauss (1965) have identified four rules that obtain during the pretense interaction episode: a dangerous topic should be avoided; if there is to be talk about a dangerous topic, it is permissible only so long as neither side breaks down; generally, the participants should focus on neutral and safe topics; when a faux pas is made, both parties will ignore the slip and even divert their attention. From these implicit rules of interaction we can see that the participants have covertly accepted mutual responsibility and even a degree of mutual trust in perpetuating the ritual.

The Transition

The transition from pretense to open awareness may occur suddenly, slowly, or oscillate. The rate of transition, if one indeed occurs, is often influenced by the hospital milieu and the specific staff-patient interaction mode. Pretense collapse is usually accelerated with increases in pain, medication/sedation, and physical deterioration. By word or gesture, patient and staff become increasingly prone to acknowledge impending death as physical deterioration increases. Pivotal anxiety now is likely to be on speaking of death and reducing fear of it rather than the previous fear of bringing the subject up. Sometimes, at this point, the staff is caught in the drama of hoping openness can be achieved before the patient expires or becomes comatose. Yet it should be recognized that maintenance of pretense may be the patient's way of preserving dignity (Glaser & Strauss, 1965). Stress, especially for nursing staff, may be at a high point during transition periods since nurses must cope with care agendas as well as the emotional oscillations of the patient and family.

There are at least two major factors that have to be considered when evaluating the proper communication modes with patient and family. One already alluded to is the type of illness involved, and the other is the patient's psychological coping pattern. The first factor concerns prolonged dying vs. sudden death. Cancer tends to carry stereotypic expectations, anticipations, and fears: lingering, painful illness and disfiguring or mutilative surgery. Heart disease and accidental death prompt other typical fears of sudden death and unconsciousness. In between these extremes lie such conditions as muscular dystrophy, which is slow and disfiguring, but not perceived as being markedly painful or mutilative.

Kübler-Ross (1969, p. 152) has perceptively drawn attention to the differentiated grief patterns associated with prolonged illness and swift death. She reported that it is easier to talk with a cancer patient about death and dying than it is with cardiac patients. With the cardiac patient health professionals may well feel afraid to broach anxiety-provoking topics lest they trigger a coronary and be responsible for a death. This appears to hold true for the families of such patients as well. Cardiac families are generally reluctant to discuss death and dying even considerably after the patient's resumption of an ordinary lifestyle. In some families this reluctance becomes a chronic family pattern where family members automatically avoid discussion of any death-related topics.

The second factor—the psychological quality of the patient's coping pattern—may sometimes be discerned from knowledge of the person's past but sometimes is unexpected. The general rule—that a person who relates to reality easily, is generally happy, forms substantial friendships and warm family ties, and is a model of good adjustment can cope with death best—may not be the case. The less happy person may be better prepared to die (Aldrich, 1963, p. 329). This dimension of the coping pattern is best monitored through the period of acute coping so that appropriate reaction to patient or family needs can be implemented.

One example of a bizarre parental coping pattern I recall is that of a father who wanted to keep the amputated leg of his son. Although this may not at first seem much of a problem, one can, after a moment of reflection, see the potentially traumatic ramifications for the child. In another instance, a usually quiet female patient would become anxious and agitated daily at mid-morning and need tranquilizers. Eventually, it was discovered that she routinely administered herself a coffee enema. While this patient was compulsive in following treatment, even adding an extra dimension of her own, some patients may commit a form of suicide by not following prescribed chemotherapy, especially after leaving the hospital. Physicians remark that one reason for the diverse effectiveness level of certain medicines is related to how well the patient follows medication and diet instructions.

We now come to how a patient or family is told. I recall an instance when a high school football player was injured and brought to the hospital. During the relatively minor surgery cancer was discovered. The physicians along with the parents decided the optimal procedure was immediate removal of the entire right leg. Later, when the patient awoke, only his nurse was present. She was new on the service. He discovered that his leg was missing and broke into tears of anguish. The nurse said later that she was paralyzed with fear and her first impulse was to tell him to wait while she went to find somebody who would know what to say. Fortunately, she overcame her own fears, stayed beside him, and comforted him.

Even staffs armed with the experience and sensitivity essential for such a situation are not assured of successful communication. Basically, it seems that doctors tell a patient or relative in one of three ways:

1. Terminological method (diagnostic labeling), wherein the physician informs the patient and/or family of the diagnosis in medical terms without embellishment. In using this approach, the doctor usually tells the family and allows the family to tell the patient, giving them the responsibility of explaining details.

2. The oblique approach, wherein the physician attempts to plant ideas that will allow awareness to grow—hopefully at a pace compatible with and determined by the patient's (or family's) emotional strength. The patient's emotional strength level will be known by his or her awareness growth rate. Surgeons sometimes tell patients before operations that serious operations require extensive surgery. When patients awaken they can then begin to evolve conclusions consistent with their emotional state. Hope is never excluded nor is misleading information given (Gavey, 1955, p. 705). Staff who employ this mode of patient care should be attuned to patient and family needs as awareness grows. The staff should be capable of answering questions, providing emotional support, and should know how to deal with various emotional stages of dying.

3. The statistical approach is that in which the physician points out statistical outcomes of cure and remission relative to the specific disease and medical factors unique to the patient. Some facilities utilize this approach with patients and/or family from the outset—as soon after diagnosis as possible. Others combine the two approaches starting with an oblique approach and then, as patients and families become more aware and want more information, resort to statistical and probability outcomes of treatment.

All of these approaches leave something to be desired. It might seem that openness and immediate dealing with emotional reactions is desirable, but this often is not feasible and, therefore, the only choices may be the oblique or statistical modes. These two approaches often leave the attending staff open targets for resentment as patients attempt to work through anger stages. Frequently, patients accuse the staff of being deceptive and not "simply telling me how it is." On the other hand, the physician quickly becomes sensitive to surefire failures and opts for the approach that tends to have the better long-term odds. Thus, in some respects, the patient and family are right—answers have been hedged because the staff interpreted the cues that were available and as the patient and family seemed to be able to deal with the facts, they were told. In theory these approaches sound conservative but reasonable.

As Shands et al. (1951, p. 1160) have pointed out, the United States is an especially blame-oriented society and, moreover, a society looking for ways or people who can "fix" its ills. These two orientations arbitrate conditions whereby one in great need of having something "fixed" will want to place that responsibility in the hands of someone who does that sort of thing. The doctor like the mechanic or plumber can become the target of anger and resentment if he or she accepts the all-knowing authority role and encourages the patient and family to become markedly dependent. To minimize and avert such a counter-productive relationship, the oblique and statistical approaches can be beneficial. Again, the hospital staff strategy should not be calculating, distant, and manipulating, but rather empathetic, supportive, and consistent. The patient may begin indirect probing which may prompt a staff member to guess at outcomes. Such a response could diminish patient hope instead of alleviating the patient's worry. Helping the patient to verbalize his or her feelings and occasionally reiterating probable eventualities, as the patient asks in realistic but positive ways, may be more burdensome but tends to force the patient to maintain a decision-making identity. The preservation of this level of identity is important to the patient going through cycles in the various states of coping with dying. The patient's eventual realistic understanding of the skills and limitations of the care team will be influenced by this factor. Family members feel more useful and less guilty when they are allowed to maintain a level of responsibility. Family communication is enhanced as family members begin to deal with the reality of inexactitude and uncertainty and learn to coexist. Uncertainty no longer means no hope.

As openness in communication grows the patient and/or family may select one or perhaps two people with whom they feel especially close. The chosen health care member would ideally have the skill and administrative license to respond in the appropriate fashion. As openness grows the care team will begin to be seen in a different light. Perhaps even certain shifts of hospital staff will be greatly favored. It is generally at this point that the involved care team members can intuitively grasp the deep emotional turmoil of the patient or family. The involved team members can be most effective in assisting their charge in achieving the most desirable medium of adjustment. They may also find themselves overcome with grief. The old nursing care formula "empathy without sympathy" may be difficult to follow when empathy is too profound. It is therefore advisable to have staff members meet in discussion groups, especially where there are high patient death rates. A means of emotional ventilation is needed.

Weaknesses of the Terminological, Oblique, and Statistical Approaches

Unfortunately limitations hamper the effective use of these techniques in guiding patients toward emotional stabilization. Some of these limitations we might call "systems" problems. For example, it is more than just awkward when a patient asks a nurse or other health care team member a question about his or her condition and prognosis if the physician alone wishes to articulate anything bearing on those topics. This problem of "domain" is not usually well understood by the patient. The patient does, however, often detect hedging and edginess in a guarded reply and may misinterpret the reasons for the guarded answer.

A limitation of the statistical approach is that staff does not always know the long-term statistical probabilities and may have to guess or hedge. Sometimes statistical estimates are so involved that it is impractical to attempt to explain details with the patient or family. Sometimes the staff misjudges the intellectual capabilities of the patient or family. The physician or care team may interpret nonverbal cues that the patient will absorb information readily when emotionally prepared. Yet, if the patient is not as intellectually facile as estimated, he or she will be denied a chance to progress because of this error.

Another limitation is the possibility that the oblique approach will be used simply to postpone any emotional reaction and coping until the patient is sufficiently out of care range. That way someone else will have to worry about his or her responses.

There may be a problem of staff "jealousy" when the patient chooses one staff person as confidant over the others. These rivalries are best dealt with in staff therapy groups. Finally, after the oblique or statistical approach is decided upon, all team members may not agree that the approach chosen will benefit a particular patient. Patterns of resentment may build up among the treatment team and nullify any possible benefits. Sometimes this problem is fostered when the physician dominates and refuses to allow other team members to offer their feelings and suggestions.

SPECIAL PROBLEM SITUATIONS

I have discussed talking to the patient and family about dying but there are other considerations that are sometimes of overshadowing importance—even to the momentary topic of death. These are special problems that a health care professional will encounter.

Rejection

It is not altogether infrequent that a cancer patient, a quadriplegic, mentally impaired person, or other disfigured patient begins to experience difficulties with a lover or spouse. These cases are more traumatic when there are healthy children involved. A cancer patient may have substantial facial or sex-organ disfigurement. The spouse sometimes finds it increasingly difficult to respond in caressing ways. In some cases the spouse makes an open break and seeks separation or divorce. This additional trauma to the patient can hamper treatment. All too often patients suffering such strife do not have access to counseling resources and come to harbor emotional conflicts that propagate depression or even self-destructive habits. Such problems should be evaluated by the health care team and efforts made to assist the patient.

The patient may sometimes feel rejected when a nurse with whom he or she has grown attached is transferred to another service. Should the nurse occasionally drop by for a visit? Definitely. Nursing staff should be actively encouraged in such endeavors.

Sometimes the patient will confide in the nurse that he or she feels rejected by the doctor who never seems to really have time to talk. Should the nurse mention this to the doctor? This question must be evaluated by the nurse. Does the physician allow such openness or will he or she become angry, threatened, and vindictive. Hopefully, not. Perhaps, problems similar to this could be discussed in staff groups or with supervisors.

Helplessness may be an embarrassing and humiliating aspect of a terminal disease. Some patients will struggle with their embarrassment and go without attention before asking for necessities. Patients with these tendencies are usually easily recognized and staff efforts to overcome these inhibitions would greatly relieve the patient's tension.

There are some categories of disease which are associated with life-threatening processes that are not as "socially acceptable" to have and talk about. Examples of these are certain kinds of cancer or residual disfigurement and dysfunction of sexual and eliminative systems: colostomy, cancer of the cervix or scrotum. Patients with these difficulties often need special appliances and it is important to assist them in accepting the appliance as a necessary helping device. Some often continue to express subtly what they covertly may feel to be social stigma. Such expressions are manifested when patients refuse or frequently "forget" to use properly or clean the appliance. Sometimes such poor utilization is the result of poor patient preparation, poor comprehension of the necessity for the device, and sometimes it is a form of self-inflicted punishment. Some patients incessantly "tinker" with appliances and perpetually require attention—which may also be the underlying motivation. Staff may, in that case, engineer alternate routes by which the patient can get attention.

Occasionally, the care staff will encounter a patient who seems bright, responsive, and potentially reliable. But this very patient who seems to have a probing and fertile mind obviously does not want to face or discuss death or dying. As a care team member one may feel that this patient—perhaps with children—of all people needs to face finality, work through the anxieties and conflicts, and prepare him- or herself and family to carry out financial planning. Even with repeated "nudging" and cue dropping the patient exhibits no realistic recognition. What should one do? This tacit rejection of reality may seem a spiteful act on the part of the patient to inflict feelings of guilt, helplessness, and failure on the staff. The staff may feel gripped with a fear that the patient is going to die unhappy unless they recognize what is happening and allow everyone the freedom to express emotion. Sometimes a staff person cannot deal alone with this kind of pressure. Verbalizing these tensions to other staff members may help relieve anxiety and illuminate more fully needs and attitudes. The staff member may be identifying in such a case with the anticipated guilt and anger that will be a legacy of relatives. One may therefore be prompted to feel anger at the patient for selfishly binding those who remain with guilt that cannot be fully ventilated after the patient's death. Even so, the patient's right to die at peace, with self-esteem intact, should be preserved. Forcing a patient to talk about death and dying may violate this right. A zeal to share and know dying patients may become an intrusion in the name of training and experience.

Psychological death of a patient may occur when the family looks upon the patient's demise as inevitable and essentially withdraws emotional support and even physical presence. Nursing staff at these times may be especially taxed with care needs. Although attempts may be initiated to reinstate family support, such efforts are often to no avail and may even engender hostility from the family. Van Eys has referred to similar circumstances as the Lazarus syndrome. In such cases parents and family show irritation and resentment toward the patient who was supposed to have died but lingers or gets better. Relatives may be resentful of their continued burden.

Sudden Infant Death Syndrome (SID) is a relatively illusive phenomenon that results in infant deaths, about 10,000 in the United States annually. Such a death may cause undue parental guilt and staff should inform and support family regarding the nature of the illness which is not an outcome of neglect.

Now let us consider coping with the individual who is dying and review some behaviors which can guide our approach in assisting the patient. Kübler-Ross (1969) has delineated several basic stages of coping. Although these stages do not always appear in a particular order or for predictable time spans, the following prominent features have been noted.

Psychological Coping Stage	Prominent Features	Staff Intervention Mode
Denial and Isolation Shock to defenses, necessitates time for patient to restructure coping mechanisms.	" . . . not me . . . must be some mistake, a mix up." Shock, numbness, doesn't hear. Begins to blame others. Is selective in giving permission to others to communicate. Make-believe that everything is going to be all right.	Attempt to identify permission level allowed. Be reflective with anger and avoid taking it as personal attack. Be available to listen.
Stages of Anger Overt venting of frustration culminates in expressions of anger.	Make-believe fails. Resentment and rage expressed. View of unfairness may be expressed. Envy of others	Listen and allow for expression of initial anger and feeling. Avoid feeling anger is personally directed.

Psychological Coping Stage	Prominent Features	Staff Intervention Mode
	who are healthy: "Why me—why not them, just when I was about to get. . ." Patient's mood may exacerbate family guilt.	Nurses and staff may also experience anger toward patient and feel guilty over their destructive wishes. Assist family in coping with patient's anger and their guilt.
Bargaining Usually an attempt to postpone. It may include offerings of appeasement, promises to God, and self-imposed deadlines.	Most bargains attempt to postpone occurrence of death. Such bargains include offerings, self-imposed deadlines, and once-in-a-lifetime promises: "I'll never ask again." Bargains are made with God and promises stem from guilt—not attending church, etc.	Patient may show need for punishment and atonement. Attempt to alleviate and relieve fears and guilt if promises and deadlines cannot be kept.
Depression Unrelenting disease results in recognition of loss of life. *Preparatory Depression* Patient may focus upon future loss.	Future orientation, Preparation for final separation. Often patient is quiet and reflective.	Help alleviate guilts: over leaving children, over leaving spouse, over leaving debts. Allow ample silence. Avoid "cheering up" since it may amplify what is being left and lost.
Reactive Depression Patient's focus is often on past.	Attention often on past. Sad, mournful quality, regrets, and guilt over	Reassure patient of self-esteem. Help alleviate fears of

Psychological Coping Stage	Prominent Features	Staff Intervention Mode
	leaving unfinished parts of life.	vital issues such as welfare of children, spouse, etc. Assist in alleviating guilt and shame.
Acceptance or Resignation A period of increased tranquility.	Tendency to have flattened effect. May appear somewhat like depression but absence of somber, mournful quality. Verbal communication diminishes and patient seems less stirred by worldly events.	Be available but be comfortable with silences. Family and friends may now need increased help and attention. Assist family in grasping patient's needs for quietude.
Hope	May verbalize faith in possible last-minute recovery. Reliance upon God to see patient through.	Attempt to manage patient and family so hope can be preserved within a realistic framework. Convey to patient that every means that is desirable will be used to comfort and treat patient. Avoid conveying abandonment when patient's death is near.

ALTERNATE CURATIVE PROCEDURES

The discussion of curative procedures above generally follows contemporary medical, psychological, and psychiatric models. However, there are alternate curative procedures available to patients. These alternate curative procedures include faith-healing; consumption of restricted, prohibited, or unrecognized drugs; psychic surgery; disease-combatting meditation; special diets; rejuvenation techniques; and many other controversial tactics. Some of the criteria that set these practices apart from those discussed earlier are: the absence of endorsement by a public sanctioning body (such as a government agency or medical society); the lack of demonstrated adherence to principles of scientific investigation and procedure; the lack of sufficient data demonstrating statistical effectiveness; the lack of operational definitions (treatment protocols) that lead to consistent, predictable results; and the lack of statistically demonstrated health safety margins.

Throughout the ages persons afflicted with life-threatening disease have sought consultation with those involved in the healing arts. Modern man is no different. Even though the impact of modern medicine has been monumental there are still tens of thousands that annually seek alternate curative modalities. Some persons spend thousands of dollars and go as far as the Philippine Islands to seek psychic surgery. Many try DSMO, peach pits, and apricot pit extracts. Quackery is not a myth. Yet there are inexplicable remissions. The unanswerable question is what caused the remission—spontaneous immunity reactions of the body or the "unproved" healer's art. Not all such practitioners are high-school dropouts, or from lower socioeconomic levels. Dr. Carl Simonton of Dallas, a physician and radiologist, has established a cancer treatment clinic which utilizes "psychological warfare" against the disease. Patients are counseled and given instruction in procedures which Dr. Simonton maintains eventuates in a high cure rate. He maintains that the patient's and family's belief systems influence recovery. Laetrile, an extract of apricot pits, has recently been legalized in Texas even though the Food and Drug Administration prohibits interstate commerce in it and the medical community questions its effectiveness. One interesting treatment approach administered in a hospital setting was the administration of lysergic acid diethylamide (LSD) and music to terminal patients in order to minimize dehumanization of the death event. The investigators report that none seemed harmed. One-third felt helped, one-third somewhat helped and one-third felt no help (Pahnke, 1970).

Cellular therapy is another approach at healing that is beset with controversy. Some clinics in the Bahamas, Yugoslavia, South America, and Switzerland have dedicated followings. Brinkley was an early proponent of using goat glands in the United States. More recently (Lindeman, 1975, p. 41) the New Life Clinic of Florida drew attention when Doctor Bob was indicted by a federal Grand Jury for mail fraud and income-tax evasion. The Fort Myers medical examiner studied some of the clinic's ex-patients who had died of gas gangrene and reported that it was no wonder they died because of the sloppy conditions of the clinic. It turned out that some of Doctor Bob's lab work was performed by Frances Farrelly, a psychic who tested blood samples for vibrations.

One of the most frustrating problems in the field of cancer treatment is the patient who detours to unsafe curative practitioners (Cobb, 1955, p. 10). When the detour to alternative treatment occurs early in the disease, it may be a deciding factor in the patient's longevity. Cobb (1955, p. 10) stated that there are four categories of patients who make unsafe detours: miracle seekers, the uninformed, the restless, and straw graspers. They detour prior, during, or after orthodox treatment. She reports that the miracle seekers and the uninformed are the two groups most likely to seek unsafe help prior to orthodox help. Since overall cure rates of unorthodox approaches are not substantiated as being equal to orthodox modes, why do patients sometimes manifest stubborn adherence to the former? Typical of the loyal patient is optimism, appreciation for concern shown, and desire to relieve pain These features reflect patient needs that are not being met in orthodox settings and do not necessarily reflect a self-destructive instinct. Thus, instead of admonishing patients for seeking high-risk treatment, perhaps we should examine our orthodox services and service-delivery systems.

HEALTH CARE TEAM MEMBERS' REACTIONS TO CARING FOR ACUTE CASES AND THE TERMINALLY ILL: TRANSCRIPT OF A GROUP INTERACTION*

This is a discussion rather than a lecture. I have some questions that I would like to ask you. First, has everyone here worked with cancer patients? Yes.

DR. BENTON   Have you ever been in a situation where you feel that you have lied to a patient?

RESPONDENT   Yes.

DR. BENTON   What happened to you?

RESPONDENT   You don't exactly lie but you don't exactly tell the truth (tape fades).

*Audio recordings of this session may be obtained from IBQ P.O. Box 19843, Houston, TX 77024.

DR. BENTON	Has anyone else had that experience?
RESPONDENT	You just feel as if you haven't really answered the patient's questions when he asks because you skirt around the issue.
DR. BENTON	Do you think the patient knows that you are being evasive? How does he interpret that?
RESPONDENT	With more fears.
DR. BENTON	So at that moment you don't feel that you are being totally effective in your care for the patient? How would you rather have it?
RESPONDENT	To me it is an ethical problem, because you have this feeling that this patient is entitled to the honesty of preparing himself for death if this is the situation, and you do not feel you should be the one who tells him this, that it should be someone who has more expertise than yourself. Consequently, you are on the boundary where you want to be honest with this patient, you feel he should be entitled to this, but it is not truly your responsibility to do this.
DR. BENTON	I guess we are talking now mostly about patients who have a poor prognosis. What if the patient has a relatively favorable prognosis?
RESPONDENT	I think he should have an honest reaction, honest encouragement, he should be treated with realistic optimism.
DR. BENTON	When you felt that the prognosis was very poor, have you ever asked a patient, "How do you think you are going to do?" Did you ever ask that and get an answer which would indicate to you his or her level of knowledge?
RESPONDENT	I prefer to let the patient broach this himself. If he is willing to talk about it, I prefer to listen to what he has to say.
DR. BENTON	Suppose you have a patient with a very poor prognosis, and the attending staff has said that he has been informed, and in talking with the patient you feel that as you perceive it, the patient really does not grasp the gravity of his situation. What would you then do?

RESPONDENT   I have only had experience with two terminal patients. The first patient was alert, was informed, was able to make his last few days meaningful with his friends and to prepare his remaining family for the debts that would be incurred. In other words, he was organizing himself, and my role with him was mostly supportive. I didn't have anything to do, whereas the other patient that I encountered had brain tumors, she was in intense pain, and there was no true communication with this person. So I don't really know how I would react.

RESPONDENT   I was discussing with another therapist that a lot of patients have denial, and it has been my experience that if you try, whether for your own comfort or for the nurses' or doctor's comfort to combat that denial, in a way you are killing hope. Maybe the denial process is something the patient really needs and needs to verbalize about, and even though it makes us uncomfortable to hear them deny, if you listen and try not to come across with so many opinions, but just listen, occasionally they get around to the point where they are really not expressing denial in their conversation, and then they will go back to the denial to maintain hopes. I am very much against trying to change anybody's denial patterns. I think they are important.

RESPONDENT   I agree with that, and I also think it is important not to strip away whatever defense they are using. They may be left without anything, and the time that they come to that realization might be at, say, six o'clock at night when I have gone home.

DR. BENTON   Do most of you in fact work during day shifts? Who is taking care of the patients' emotional needs at night?

RESPONDENT   We have social workers who are there quite late in the evenings and available to come in on twenty-four-hour call.

DR. BENTON   Shifting to another area, have you ever been working with patients and tried to encourage them to get into something you were interested in, but they became more withdrawn or didn't participate? Did you ever get angry with them? Did you ever express your anger to them or did you just let it go by? Do you feel guilty if you get angry with a patient?

RESPONDENT   I think some of the feelings I've had have changed as I get older and have more experience, but initially I have become angry, and taken it personally, and think, you know, here you are refusing these remarkable skills I have to offer, and so on, but later you grow to realize it isn't directed at you personally. I can handle it without feeling guilty now, except that there are times when I have confronted a patient with it, usually with a patient I've begun to care about a great deal, and what happens to them, and in that case saying that when you shut me out, I have nothing to go on, and I feel that there are things to offer that can help him. Sometimes that can set up a situation that I can progress from, if they listen to me.

DR. BENTON   Do you feel that if you had some way of communicating more freely with the occasional physician you feel you may be having some problems with in terms of this, would this help, or do you ever feel this as a problem?

RESPONDENT   I have had the experience where the physician wasn't honest with the patient. Now where does that put me, the therapist? It's difficult. The attitude at this hospital, from the doctors we've heard from, is honesty to the patient. This is another hospital in another part of the country, where this particular staff has quite a different attitude, where the less that is told the patient, it seems that this is their defense. I found it very difficult there for me to step out and speak, which I do not do. But how do you handle a thing like that?

DR. BENTON   What do you do? Does anyone have any answers?

RESPONDENT   I think this is the most difficult area for me because I have been brought up in the era that believed doctors know everything. It is very hard to confront a doctor, to go into the room and say, "You know, I'm not trying to demote your skills or this type of thing, but why aren't you giving more pain medicine, or what in the name of Pete are your goals with this patient?" I think it's very difficult, and a lot of times you find that doctors are at a loss in their own emotional feelings about the patient and they really have been tormented with how to handle the situation. And even though I don't resolve anything a lot of the time, I walk away feeling a lot more relaxed for having verbalized how I feel.

RESPONDENT   I think there are two things here. One, I think you are on fairly safe ground if you are honest with your patient, but along with giving information to that patient, I think you have to take the responsibility for giving that information. To make sure that you remain on safe ground, you must make sure that you have communication with the physician.

RESPONDENT   I have a comment in defense of some physicians. We had a psychiatrist talk to us about dealing with cancer and patients dying, and he says that in his experience early in his career when he got to the cancer patient he wanted to shy away because he didn't know how to talk to him, and he found that as he developed his own ideas and personal beliefs about dying, he was a lot more comfortable dealing with the patient and therefore could relate a lot better. As staff people, he suggested to us that we think about these kinds of things ourselves so we can come to our own realizations about how we feel about death and we can then put them in our own perspectives. But we would do a lot better dealing with a patient in a similar situation.

DR. BENTON   Have you ever dealt with a patient who had a brain tumor, perhaps, whose behavior was not quite in accord with what the ward or the facility felt was reasonable? What happens if the patient starts crying or gets very upset? Do you feel that you need to quiet the patient down? Do you try to talk to the patient, or do you indicate to the patient that what he is doing is trying to get a lot of attention and disrupting services? Have you ever seen that, or been involved in that sort of thing?

RESPONDENT   What concerns me is, generally, in hospitals I have worked in, expressions of emotion are considered abnormal and the patient gets a label immediately as depressed, agitated, or combative, all kinds of words that I hate to use. I suppose some of us tend to do the same as others, "Don't cry, everything will be all right," kind of thing, but for me, I can't handle it that way. I would hope that, as the chaplains pointed out earlier, listening to the patient and letting him verbalize his feeling may prevent an acting-out kind of thing from letting feelings build up. I think the emotions that are in a hospital are natural, for the patients to feel depressed or to get angry or to cry, and to suppress them is immoral in my view.

DR. BENTON   To digress for a moment, I think we are saying it would be nice to break up the association between death and cancer or a diagnosis of cancer. Right? We feel it would be desirable for people who have a diagnosis of cancer, not to feel that that also means death. Right? What would you feel if you had a diagnosis of cancer? Would you be able to make the distinction? Would you make the distinction?

RESPONDENT   I can't be sure how I'd react if I really had the diagnosis, except that I think it would depend a lot on what type of cancer I had. I work a lot with patients with brain tumors, and there are different types and different grades. Certainly, with certain ones I would make the association. At least half of my case load and more are persons with brain tumors, and I have seen most of them die.

DR. BENTON   If you were a patient and you were told that you had a diagnosis of some type of brain cancer, would you want to be told the statistical probabilities, your survival rate and the statistical length of time, etcetera?

RESPONDENT   I would want to be dealt with honestly and to know pretty much of the success of treatment. I don't think I would have to know exact numbers, how many died of a group, but I wouldn't want a length of time because that usually isn't right. People have lived longer and people have lived not as long.

RESPONDENT   I think I would want honest answers to the questions I was willing to ask at that time. It's like the little boy who asks his mother where he comes from, and he just wanted to know whether or not he was born in Arkansas. He didn't want to know about the birds and the bees. I think if I got my answer to the question I was asking, then I would be more free to ask the next question. I would probably, at least in the beginning or maybe never, want to know the statistics of it.

RESPONDENT   I would like also to have an open relationship where I could talk with the physician. I work with children and the parents so often. I'm thinking particularly of one case, a teenage girl with the diagnosis of carcinoma. She was with her parents when the doctor told her this, and they went home, and she told her dad later in the evening, "You know, one of the girls at school told me they had heard I had cancer." He said, "Didn't you hear the doctor?" She had completely blocked the whole thing. It is such an emotionally laden word that I think once the person adjusted to the idea there would be more room to discuss, but the original diagnosis is so loaded that all of us have said, "Well, I have told the patient this." You have to keep repeating and reinforcing, because you may have told them a lot of things but you don't know what has filtered through for their acceptance.

DR. BENTON   So, how do you deal with a patient? How do you talk to a patient who does know of the diagnosis? It seems there are two major parts to a question that keeps coming back up. How do you deal with a patient who may not fully know because he may not have been fully informed, for whatever reasons, whether doctor's, or yours, or family's? Secondly, how do you relate to a patient who does know. Do you try to relate to them differently?

RESPONDENT   I'm just responding off the top of my head, but the main thing is to listen to your patient and find out where that patient is. How much of a question is he willing to ask, and once you've decided that, you have to be honest and ask, "Am I really capable of giving this information? Is it something that I can give, honestly, or is it something that I really think the patient is prepared to get from a direct source, his physician?" I say, "These are things that I think are important, and that you should talk out with your doctor. Why don't you just make a list of things that are really bothering you, and ask him to sit down and talk to you until you are satisfied about them?" That is the primary reaction I have to it.

DR. BENTON   I think in some ways what we are saying is that we represent ourselves as purveyors of expertise, information, and services. The extent that we don't fulfill that is the extent that we are being somewhat counterfeit. That makes us feel guilty, I think, for whatever reasons. So the information we try to convey is information that, hopefully, will be useful to the patient. Sometimes it doesn't even have to be textbook information, but rather, information that the patient can use, as your example amply illustrated. "What do you tell the patient?" is the question that keeps coming up. Maybe you don't have to tell the patient, period. Maybe part of what you have to do is hear the patient, and then respond, maybe not in terms of providing them with concrete information.

RESPONDENT   In terms of talking with the patient who knows versus one who doesn't, I usually don't see a lot of difference. I think there are questions that can be asked by a therapist when a person doesn't know that don't really speak to what they have, but how they are feeling, and it has been my experience that most patients who have a poor prognosis or a serious diagnosis know, even though they haven't been told. They know something is wrong, and they may or may not talk about it. I often ask a question like, "What really worries you the most right now? What is your biggest concern right now?" Often that leads to other things, so I think there are ways to question the people and get at those things without saying, "Now you know you have cancer and you are going to have to deal with it."

DR. BENTON   The thing that keeps coming across is that in dealing with these people with poor prognoses we are walking on eggshells, and when we walk on eggshells we want a leader, an expert, somebody who can show us the way out of the woods, and perhaps part of the way out of the woods is understanding ourselves a little better and relying upon ourselves and our judgment. What if you make a mistake, though? Is the mistake your problem or the patient's?

RESPONDENT   Both. It is a learning experience.

DR. BENTON   Right. Except, the problem with a learning experience is that we keep feeling guilty. This person may have only this one shot. It may be a learning experience for us but what about him?

RESPONDENT   We are people, and so is the patient, and sometimes, especially in dealing with disabilities of any kind, be it cancer or anything else, we have to remember that. I remember an example that happened in our rehab center where a patient said to another patient something out of the way, and my staff really got upset. I said, "Remember, that fellow is going to be living in the world. Don't you think someone in the world is going to come up to him and say something a little out of line?" We are people too. We make boners, as people, especially if we are reacting at that level and not trying to make it always thinking of ourselves as therapist-patient, because it seems that we've all been saying you've got to deal with the people as people. We shouldn't feel guilty if we make an honest mistake.

DR. BENTON   Right. Therefore, why try to present yourself as an expert? I'm not sure there are any experts in this area. Why not just be a person and assume that the only responsibility you have is for your knowledge, as best you have it. From another standpoint, this is very interesting too, we are talking about being very compassionate and human, yet, suppose we have a patient all prepared to die, and he doesn't die. Have you ever been angry about that? Some people have. In fact, families sometimes come in and say all kinds of things. Another week of this, my God. Christ, when is this going to end?

RESPONDENT   We often have more problems with the family than we do with the patient. It could stem from any number of things, where the doctor won't be honest with the family where he has been honest with the patient. For example we start to make discharge plans for the patient and the family is waiting for him to die, and if something doesn't happen it's a bad situation because the patient doesn't want to be honest with his family because they are not ready to talk to him, and he has to make the break from the staff, so it leaves the patient in a really bad situation.

RESPONDENT   I had one quite satisfying experience with a cancer patient. My exercise periods had diminished to about a twenty- to twenty-five-minute session in the afternoons during which I couldn't really help him move much of anything without extreme pain and he was very, very terminal. His wife would come at the same time that I got there, and we fell into the habit of going back in his past. He happened to have been a homesteader out in our area, and he got to the point where every afternoon there would be this session where he talked. I should really have taken notes, because between him and his wife, they recounted some of the most fantastic stories, and it left the impression with me that he felt good at the end of that session, and looked forward to it every afternoon.

RESPONDENT   I overheard a lady here say in the hall to another lady, "Well, we did have a lot of good years together." I had the impression her husband was going to die.

DR. BENTON   Are you all familiar with Kübler-Ross's stages of death and dying, etc.? Have you seen those kinds of reactions in patients?

RESPONDENT   I had a very frustrating experience with a brain tumor patient who was aphasic. Looking at his face and his eyes, I knew that he was going through extreme anger, and was not able to convey it. I was trying as best I could to say some of the words for him. When we talked about his anger, he shouted the only word he could: "NO!" At least he found some way, but it was a very, very difficult experience for me because I was so helpless. I knew the patient had something that he couldn't get out.

DR. BENTON   Let me go back to one last thing. Do you feel that there is any way you can identify to improve your communication with other staff people, if you feel that you are not being able to relate effectively to the patient?

RESPONDENT   I want to go back a little, to when we talked about anger. It has been my experience that many of us try to repress anger against the patient, against ourselves, but the families are sometimes very severely criticized by many members of the staff, and they are going through all the same things that the patient is. I guess because they are healthy, somehow we feel that they should be able to take it all.

DR. BENTON   I guess in an odd sort of way this ties in to my last point, too, which is that different specialty areas tend to vent their anger and their frustrations upon another specialty area more than within the group. That is what I think I sometimes see.

RESPONDENT   I just want to make a comment that we as physical therapists and occupational therapists, once our patients are ready to be discharged, we feel now we have done all we can, we've done tremendous things, as the saying goes (I've heard it twice), the patients feel that we walk on water, and patients with visible disabilities (I feel at home here, I feel I'm in the in crowd, in this hospital). But it's great when you're in the hospital but your biggest adjustment is when the patient leaves and some patients ask us, "Will people stare, will people make comments?" and many times we'll say, "No, don't worry about it." Well [after I had a mastectomy], I found out people will make comments, people do stare. About three weeks ago, in my vast preparation to come here, I bought a blouse and I was trying it on in the dressing room at the department store. You know these little salesladies in department stores can be such busy-bodies, and she opened up the curtain to come in and when she saw me she immediately closed the curtain and took the blouse from me and as I was leaving the store she was spraying it with Lysol. So these things do happen and I think you should be very honest with the patient that these are the things which you have to be prepared for. The biggest adjustment is after you leave the building and you're out on the street.

DR. BENTON   Yes, you come into contact with people who are not trained to be aware of your sensitivities. There is a young boy that I can remember who had some secondary problems. His cancer was visible and the teacher required that he use separate washing facilities, and so on.

RESPONDENT   I think sometimes you can help a patient prepare for something like that (this is opposed to a terminal thing; where they are going to go back out). You can help them with some pat answers for some of these people. After all, the people you're going out to be with are normal people. You stick out, you do stick out like a sore thumb. They are as uncomfortable as you. It's hard if somebody comes in with one leg. We had a one-legged girl in our class in high school. I felt uncomfortable with her through four years of high school. I never knew how to act around her, and yet she was perfectly natural. She didn't have any hangups. I was the one with the hangup. Several of us around the hospital try to give the guys some kind of a flip answer when someone asks them about their cancer or point blank stares at them, to come up with something clever that turns it off to a laugh and everybody relaxes.

DR. BENTON   Why do you think people make these little gestures and comments toward someone who is a little different from themselves?

RESPONDENT   I think it's because in our society we are so geared toward the physical, and the outward appearance, it's hard to really think it's the person who counts, it's the person on the inside, and what you do and what you think, and not the clothes you wear or how you look or anything like that. I don't know how to overcome that problem because even little children. . . . I was just in the ladies' room and there was this little kid, about two or three years old, saying "There's too many people in here, I want to get out of here," and another lady was in there, and in order to pacify her she said, "Oh, you are so cute. That's such a pretty dress. You have such pretty hair." We are so geared, from little children, to outward appearance, that that's a lot of our self-image. I think we are offended by someone else who is handicapped because you know it is hard to realize that it is the person inside that is who we are. I don't know whether it is something the human race can ever overcome. But I think it is, like death, something you have to have your own feelings about to deal with it.

DR. BENTON   This is the time of Halloween, and if you'll notice, these are the things that really spook us, the disfigurements.

RESPONDENT   I work with two little girls who have a disease process. This has nothing to do with cancer but it is terminal. Their disease, to give a comparison, looks like leprosy and burns, together. Their deformities are very overtly evident. What comes to mind with these children is the fact that they put you at ease with them. When you are with them, suddenly you get to know them and you don't even realize how deformed they are. Unfortunately, when people are handicapped, this is an added burden, that they have to learn how to put people at ease and be stronger people. This is another thing that we have to work on, as therapists.

RESPONDENT   I really agree with everything that has been said, and I wish that I could always act in ways that intellectually I would like to. It is hard, sometimes, to accept the fact when a terminal patient picks someone else to be close to and asks me to participate in his denial. I am wondering how you help people like us in situations like that. Is this your primary function with the cancer patient, where you interact with them directly, or can you help us with that kind of thing?

DR. BENTON   Well, primarily, I see patients here on a referral basis. I talk to anybody that will talk to me. I try to help anybody that I can, but you see, in some ways I have the same limitations you have. I don't know sometimes whether I have the answers. I don't know if what I'm saying is the right answer, because sometimes perhaps there is no right or wrong answer. Sometimes all there is is what you're feeling, and what you can say. And you have to live with that. That gets back to the topic I mentioned awhile ago. In a sense we are a nation who continues to look for gurus, and perhaps that is all right, but sometimes in some areas it is difficult to determine who is really the guru, who really has the answer. It reminds me of the guru who once said, "When it comes to humility, I'm the world's greatest."

RESPONDENT   I feel, when in this course, for instance, with all the pictures we have seen, I don't get appalled by the looks of people, but it is more, this could happen to me, and that gives me the scare. Probably that's why I would only want to have answered exactly what I asked.

DR. BENTON   But you see, what you are saying is, "I don't trust a lot of the things I learned as I grew up. I must go somewhere and learn the right things." Perhaps some of the things you did learn as a person were the right things.

SUMMARY

Patient care techniques have become increasingly hospital oriented in the past 75 years. These health delivery changes have had marked effects upon the patient, family, and the health care team. The hospital care orientation is seen to have facilitated a modern propensity to view death as the ultimate enemy and has propagated an emphasis on biological functions almost to the exclusion of attention toward the psychological needs of patient and survivors. Moreover, the ignorance that permeates the final arena of the personal life of a patient is encumbered by ill-prepared health care persons. A common patient fear—fear of dying alone in the psychological sense—is a frequent occurrence.

Even though several investigators have indicated results that signal the need for more study of children, death, and dying, very little has actually been carried out. The lack of evidence and knowledge has, perhaps, increased the tendency of health care persons to avoid or evade the inquisitiveness of children.

Recent investigators and practitioners have encouraged an open and direct fashion of dealing with questions concerning death and dying. Proponents of this approach suggest that the imaginative process of children should be provided with realistic, supportive, and factual information. The informative and supportive approach with child, adult, and family alike may be the favored option for maintaining guilt at tolerable levels. Although there are some areas in which detailed facts do not exist, such as experimental drugs, the parents and physician may need to evaluate the short-term and long-term outcomes. Iatrogenic disease is not uncommon in some treatment intervention modes and may give rise to problems with self-image. Still, some of the disfiguring effects of treatment can be corrected cosmetically or subside with time.

Not only does staff need to deal with life threatening disease but often they also must deal with unrealistic expectations of the family. Such expectation levels may invoke patient guilt and seriously hamper psychological well-being. Thus, the staff should be aware of all the major conflict areas that a family experiences when life-threatening disease strikes a member.

The care staff is frequently perplexed by what, when, and how to tell terminal patients. In efforts to deal with this perplexing situation several approaches have evolved. The several more common approaches of assisting patients and family in evolving knowledgeability are discussed. Limitations of each of these techniques are briefly outlined.

There are always special situations that occur which are not easily categorized. Several such situations are discussed which often cause considerable consternation.

Part II of the chapter provides the reader an indepth interview with a group of health care providers. Their personal reactions to their work gives an illuminating view of the emotional feelings of care staff. The final portion of Chapter 6 deals with curative procedures that are more or less controversial. Motivational factors that lead patients to seek such care procedures are reviewed.

REFERENCES

Aldrich, C. K. "The Dying Patient's Grief." *Journal of the American Medical Association, 184 (1963), 329.*

Alvarez, W. C. "*Caring of the Dying.*" *Journal of the American Medical Association,* 150(1952), 86.

Aries, P. *Western Attitudes Toward Death.* Baltimore, Maryland: The Johns Hopkins University Press, 1974.

Asher, R. "Management of Advanced Cancer." *Proceedings of the Royal Society of Medicine,* 48 (1955), 373.

Cobb, Bz. "Psychological Impact of Long Illness and Death of Child in Family Circle." *The Journal of Pediatrics,* Special Article (1954), 746–751.

Cobb, Bz. "Why Do People Detour to Quacks?" *New Horizons* (Winter, 1955), 10 – 12.

Cramond, W. A. "Psychotherapy of the Dying Patient." *British Medical Journal,* 3 (1970), 389–393.

Futterman, E., and Hoffman, I. "Crises and Adaptation in Families of Fatally Ill Children," in *The Child in His Family.* New York: John Wiley and Sons, 1973.

Gavey, C. J. "Discussion on Palliation in Cancer." *Proceedings of the Royal Society of Medicine,* 48(1955), 705.

Gerle, B., Lunden, G. and Sandblom, P. "The Patient with Inoperable Cancer from the Psychiatric and Social Standpoints." *Cancer,* 13 (1960), 1206.

Gilbertsen, V. A., and Wangensteen, O. H. "Should the Doctor Tell The Patient that the Disease is Cancer?" in *The Physician and the Total Care of the Cancer Patient.* New York: American Cancer Society, 1961.

Glaser, B. G., and Strauss, A. L. *Awareness of Dying.* Chicago: Aldine Press, 1965.

Grollman, E. A., ed. *Concerning Death: A Practical Guide for the Living.* Boston: Beacon Press, 1974.

Jury, M. "The Nobility in Our Gramp's Decision to Die." *Today's Health* (January 1975), 18–23.

Kavanaugh, R. *Facing Death.* Baltimore, Maryland: Penguin Books, 1974.

Kübler-Ross, E. *On Death and Dying.* New York: MacMillan and Co., 1969.

Leventhal, B., and Hersh, S. "Modern Treatment of Childhood Leukemia: The Patient and His Family." *Nursing Digest,* 3(1975), 12.

Lindeman, B. "Cellular Therapy: A Shabby Clinic Offered Rejuvenation but Delivered Death." *Today's Health* (June 1975), 36–41.

Nagy, M. "The Child's Theories Concerning Death." *Genetics and Psychology,* 73 (1948).

Ogilvie, H. "Journey's End." *Practitioner,* 179 (1957), 584.

Oken, D. "What To Tell Cancer Patients." *Journal of the American Medical Association,* 175 (1961), 1120.

Pahnke, W. N. "The Psychedelic Mystical Experience in the Human Encounter with Death." *Psychedelic Review,* 11 (1970), 3–20.

Rochlin, G. "How Younger Children View Death and Themselves," in E. A. Grollman, ed., *Explaining Death to Children.* Boston: Beacon Press, 1967, p. 62.

Schilder, P., and Wechsler, D. "The Attitude of Children Towards Death." *Genetics and Psychology,* 45 (1935).

Shands, H. C., Finesinger, J. E., Cobb, S., and Abrams, R. "Psychological Mechanisms in Patients with Cancer." *Cancer* (November 1951), 1159–1170.

van Eys, J. "What Do We Mean by 'The Truly Cured Child'?," in J. van Eys, ed., *The Truly Cured Child—The New Challenge in Pediatric Cancer Care.* Baltimore, Maryland: University Park Press, 1976, pp. 84–85.

Case Studies: Professional and Personal Reports

This chapter is a compilation of personal experiences of the various contributors. Editing and interpretation have been kept at a minimum so that the reader may better focus upon the personal emotional experiences of each contributor.

The Family

This material is the transcript of a taped interview session. Clearly, this family has extensive experience with the grief process. While this family's experience of multiple deaths was unique in particular aspects, there are areas common to other bereaved families in their learning to live with death. Their willingness to share the details of their tragedies and personal consequences is deeply appreciated.

DR. BENTON	How many years have you been married?
MR. D	Eighteen years.
DR. BENTON	You work for the postal service as a mail carrier?
MR. D	Yes.
DR. BENTON	Mrs. D, you're a housewife?
MRS. D	Yes.
DR. BENTON	After you were married both of you were in good health? What were your goals in life at that time?
MRS. D	You know, being married and raising a family—

MR. D	I don't think I had any specific goals, you know—making money, to get ahead like everybody else, to get a home. I think at that time we were living in an apartment. I wanted to get a home. We were living in a garage apartment and we were real happy. It was just a small place but it had a nice tone.
DR. BENTON	And how long had you been married before you had your first child?
MRS. D	Let's see—I guess about a year.
DR. BENTON	You both planned and talked about having children?
MRS. D	Oh, I think we did vaguely but at that time when you got married you just assumed you would have children.
DR. BENTON	You like children?
MR. D	Yeah, I like children. I was real proud of my son. You know, he was a boy, the first son, and you have all these ideas about what you were going to do and this and that. Mike was huge when he was born—a ten-pounder. I was real proud of him, you know? I was really looking forward, too.
MRS. D	We probably would have been just as happy if it was a girl.
DR. BENTON	What were you looking forward to?
MR. D	Oh, I guess like every father, I wanted him to grow up and to send him to Notre Dame to be a football player. Everything I couldn't do I wanted him to do, you know? I just had a lot of ideas. I guess like every father I wanted to have somebody I could take out and look forward to. And at that time I had dreams that he would go to college and go on to Notre Dame and be a football star. They sort of become an extension of you.
MRS. D	It's like seeing yourself grow up and do the things you wanted to do but you never really got to. Mike died when he was only two.
DR. BENTON	How did he die?
MR. D	He got killed in a car wreck. It was my day off and we were going to go over to see one of my friends at work—one of the guys I work with over in Spring. He was sitting in the back seat and he was asleep. We

had just gotten him a candy bar and he was sitting there all curled up in the back seat. He was sleeping and we got in a wreck on the freeway. The car overturned and jumped two lanes and smashed the top in. I don't know why we weren't all killed because the car was all upside down. Mike was in the back and he didn't have—you know, there wasn't no seat belts there. He had a skull fracture.

DR. BENTON   Did he die immediately?

MR. D   No, he was unconscious. We got out of the car and then an ambulance came and took him over to Jeff Davis and I think he died shortly after. I don't think he ever regained consciousness.

DR. BENTON   Is it still hard to talk about it?

MR. D   It is for me.

DR. BENTON   How long ago is that now?

MR. D   Thirteen years ago. It was pretty gruesome. I re-member—you know when he was laying down there they put him on some blankets. They couldn't get his mouth opened—they had to use a stick to pry his mouth open or something.

MRS. D   They said to keep him biting the stick.

MR. D   I had to stay there and they were leaving with the am-bulance, whizzed him over to Jeff Davis and that's the last I saw of him because I had to stay.

DR. BENTON   Why did you have to stay?

MR. D   Because the police were there and they wanted to know what happened—I don't know why I stayed.

MRS. D   It was just one of those things that get mixed up. They had movie cameras out there and everyone was stopping and gawking.

MR. D   I remember this guy with a movie camera was follow-ing me around, you know? I don't know why I stayed—I shouldn't have. We should have all been killed really, because the whole top of the car was smashed in. I don't know how we got out alive.

DR. BENTON   What other kinds of feelings did you have at the mo-ment?

Mrs. D	Just blank shock.
Dr. Benton	Just blank shock?
Mr. D	Well, when he went over there I could tell by the injury that there was probably brain damage and I was just hoping that he wouldn't live because I knew that if he lived that he wouldn't be, you know, normal. I was almost sure that he wouldn't live. We were in one room and then an attendant came in and just said, "Well, I'm sorry." That's all he said. Of course, you know, I didn't expect him to live. We were in shock. We just couldn't believe it and—but I don't think he knew what happened, you know, because he was sleeping and—
Dr. Benton	Would you feel better if he didn't know what happened?
Mr. D	Oh, yeah, that he didn't—that he wasn't conscious because it would be just like blacking out.
Mrs. D	He wasn't, I guess, ever conscious or he probably never even felt, you know, where he was hurt.
Mr. D	It's something you never forget. It's like burning your dream.
Dr. Benton	What did you feel towards the other person who was driving?
Mr. D	Them? I wanted to kill them—I still do. I think, even now I think that he should have been punished, and I should have, too. Oh, I hated him.
Dr. Benton	Did you say anything to him at the time? Did you express any anger?
Mr. D	No, he didn't say a word to us. He talked to the policemen—but at that time there was just so much confusion, you know, Mike was laying down in the blanket in the middle of the street, we were waiting for the ambulance. This lady was real nice—she stopped her car and got blankets and helped my wife, and no, I didn't say a word to him. And later on I saw him—we had to go off to the attorney's office. And we had a suit against him. I saw him up there then but I never said a word to him but I—I just wanted to kill him, you know, I still do.

Dr. Benton	How did the lawsuit come out?
Mr. D	Well, they settled. The insurance companies settled. I mean it went down to the day of court and we appeared in court and they just reached a settlement, you know, instead of taking it to court. They made an offer and our attorney said that it would probably be best to accept it so we did.
Dr. Benton	Did that make you feel better?
Mr. D	No. It's like getting blood money, you know?
Mrs. D	It's just like saying, "Well, how much is your child worth?"
Dr. Benton	How much was it?
Mr. D	I think it was ten thousand. After the attorneys got through, though, we got five thousand, six hundred, and he got the rest. You know, at that time I didn't really care whether I got a cent.
Dr. Benton	You were still kind of numb?
Mr. D	I didn't feel good about the money, you know? I mean you got the money here because your son got killed and maybe you're to blame. It's like profiting off of your dead son, you know? I wanted it and I didn't want it. And then I took it. I had good ideas. I said, "Well, we'll use it for our other children, you know?" We never did. I took it and we bought another car.
Dr. Benton	After the doctor came in and told you that your son was dead, how did you go about making arrangements for the funeral and so on?
Mr. D	Well, we left and went over to her mother's. I think her mother and brother made the arrangements. We didn't have anything to do with the arrangements. Then my mother came down from Wisconsin. I think they took care of everything. But then, I think it was two or three nights later, my wife took an overdose of pills. You know, that was our only son—
Dr. Benton	So it was hitting her pretty hard, too. How did you discover she took the pills?
Mr. D	Because she wouldn't wake up. She kept sleeping. I called her doctor and we kept her walking and walk-

ing. Well, that was our first child and they were real close.

DR. BENTON   Mrs. D, what feelings did you have before you took the pills. Do you remember?

MRS. D   I guess it was just unbearable.

DR. BENTON   Is it still painful thirteen years later?

MRS. D   It comes and goes. Some days it's like a dream. It's like it just happened.

MR. D   Yeah, that's funny—it doesn't matter how long ago, it just seems like yesterday, you know? And I just don't try to think about it anymore, you know, because it's just—

MRS. D   Some days you can talk about it and it doesn't bother you and sometimes just thinking about it drives you crazy.

MR. D   I never could talk about it, you know. I don't even like to think that when my mother-in-law comes over and mentions his name—I don't care for it. I just walk out of the room. It's dumb and it's over with and I'd just as soon forget it as best I can.

MRS. D   The trouble is you can't forget it and if you don't talk about it you'll never get used to the idea.

MR. D   Well, that's your way. That's not my way. Well, you know, that's part of life. I just hate to have it happen that way.

DR. BENTON   Why? Because you have the lingering feeling that he didn't get a chance in life, or an unfinished kind of life?

MR. D   Yeah, I think he was cheated out of his life. I don't know, since we lost two of them, I guess—I lose a lot of sense of feeling that I can protect my family, you know? I guess because you're brought up so the man's supposed to protect the family and here my son died in an auto accident and my daughter died and I couldn't do a thing. So what the hell good am I? I mean, it shows you how helpless you are. Because I guess every man's got the sense that he wants to protect his family, but I couldn't do it, you see? I mean, he died and there was nothing I could do about it. It was the same way with our daughter. She died and there wasn't a thing I could do. So what the hell good am I?

DR. BENTON   What about your daughter?

MR. D   Carl was born first, in 1963. Cathy was born in 1965—two years after. We were happy with Carl because we had just lost a son and we got another one.

DR. BENTON   Did you look upon him as a replacement?

MR. D   We did at first because—in fact, she wanted to name him Michael, after our first son. Then doctor Felps, our pediatrician, came in and said he didn't think that was a good idea. So we changed the name to Carl. He said, you know, we'd just try to be—it wouldn't be fair to the child, you know?

MRS. D   It was already on the birth certificate, so we had to go and have it changed. At the time you think you're replacing that child, but you're not. It's a different child, a different personality, a different way to be. And he just can't replace a child. He may fill up that space—when you have other children and you lose one, it's a little easier because you just can't let go. You've still got somebody depending on you to be taken care of.

DR. BENTON   And Carl was healthy at that time?

MR. D   Yeah, at the time he was real healthy.

MRS. D   We had no problems with any of our children. They were born normal, you know, everything was perfect.

DR. BENTON   And then your daughter was born in 1965?

MRS. D   Yeah, and she was all right. She used to get a lot of colds, though. But when she was about a year old, she began to cough at night and she didn't have a cold, she just coughed. And it would go away, and then, the next night, the same thing. I took her in and had her checked. Nothing wrong, nothing showed up. She had—so they'd give me cough medicine, which didn't work. Finally the doctors said she had asthma.

MR. D   Well, they thought it was an allergy, at first.

MRS. D   Well, that's what triggers the asthma are the allergies.

MR. D	She was healthy until she went into these asthmatic attacks, you know?
MRS. D	And her asthma just got progressively worse. And she had pneumonia I think about four times. You know, you could just almost count on it. And there was no freedom for her because she couldn't go outside. I think she was allergic to everything under the sun. But she had to be exposed to three things before it would trigger an attack. And two of them are always present: pollen and dust and mold and what have you. And, you know, you expose her to a third one and she's got an attack. But she had had attacks daily. Sometimes it would go like—she'd have one every three or four hours around the clock for maybe a week.
MR. D	Oh, it was terrible. She'd get so she couldn't breathe, you know, just (wheezing noise).
MRS. D	She was a very good child, but it was just a continuous battle with no let-up.
MR. D	We'd have to take her and put her on this board and pat her on the back to try and get all that fluid out of her lungs.
MRS. D	But she had attacks where we couldn't control it. She'd be in intensive care. They'd have to have tubes through her lungs and her stomach and everywhere else.
MR. D	And then, like, she could get those attacks at night— we'd call up the clinic and try and get a hold of somebody and they'd say, "Well, do this and do that." And here she is, just gasping to breathe and turning different colors.
DR. BENTON	How old was she at that time?
MR. D	About two years old. I don't know how many times we took her up to the hospital. I don't know how many times she was in intensive care, but like you'd have to sit up there ten days or fourteen days before you got her off. Then we'd think, "Well, maybe that's the last one, you know. She won't have them anymore." But all this time it was leaving scar tissue on her lungs. So you lived in constant fear—"When is it going to hap-

pen again?" I remember one night we had to rush her over to the Texas Children's Hospital. I stopped a policeman who was giving somebody a ticket and I said, "Could you help us get over there?" He just stood there, writing a ticket. "Soon as I'm done here," he says. And, hell, I wanted to get her over to the hospital. Well, then finally he did get her over there. That was that time, I think she almost died. Because they came out and told us that there wasn't very much of a chance, you know, and I knew as soon as the priest showed up, I knew she was pretty serious. Then she turned around and just bounced right back. Then the last time they put her in there it just got worse and worse. They had to do a trach on her.

MRS. D   Asthma puts a direct strain on your heart, too. And when you're that young, there's just so much your body can take.

MR. D   I remember the last time—God, I used to get so nervous, you know, driving to the hospital and she was gasping for breath and, you know—

MRS. D   God, you'd get petrified.

MR. D   I'd like to went out of my head, you know, because, Christ, here she's like suffocating in the car. Can't sit still because she can't breathe. That poor girl was really—I never could understand why children, you know, would have to go through that much torture like that. And the last time, when they put her in intensive care, they had her—that really hurt me because they had to tie her wrists down, you know, so she wouldn't pull the trach out. Jesus, that poor girl.

MRS. D   I think that if she had lived 'til she was grown, she never would have had a normal life. It would have been impossible for her to even consider having children. We were going to see so many doctors.

MR. D   We started out with the pediatrician and we went to the allergy clinic and then over to Dr. H who was an expert. I don't think the three of them together knew what the other one was doing. We asked Dr. H something and he'd say, "Well, why don't you ask the clinic doctor?"

MRS. D   I used to go out of there feeling like what am I supposed to do now?

MR. D   Them damn shots weren't doing her a bit of good, you know? And I even asked Dr. H once and he wouldn't say that the shots weren't doing any good, but, you know, one backs up the other. One doctor's not going to say that the other doctor is a waste of time and money, you know? But I always felt like they just didn't know. They just didn't do what they should have. And I remember this one resident when we were up there. We were sitting there and she was in intensive care and he was a new resident. I guess he was impressed with himself. And he'd come out there and give us all this, "Well, she's got this kind of a virus and we haven't determined what it was, yet, and this and that." At that time I'd never been in the intensive care, you know, so I didn't know what's going on back there. And I thought he was back there, staying with her and really taking care of her. And he was just out there trying to impress us with his knowledge, you know? And I asked him later about the virus and what was it. "Oh, it was this or that or something like that." And all he was, you know, he was just trying to impress us with what he knew. I remember another time when she was back in intensive care. God, I felt so bad because she'd look at us, you know, and she had beautiful blue eyes. And she couldn't talk, and her hands were tied down, Jesus.

DR. BENTON   You mean you felt like she was looking at you and—

MR. D   Yeah, Daddy, do something. Let me tell you what happened near the end: One day we was standing by the elevator. These two doctors come up from the clinic. One of them was Dr. T. He was experienced. The other guy was younger. We asked how Cathy was doing and Dr. T goes, "Well, so so." This other guy says, "Do y'all have any other children?" I knew right then that she wasn't going to make it. And Dr. T kind of hushed him up, you know, and said, "Well, we'll do the best we can."

MRS. D   She was beginning to show a little change and stabilize.

MR. D   They took the trach out because they could leave it in just so long and the esophagus would swell up if they didn't take it. They took it to try to let her breathe on her own. She couldn't do it. They got a little room there where they take the parents, you know, when somebody dies. And I walked in there and I said, "Is she dead?" And they said yes. And I just left (crying).

DR. BENTON   What kinds of things did you do to try to deal with the pain and loss?

MRS. D   There's no comfort anywhere.

MR. D   I don't know, it's just something you have to go through, you know? When I left the hospital I just wanted to kill myself, you know? I was just roaming around and I just wanted to kill myself, but I didn't have enough guts. I went home and, God, I saw her clothes and I tried to hold on to them. I just wanted to be alone. Later on, the father of another little girl called us. They were Belgian. He said there were some more children coming over for operations. So I went back up to the hospital, you know, to help them with what I could. I knew it was going to be hard, but I knew I had to get back up there. And this helped me. She couldn't go up there again, but it helped me because for the next two years, I was going up there. And I started taking Flemish and I was going up there and I could see these other parents that had people with heart defects. And I knew what they were going through because I had been through it. And that helped me an awful lot, and it helped me because I saw that ours weren't the only problems in the world. There's other people that have more problems than I had. You know, their children mean just as much to them. It helped me a lot because I think the time I was up there, I think there was about thirty-five children came. There were three of them died and we brought the parents over to our house. And we knew how to handle them because we had been through it twice. And it really helped them. And I felt better and I think this kind of straightened me out. I still hurt but I knew that it wasn't the end of the world. You really have a choice of what you are going to do. After it happens you either have to go on living or you just die. They say, "God, you sure were brave. You got through it." What's the alternative? You either have to keep on living or you just quit altogether. And I think after a while you realize that it's just a part of life.

DR. BENTON   What about Carl?

MR. D   Well, he was about four when we found out he had MD. He was real healthy but he had abnormal calves, you know, looked real big. I thought he was just muscular, you know? One day when I took him to the doctor, he asked me if we had a family of muscular people. And I said that I didn't think so. People used to always remark what big calf muscles he had. Then one day she took him to the doctor. She came home and told me he had muscular dystrophy.

DR. BENTON   Mrs. D, how did you know?

MRS. D   I had a brother who had MD but we didn't know it was in my family until after we were married. I had a feeling about Carl and, you know, I'd think, "Well, God, with all our problems why should I be looking for another one?" So I never said anything to my husband because it was pointless and I figured if he did have it, we'd know anyway, eventually, so why add to the bad part? You know, why add to the misery? Then I had two more children after him. I guess what happened kind of overshadowed my way of thinking, too. Of course, the last two children were girls and there's no chance of them having it.

DR. BENTON   When did you first know that you might transmit muscular dystrophy?

MRS. D   Oh, I don't know when I really began to actively think about it. I guess I'd been reading a few things here and there. When my brother was diagnosed and he had it, they still didn't say, "Your daughter will be a carrier and your sons will have it." And I'd been married quite a while before they really said, "They will have it." And I was pretty put out with the doctors and I even took it out on my mother for a while and she was real hurt.

Mr. D	Well, I still blame her, in a way.
Mrs. D	She didn't know though, Brian. She knew exactly what they knew.
Mr. D	I asked my wife one time about that and she told me that her mother said that the doctor told her that it's not hereditary.
Mrs. D	You can blame everybody—you can blame my mother, you can blame yourself, you can blame me—
Mr. D	I don't blame you. I don't blame anybody. It's just something that happened, you know? She feels guilty every day about it.
Dr. Benton	Would your first son have had it?
Mr. D	I think now that possibly he did have it. So in a way I'm glad that he did die like he did. Because I saw the way her brother died.
Dr. Benton	And how is Carl now?
Mrs. D	Fine.
Mr. D	Well, he's physically fine, but he can't move, you know? He's immobile.
Mrs. D	He can feed himself and write and do things with his hands. He's just slow.
Mr. D	He's happy with what he can do. The only thing that bothers me now is some of the children like I saw on the muscular dystrophy TV. They know that they're going to die.
Mrs. D	And they talk about it.
Mr. D	And now, Carl, he talks about when he gets out of the wheelchair, you know? When they get a cure and he gets out of the wheelchair, or like he said the other day, "When I grow up—"
Dr. Benton	So Carl is still—
Mr. D	He don't think he's going to die.
Mrs. D	No, they talk at camp about this among themselves.
Mr. D	Yeah, but Carl—let me tell you this personality he has. If it's bad news, he don't want to know about it. You know, just like fighting or—we had one bad experience one time and I tried to talk to him about it

	later and he said, "Let's not talk about that, Daddy." He doesn't want to know about things that are upsetting, you see?
Mrs. D	I really don't think one way or the other about a possible cure. If they find one, fine, I'll be happy. But I'm not going to spend years, you know, really driving myself crazy over it.
Dr. Benton	How old is Carl now?
Mrs. D	Thirteen.
Dr. Benton	What are your hopes and life expectations for Carl?
Mrs. D	Most boys that are in good health live to be about twenty. There's two boys right now in college.
Mr. D	I don't have much hope for him. And if he does go, I hope it's fast and not like her brother where they just—dragged out to the last minute. He weighed about twenty pounds.
Mrs. D	He was sick.
Dr. Benton	Having been through this two times already, do you feel like this will in any way give you a different perspective or possibly more strength in facing it the third time?
Mrs. D	Well, I always felt like this: It may give us—we may have more strength and then again it may be the straw that broke the camel's back.
Mr. D	I don't know. It depends. If he dies fast, you know, it wouldn't be as bad as if it goes slow. If it goes slow, it may be—it just may be too much.
Mrs. D	But they don't go slow. One day they're there and they go to bed, and that's that.
Mr. D	If he dies fast it's going to be a lot easier on us. You know, I mean it'll be just shock and then you can start off from there, you know? But if he goes slow, it's just going to be unbearable. I just don't know if I can go through it again. The funny thing is, you know, I expect any day for Janey to come down with something. After it's happened so many times you just expect that it's going to happen again. When she gets sick or something, I'm going to say—she's going to go to the doctor and they're going to find cancer, you know? I

mean, it seems to be a string of tragedies—just one after the other.

DR. BENTON   You have two daughters.

MR. D   We have two, yes, Cathy and Janey.

DR. BENTON   Do you feel like the difficulties you've had contributed to the way the two of you as parents and adults interact and feel?

MR. D   Definitely. I don't know how our marriage survived, you know? I don't know how many times I just wanted to get up and leave it all. The pressure just gets to you and you don't have any time to be with yourself—I mean for us to be together. We still don't because it's a constant demand with—we have to take care of Carl and get up two or three times a night to roll him over and then there's Cathy. It's just one constant demand. I'm surprised that we've stayed together this long. I know one thing for sure: If we hadn't have come down here we wouldn't have made it. I believe that if I had it to do all over again, I wouldn't have children.

DR. BENTON   Why not?

MR. D   Not because I don't love them. It's just because of the strain and—it's ruined her health, you know?

DR. BENTON   What do you mean when you say that?

MR. D   Well, her arthritis and her depression and even now she doesn't have any goals of any kind, you know? It's hard on me, too.

DR. BENTON   How about you? Do you have any goals?

MR. D   I think I'm starting to get some now. I feel a lot better now. But there's times I just want to get up and leave. It gets to be too much. God, it's just one demand after another. Sometimes I feel like I wish Carl would just die and get it over with, you know? And then I feel guilty. It doesn't bring you closer together. I don't think when a child dies it brings you closer together.

MRS. D   Well, you think you are for a while.

DR. BENTON   And you said that momentarily it does?

MR. D   I think it does because, you know, you feel so bad. But then, you kind of get into your own personal grief and

	you just forget about the other person who's suffering, too. And you just pull away. Like with Mike, I don't think she—you know, I know and she knows that it was my fault as much as the other guy's. I don't think she's ever gotten over that.
MRS. D	No, I don't think that.
DR. BENTON	Did she ever tell you that?
MR. D	No. If there's anybody that wants to help somebody that's lost a child, the best thing is to say nothing, to just be there.
MRS. D	Yeah, that's right, just do that.
MR. D	That's the best thing in the world. The people that just came and sat there and said nothing were the greatest comfort. The ones that tried to, you know, give advice and stuff, well, you want to say, "Well, how the hell do you know?"
MRS. D	Because right then you don't feel like accepting it.
MR. D	It's the emptiness, you know? Just like I wanted to hold her and she wasn't there to hold anymore, you know?
MRS. D	That's the bad—
MR. D	That's the worst part is that emptiness. It's just like your whole insides was taken out. The fact that you'll never see them again—I guess if you believe in religion you will, but—
MRS. D	But you miss that physical contact.
MR. D	I think definitely it would be hard to face death of an adult—I haven't had any experience with an adult, you know, except my father, and I didn't know him too well. But if something happened to my wife, that probably would be just as bad as the children, maybe more so. How can you say?

The Nurse*

It is probably incorrect to say that the demands made of nurses are greater today than ever before. Nevertheless, it is clear that the demands are great and preparation for such responsibility does not come from classwork alone. Chudleigh reports some of her experiences which amplify caregiver feelings and reactions that most nurses will likely experience and deal with in their careers. Recognition of these feelings can be of adjustive value for nurse, staff, and patient.

My first experience with death was in a situation where the physician was not available—he was across town and accessible only by phone. Unfortunately, when I tried to reach him, he was taking a shower. (Technology fails again.)

Bill had come to our facility because he was in severe pain associated with a soft tissue sarcoma of the lower abdominal region. He had received toxic levels of chemotherapy and as a result was sloughing the mucous lining of his internal organs, primarily his bladder and urethra. His wife was also a patient and only the evening before sat together with a nurse talking about the decisions they both needed to make since it seemed apparent the husband would not live much longer, and certainly would not outlive his wife who had a cancer of the thyroid. On this morning the man and wife were having coffee together in the lounge when the man seemed to have a stroke. As I notified the physician and arranged for transferring Bill to the acute care facility, he became comatose. By the time the ambulance arrived, Bill's heart had stopped. The ambulance team instituted resuscitation which was unsuccessful after thirty minutes. During this time I was unable to reach the on-call physician, so I called Bill's attending physician at home. He wasn't much help—his only comment I remember was: This is what makes cancer such a fascinating area of research—the outcomes are so unpredictable. I was rather shocked that he could be so callous at such a traumatic moment. I don't think I ever really trusted that doctor again.

I was pretty upset and it was sometime during all this that I realized that resuscitation is more for the benefit of the living than helpful to the dead or dying patient. The family can say they tried everything but he was too far gone to bring him back, and the act of resuscitation makes the professional staff look efficient. I decided here

*Written by Mary Kathleen Chudleigh, RN.

that it was a sacrilege to perform such violent insults on an individual in his last moments of living. I think the nurse who sat rocking and holding Bill was really in touch with life and was the only real human being in that room that morning. I was the impartial observer, Hawthorne's unpardonable sin personified. I had by far the most difficult job. It was such an earth-shattering experience to realize the actual limitations of medical science and that man is helpless to prevent death. Shaken as I was, and feeling totally inept and useless, I was astounded when the family complimented me on how competently the difficult situation had been handled.

I have lost my faith in cardiopulmonary resuscitation. I doubt very seriously that I would ever perform it for any reason. I've seen too much suffering and mutilation as a result. Even still whether to resuscitate or not presents a conflict. I remember one young girl, a leukemic in remission with an eight-month-old baby. She had an arrest while at home—her father resuscitated her and now she is fine. No one ever discovered a cause for the sudden arrest. I still don't know if I'd been there if I would have performed the resuscitation.

After seeing a person lie in a coma unresponsive for days if not weeks—it is a relief to watch them stop breathing. Yet I have seen major upheavals in research departments when the director ordered that everyone be resuscitated—across the board, no exceptions—coma or no. Fortunately one physician told the director if he wanted to resuscitate, he could do it himself. Where does research end and humanity begin—or does it ever?

A coma helps make death more easily acceptable—sort of a gradual slipping away through sleep—if it's not prolonged. It becomes tragic when prolonged; a useless body that occupies space, but still breathes—comparable to a Mary Shelley monster reject.

The most difficult death to watch was a patient who developed cardiogenic shock and took one week to die. He was awake and terrified the whole time. He knew exactly what was happening and never knew if the next heartbeat would be his last. It was with great relief that the family and professional staff welcomed his death. It is very difficult to accept that the time comes when modern medicine is useless.

Most people I've worked with feel that by the time they've been through all the phases of the disease process in a terminal illness, they are ready to die. Life for them has generally become very complicated: They have incurred tremendous debts; they are beginning to malfunction as independent human entities, and are very dependent for physical protection and well-being on those close to them. Sometimes patients with cancer require an excess of five thousand calories a day to maintain a stable body weight. Do you realize how many steak dinners replete with baked potato, etc. a day that is? Unfortunately, if they did have the food to eat, most patients have neither the energy to fix the food, eat it or digest it.

The most difficult problem to handle in coping with the dying is the ever-present ethical question: Which has priority, to relieve suffering or to prolong life? Both concepts are present in most codes of ethics which influence professional behavior. However, no one seems to know which is most important. Because my experience has been primarily with the dying, I hesitate whenever a measure calls for action that will prolong life which not only I question the validity of, but so does the patient and family.

The unfortunate result of giving priority to relieving suffering is the question of suicide. The idea of having to suffer through a debilitating disease is more than some people can stomach. I'd imagine that suicide is prevalent in early stages of terminal disease when a patient is still independent enough to perform one last conscious purely self-centered act. Many patients have threatened suicide, but, few have actually attempted it. One young girl, a twenty-three-year-old from the South was diagnosed with choriocarcinoma. She was eventually cured and is now disease-free. However, her problems began when her husband was told that the disease was pregnancy related. He had just recently discovered he was sterile, but had not told his wife of it. For the next two years, the couple had quite a few difficulties to overcome and the extensive chemotherapy necessary for the treatment of choriocarcinoma was hardly a welcome experience to them. The marriage finally ended in divorce, but not before the wife had attempted suicide by overdose of narcotics and barbiturates. She was not harmed. But it is a sad indictment of the health care providers that knowing the wife's problems, she had to attempt suicide before psychiatric help was sought.

Another example of threatening suicide was a very personable, intelligent thirty-year-old who had seen many of his friends die from the same disease he had—carcinoma of the testis. When he knew he was no longer responding to chemotherapy as he wished, he used to frequently threaten to overdose himself with narcotics—not grossly, but since he did have lung involvement with his disease—just take a few too many pain pills and induce carbon dioxide narcosis. He almost did, too. During the late stages of his disease, his lungs became so non-functional that even mild doses of narcotics depressed his respirations so that his oxygen supply was curtailed.

I suppose the most bizarre incident I ever encountered was the man who had a recurrence of cancer in his trachea and was being seen daily by the physician to ream out the new growth so that he would not suffocate. As this treatment continued for several weeks, the patient became somewhat confused, quite depressed. One night he was found putting a pocket knife down his laryngectomy. He had (I assume inadvertently) severed several major blood vessels and created a really bloody mess. He died from aspiration pneumonia and sepsis. At the time I was asked to judge whether the attempt was suicide or not—a very difficult decision.

Dealing with the dying on their deathbed is one facet of caring for the dying; the most taxing role for the nurse is in caring for individuals between the time they are first diagnosed and the time they will be really terminal; years may elapse. The nurse's position in caring for the dying is very human. Nurses must care about people if they are to function well in this setting. It is emotionally exhausting. From the patient's point of view, being told that one's life is being cut short is a rather traumatic revelation. Generally, it is the nurse who copes with the long-term effects of the physician's talk with patients when they are told they have a terminal illness. Everyone reacts differently. Young people (late teens, early twenties) tend to be nonresponsive at first to being told they have a terminal illness. However, these persons generally have family who react strongly to the possible demise of the young family member.

One example is a fifteen-year-old Mexican-American female who was diagnosed with acute leukemia. She had virtually no response to being told of the disease—only slight disappointment showed. The sort of reaction one would expect if she had been told she could not go out that evening with her friends. In contrast, the father and mother were very shaken. It wasn't until several months into the treatment (intensive chemotherapy) in a laminar air flow unit with strict sterile isolation that the patient became almost catatonic, a state induced possibly by several problems in family relations and isolation from her friends. Again, it is sad that severe psychological problems cannot be picked up earlier and treated. In this case, it was the nursing staff who provided the psychological support and who designed the necessary care and treatment plans. The physicians were aware of the problems and called in a psychiatrist to evaluate the problem which is exactly what he did. He diagnosed her emotional problem then removed himself from the case with the suggestion he be contacted for another consult if the patient's condition changed.

A similar case where the patient seemed to underreact initially was a twenty-three-year-old auto mechanic with osteogenic sarcoma in his pelvic bone. He was scheduled to undergo an hemipelvectomy. He kept referring to the procedure as a little surgery—even after the rehabilitation team explained to him in detail the ramifications of the surgery: he would no longer be able to work as an auto mechanic which required going underneath cars, and the surgical recovery and rehabilitation period would be extensive, taking the better part of a year, possibly more with a fair chance the sarcoma would recur in several years.

Another reaction of young people that thoroughly exhausts the nursing staff is dependence on their family even in early stages of the disease when they would be able to be quite independent. A typical dependent response is a nineteen-year-old girl who brings her stuffed animals and her own special pillows and blankets from home. Her mother stays with her twenty-four hours a day. The child is very apprehensive and whiney about her treatment, but very seldom assertively demanding. These types of patients and their dependency tactics can easily undermine the morale of the nursing staff on the unit with terminal patients. It is generally the role of the professional nursing personnel to support the ancillary personnel in understanding the bases for these behaviors and teach them to cope with life among the population of cancer patients. Some of these dependency problems might be helped by counseling and either preoperative or early diagnosis teaching on the part of the nurse. But, the nurse is frequently rushed, and does not have time to talk with these patients although she realizes it would be useful or helpful.

Older patients tend to be more protective of themselves, more demanding of health care standards and less trusting of the established medical protocols. Lengthy explanations are given by the physicians who generally go into great detail in explaining the disease process and plans for treatment. At such a time, these patients do not ask very many questions. But shortly after the physician leaves, the nursing staff is bombarded with questions. One woman, Peggy, around thirty-eight, was extremely difficult to handle in a ward situation because of her negative and depressing attitude toward the "cure" she and doctors were striving for. Her attitude was that in spite of all the treatments, the whole situation was futile and she did not mince words when discussing this with the professional staff. Any patients who came into contact with her and her views became very depressed or very angry. This woman was usually in a room with leukemia patients who had relapsed and who were in the terminal phases of the disease. It seems odd that someone as negative as this toward her treatment and therapy would consent freely to having such treatment done at all.

Her family situation did not help much. Her mother was present during most of her treatment and provided a great deal of the primary care. When Peggy was discharged between treatments, she usually spent the time at her mother's. Her husband was contemplating divorce. Apparently they had had a marriage in which each person was very individual and independent. When the wife became very dependent due to her disease, the husband considered it more a play for sympathy even though she remained independent longer than most leukemia patients. Her disease really cramped his social style. Peggy's two grown children in their early twenties visited her at the hospital only twice in the course of treatment (multiple hospital admissions) in the year she was ill. As she was dying, her whole family was in attendance and she dismissed them all—sent them home because she did not want them to see her die. Her mother insisted on staying and Peggy agreed to let her. The husband and children left to resume their home lives. In this case, Peggy's attitude changed from a resentful protective independent function to a totally dependent childlike inability to make any decision even so simple as to what time she wanted her daily bath. Contributing to this was the fact that she was paralyzed below the waist due to leukemic infiltration of her lower spine.

Dependency in the sick role is a devastating behavior to watch develop. Hospitalization itself demands increased dependency. Just being flat in bed for several days will weaken a person. Add to this several IV lines to manipulate, lack of privacy in a two- to four-bed ward with only one bathroom, either no family to help or very poor staffing of nursing personnel, and the patient is then discouraged from attempting so simple a task as walking to the bathroom alone.

To further compound the dependency problems, patients are not allowed to make independent judgments on their own regarding their health care. Physicians have a tendency to dictate treatment plans and although they may forward alternative plans, they generally emphasize and are prejudiced toward the original plan presented. If the patient chooses an alternative plan, the physician will frequently leave the case and have someone else take over. Some physicians consider it a personal affront for a patient to select an alternative plan which may include refusing treatment entirely. There was a case with a twenty-one-year-old with leukemia who relapsed and was being considered for a bone-marrow transplant. The girl would have preferred to be left alone and allowed to die in peace at home. This was totally unacceptable to her family. They insisted she return to the research center for treatment. The only treatment left was the bone-marrow transplant. The physicians wasted no time in engaging the parents influence to talk the girl into a transplant procedure. Even though the patient and family were aware of the deleterious effects of the procedure, it was not until the effects were exhibited that the family suddenly was concerned about what all the medical terminology really meant—irreparable bone-marrow suppression, graft versus host disease. I generally do not watch horror shows, but I certainly hope I never encounter as macabre a circus act as this young girl experiences: toxic levels of potent chemotherapy, total body irradiation, allergic reactions to blood products/antifungal agents where steroids are used sparingly if at all, strict sterile isolation where human contact is virtually forbidden and regular good old food is boiled into an oblivion of sterility only to lead to brain damage, coma, and mercifully, death.

How does a nurse cope with death on a daily basis? One becomes accustomed to it, indifferent, peeved with the family who refuses to recognize impending death, astounded at the highly emotional outbreaks of family members, amazed at the varying cultural responses to death. Each nurse reacts differently, but generally defense mechanisms are rampant: Intellectualization, rationalization, repression, anger, hostility, displacement, depression, futility, exasperation, relief, suffering, exhaustion (mental and physical), to mention a few. Dealing with death is a rewarding, gratifying experience. But I suppose most nurses have high nurturance needs and this provides a ready-made outlet for it.

Death is a relief for the nursing staff as well as the family. August Kasper in *The Doctor and Death* talks of caring for others by physicians as a vicarious dependency—I suspect the same is true of nurses. Sometimes death is a routine activity. Two nurses on their way for coffee suddenly remember they have a body to prepare for the morgue and so prepare the body keeping up the giggly, gossipy conversation of a coffee klatch.

The act of dying in a long-term disease process where there is severe pain, agony, and suffering serves as a merciful act to those who must live with the suffering person. One older patient, Ola, aged sixty-two with grown daughters all married and with young children, swore she would never return for further treatment if she relapsed. However, when she did, her family insisted she return for treatment even though it would be purely research, that she not give up hope so easily.

When given the Phase I research drug within twenty-four hours after hospital admission, Ola went into shock. The physician was on the floor when it happened so she was stabilized—except she remained comatose and it was necessary to maintain her blood pressure with potent vasopressors. Ola never regained consciousness and it took her two weeks to die. Her family was with her twenty-four hours a day—all members all the time including one daughter who was pregnant and had a history of difficult pregnancies. During this two-week period, the patient breathed two to four times a minute; she would groan every few hours which was the signal to give her high doses of morphine intravenously. For two weeks the professional staff was sure that her next breath would be her last. After the first few days without response, the physician gradually withdrew the vasopressors without any effect. It was a perverse form of torture to watch this woman slowly quit breathing. And a great relief when she finally died. Is it any wonder people avoid deathbed scenes when possible? It was of some comfort to know that the physician and nursing staff had enough respect for the temporary condition of human life not to attempt resuscitation.

There are similar cases when resuscitation was attempted and, if successful, served no purpose other than prolonging the agony before the final death pronouncement. Ola was a case in which the family regretted pressuring their mother into further treatment. Many times the disease progresses in a like manner, but the closer family refuses to accept the impending death. Such was the case of a young college professor who had both leukemia and lymphoma. His leukemia was cured by a successful bone-marrow transplant from an identical twin. However, the lymphoma did not respond to the transplant. He developed pericarditis, pleural effusion, malnutrition, and congestive heart failure. Further attempts with chemotherapy to treat the lymphoma totally wiped out his bone marrow. A second bone-marrow transplant was attempted but did not take. It was at this point that his wife flew to Mexico to get Laetrile for him but he was unable to take it because the injections would be too risky, possibly causing bleeding and infection. To the professional staff, treatment at this point was strictly supportive. His wife insisted he wasn't ready to die yet. She approved one more course of chemotherapy which was given. By this time the husband was receiving continuous feedings through a tube he would yank out if he wasn't tied down or someone wasn't there to restrain him. He was on a respirator and receiving vasopressors to maintain his blood pressure. It was at this point in his disease that the director of one of the research programs announced on local television that he had the cure not only for lymphoma but several other types of cancer, but the government wouldn't allow him to use the necessary drugs. When this patient's wife confronted the director with this, knowing that her husband would not live, the director still maintained he could cure him if he were allowed to use the drugs. After several more days without change and no further treatment, the patient died, in spite of all the life-support systems. His wife was shocked, astounded, totally unable to grasp the reality of the situation which had been developing for months. The patient died in the middle of the night. Fortunately one of the staff nurses who had a good rapport with the wife was on duty and sat talking with the family members. Later when she was asked about the wife's reaction she said: "It was unbelievable. I don't think she ever did comprehend that he'd been dying for the past year." The day he died—she was planning to take him out to the park. (Respirator and all?)

Treatment in a research center makes handling the emotional aspects of the disease easier for the staff, but much more complex to cope with for the family and patients. By the time patients reach the research facility, they have a good idea of why they are there. It is a great relief to the nursing staff for a patient to know his or her diagnosis; it is probably a relief to the patient also. It prevents many of the feelings of being isolated, not being told the truth, and being treated as a grotesque side show. But on the other hand, with all the research and the physicians always coming up with a promising research program to cure God only knows what else—it makes it difficult for the patient and the family to accept death. If only the patient can be kept alive long enough, any minute they'll discover the ultimate cure. The research facility induces the family to believe this, and this is the reason such extreme measures are considered in resuscitation and coma. To a certain extent research centers prey on the dying person's reaction to the idea of death.

Nursing provides continuous twenty-four-hour-a-day monitoring of the institutionalized patient. The duties of a nurse are intrusive; there is no way to avoid personal contact of this sort without emotional involvement. The act of bathing patients, feeding them or just seeing that they are eating enough, changing the bed when it's dirty, monitoring equipment to make sure it's functioning, making sure intake and output are adequate and balanced, just these physical duties bring the nurse and patient into a close interpersonal relationship. Because of this relationship, the nurse is usually the one to explain what the physician really says: the prognosis is poor with a six-month life expectancy. It is the nurse who explains how the patient is supposed to live without an arm or leg or with a stoma of some kind. If the doctor goes ahead with surgery, what it really will entail—how long the patient will be laid off (if he or she will ever be able to return to work at all.)

People with cancer have such problems: the forty-two-year-old lady with two teenagers who refused a total pelvic exenteration for metastatic carcinoma of the cervix. She couldn't leave her children alone during the time necessary for the surgery and recuperation period but returned six months later for the surgery when her pelvis had become so necrotic and she felt so "unclean." She was told there is nothing anyone has to offer except palliation and supportive care until she dies—it must be a frightening experience.

What are the long-term reactions of the business executive with melanoma which was surgically removed, but not before it had metastasized to the axillary lymph nodes. After chemotherapy with no response and an axillary lymph node dissection, he finds it impossible to believe that someone as healthy as he is, with his active social life and no real physical problems will probably be dead in five years. What of the reactions of this man's wife when the doctor tells her she can believe what she likes but she's a fool if she doesn't listen to reason?

How do you manage the independent but feisty old bachelor who lives thirty miles from the nearest civilized outpost, cured of his cancer by surgery and radiotherapy, who always finds an excuse to return for his check-up months before he is due just to frustrate the nursing staff—performing outrageously and abominably (exposing himself to little old ladies) just to get attention.

Or the man whose wife just died that is diagnosed with a slow-growing tumor—untreatable. But he can probably live several years. His family does not want him, he has no place he really wants to go. So he dies in a matter of a few weeks. A blessing for the medical social worker involved.

How can nurses be indifferent, objective toward the man who refused to allow his wife to have a radical mastectomy, but finally decides she may undergo the surgery when she develops lung metastasis, pericarditis, congestive heart failure, and the only open avenue of treatment is palliative?

What is the nurse's responsibility when someone else's behavior severely conflicts with her or his own value system? The nurse is frequently confronted with the patient who wants to go home and die peacefully from cancer when it could be easily cured with surgery; or the patient who would rather die than let a licensed physician touch him—quack, witch doctor, faith healer—all are preferable to the scientifically based practitioner. Yet the physician is the only one who can offer a real cure.

Each nurse reacts differently in each case and it is a relief to both the patient and the nurse to have a variety of relationships for the patient to respond to. One nurse on staff is frequently used as scapegoat—generally the one the patient has little regard for. Then there is the nurse who is the gossip that collects all the tidbits of information which patients tend to drop. Then the care provider appears and finally the counselor who is someone both the family and patient relate to well. These roles are generally not static and are passed among the nursing staff. My least favorite is scapegoat. However, even this role can be effective in the management of a unit and effective management is a goal in an institutional setting. I am amused when I remember the time I was elected to confront a sixty-four-year-old man who was rather vulgarly propositioning not only the staff but the female patients most of whom were senile, helpless women from some of the more backward, protected areas of the South. I simply told the man I did not appreciate his behavior at all and asked him to please refrain from such behavior in the future. First he was kind of shocked; then he became angry especially when I refused to listen to his side of the story. Afterward though, he made it a point to bring me a token gift every time he came in. I never had any further problem with the unsolicited proposition either.

On the other hand, there was a patient who was solving the problems of another patient's itinerant alcoholic husband. I told this man that I appreciated his thoughtfulness and helpfulness but I felt the social worker had better handle the situation since the husband was from out of town and AA was involved. That man never forgave me: he was really upset. Of course he is dead now, as are most of these people.

One man was in a work-up to determine the extent of his newly diagnosed cancer. One night he pulled a knife on a nurse when she was making rounds. "I'll kill you if you don't let me out of here now— I've been in prison for killing before so just let me out." He was happily escorted out—but he was never allowed to return. I knew work-ups were frustrating but I really never suspected frustration like this.

Or what about the man, a newly diagnosed acute leukemic who had been given extensive instructions and general information on living in the sterile environments—all the dos and don'ts and how tos. After he'd been in about four hours, he pipes up with "This reminds me of the time I was in solitary confinement."

I was the sweet, rather unsuspecting child who was not even

allowed to go out by myself for fear I'd be kidnapped. How I ever ended up in situations like these is beyond my comprehension. It is certainly nothing along the lines of my once youthful aspirations.

Some of the most memorable patients are those who had extensive mutilative surgery.

One man I particularly like—but of course you simply don't develop close friendly relationships with these kinds of patients unless you can't avoid it. This man had his mandible removed, was cured of cancer, but did look particularly grotesque without a chin. In the next year, he had plastic reconstruction and the finished product looked remarkably normal. But he had a common-law wife who didn't stay around long enough to be of much help to him. He never really talked about his problems to the nurses but I gathered from the social worker things were pretty nasty in his home town.

One unfortunate man had massive facial surgery—one-half of his maxilla removed, right septum exposed, and right orbital exenteration. I never decided whether this man was senile or whether he was just a stubborn, headstrong old cuss who knew everything anyway.

He had had several facial prostheses made, but wouldn't wear any of them because they just didn't fit right. So he walked around with his deformed features exposed, scaring people to death. The man was an embarrassment to his family. They just couldn't cope with this sort of antisocial behavior. But then, as a nursing staff, I don't think we fared much better. I often wonder what really happened to the man. He wasn't a happy man, but he was independent. The problem with the prosthetic devices was that they were too complicated to apply, and took way too much time. It really took two people to apply them correctly. I still remember the maxillofacial specialist calling me into the office to learn how to apply the prosthesis so that the man could get used to wearing the thing ten minutes at a time. His real concern however was that the nursing staff see that his prosthesis didn't get "lost." I think he finally gave up after four prostheses disappeared in a matter of days, if not hours, after they were completed. On the other hand, I knew several women who had had extensive facial surgery who had no difficulty applying their prostheses, but they were both very active socially in their own communities. At least they could resume their activities at home until plastic reconstruction could be completed.

America's health-care system provides an interesting backdrop for the foreground of melodrama exhibited in health-care institutions. Is it any wonder that medicine is a hot subject for the daytime soaps? The problems of patients are only one facet of the whole network of relationships. Things would be much simpler in the long run if it were only the patients who had problems. Unfortunately, the people who make the institution function have equally traumatic sets of problems to work with and within that setting they solve all their problems as best they can. Things generally are not in reality as any one individual perceives them. Many a nurse, doctor, patient, administrator, etc. ad infinitum goes home frustrated, convinced that the whole system exists just to confound his or her life as a personal vendetta. Cancer nursing wouldn't be a bad profession if there only weren't all the people around to screw up the works. It is exhausting. If physicians and nurses could not only define their respective roles, but also come to agreement on who is to scratch whose back in delivering health care; if administrators and owners could be more oriented to health-care delivery rather than money making; if there weren't so many shysters trying to figure out new ways to screw the government out of their money—if there weren't any cancer.

Scientifically oriented medicine has always had difficulty in dealing with the dying patient. People die in spite of every convenience and miracle modern medicine has to offer. The tremendous problem of medical research is that for every cure that is found, several "new" diseases develop to take the place of the one disease that has been cured. There seems to be no way even to begin to attack all the incurable chronic illnesses which now devastate the population. The germ theory provided a pasture for growth in the area of communicable-disease control and surgical techniques. But no similar theory seems evident for dealing with the chronic and terminal illnesses which are a socioeconomic anathema. Try as they might—and the scientists have tried hard—human contact, human caring, humanity in medicine will not be replaced.

REFERENCES

Illich, I. *Medical Nemesis: The Expropriation of Health.* New York: Pantheon Books, 1976, pp. 174–200.

Kasper, A. M. "The Doctor and Death," in Samuel Gorovitz et al., eds., *Moral Problems in Medicine.* Englewood Cliffs, New Jersey: Prentice-Hall, 1976, p. 70.

Mothersill, M. "Death," in James Rachel, ed., *Moral Problems: A Collection of Philosophical Essays.* New York: Harper & Row, 1971, p. 378.

Life and Death Decisions on a Pediatric Cancer Ward: The Doctor*

Dr. Jan van Eys shares his views and experiences on issues that are faced by a caregiver-administrator. Many features of his professional role are unique and foster a reflective concern for the choices which are made in treatment procedures.

His charge is a sensitive one: it deals with children; with death; with the pursuit of life; with legal, philosophical, and medical systems; and it deals with persons and personalities.

Cancer at the pediatric age is not an uncommon disease. Until recently, cancer was the most common cause of death from disease in childhood after the immediate neonatal period. This is no longer so, because great inroads have been made in the treatment of childhood cancer. The annual new cases in the United States can be expected to number around 6,500. The annual death rate will be around 3,000. This implies a very prolonged survival in children with cancer. Therefore, a child with cancer is a child who might die, but who also might live. That is the reality against which any decision regarding life prolongation must be made. In fact, since the indefinite survival rate exceeds 50 percent, all children should be initially approached as children who will live, rather than children who will die. This means that the death of a child is conceptually a failure. But unless that is acknowledged, the child will not develop normally during the period of his or her chronic illness. Such delay in development cannot be overcome. Therefore, a biological cure might be achieved, but a truly cured child, a child on par in development with peers and potential, will not have resulted (van Eys, 1977a). Such considerations put life-and-death decisions immediately in perspective. It is so much easier to expect a child to die and accept the cure as a reward than to expect the child to live and then to accept the death as failure. The latter stance is essential for the child, but it puts the onus of accepting death, when it has become inevitable, on the shoulder of the care giver.

The decision that a child is ready to die rests of course entirely with the child. Herein lies a serious conflict. We are apt to view the

*Written by Jan van Eys, Ph.D., M.D. Pediatrician and Professor of Pediatrics and Head of the Department, The University of Texas System Cancer Center, M.D. Anderson Hospital and Tumor Institute, Houston, Texas 77030.

child as totally dependent, as a ward that must be protected at all cost against the scourge of cancer. We adults, in fact, impose our concept of quality of life on the child because the child is not truly perceived as a person, an individual separate from us. The child is seen as human, and requires all our protection, but personhood is granted very slowly indeed (van Eys, 1977b). Only when we see a child as a person can we allow the child to die with all the appropriate grief, without a sense of true failure. And that child must be accepted as a person with cancer. The cancer cannot be considered independent from the child. The child would not be the same person if he or she had not experienced the cancer. The cancer is that child's reality. If we accept the child's individuality, then the cancer is an unremovable and integral part of that person.

When medical care cannot further avert physical deterioration, and the child-person perceives this, then the child is dying. No questions arise, no true decision making needs to be done. Medical science cannot help, therefore extreme measures become poor medicine. A physician should be severely censored if he or she used an antibiotic for heart failure. It is ineffective, costly, and might have detrimental side effects. By the same token, resuscitation might make a failing heart keep going for a while, but it is bad medicine if the basic cancer is untreatable. It is ineffective, costly, and does have side effects. There is no benefit. Therefore we do very few resuscitations on our ward, because we try not to apply erroneous medical procedures (van Eys, 1977b). A patient on a respirator might have a heartbeat for a prolonged period of time without any cerebral function. The dilemma of discontinuing a respirator is not often encountered if the respirator is used only in medically justified circumstances.

This point is not often thought through, even by experienced medical personnel. An example might be given to illustrate this. This case comes from a general pediatric service so that death was not quite as familiar as it is on the cancer ward. The case was a six-year-old boy who had undergone a tonsillectomy elsewhere. The hospital where he was treated was understaffed, and the only registered nurse on duty had the signs and symptoms of a heart attack. The child was largely unattended, so that intravenous fluids were inappropriately administered, resulting in a grand mal convulsion. He aspirated and asphyxiated. He was resuscitated and transferred on a respirator to the intensive care unit of a tertiary hospital. There he was found to have electrolyte imbalance which could be corrected. But he had no ability to breathe on his own. An EGG was isoelectric (flat). While there was no difficulty with declaring a brain death if sequential EEG tracings were flat, there was a period of time for which support had to be continued. One of the intensive care nurses asked whether he should be resuscitated if his heart were to fail. An intensive care unit is used to allow prompt response to cardiorespiratory failure, so the question may seem natural. But after only a very short discussion the nurses realized that he already had been resuscitated once. If his heart were to fail now, repeated resuscitation would be repeating a medical measure that already was proved ineffective. Resuscitation attempts would be inappropriate. Interestingly, no member of the medical and nursing team had any qualms about discontinuing the respirator. The ultimate cause of brain death only invoked anger, but little if any guilt, so that the decision could be made dispassionately.

The decision whether to apply the final measure, an attempt at resuscitation is rarely truely difficult. The measure is the availability of realistic therapy for the underlying disease. Only on occasion are resuscitation measures instituted because the question of potentially definitive therapy could not be answered in the short time available to make the resuscitation decision. Some guidelines are therefore often helpful. That does not mean that a checklist or an absolute manual for resuscitation decisions should exist, but rather that specific concepts must be clear. The first understanding is that the physician should not usually make that decision. Rather it is up to patient and family. If you do not know the patient, you don't come in charging like a defender of life. Resuscitation teams that impersonally administer medicine's last gesture have no place in a cancer hospital, or in any institution treating chronic disease. This ultimate decision must be made against a background of medical advice, mutual trust, and patient's and family's desires. It is rare that death comes unexpectedly, even to the patient. A second understanding is implied in the first. Physicians only advise, they never coerce a patient. That is even true when the patients and parents say: "Do what you think best." The physician should always involve the patient as the decision maker. It is a mistake to assume that patients are requesting resuscitation when they ask that everything should be done. They simply want the doctor to try everything that might be effective. The decision as to the effectiveness of a particular treatment such as resuscitation is the prerogative of the physician. He or she has that knowledge. The physician contributes facts to a dialogue with patients just as patients contribute facts and insight relevant to their reasoning that only they can give. A last concept in pediatrics is that the child should not be viewed as the adult fantasizes the child to be. Our concepts of life and death are not much more advanced than those of children. Therefore, we should not load our uncertainties on their shoulders (van Eys, 1975).

Even if this line of reasoning will make it possible to deal with the final moments of life in a sensitive way, that does not mean that the decisions over life-and-death matters become less difficult. Prolongation of life can occur at other times than cardiorespiratory arrest. First of all, the question in cancer care of whether extreme measures against the cancer are justified comes up frequently. While many children are able to continue living indefinitely, death still occurs often. The initial therapy is easy. Many children respond favorably. But when therapy fails repeatedly, less and less effective drugs are available, until at last only Phase II drugs can be offered in therapy. Such drugs are known to be effective sometimes in animal tests. Toxicity in humans is known. But effectiveness is only a possibility; these drugs are not known to affect cancer in human beings significantly. The motives of all persons involved must be kept clearly in mind. Even though the patient may be very sick and very likely irretrievably overcome by cancer, as long as the patient has a theoretically realistic hope, that patient is not dying. What degree of hope is realistic and should be supported is only for the patient to decide. There is an almost infinite distinction between false hope and a last glimmer of real hope. As long as the patient and the parents understand that a new drug may not be effective at all, but might be beneficial, then it is up to the parents to decide whether the prolongation of life is worth risking the possibility of increased physical suffering.

Even though facts will never in themselves sway the decision, clearly facts are required. The main source of facts is the physician. The physician can easily influence the outcome of the final decision. Since such drugs are experimental, it is essential for the progress of medicine that experience be gained. Since only a few physicians are allowed clinical trials, it is essential to the physicians' careers that experience with these drugs be gained rapidly and in a scientifically sound manner. Some patients are ideal candidates to meet the latter requirement. Therefore, the physician who has to offer the drug as a potential therapy is not without bias. Most of the time there is little question or difficulty. The parents keep pushing to try something and the drugs are offered even reluctantly by the physician. However, problems can arise. As an example, a five-year-old child was admitted with a lymphoma. Chemotherapy programs were always somewhat effective. The disease regressed but never disappeared and regimen after regimen was tried. The hospitalization extended into months. The mother and the child were always cooperative, always inquired about the next possible therapy with apparent expectation. Finally a Phase II drug had the usual marginal success. It happened to be an oral drug so that it was technically feasible and convenient for the child to go home. This was offered to the parents and they eagerly planned their departure from the ward. However, the day before leaving the mother asked if we were not angry at their leaving. Clearly something was misinterpreted in the communication. We did not hear the family and the family misinterpreted or maybe overinterpreted our role.

Even if the physician is very clear about his or her role in the process of extreme and experimental therapy, there still remains a significant problem. When all participants, physicians, nurses, parents, and patients, decline extraordinary attempts at treating the cancer, there still remains the question of what care is required to meet the demands of comfort. A child who by choice is not being treated any longer for cancer is dying. That is, it is known what the ultimate cause of death will be, and that death is in the foreseeable future. Dying is a state to be perceived by all participants. We cannot declare that another person is dying. We might be able to say that we would be dying, were we to find ourselves in those circumstances, but that remains a personal view of life. Many of our perceptions concerning death and dying grew from the inability of care givers to accept the dying of a patient. But the efforts initiated by Kübler-Ross (1969) have made the pendulum swing the other way. We insist that the patient is dying before the patient actually perceives that reality. That we are talking about children makes no difference whatsoever. It only complicates communication and often thwarts empathy.

There are times when the patient acknowledges dying and the staff recognizes that reality. Then the most difficult set of decisions comes up. What kind of life does the patient desire. What is the quality that makes life optimal. There is no crisis anymore. The patient acknowledges the inevitability of the event of death. But the dying, the knowingly living toward death, can be affected by our medical ministrations. Not infrequently parents and patient want to stay in the hospital for terminal care. Therefore, the first decision is whether our limited resources are best utilized by allowing prolonged dying in the hospital. That is often translated into a question whether the patient is not better served by dying at home. But again, the patient does not think so; otherwise the question would never have been asked. Physicians only serve. Therefore, while death at home can be considered, the physician's judgment that it is desirable cannot be used as an excuse for removing the patient from the ward. Resources are limited, and the economic consequences of terminal care are rarely understood by parents when such a decision is made. But one cannot abandon a terminally ill patient. One can help patients view the question of terminal care in full perspective. If after that, the patient and parents ask to stay in the hospital, that is a responsibility the hospital assumed when first care was given. Death was known to be a possible outcome right from the beginning.

Granted then that terminal care be given, what constitutes reasonable rather than extraordinary care? The line where unnecessary care stops and benign neglect (i.e., passive euthanasia) begins is very fine indeed. It would be easy if the distinction could be left totally to the patient. Care would be solely defined as the patient's comfort. But first of all, how does one communicate about comfort with a toddler. Secondly, what are the consequences of the actions of the physician. Even the use of painkilling medication is not without complications. Much analgesia interferes with consciousness. Not infrequently a child wants to stay awake. Pain is subjective. Perceived pain is not always suffered pain. Should one give pain medication "as needed" on request of the child or parent? Much of the time we listen more to the parent than the child, because we speak the parent's language. But the child is the patient.

Analgesia does not alter the course of the physical disease. But most patients with cancer do not die of the disease directly. Rather, they die of infection, bleeding, or malnutrition. Suppose a cancer becomes untreatable, and that fact is acknowledged by the patient. The decision is made to treat for comfort as a goal. Suddenly the child begins to bleed overtly from nose or mouth. The platelet count is very low and platelet transfusions can stop the bleeding; this will clearly prolong life because the bleeding is severe enough to result in death quickly if left unchecked. Should you administer platelets? It is extremely uncomfortable to be bleeding overtly. Even if the patient does not suffer physically, an actively bleeding patient cannot have an undisturbed communication with loved ones. The dying is made uncomfortable because human interaction is seriously disrupted. We usually accept that as an overwhelming cause of discomfort and give platelets in such circumstances. But patient, parent, and doctor often realize that we do not just comfort, we also choose the mode of demise, since we declare bleeding as an undesirable death.

Blocking human interaction, where it could be maintained through a painless medical intervention, i.e., giving platelets, is intuitively considered very poor care. Therefore, the decision to stop bleeding rarely causes controversy on the ward. But consider the patient who becomes septic: a bloodstream infection sets in. The child is symptomatically uncomfortable from fever, general malaise, and muscle ache. This could possibly be averted by antibiotic therapy. Antibiotics often do not work because the patient is in such a poor physical state that necessary natural resistance is insufficient to combat the bloodstream invasion by bacteria. Nevertheless, the antibiotics might be effective and in that case they significantly prolong life. While the issue may be said to be one of discomfort, that is not a reality. Furthermore, the patient or parents rarely can select antibiotic therapy in the same way that they are knowledgeable about blood-component replacement therapy. Parents and children learn fast on a cancer ward. But the details of infection-specific antimicrobial therapy are not usually discussed. Therefore, this is an area where the need for judgment falls heavily on the physician. It is very rare that the patient specifically requests the physician not to treat the infection, though it does happen and the physician should always listen. But if the only request is that the doctor not allow the patient to be uncomfortable, the issue becomes one of passive euthanasia—the making of a unilateral life-or-death decision. Most physicians make that decision in a negative way. We select which mode of death we do not like (e.g., bleeding), but we have no judgment concerning which way of dying we would actively seek for the patient. Most physicians actively decide to give antibiotics. After all, the giving of antibiotics is a trivial intervention in relation to the total disease process. Physical suffering is not significantly enhanced, and physical pain and discomfort may be significantly diminished. Fever may decrease, malaise may disappear. But the physician must remain clear about the process of decision making here. No end of rationalization can avoid the spectre of passive euthanasia. There is no clear-cut positive issue as is present in overt bleeding. Pneumonia used to be called the old man's friend in days before effective antibiotics. Why then do we not call sepsis the friend of the child with cancer. The answer should be realized and accepted.

The issues so far are rarely controversial in practice, even though they should be discussed at length among the care givers. But the third mode of demise of the cancer patient raises a difficult issue. Many patients now die of malnutrition (van Eys, 1977c). This is a consequence of the heavy metabolic demand of the cancer, compounded by malabsorption and anorexia, even food aversion. If oral feeding were the only modality available there would be no issue. What you cannot change should be accepted. But now intravenous hyperalimentation has become a realistic mode of treatment. That is beyond single standard feeding. To get enough calories into the patient without excessive volume, a hypertonic solution has to be infused in a large vein. This requires insertion of an infusion line close to the veins into the heart, with serious infection danger. There is a necessity of very frequent monitoring of blood chemistry values. Now fat emulsions are becoming more easily available and nutrition can often be given in near adequate amounts in a peripheral vein. In either case, however, close biochemical monitoring is essential, and some extra procedures are performed for the patient that are not strictly necessary except for the intravenous hyperalimentation. There is no doubt that hyperalimentation will keep the patient alive longer. The patient feels no real hunger, so the feeding does not usually alleviate a real discomfort. The method of feeding is "unnatural," it is a true medical intervention. But feeding is close to our basic instincts. If the question is put: "Should the patient be allowed to starve to death?" the answer is: "No, of course not." If the question is asked: "This patient cannot eat nor does he desire to eat any more. Should we keep him alive by artificial feeding?" The answer is likely to be: "No, that is clearly in the realm of extraordinary measures." Few physicians have consistently reasoned an ethical stance on this dilemma to date. As more attention is paid to nutrition, hyperalimentation will be used at times when cures are clearly still possible. In that case, refusing to use hyperalimentation for the terminally ill is going to be even more difficult. Clearly the patient must understand a great deal of information to make decisions concerning nutrition.

The case has been made that life-and-death decisions do occur regularly on a pediatric cancer ward. However, the decisions are not made in a crisis atmosphere during the terminal event. They are made earlier. The decisions are no less difficult then, because one must be aware of the implications of all of one's actions. Each time a decision is made in a given case, few irrevocable principles can be used. In a sense, the illusion is created that a "situation ethics" (Fletcher,1966) is at work. To a degree that is indeed true. But fundamental principles are used for guidance, because in the patient-physician encounter, both have active roles. Even though the physician only advises, that does not imply that all advice is exclusively on the specific basis of ir-refutable facts; often opinions are requested by the patient. And even if only facts are communicated, the way in which they are com-municated will reflect the feelings, principles, and concepts by which the physician lives. The patient-physician encounter has to be dealt with according to the situation, but the physician must enter that situation voluntarily and with an idea of what the basis of his or her de-cision making is. To be an oncologist in the first place was a positive decision. The oncologist has had some real struggles with the concepts of mortality, dying, quality of life, appropriate death, and their metaphysical implications (van Eys, 1977d). Fletcher states that love is the only measure (1966). Oncologists must know what love is to them.

Not every patient or family approaches death and dying mentally healthy. But most families cope somehow, and children tolerate the stress of the crisis of dying often better than adults. Therefore, it is imperative that the care givers also are prepared for the stresses of the repeated crisis of confronting death in children who truly deserved a better fate in our eyes. One should be at ease with not knowing why, so that the interaction of child-parent-physician becomes a dialogue of equal persons.

REFERENCES

Fletcher, J. *Situation Ethics*.Philadelphia: The Westminster Press, 1966.

Kübler-Ross, E. *On Death and Dying*. New York: Macmillan Co., 1969.

van Eys, J. "The Dying Child." *Cancer Bulletin*, 26 (1975), 105–106.

———. "Perspective of a Pediatrician," in D. G. McCarthy, ed., *Responsible Stewardship of Human Life*. St. Louis: The Catholic Hospital Association, 1976, pp. 3–5.

———. "What Do We Mean by 'The Truly Cured Child'?," in J. van Eys, ed., *The Truly Cured Child*. Baltimore: University Park Press, 1977(a), pp. 81–98.

———. "Caring for the Child Who Might Die," in D. E. Barton, ed., *Care for the Dying*. Baltimore: Williams and Wilkins, 1977 (b), in press.

———. "Nutritional Therapy in Children with Malignancies: Rationale, Promises and Problems." *Cancer Research*, 1977 (c), in press.

———. "Being an Oncologist." *Cancer Bulletin*, 1977 (d), in press.

Warriors

There are relatively few occupations whose practitioners capitalize upon death: soldiers, executioners, secret agents, "hit men," and members of torture squads.

Some have legal sanction or popular sanction, and some temporarily, may have one, both, or neither.

In the relatively small and therefore perhaps biased sample of persons I interviewed who had participated in this area of behavior, the principal responses were: "It was a job," "I did what I was told even if I didn't especially like it. I felt it was my job," "Even if what I was doing was 'bad,' those I did it to were worse," and "If you're being shot at you don't have time to be analytical and philosophical."

We are reminded of the Milgram studies on patterns of obedience to authority, in which it was learned that participants tended to follow instructions even if they felt their action brought pain to an experimental subject. The request, or directive, to kill evokes a spectrum of responses from "no emotion" to "incapacitating guilt." The testimony of the "warriors" illustrates the impact war deaths have on survivors. Personality factors influence postwar adjustments to life.

Soldiering is the only occupation where one primary objective is to inflict death or destruction upon the adversary. Other related occupations are guards and police. Police work, however, is different in important ways. Police are generally enforcers of the prevailing law and social structure and although dealing with or inflicting death comes under the purview of police work, it's not an objective as in soldiering. Soldiering may be viewed as a continuum: at one end are people that are conscripted and at the other people that choose soldiering as a career. Some do battle as mercenaries and some as patriots. The two soldiers interviewed reflect divergent reactions of substantial interest.

THE HUMANIST WARRIOR

DR. BENTON	Tell me briefly about your youth.
RESPONDENT	I grew up in a middle-sized southern town. My family was middle class.
DR. BENTON	Was your father employed? What was his occupation?
RESPONDENT	Well, he worked for XYZ Corporation in Baytown and he was canned. All the employees were.
DR. BENTON	And your mother's not employed?
RESPONDENT	No, she never was.
DR. BENTON	And how many children are in your family?
RESPONDENT	My twin sister and an older brother. In high school I was popular. I was class president, most handsome, and all this bullshit, you know? Also I ran track. I was

on the Allstate Track Team. I played football. I made the grades and that's about it. I finished high school and then I went to the services—the Navy.

DR. BENTON   You joined? How old were you when you joined?

RESPONDENT   I was eighteen years old when I joined the Navy.

DR. BENTON   Why did you join?

RESPONDENT   Everyone else had left so why shouldn't I? I didn't really care for college that much. I didn't want to start that stuff so . . . I wanted something different.

DR. BENTON   Why did you decide on the Navy?

RESPONDENT   Well, I had a good friend who had joined the Navy a year before me and he became a corpsman. So I joined the service and then went to corps school and then I was on a ship for about nine months—kind of working out as an apprentice in the corpsman field. I learned how to suture—minor surgery, more or less, give the injections. It was much of a challenge, is what it was. Then I went to school. I was an apprentice there for about nine months. I was stationed at a naval hospital. A lot of the casualties were coming back from Vietnam and a lot of them were orthopedic casualties.

DR. BENTON   Were you ready to go to Vietnam?

RESPONDENT   Yeah, really. Of course I was tired of that day-in-and-day-out situation as far as the hospital, you know?

DR. BENTON   Tell me about your first casualty.

RESPONDENT   The first casualty? I had been over there for about a month. The reason it had been so long was because our unit was assigned to a rear area at the time. And then we started moving out of the battalion area into bigger territory and less secure where there were more V.C.'s. And it was a—what you call a sweep. You line up and then you sweep the field. A corpsman, the platoon sergeant, and the radio man always kind of walk behind the battle people. That's where you have your grunts. The first casualty was sweeping a field. We were going into a field and there was a hedgerow. Somebody tripped and this guy said "booby trap," you know, he knew what he had done. And everybody just kind of froze and it went off. And it just kind of goes up in the air and explodes. A "bouncing Betty" is what it was. A lot of shrapnel hit him in the face. It hit him in the face and another guy behind him caught a lot of it, too, in his hand, you know, and I was scared to death. I didn't know what the hell to do.

DR. BENTON   Did somebody yell for you or did you just know that when you—

RESPONDENT   Well, no, somebody hollered for me because I couldn't see from where I was standing what had actually happened. I heard the explosion and somebody hollered "corpsman." I think it might have been the man who was hit—the casualty himself. And I was kind of petrified, really scared, you know, because that's my first confirmation with an actual casualty up there. And I was scared to death. And like I said, everything seemed to go blank. While I treated him I was just shaking, shaking so much, you know—really numb and I couldn't really put it together. I didn't know what they were—if they would start shooting at us or whether I would hit a booby trap myself. The V.C. would plant one booby trap here and one over there just within a few feet of each other. They knew when a man was hit he would require aid from either a corpsman or a buddy. And of course once you start congregating over there they start picking you off.

DR. BENTON   Did he die?

RESPONDENT   No, he lived. In fact, both of them lived—the black guy lost his hand.

DR. BENTON   What did you do specifically?

RESPONDENT   I put a tourniquet on it and I put a bottle dressing on it. A bottle dressing is similar to a kotex—a dressing type of bandage which is used in the field. We called for a meditaxi which is a helicopter which is always on standby. We'd pop a green smoke hand grenade or something like that—a marker.

DR. BENTON   What was your next major experience with death in battle?

RESPONDENT   Well, I guess when we had those three die on us. I can still hear them screaming. We were sitting around. We had just moved back into an area where we had been once before, a couple of weeks before which was bad because the Americans had a bad habit of coming back to an old area where we had been before. The V.C. were very effective—once you would leave a camp they would booby trap the damn place. And then when you came back, they'd be waiting. And this is exactly what happened. The platoon leader had called a meeting for the squad going out that night. The other corpsmen and I usually would listen and be briefed on patrol briefs, too. A good friend of mine from Dallas, a marine, was sitting there and we heard a loud explosion. Somebody hollered, "incomin'." We thought mortars. Everybody snapped and all a sudden started diving for holes—it was a natural reflex. And then I hear these screams. There was just such a mess of human bodies. It was really terrible. We had two corpsmen at the time in the platoon and really tried our best. All the guys pitched in and tried to help us because we had traumatic amputations of legs and things. There really wasn't a whole lot we could do for them. And there is something about blood—as far as human blood. I remember on every casualty in Vietnam there was always that certain odor. Something I never smelled in an O.R. Picking up the body parts and putting them in a plastic sack really bothered me.

DR. BENTON   What does the corpsman do when he has more casualties than he can attend to? Do you have some kind of priority?

RESPONDENT   You are supposed to treat the less wounded first and the main reason for that is so they can get back to defend the situation. And your most seriously wounded are the ones you treat last because, you know, they can't get back to the gun. It is human nature for me to treat the most wounded, however. The one who's wounded the most—it's part of human nature to me. You know, they can teach you to treat the guy with the broken finger or shot-off arm first, but I always treated the one who was the worst wounded. If you've got a guy laying out here to where he was shot through the chest or something, and you had a guy over here who was shot through the hand, it was always the one who was shot through the chest first because you knew he needed you and you knew his chances were less if you didn't treat him.

DR. BENTON   You mentioned some cultural or social patterns that the soldiers of the United States did, like returning to an old campsite. What are other kinds of national behavioral patterns that you noted that influence the way the soldier from the United States would fight?

RESPONDENT   Well, the American soldier had more respect for small children and older people—sixty years and up. I think I saw a distinction there.

DR. BENTON   By distinction do you mean a greater reluctance to inflict death or harm? So there's kind of an eligibility gradient.

RESPONDENT   More or less.

DR. BENTON   What would you do if a child came at you or aimed a gun at you?

RESPONDENT   Well, that happened one time. How old this child was, I'll never know, but I'd say he was probably thirteen or fourteen years old. I saw him aim his gun and shoot a guy and he hit him in the helmet—he didn't hit him, but within a fraction of an inch he would have killed him. But my feelings then and as they are now was that I can't really hold anything against him. I don't think a kid is an adult. I think he was indoctrinated. He was doing his thing and he was doing a damn good job of it, too. And I think by now, you almost have to be proud of him. You see a kid that old, being a Vietnamese, and you see a kid like that in the same situation from America—it's two different worlds completely. Another time I saw a child planting a hand grenade and booby traps and when he was shot and wounded by your own troops and you're asked if you want to save him or kill him—

DR. BENTON   What did you do in that type of situation?

RESPONDENT   I had to go ahead and kill him. And that's what we did.

DR. BENTON   How old was he?

RESPONDENT   He was about nine or ten years old—a child.

DR. BENTON   Did that ever bother you after that?

RESPONDENT   Sure it did but I doubt it very seriously if he would have ever survived in that type of terrain and what we had as far as medical treatment for him, because if you called a meditaxi and said we got a gook kid out here that needs medical treatment, you see them four or five hours later. They had American casualties in the field and they had priority and I knew that. Why make a fool of yourself and call a meditaxi? They would think I was crazy.

DR. BENTON   Why would you think a corpsman might get hit?

RESPONDENT   Well, that was probably one of the highest casualty rates in Vietnam, was the corpsmen because the enemy knew quite well that when—once you have a casualty, the first one there is the corpsman and once you put the corpsman off, or a medic, as far as the Army, then you've lost a lot of morale right there. You know, once you see the corpsman's bombed, forty guys are saying, "Who's going to take care of me if I get hit?" And that's not a crowd pleaser, I'll tell you that.

DR. BENTON   Do you feel like the experiences of war have had an impact on your life?

RESPONDENT   Sure they have. In a lot of ways. I've become very much more sensitive toward people and toward myself in a lot of ways.

DR. BENTON   Did you or do you or have you looked upon the Vietnamese or the North Vietnamese as the "bad guys" and were you committed patriotically to what you were doing—to the fighting, to the cause, esprit de corps? Those kinds of things?

RESPONDENT   Well, I can't really say that because, like I said, I was nineteen, almost twenty years old, when I went overseas. I turned twenty-one in Vietnam and I didn't know what the hell was going on, I really didn't. I don't think half those people did.

THE PROFESSIONAL WARRIOR

DR. BENTON	Bill, let's start with some background; you were born and reared in a moderately large city in the South, right?
RESPONDENT	That's right.
DR. BENTON	And do you have any brothers and sisters?
RESPONDENT	I have one younger brother.
DR. BENTON	You went to school and when you graduated from high school what were your desires and what did you do?
RESPONDENT	I went out to college for about two years. After two-and-a-half years in college, then I went into the service. I joined the Army.
DR. BENTON	And then what happened?
RESPONDENT	I volunteered for Vietnam.
DR. BENTON	How did you feel about going?
RESPONDENT	Well, to be honest, I felt two ways about it. The type of unit that I was in, it was just a—the thing was not whether you went to Vietnam, but how many times. It was a volunteer type of unit and you just listened to the old sergeants and the ones that had already been over there twice by the time 1967 rolled around. Some of them had been over there as many as three times between '62 and '67 and the young soldier who was in Special Forces couldn't wait to get over there. Honestly, I have to say that I felt a little apprehension but I looked forward to getting over there and they needed volunteers.
DR. BENTON	And tell me about some of your experiences as a soldier—being one of the few people whose primary duty and responsibility is to perhaps disable the enemy. What do you see as the responsibility of a soldier and then tell me about some experiences—
RESPONDENT	Okay, the mission for the Special Forces in which I was trained and a part of is to go into a country and work with the indigenous population in a group of twelve Americans and you train, equip, and organize

and grow a band, if you care to call it that, to conduct covert and overt actions against the enemy forces. Vietnam for the Americans was not a typical guerilla warfare setting but we did act in that way. I was over there as an Executive Officer on what is called the Special Forces A Team and that team is equipped with operations in intelligence personnel. It is equipped with medics, communications personnel, engineer personnel, and medical personnel. Our job was strictly to take bands, and in our case we had about 600 that we trained, equipped, and organized into a fighting force. We conducted missions against the Viet Cong and the North Vietnamese department.

DR. BENTON   Did you ever feel guilty or remorseful about killing people? Did you ever eyeball to eyeball kill someone?

RESPONDENT   I only killed one individual eyeball to eyeball. The rest of the time we called in air strikes, we called in artillery strikes, we set up ambushes, we sent out patrols of the troops that we were doing, and I guess we justified it by the fact that it was a job. It was a dirty job, it was an unpleasant job, but we had to do it.

DR. BENTON   Would it bother you or would you be hesitant to shoot at an eight-year-old child who was about to shoot at you?

RESPONDENT   We were psyched up enough to where if the child would appear to shoot us or throw a grenade at us or something we would have killed them, even though it was a child, without hesitation.

DR. BENTON   Can you tell me about the incident in which you did kill a person?

RESPONDENT   We had been out on the patrol about eight days and were coming back in. We converged into an open area at approximately the same time as the Vietnamese. I happened to be very close to the point at that time and I don't know who opened fire first. All of the sudden there was a guy that was pointing in my general direction and I just cut loose on him. I had my weapon on automatic fire and caught him with a burst across the rib section. I responded, I did what I had been trained to do. At the time that was the only way I could look at it.

DR. BENTON   Did you have any particular attitude toward the Viet Cong?

RESPONDENT   Well, the average Viet Cong soldier was fighting for his life, okay? The ones we captured and interrogated were deathly afraid that the Americans were going to cut off their ears or cut off a part of their body. And most of them, being Buddhists, felt that they could not enter their happy land, wherever they go, unless they're in one piece. So the ones we captured and interrogated were really afraid of the Americans because they felt that we would be mutilating them in some way.

DR. BENTON   Could you see yourself as having continued a career in Special Service of some type for the government in which the taking of lives could have been a part? For example, a special agent or something along those lines?

RESPONDENT   I guess I can say yes. I think that perhaps if that was the job and that was what was required of me and I knew this, I think yes, I could have.

DR. BENTON   Is there anything else that you can think of or that you remember that sort of stood out or stands out relative to your career as a soldier and has it had any impact upon your life and adjustment after the war?

RESPONDENT   I lost several friends in Vietnam and that had an impact on me. Anytime you lose a friend. I did see numerous Vietnamese killed in different ways and that had an impact on me. A couple of times I saw Viet Cong hit the village near where we were and actually mutilate and string someone up. I saw some pretty bloody gunshot wounds and some pretty bloody burn cases and I worked with our medic a lot. I guess some of the gut-shot men were some of the worst. The only time that I feel that I was really scared in Vietnam, that it really got to me, was the night before I went to Australia. I was staying at the Special Forces' main compound and I had turned in my weapon and I was visiting with them and I was to go to the air base the next morning to catch the flight for Sydney, Australia. We were mortared that night and received incoming small-arms fire at about midnight. I did not have a job to do. I was not part of that compound. I was a guest, a visitor, in that compound. I was shown the bunker that I had to go to and I sat in the bunker for about an hour with three other people while we received incoming fire. That scared the devil out of me because all I had to do was to sit there and think about it and I didn't know whether we would be overrun, whether we were winning, losing, or what. That scared the hell out of me, to be quite honest. But I guess one of the things that sort of a lot of us adopted in our A camp was a little model we had and it was kind of meaningful and it goes something like this, "For those who fight for it, life has a flavor the protected will never know." I guess that sort of sums it up.

The Undertaker's Assistant

Some occupations are looked upon as areas of accomplishment and those who aspire to them viewed with admiration and awe. Some occupations are scarcely regarded at all. But the undertaker is typically regarded with a "mixed bag" of views and emotions. Rarely does one announce "I'm an undertaker" at a party. It is poor taste to boast of certain occupations. As the undertaker's assistant indicates, there is "inside" humor in the work.

DR. BENTON   There are two reasons that I wanted to interview you for this chapter. One was because you were very close to a sister who died and the second reason was because your family, or at least part of your family, has been in the funeral industry for years and you've had close relationships in working with—personal involvement with someone who died under conditions similar to Karen Ann Quinlan as well as working with cadavers, preparing them for one type of burial or another. Let's start with your sister, Julie.

RESPONDENT   Julie was thirty-two when she died and I was thirty.

DR. BENTON   How did she die?

RESPONDENT   She was pregnant and my understanding of what she died with, the sickness or illness or disease is called fatty infiltration of the liver which only occurs in pregnant women. We were told that she was the forty-second recorded case with this type sickness.

DR. BENTON   Fatty infiltration of the liver?

RESPONDENT   Yes, I guess fatty metamorphosis of the liver would mean the same thing. And there is no recovery for the patient. There have been times where they've saved the child or children or whatever, but never the mother.

I was out of the country when Julie first got sick and her husband was the one who told me that they had taken the babies. Both of them were dead. Then, like twenty-four hours later, they started coming in her room and asking her who the president of the United States was and, you know, at that time it seemed like ridiculous questions even to Julie. Within another twenty-four-hour period she was co-matose. Just gone—and they put her in intensive care and then I came home and I think she had been in intensive care at that time for like two weeks. When I walked in it was like looking at a—I guess mongoloid child, you know? This girl was just perfectly beautiful and alive and everything about her was dead—the shape of her face, the look in her eyes. The nurse went over and said, "Patsy's here." And Julie patted my hand and said my name. I don't know whether due to control or whatever it was, you know, but I didn't fall apart then, but I was furious. I was absolutely furious that she was in this condition plus the fact that they had parted her hair down the middle and put these pigtails on both sides and made her look like a little kid. A couple of days later she had advanced to another stage of this thing and there was no reaction from her whatsoever except when they would try to take blood from her veins. She didn't want that but she couldn't talk, couldn't communicate. Leslie, my older sister, says that Julie wrote for her. She wrote her name and the word "heaven" on a piece of paper. I assume that Leslie destroyed it. Anyway, from that point on, Julie never did get any better and then they finally wound up putting her in the bed and that's where she'd stay. You could go lift her eyelid and there was nothing there. As far as I was concerned she was dead. Finally the doctors came out and told us we were going to have to make the decision of whether they took these life-support systems out or not 'cause that's all they were doing. And my feelings are, we were going to make a big pow-wow out of it and each one of us hated to have that decision put on us, you know, and yet everybody knew that the plugs needed to be unplugged. Well, maybe an hour had passed and the nurse called and said, "Mrs. Briggs, you can come in and see your daughter now," which just shocked the daylight out of all of us. And when we got back to intensive care, the doctor came around the corner and he almost turned pale and he said, "You don't want to go back there now." And my mother said something like, you know, "This must be it. Yes, I want to go say good-bye to her." And I looked up and they had already unplugged everything and Julie was in the last throes of death which is really gruesome as far as I'm concerned. Maybe if it was somebody I didn't know I could handle it but it was really bad. And then we turned around and walked out. Now whether my mother was aware that these things were unplugged, I don't know. I don't know whether something happened in that hour's time that made—that she died even with machines on or what. I'm just grateful that it happened that way and we didn't have to make a decision. And then they put us all in that little room they've got. We sat there for about ten minutes and they came in and said that she had been pronounced dead. But, you know, the feeling that I had when I first walked in and saw her was "My God, you know, just don't do this crap." Because my understanding of the sickness is that if the liver deteriorates, your mind deteriorates, always. And then there's a point that you pass where your liver can regenerate but the brain will not and this is what was happening to Julie. Her liver was getting better but her mind was just obviously gone, you know? She wouldn't have wanted it and we certainly didn't want it.

DR. BENTON	Were you close to your sister? In terms of mourning, did it take you a while to work through it?
RESPONDENT	She had to work real hard to get her goals and there was a lot of anger in me when she died directed at, you know, why Julie, the best one out of the whole bunch (of siblings)? Why not me, egomaniac that I am? And why didn't they get her to the doctor before this?
DR. BENTON	Could the doctor have possibly prevented this?
RESPONDENT	No, he became very involved in this. It really got next to him and he—they know so little of this sickness, it just happens. At this point there's nothing that they know to do to trace it or to see it, you know, before it's there. It took me quite some time to get over it. Even today, you know, I can just be driving along and all of the sudden the thought will pop into my mind, you know, where is she? Or something will remind me of her and I'll get all choked up. Those times are getting fewer and farther between.
DR. BENTON	Had she also worked in the funeral home?
RESPONDENT	No, she didn't. Leslie didn't, Brad didn't—just me.
DR. BENTON	I wonder why that difference?
RESPONDENT	I don't know. That would be interesting to study. It didn't seem to bother Brad. Leslie just didn't like to be around it and neither did Julie.
DR. BENTON	How did you get started working in the funeral home?
RESPONDENT	Let's see, the funeral home was near our house.
DR. BENTON	What age did you first start working there?
RESPONDENT	I must have been eighteen when I actually went to work and wasn't just playing there anymore.
DR. BENTON	But before that you did play at the funeral home?
RESPONDENT	Oh, yes, all the time. We played in and out of the boxes that the caskets came in and up in the casket room we played hide and seek and—
DR. BENTON	Did that ever bother you kids?
RESPONDENT	We'd sit around and tell ghost stories.
DR. BENTON	Did you ever watch them care for the bodies in that period of time?

RESPONDENT   No, they seemed to be very cautious of that sort of thing around kids—us in particular.

DR. BENTON   But then when you were eighteen, you had the opportunity to go and do some work there. What kind of work was it?

RESPONDENT   Answer the phone, help arrange the flowers, put the flowers in the different chapels, and then my cousin, who was doing all that work at that time, asked me if I'd be interested in learning how to do hair.

DR. BENTON   You mean preparing or fixing hair?

RESPONDENT   Fixing hair on the bodies. And I said yes, and the cosmetics. So she taught me, you know, she started out teaching me what she knew.

DR. BENTON   And did you have any reactions to doing it or any problems at all?

RESPONDENT   I loved it. It was different, you know, from anything anybody else I knew was doing. Yeah, I really liked it and I don't remember then having any reaction to, say, young kids dying. But, you know, the last experience I had—small children really got next to me. I was repulsed by a burned victim, you know? I didn't want to be in the embalming room with the burned victim.

DR. BENTON   Why did it bother you?

RESPONDENT   I think it was the smell more than anything else.

DR. BENTON   When you began to find yourself having trouble dealing with children in the embalming room, was this after you were a mother or before you were a mother?

RESPONDENT   After.

DR. BENTON   You had mentioned earlier that you didn't seem to have any trouble with almost anything in the embalming room or in the preparation of the bodies before you were in your thirties and certainly in your younger years, but then afterwards, you began to have some trouble. What kinds of things were you having trouble with?

RESPONDENT   I didn't want to be in the room when they were doing a postmortem. Now, the embalmers wouldn't do that—the doctors would come in.

DR. BENTON   Did it bother you to be around the embalmers?

RESPONDENT   No.

DR. BENTON   Did it bother you when they drained the blood from the bodies?

RESPONDENT   Only when they used a trocar.

DR. BENTON   I see. What is a trocar?

RESPONDENT   It's a long stick like a spear that has a sharp point and they attach it to a tube and it has suction on it. And they jab it into the stomach and just, you know, jab it around in there.

DR. BENTON   Sort of suction out all of the fluid?

RESPONDENT   Yeah, it still nauseates me to think about it but before that it didn't bother me. "Posts" didn't bother me at all.

DR. BENTON   What bothers you most about the postmortem?

RESPONDENT   I think just putting myself in the place of the family member, you know, and I just wasn't able not to and knowing that, you know, really that the doctors who are in there performing the autopsy just are there to perform a service and get their job done and get out of there so they don't care who Joe Blow is. And they do a slipshod job of it and then leave. And here's whoever, you know, laying there just all cut up which nobody's going to see after they're dressed but still I know what they've done.

DR. BENTON   And you were saying that, you know, when you were younger, the whining of the saw as it cut through the skull didn't bother you, then later—

RESPONDENT   Well, that was a determining factor when Julie died. They wanted to do an autopsy on her and we—I was just very vocal about it, you know, they had already cut her stomach with a cesarean section and I said just, you know don't let them do anything else to her except on her—in the stomach area. Don't touch her head—and it wasn't necessary to touch her head, so they didn't. But just the thought of them going in there and doing a slipshod job, just cutting her up was just hard to handle and I don't know whether it's because I'm getting closer to it or—

DR. BENTON   Do you have any feelings about the way you said that earlier you acted in some fashion as a receptionist? Did you have any feelings or thoughts or reactions about the terms that are used like "deceased" or the "loved one" instead of the "body" or the "corpse" or the "cadaver" and things like that?

RESPONDENT   The term that appealed to me and I could handle best was the "deceased." The "loved one" I think is not my own certainly but I think it's used in a more joking manner in the funeral business.

DR. BENTON   Do you feel like a little bit of "put-on" goes on in the funeral business or salesmanship?

RESPONDENT   Yeah, I sure do. See, now that's an area of the funeral business I don't approve of and they don't have my stamp of approval.

DR. BENTON   So you feel that in some ways they do sort of make mileage out of people's emotions?

RESPONDENT   There are several funeral directors who are average, everyday people who handle families in an average way. They don't make it morose or anything but then—that reminds me of Digger Odell, the friendly undertaker, you know, and I don't approve of that at all. That's their style and you're dealing with people that are so emotionally distraught that probably five days later they don't even remember who the funeral director was, you know, so it probably doesn't bother the family.

DR. BENTON   What kind of people are the families that are in the funeral business?

RESPONDENT   I think they have a big burden to carry around with them but—

DR. BENTON   How do you mean that?

RESPONDENT   "What does your daddy do?" He's a funeral director.

DR. BENTON   Do you feel that that is kind of a problem with the kids growing up?

RESPONDENT   I don't know. It used to not bother me to say, you know, that my relatives had a funeral home but to-day—

DR. BENTON   You don't tell everybody, right?

RESPONDENT	I don't tell everybody.
DR. BENTON	Do you feel that a funeral director and his family are somewhat ostracized?
RESPONDENT	Well, I think maybe they—I can only speak for the family point of view. When my grandfather started this and my grandmother was certainly involved in it and she took over after he died, the idea being it was a service as well as making a profit, but the main idea was to perform a service for people in need. Well, it just seems that this has been overshadowed today. That's how I feel about it. They may tell you something entirely different with the money aspect. And I think in terms of myself, looking at it and that just knowing myself, I can handle the idea that they were service-oriented people.
DR. BENTON	Does the general "run-of-the-mill" funeral home still take on pauper burying?
RESPONDENT	Not anymore, not like they used to.
DR. BENTON	Is there good money in that business?
RESPONDENT	Apparently there is. I don't really know what the mark-up is but I think it's too damn much.
DR. BENTON	Why do they embalm the bodies?
RESPONDENT	It's a state requirement, that's all I know. (Actually it is not, unless the body is not to be buried or cremated within a certain time period—author.)
DR. BENTON	You mentioned that there is levity that goes on in the funeral homes. Can you recall some examples that were interesting?
RESPONDENT	I remember Mr. Hubbard talking about an embalmer named Tex who was apparently a giant of a man who had walked into the embalming room to inject this body and he turned around to turn on the machine and the fluid started into the body and it tremored. And the hand jumped up and grabbed him behind the collar and he was standing there and he was saying to himself, "I know that this person is dead and his hand has jumped up and it's in my collar." And he took the hand off the collar and let it down and walked out of the embalming room and never went back. And then

Mr. Hubbard always carried a yardstick, always had a yardstick. And he'd come back there and he'd pop somebody, you know, he'd pop one of the bodies back there and he'd say, "Oh, excuse me," or whatever, you know, he'd talk to them and have them talk back or if you were combing their hair he'd get back and he'd mimic the woman—move their hands or something.

DR. BENTON   Did everybody laugh?

RESPONDENT   Oh, yes.

DR. BENTON   Do you think that was sort of a tension release perhaps?

RESPONDENT   I think so—for all of us.

DR. BENTON   Do you see some of the reactions that people have in those kinds of situations as callous, uncaring, or just some type of adaptation?

RESPONDENT   I think to some point they—you know, they don't become callous. It's probably like driving a car, it's just something they get used to doing and I have seen emotional reactions, you know, depending on the circumstances from each of the embalmers that I work with. You know, being upset over a useless murder. Do you remember, I guess this was close to four years ago, when this young boy was supposed to be doped up on marijuana, he went to Westbury and he shot a little girl and an older woman—I think there were three people that died. He was just shooting at random. Well, we got the little girl and it was like she was every woman's conception of what they would want their little daughter to look like. She was absolutely gorgeous. And the bullet was right in the middle of her forehead. And you just resent such a waste. So there were times when you would get an emotional reaction out of, you know, everybody that was involved but on the whole it was a job they did, kind of a run 'em through an assembly line type thing.

DR. BENTON   Did you ever see or assist with cremations?

RESPONDENT   I never saw a cremation. Something else interesting—at this particular funeral home and it would never fail, it was always at lunchtime, a little man from the hospital would come by with a limb—maybe a leg, maybe an arm—it was wrapped and wrapped and wrapped and finally done in something that looked like Saran wrap. He would carry it through where we were eating lunch and put it on the side and what we would do was just bury it, you know? It may be Jane Doe and her family doesn't even know it.

DR. BENTON   Is that right! That's interesting. I hadn't really thought about what they do with detached limbs.

RESPONDENT   One woman was buried with her dog. Now, you have to have special permits I think to do something like that. They don't approve of that.

DR. BENTON   Who doesn't approve of it?

RESPONDENT   The state.

DR. BENTON   Why?

RESPONDENT   I don't know. But they had her dog put to sleep and buried with her. Those were her last wishes. One thing that did impress me was that whatever the request of the family, the funeral home really tries to meet it. It doesn't matter how ridiculous it might be.

DR. BENTON   Are there some ridiculous requests?

RESPONDENT   Oh, as far as I'm concerned, yes. I think all of the folderol at a funeral is ridiculous. Psychologically it may be good for the family. I don't know, it's not good for me to sit and mourn for three days. And the Italians go and celebrate and they come inevitably with just barrels and barrels of food and wine to drink and that sort of thing. They go to the back room and cry over mama and try to jump in the casket with her and beat their breasts and wail and then walk into the room where the food is and just start laughing and carrying on and eating and then they go right back in and play this other role, "Oh, mama, I'm so sorry."

DR. BENTON   What about other nationalities?

RESPONDENT   I wasn't there when they had a certain Chinese funeral. The XYZ funeral home did that one and they gave out fortune cookies and were very happy.

DR. BENTON   Any other ethnic differences?

RESPONDENT   No, Mexicans and Irish and Italians all pretty well scream and holler.

DR. BENTON   Have you noticed any economic differences? Do the people with less worldly means have any displays that are different from—

RESPONDENT   I think the more affluent people are, the more showy they are.

DR. BENTON   Showy in what way?

RESPONDENT   This, you know, ridiculous carrying on and the less affluent they just are—you can see them trying to accept what has happened. Now, you know, you said something about the embalming and it just occurred to me that Jews don't embalm—Orthodox Jews don't embalm. So maybe embalming is not a state law. Maybe if you're buried within a certain period of time you don't have to be—that would be the best way to go, as far as I'm concerned.

DR. BENTON   What? Just not embalming?

RESPONDENT   Just not embalming. Just bury you and get it over with. But then maybe, see, the funeral service is designed specifically to help the family through the emotional trauma of death just simply because people don't face it. They had me wait on a family one time. I don't have a funeral director's license so I could only take them up to a certain point. This young boy had died of leukemia and I went up there. I was so nervous. The one thing I do remember is that the father, who was an athletic coach, handed me this swiss knife that had all these little blades and things on it. And he handed it to me and said, you know, "Would you put this in my son's hand?" Well, that just undid me completely and I thought, "You can't cry with this family here," so I just didn't say another word and got up and walked out, you know. I got downstairs and started running, you know, and went to the back room and just bawled. So if I can look at it in terms of that, you know, this family apparently needed to go through seeing their son in the coffin which was all right. That part I can handle, but it's the show that really turns me off.

DR. BENTON	A large percentage of cemeteries and funeral homes appear to be owned by insurance companies and SCI or some conglomerate like that which suggests a good profit margin probably exists.
RESPONDENT	Tremendous, I'm sure. I've not looked but I can well imagine. It would probably just, you know, stir my ire some more if I really knew. I think mausoleums are absolutely ridiculous. I think headstones are just a nice little marker to let them know that I'm here. That's one thing but to go get some huge monument carved is just insanity, but then I think that goes along with some of the insanity that I have seen in preparation for funerals. You're catching people at emotional times.
DR. BENTON	Why do you say mausoleums are—
RESPONDENT	Because they're so outrageously expensive.
DR. BENTON	Are they?
RESPONDENT	Yeah, you know, and at that time it just seems like there are people who would sell their souls and bodies to give the dead person things that really should have been given to them while they were alive.

Medical Examiner's Office*

To some it may seem inconsistent and contradictory to deal with the emotional aspects of loss, love, caring, and autopsy in the same book. Yet, all are features of death and dying. Our abhorrence of pain and dislike of disfiguring the deceased may account for part of our denial reaction to autopsy. Nevertheless, for the student and survivor alike some understanding of the medical examiner's process is essential. Most of us in our lifetime as surviving family or health care professionals will be faced with decisions that deal with this matter. The materials presented here concern the postmortem process.

This section is an amplification of a lecture delivered to various college and high school student groups interested in the duties of a medical examiner.

---

*Written by William E. Korndorffer, M.D., Chief Medical Examiner, Galveston County, Texas.

MEDICAL EXAMINER SYSTEM

In the case of every human death someone has to decide if the death is in anyway connected with a crime. The private physician plays this role as a public official every time he or she signs a death certificate. When the manner of death is not natural or the cause is unknown or due to violence, the death must be investigated by a representative of society. The legal system set up for this purpose has varied over the years and continues to vary from country to country and state to state. In Texas the system varies from county to county. In the smaller counties the local elected Justice of the Peace acts as the coroner. The larger counties have medical examiners.

The Justice of the Peace is an elected official and is usually not trained in medical matters. If the cause of death appears to be obvious—automobile accident, suicide, heart attack (myocardial infarction)—the Justice of the Peace can fill out and sign the death certificate. A person can die and be buried without ever having been seen by a physician! That this system is inadequate can be illustrated by the following three cases:

Example 1. A 24-year-old girl had a fight with her boyfriend. She grabbed a pistol and locked herself in the bathroom saying that she was going to shoot herself. The boyfriend did not believe she was suicidal and was walking out of the room when he heard a gunshot. He broke into the bathroom and found the girl with the gun in her right hand and a bullet hole in her right temple. It was presumed that she had killed herself. The bullet that was recovered from the brain had specs of enamel embedded on it. This, along with the samples of enamel from the bathroom fixtures, led the medical examiner to conclude that the death was accidental rather than suicide. The girl had evidently tried to scare her boyfriend and had accidentally discharged the weapon. The bullet ricocheted off the bathroom fixtures and struck her in the head.

Example 2. A 40-year-old man was involved in a fight in a bar where he was shot in the left side under the arm by a small calibre pistol. He got into his car and drove several blocks down the street when he collapsed. Going at a slow rate of speed, the car ran into a telephone pole. A passerby called an ambulance and the man was taken to the hospital where he was treated in the emergency room for a heart attack. When he died a few minutes later he was signed out as having died from a massive myocardial infarction. Because he died in the emergency room he was a medical examiner's case. The autopsy examination revealed the small pencil-sized hole in the left armpit (axilla). The bullet had entered the heart, and death was because the sac surrounding the heart (pericardium) had filled with blood so that the heart did not have room to beat (cardiac tamponade). The death was by homicide and not by natural causes.

Example 3. A 60-year-old woman was involved in what appeared to be a minor automobile accident. She was dead on arrival at the hospital (DOA). Because she was DOA at the hospital she was, by law, a medical examiner case. The autopsy revealed a massive heart attack and a completely plugged up heart vessel. The woman had had the accident because of the heart attack and death was by natural causes and not due to the accident.

An experienced Justice of the Peace probably would not have made a mistake in diagnosis, but one can see how these cases could have been missed if the obvious had just been accepted as the obvious and the elected official had tried to save the voting taxpayer $300 or $400 an autopsy investigation would have cost.

Dissatisfaction with the elective Coroner's system led to the introduction of the Medical Examiner system in Massachusetts in 1880. Since then, many states have followed this pattern. The medical examiner is charged with the responsibility of conducting an inquest into the death of any person where crime may have been committed.

Specifically, the following cases fall under the jurisdiction of the medical examiner:

1. when a person shall die within 24 hours after admission to a hospital or institution or in a jail;
2. when any person is killed, or from any cause dies an unnatural death, except under the sentence of the law, or dies in the absence of one or more good witnesses;
3. when the body of a human being is found and the circumstances of death are unknown;
4. when circumstances of the death of any person are such as to lead to suspicion that the person came to his or her death by unlawful means;

5. when any person commits suicide, or the circumstances of death are such as to lead to suspicion that he or she committed suicide;

6. when a person dies without having been attended by a duly licensed and practicing physician, and the local health officer or registrar required to report the cause of death does not know the cause of death;

7. when a person dies who has been attended immediately preceding death by a duly licensed and practicing physician or physicians, and such physicians are not certain as to the cause of death.

The Medical Examiner's Office is set up to be independent of the other political bodies. It can issue subpoenas, call witnesses to testify, carry out investigations, and fine or jail those who give false testimony or hinder the official investigation of a death. The medical examiner may also exhume (disinter) a body at any time if there is reason to believe an inquest ought to have been held.

The purpose of a coroner's inquest is to obtain information as to whether a death was caused by some criminal act and to obtain information to prevent escape of the guilty as well as to furnish foundation for criminal prosecution in case death is shown to be felonious.

Medical examiner investigators, appointed by the chief medical examiner, go to the scene of the death of every medical examiner case before the body is moved. By law a body can only be moved if it is to protect the body from further damage or to prevent it from blocking traffic on a highway. When on the scene, the medical examiner investigator takes charge of the body and all property found with it.

The report prepared by the medical examiner investigator goes with the body to the morgue where the medical examiner conducts the investigation and autopsy. Ideally, a complete autopsy should be performed in every case. Unfortunately, the funds usually available only allow autopsies when the medical examiner believes the autopsy findings will contribute to the decision as to the cause and manner of death. In all cases photographs and a careful external examination of the body are made. A blood specimen is always collected and saved for examination if a poison is later suspected as the cause of death (toxicology). If, in any specific case, the medical examiner questions whether an autopsy should or should not be done he or she is usually well advised to perform the autopsy. Only rarely does the medical examiner find it necessary to conduct an official formal inquest where a jury is needed to weigh the evidence. Usually the medical examiner personally makes the decision as to whether death was by natural or unnatural causes, and if unnatural, by suicide, accident, or homicide. It takes a great deal of training, experience, and skill to make the decision.

The medical examiner and deputies are, by law, licensed physicians with specialized training in pathology. Following graduation from high school a person spends four years as an undergraduate in a college or university leading to a B.A. or B.S. degree. After four years of medical school and receipt of an M.D. degree the person takes a medical examination given by the state. If he or she is successful in passing the examination, the person is then considered a licensed physician legally capable of practicing medicine in that state.

However, one ordinarily continues in training as an intern in a hospital for a year. Following this, the physician completes four additional years as a resident in pathology. All interns and residents are M.D.'s and most are licensed in one or more states to practice medicine.

Following the four years as a pathology resident the physician takes an examination given by the American Board of Pathology. If the exam is passed, the person is "certified" as a specialist in pathology. Forensic pathology is a subspecialty of pathology. The forensic pathologist is a physician certified in pathology with additional specialized training or experience in forensic medicine.

AUTOPSY

The autopsy is still the basis of all medical knowledge. The pathologist performing the autopsy is somewhat like a skilled mechanic examining a very complicated piece of machinery. He or she approaches the autopsy with the assumption that there is a mechanical, physical reason the person dies. Often the reason is obvious. It may be a hole through the aorta (a garden-hose sized artery), or it may be a plugged-up, occluded blood vessel going to the heart or brain. The defect may be on a microscopic or submicroscopic level. Then, because there is still so much we do not know about the "incredible machine" we call the human body, the pathologist frequently cannot find the cause of death.

Any examination of the body after death (postmortem) is an autopsy. There is no such thing as a "complete autopsy." No matter what is done, something else could have been done. The repeated request for more to be done in the case of President John F. Kennedy is one example. The term "complete autopsy" refers to an examination of the organs of the three major cavities of the body—the abdomen (peritoneal cavity), the chest (thoracic cavity), and the head (cranial cavity). The spinal cord is not ordinarily removed and examined; and the muscles and blood vessels of the arms and legs (extremities) are not examined. The voice box and neck (larynx, pharynx, trachea, thyroid, parathyroid) are removed with the organs from the chest (heart, lungs, thymus). The female sex organs (uterus, fallopian tubes, ovaries) and male sex organs (testes, prostate) are examined with the abdominal organs.

Autopsy techniques differ from each other in the order in which organs are examined, or as to whether single organs or intact organ systems are removed from the body. In the Virchow technique the organs are examined one by one. The Rokitansky technique is characterized by in-situ dissection, in part combined with en bloc removal. The actual technique used in any specific autopsy is usually a variation or combination depending upon the preference of the pathologist and the circumstances surrounding the case at hand.

The cut (incision) used to open the body is referred to as a "Y" incision because of its shape. An incision is made from each armpit (axilla) to the lower end of the sternum or breast bone (xyphoid process). These two incisions make the upper part of the "Y" incision. The incision is then carried down the midline past the naval (umbilicus) to the pubic bone. The primary incision cuts through the skin, subcutaneous tissue, and muscle. In the female, the "Y" incision is made on the outside of the breast. By folding this flap of skin, subcutaneous tissue, and muscle of the chest back and up (along with the breast in the female), and removing the rib cage with a saw along the sides, all of the organs of the chest and abdomen are exposed. When the autopsy is completed, the rib cage is placed back and the skin flaps are sewn together as in a surgical procedure. After the body has been embalmed and prepared for viewing at the funeral home, one cannot tell by looking at the body that an autopsy has been done.

The brain is examined by making an incision or cut behind the ears over the top of the head. The incision extends from ear to ear over the convexity of the head (coronal incision). The scalp is then peeled away and separated from the skull and pulled forward over the face. The top of the skull is removed with a saw and the brain is exposed for examination. When the top of the skull is replaced, the scalp is pulled back over the skull and sewn together as in a surgical procedure. When the embalmer has completed the work, one cannot tell by looking at the body in the casket that the brain has been removed and examined.

Although it may not be common knowledge, the usual procedure is to bury the body without the organs. After the organs have been examined, they are disposed of by incineration in the same manner as organs removed at surgery, such as the appendix, gallbladder, and tonsils. The brain in the fresh state is soft and mushy. For this reason, it is usually fixed or preserved in formaldehyde for several weeks before it becomes firm enough to be properly examined. This is part of the reason it takes a seemingly long time to get an autopsy report from the pathologist.

When autopsies are performed in the funeral home or smaller hospitals without incineration facilities, the organs are examined and placed back in the body where they are preserved or embalmed by the funeral home. Sometimes the family will specifically request that the organs be buried with the body. Small pieces of the organs are removed and saved by the pathologist to make microscopic slides and to study the tissues under the microscope. Blood, gastric contents, urine, bile, and sometimes fluid from the eyes (vitreous humor) are also collected for examination by the laboratory.

Whether an autopsy is to be performed or not is up to the next of kin unless the death is a medical examiner's case. Then it is performed as a matter of law. The rank of next of kin is spelled out by the various state laws. In Texas, consent to conduct an autopsy of the body of a deceased person is deemed to be sufficient when given by the following:

> In the case of a married person, the surviving spouse, or if no spouse survives him, by a child of such marriage, or in the event of a minor child of such marriage, the guardian of such child if any there be, or in the absence of such guardian, the court having jurisdiction of the person of such minor; in the event that neither spouse or child survives such deceased, then permission for an autopsy shall be valid when given by a person who would be allowed to give such permission in the case of an unmarried deceased.
>
> If the deceased be unmarried, then permission shall be given by the following for such autopsy, in the order stated: father, mother, guardian, or next of kin, and in the absence of any of the foregoing, by any natural person assuming custody of and responsibility for burial of the body of such deceased. If two or more of the above-named persons assume custody of the body, consent of one of them is sufficient. (Texas Law, Article 49.05: Vernon's Annotated Code of Criminal Procedure. Consent to autopsy.)

Autopsy Permission

1. Spouse
2. Child of legal age
3. Legal guardian of minor child
4. Father
5. Mother
6. Sibling (brother or sister)
7. Other relative
8. Friend (one willing to assume costs)

The information obtained by an autopsy on a private basis is personal and privileged information. The next of kin who authorized the autopsy should be the only one who decides who should be given an autopsy report. The information obtained from the autopsy report is used by the physician in filling out the death certificate but the report itself is treated as privileged information.

There is a difference between a private death and a public death. By nature death is a private affair. Animals tend to go away to be alone when they die. A person has that same right. When the cause of death is natural and the manner of death is of no interest to society, the death and the autopsy are private. There is controversy over just how much information about a person and that person's death should be placed on the death certificate. At times there is conflict between what is legally right and what is morally right.

When Howard Hughes, the much celebrated reclusive billionaire, was brought to Methodist Hospital in Houston he was already dead. Because he was dead on arrival he was, by law, a medical examiner's case. The medical examiner conducted his investigation and—without performing an autopsy—concluded that the deceased was indeed Howard Hughes and that no crime had been committed. The next of kin then gave permission for an autopsy to be performed by the hospital pathologist. In this manner the autopsy itself—with the photographs, and other relevant materials—became private, privileged information not available to the public. Certainly a man who wanted so much to be private in life had the right (in the absence of any crime) to be private in death!

CHANGES AFTER DEATH

Death is usually described in a negative fashion because it is hard to do otherwise. "Death" is the cessation of life and "dead" is the absence of life. In this age of transplanting organs (heart, kidney) from a "dead" donor to a "live" recipient, the question of when a person is "dead" has not yet really been satisfactorily answered. The Harvard Medical School Committee's definition of death is the one most often quoted. It simply states that a person is dead when the brain is dead. The brain can be pronounced dead when there is no electrical activity as shown by a flat electroencephalogram (EEG) for 24 hours when hypothermia and central nervous system depressants are excluded.

Cells composing the human organism do not die simultaneously, but in a piece-meal process. When a person or animal dies, some of the cells die before other cells. Individual organs also vary in their ability to survive. The brain is one of the first organs to die. The liver may be dead while the kidneys still live, etc. Individual cells of an organ may outlive the functioning state of the organ they compose. The individual cells of a kidney may still live, whereas the kidney itself can no longer function as a kidney—doing the job of cleaning blood pumped through it.

The medical, legal, and philosophical questions of life and death are fascinating. If a bacterium divides into two daughter cells, is the parent bacterium dead? If a one-cell, fertilized, human ovum dies, has a person died? Two cells? Two hundred cells? Two million cells? Two billion cells? More than 20 years ago, a patient named Helen Lane died of carcinoma of the cervix. Cells from this cancer have been propagated in research laboratories throughout the world. This cancer research line is known as the He La Cell Line. While Helen Lane is dead, her cells still live! In the final analysis, somatic death may be considered a relative state.

Changes after Death

Ocular signs
Cessation of circulation
Cessation of respiration
Cooling of the body
Livor mortis (Postmortem hypostasis or Lividity)

Rigor mortis

Putrifaction

Mummification

The first changes of death are not reliable. The person ceases to breathe and the heart ceases to pump blood through the body. Within a few minutes, blood drains from the capillaries of the skin and the muscles relax. The corneal and light reflexes of the eyes disappear. Of interest is the fact that an injection of the appropriate drug directly into the eye with a needle will cause the pupil to react many hours after death! If one has an ophthalmoscope and can look at the blood in the veins of the retina, one can find a more reliable early sign of death. The blood in the retinal veins breaks up into segments looking somewhat like railroad box cars lined up on a track.

The disappearance of the body warmth begins as soon as death occurs. Theoretically, the exact time of death can be calculated from the body temperature by using certain formulas. Unfortunately, there are too many factors that can influence the rate of cooling for this to be of much help.

Once the blood ceases to circulate, gravity pulls it to the dependent parts of the body. The blood fills and distends the small veins and capillaries imparting a purple or reddish-purple color to the skin. At first it appears as splotchy areas that can easily be mistaken for bruises. These splotchy areas first appear in 20 to 30 minutes after death. After 6 to 10 hours, it becomes fixed. Small veins and capillaries rupture and the blood stains the tissues by hemolysis. The membrane covering of the red blood cells ruptures, and the hemoglobin pigment causes the same colors in the skin one sees in a bruise. This change after death is known as hypostasis or postmortem lividity (livor mortis).

Any form of pressure will cause the area to be pale because the veins and capillaries are compressed and contain no blood. The pale areas surrounded by the purple livor mortis are important to the pathologist because they tell of the position of the body after death (Figure 7.1). The appearance of livor mortis also gives some indication of the duration of death.

The differentiation of hypostasis from bruising can be of importance. The blood will be found confined to the blood vessels in livor mortis. Pressure on the area can cause the area to blanch by pushing the blood from the underlying vessels much the same as one can do in a simple first degree sunburn (Figure 7.2).

Although clotted blood is found in the heart and great vessels of

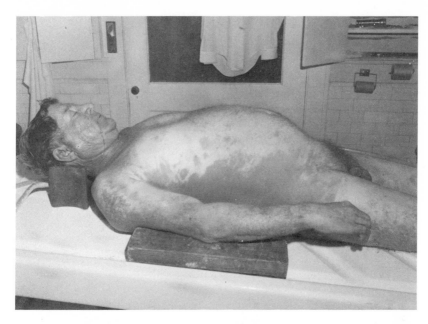

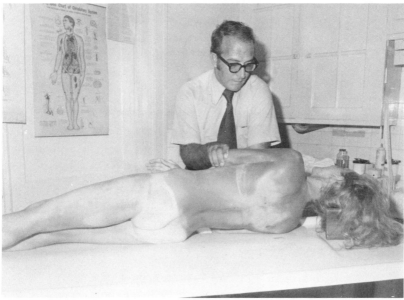

Figure 7.1   Livor mortis with pressure blanch areas, shows the position of the body. (William E. Korndorffer)

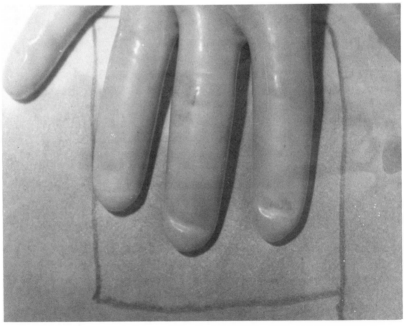

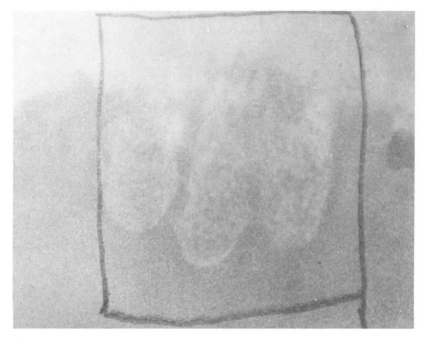

Figure 7.2 Livor mortis can be differentiated from a bruise by pressing the blood from the capillaries of the skin. (William E. Korndorffer)

the body, blood does not normally clot in the venules and capillaries after death. The lining of the small venules and capillaries (vascular endothelium) releases a substance (fibrinolysin) that dissolves blood clots. The blood soon loses its fibrinogen. Any clots formed within the first hour or so after death redissolve, leaving most of the blood permanently fluid. Most of the blood in a dead body is in a liquid form. Embalming is simply pumping out the liquid blood and replacing it with embalming fluid (formaldehyde) mixed with stains to make the skin look more natural.

Rigor mortis is the stiffening of the muscles. It is due to chemical changes involving the proteins of the muscle fibers. Every muscle in the body undergoes the change of rigor mortis. Rigor mortis will fix the body in the attitude adopted by the corpse at death. It is important also as an indication of how long the decedent has been dead. The change is first seen in the smaller muscle masses of the body. Although the stiffening takes place in all of the muscles simultaneously, it appears to the observer first in the face. It then spreads to the neck, arms, trunk, and legs. The delay in the appearance of rigor mortis after death can vary considerably. It usually first appears in two to three hours. It is usually complete within six to eight hours.

Example 4. A 26-year-old man was found dead by the side of a deserted road. He was the apparent victim of a hit-and-run accident, but the body was fixed with rigor mortis in a manner with the knees bent up and the body in a sitting position. The decedent's body had been propped up in an automobile while the car was driven for many hours. It then was dumped out and run over so as to make it appear to be an accident (Figure 7.3).

Cadaveric spasm or instantaneous rigor is a rarely seen, but interesting, phenomenon. It is a form of muscular stiffening which occurs at the moment of death and persists until true rigor mortis develops. When seen it is associated with violent deaths in circumstances of intense emotion. A soldier was found sitting on his horse after being killed by a shell. Another was found in a kneeling posture taking aim with his rifle. (This medical examiner has never seen a case of instantaneous rigor.)

Heat stiffening is seen when a dead body is exposed to intense heat as in a house fire. The heat causes the muscle protein to coagulate and flex the muscles. The large muscle masses outpull the smaller muscle masses so that the body assumes a "pugilistic attitude." The

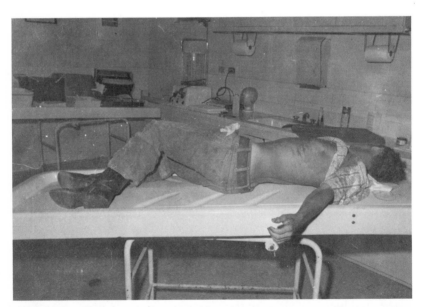

Figure 7.3 Rigor mortis indicates that this body was in a sitting position. (William E. Korndorffer)

fists are clinched and the arms are brought up with the head pulled back. The posture is that taken by strong men or weight lifters when they show their muscles. When bodies are brought from a house fire, onlookers think the posture of the burned victims shows fear. Usually the victims have actually been killed or rendered unconscious by carbon monoxide poisoning and never knew they were being burned.

After death the bacteria normally inhabiting the body invades the tissues and causes putrifaction. One of the first changes is a greenish discoloration of the skin overlying the area of the lower right side of the abdomen. This is because the skin in this area is over the first part of the large colon (cecum) where there are large numbers of bacteria. The discoloration gradually spreads from the lower right side of the abdomen to the rest of the trunk of the body. Within three or four days, the rest of the trunk is discolored. Gas from bacterial action causes the body to bloat and become distended.

The outer layers of skin loosen and separate causing large blisters. The blisters or areas of "skin slippage" can look like burns. The outer layer of skin of the hands and feet with the fingernails and toenails peels off in a glovelike and socklike fashion (Figures 7.4, 7.5, 7.6).

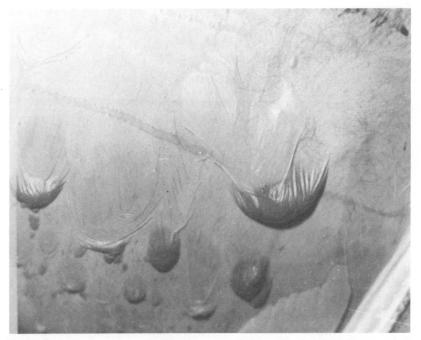

Figure 7.4 Postmortem putrefaction causes blisters that can look like areas of a bad burn. (William E. Korndorffer)

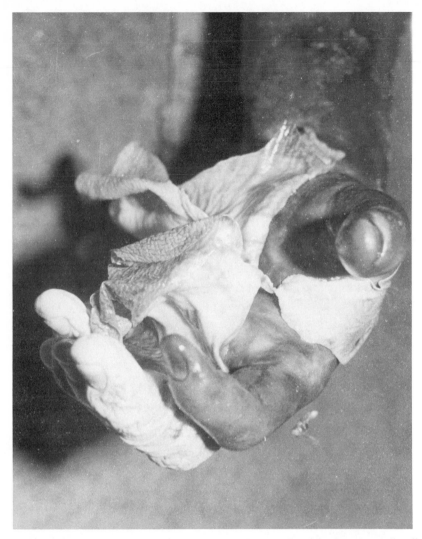

Figure 7.5 After several days, the skin and fingernails of the hand can slip off in a glove-like fashion. (William E. Korndorffer)

Under special environmental circumstances, the body can become mummified. This occurs when the bacterial action is prevented and the body is in a very dry and warm place where there is considerable air movement.

The changes of death occur in a generally predictable fashion. From it, the pathologist is able to estimate the time of death. It is,

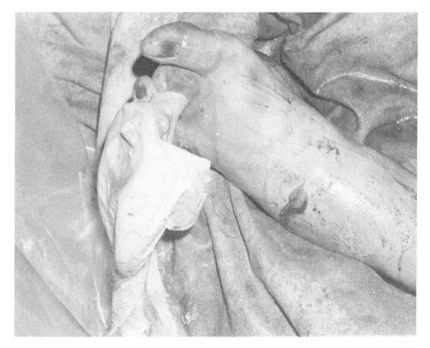

Figure 7.6   After several days, the skin and toenails of the feet can slip off in a sock-like fashion. (William E. Korndorffer)

however, only an estimate and as the time increases from the moment of death to discovery of the body, the estimate becomes less accurate. Other factors such as changes in the fluid from the eyes (vitreous humor) is of help. Perhaps someday a scientist will discover a way in which the pathologist can tell the police exactly when a person was killed or died, but this cannot be done with present scientific knowledge.

IDENTIFICATION

Identification of the dead body is usually by personal impressions. A next-of-kin recognizes the deceased person and identifies the body because it "looks like" the person they believe it to be. The unsatisfactory nature of this type of identification has been repeatedly stressed. Ideally, everybody would be fingerprinted sometime early in life. Then, the identification of the dead could be confirmed with some degree of accuracy. Even here, of course, mistakes could theoretically occur.

Unfortunately, many people, particularly children, have never been fingerprinted, and the identification of a destroyed, unknown person will always be a challenge.

The identity of a homicide victim is usually confirmed by fingerprints. Fingerprints can be classified and filed so that a person can be identified by looking up fingerprints in a file much as a name can be found in an alphabetical index file. Dental records have not yet been classified and filed in a similar manner. A person's identity can be confirmed or disproven through the use of a dental record or chart; but there is no satisfactory way to find out an unidentified person's name through the use of a dental record or chart.

The medical examiner always tries to identify a dead body by physical characteristics that are part of the person. The sex, race, and physical stature are considered primary characteristics. Fingerprints, teeth, scars, hair, tattooing, etc., are secondary characteristics. Clothing on the body, rings, and objects on or near the body cannot be used as real proof of identification. The person may have been wearing someone else's clothing at the time of death. A wallet with false identification could have been planted on a body. Occasionally, this circumstantial type of evidence is the best that is available.

Example 5. Eight persons were found burned to death following a tragic fire of a small hotel. Two adult males have not yet been identified. The bodies have been shown not to be those of a number of missing persons through the use of dental charts and other physical characteristics. The body of an infant, however, was identified by fragments of clothing remaining on the body. Another infant was identified by the shoes on its feet.

The age, sex, and stature of an individual can be determined with some degree of accuracy from the study of a number of different bones of the skeleton. Only the skull, however, gives reliable information as to what race the deceased belonged. There are sex differences in the lower jaw (mandible) and in the hip bone (pelvis). The chin is more square in the male than in the female. The various notches and angles of the female hip bone are wider and more curved than those of the male.

The skeleton and, when present, teeth are the principle sources of information upon which estimates of sex and age are based. The various bones of the body develop at different ages. The soft cartilage is radiolucent so X rays pass through it without difficulty. As the cartilage changes to bone, they are seen as dark spots on the X rays of the skeleton. These ossification centers appear in the various bones of the body at different times. Even different parts of the same bone develop and mature at different ages. Then, as the bones mature, the bony (osseous) parts grow together and the bone then stops growing larger. This union of different parts of the same bone (epiphysial union) occurs at different ages.

The ability to identify an unknown person through the use of skeletal structures and dental charting (forensic odontology) depends on the ability or opportunity to compare the findings with those of a missing person. Some medical examiner offices have facilities to keep unidentified remains for years in the hope of establishing the identity. There is a sense of defeat when the remains of a person must be buried as "unknown."

As a rule, the smaller medical examiner offices operate without sufficient funds to conduct an adequate search for the correct identity. By recording the remains through photographs, X rays, measurements, etc., it is hoped that the record itself is adequate to compare to various missing persons.

An interesting example of this was an unknown victim referred to as "Jonah."

Example 6. On the morning of April 28, 1976, a shrimp boat captain caught a 400 pound shark in his nets off the south jetty in Galveston Bay. After killing the shark, the jaws were cut out and the shark hoisted up to be thrown overboard. Just as the carcass was being thrown over the side of the ship, a human skull and other skeletal remains fell out of the shark's mouth. The captain put the human remains in a plastic bag and turned them over to the medical examiner. Examination of the remains indicated that the victim was a brown-haired, Caucasian male in his late teens or early twenties. The jaw bone (mandible) showed considerable dental work so there was real hope that the body could be positively identified. Unfortunately, to date, the body remains unknown (Figures 7.7 and 7.8).

Another less bizarre case is that of a teenager who was accidentally shot while hunting. When the case was investigated, it was discovered that the boy had used a fictitious name. In spite of extensive investigation, the body had to be buried as unknown.

Perhaps someday, a centralized, computerized roster of missing persons can be set up and classified by age, race, sex, scars, operations, tatoos, and other characteristics. The medical examiner's office would then be able to send a record of the primary and second-

Figure 7.7 The near complete skeleton of an unidentified, brown-haired, 18–20 year old male "Jonah" fell from the jaws of a shark. (William E. Korndorffer)

ary physical characteristics to this centralized agency for possible identification. A list of names of missing persons fitting the description of the unknown corpse would be made available to the medical examiner. Until such a system is devised, unfortunately, hundreds (possibly thousands) of persons shall be buried as "unknown."

REFERENCES

Camps, F. E. *Gradwohl's Legal Medicine*. Third edition. Chicago: Year Book Medical Publications, 1976.

Fatteh, A. *Medicolegal Investigation of Gunshot Wounds*. Philadelphia: J. B. Lippincott, 1976.

Ludwig, J., M.D. *Current Methods of Autopsy Practice*. Philadelphia: W. B. Saunders, 1972.

Polson, C. J. *The Essentials of Forensic Medicine*. Second edition. Springfield: Charles C. Thomas, 1965.

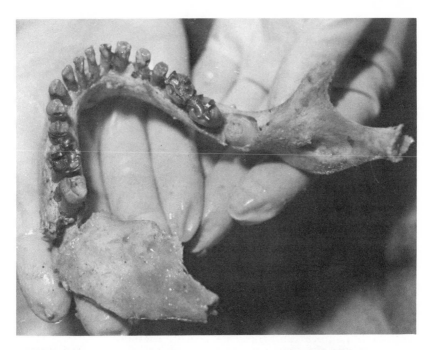

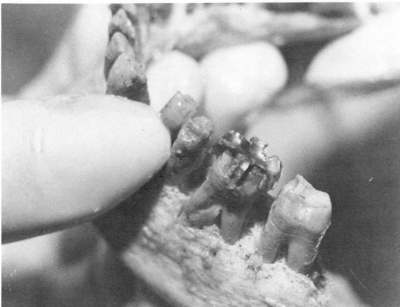

Figure 7.8 Through dental work, the body of "Jonah" may someday be identified. (William E. Korndorffer)

A Teacher Teaching Nurses*

Teaching a death and dying course is unlike presenting any other course. Often you can see the emotional growth process in the class. This becomes an especially rewarding experience giving the class and instructor the positive and immediate feedback of learning. This section details some typical class responses.

Death education is becoming an integral part of the curricula in schools of nursing. What I would like to share with you are some of my ideas and experiences in teaching about death and dying, in hopes that they may be useful to you. This course came about at the request of senior nursing students who were interested in cancer nursing. They felt that they were confronted, almost daily, with people who were dying. They felt that their own feelings got in the way of dealing effectively with the patient. They asked for specific content to help them deal with their feelings. The class pointed out that part of their problem in dealing with the patient was inadequate communication skills.

The students within the class provide each other with a unique support group. Some of the students come into the class knowing no one intimately. Within the first two weeks, I have found that they have begun to discuss intimate feelings within the group, and are increasingly caring and supportive of each other.

Many students enrolled in the course have had some experience with death—personal or professional. There are often unresolved feelings that will come to fore as the course progresses. In most instances, the students with whom I have worked have only needed someone to listen, but I am sure that the situation may well be different as the number of students with whom I have worked increases.

Below are some of the students' reactions that have resulted from heightened awareness through death education:

"The other night when I was working night duty I got so pissed. I got pulled to Head and Neck, which I really like, but the staff is a bit strange and it took until this happened for me to put my finger on it. They've all been working at the hospital for so long that they've decided that to be effective in dealing with some patients you have to be very cold and unfeeling. This situation happened when one of the housekeeping women came out and told the team leader that the

*Written by Jane Dresser, RN, Texas Woman's University, Houston.

patient in 3D was vomiting and needed help—well, I just got in on the last of it and everyone just stood there and the aide said, 'He's not my patient, is he yours?'—well at this point I could see they couldn't care less about whoever it was so I just told her to blow it off and I'd go see what was going on. (The man wasn't my patient and I knew nothing about him other than that he needed help.) So I go into this four-bed ward and here's this little old black man sitting on the edge of the bed gagging like he can't breathe with what looked like a huge tumor—mandible or maxillo—could hardly open his mouth and had a naso-gastric tube in. I reached for the emesis basin and Kleenex to help him and the RN walks in and says nothing at all to me, and when I alerted her to the man's difficulty in breathing she SCREAMED: 'You really don't have to mess with him, he doesn't know what is going on! You had better put on gloves if you are 'cause he's had everything in the world including syphillis—so put on gloves at least!' All of this in front of the poor man who now has tears in his eyes, is getting more hypoxic as the minutes go by, and the RN pushes me into the supply room to get gloves saying, 'You just don't understand, he's not with it anyway, he always has a lot of mucous. I just hate doing his treatments!' I was SO MAD I wanted to cry and stomp my foot, but all I could say was, 'Could you MOVE—the man needs help.' I went back and suctioned him of so much stuff that I'm surprised that he hadn't just passed out. I don't honestly believe I've ever been so ashamed of my own profession and so angry in my life! I hope to God I never become so hard and unfeeling. I'll always remember that poor little man sitting there, so helpless with tears running down his face, and nothing I could do to erase that woman's behavior. It just made me really sick to know how mean people can be."

Andree

"Are we going to talk about our own feelings of death—like what we think about *our* death? I've thought a lot about it and the results are amazing. I keep thinking I'm indestructible and that death is only something that happens to other people. This summer I was diagnosed as having Lupus which was seriously affecting my kidneys. Death was then very real. All the feelings of denial (I still have to go to school regardless) and being cheated (Why me?) decreased faith in God (My mother prayed constantly. I prayed but not for my health.) My boy-friend for the first time talked of marriage and I couldn't even discuss it as a future possibility because I felt I could not plan when I didn't know what would happen to me.

Well it seems it was a misdiagnosis and I have a little glomerulonephritis. So now I *still don't know* what's in my future, but I don't think I am going to die—it seems to take a definite diagnosis to even get me to think about my death.

Oh, well!"

Cynthia

"I enjoyed our field trip to the funeral home and felt it was a nice experience. However, I've been exposed to a lot of funeral homes and it was interesting to note how they all work pretty much the same. Tradition doesn't always have to be so important. The father of one of my best friends owns a funeral home and she's told me a lot about how they run. (They live above the funeral parlor and she says one *does not* cook cabbage or fish on the day of the funeral.) I think the idea of letting one of the family dress the 'loved one' is a great idea. Knowing my mom, if she were dead, I know she wouldn't like some complete stranger to dress her. I think it's a great idea! I think I would like to participate more in the funeral than conventional methods set presently."

Cynthia

"Visiting that funeral home was something else! I really felt it was worthwhile. How many people can think about that situation calmly, ask sensible questions, or be knowledgeable prior to making funeral arrangements?

I couldn't believe the actual cost involved! That night I discussed with my fiancé what I wanted when I died. I'm not sure how ready he was to cope with all this sudden talk about cremation, funerals, etc. I'm sure he had never thought about it. I think he wasn't sure I was telling him all the facts. He wanted to know whether I was sure I was all right!"

Nancy

"Here I am in this great class about death and dying and think I'm getting so good at dealing with it and ZONK—this happens and I felt totally helpless. A very close friend's father had an MI (myocardial infarction) two to three weeks ago. She rushed home, he got better. She came back. Friday night he started cerebral hemorrhaging, then left-sided paralysis, then coma. What do you say when your best friend's father is dying and she can't go to him and you're the only support she has for the moment? All I could do was sit and listen and cry with her.

He's gone. I felt so inadequate. All I could say was I'm sorry etc. I may be better with patients dying, but when it's close to home I guess it's a different story. When she called to say he'd died Sunday it made it even worse because he died about the time her plane landed and she didn't get to see him before he died."

Andree

The Unusual

The inclination to wonder does not end with death. People seek to interpret all the events that concern them. Even the absence of an event requires interpretation. And so it is with the absence of a life. Regardless of how it came to be, it is fact that millions of people—the majority of world population—believe in some form of afterlife phenomena. The variety of such beliefs and the amount of skepticism concerning them are enormous. Generally, it is the scientific community who expresses skepticism. Interestingly, some of the phenomena that are more difficult to explain have originated in scientific areas. A notable example is the "ghost image" that results from using Kirlian photography. This is illustrated in Figure 7.9. Moments before the photograph "Phantom Leaf" was taken, the leaf 's right portion had been severed.

Attention on afterlife phenomena occurred recently when Drs. Kübler-Ross and Moody reported in considerable detail the experiences of persons who had been very near death and subsequently reported out-of-body experiences. I have illustrated similar phenomena with hypnosis and, in one case, with the testimony of a person who reports out-of-body sensations as she goes to sleep. The scientific instruments of measure do not give us an unequivocal means of forming an opinion of these reports. Thus, we must each arrive at our own conclusions concerning afterlife phenomena.

Although the scientific community is cautious or skeptical regarding available evidence of afterlife phenomena and reincarnation, it is a fact that a large proportion of the world's population ascribes to some form of belief system that incorporates such notions. The reincarnation studies reported here are an attempt to illustrate the variety of phenomena that can be elicited under certain conditions. The skeptics will point out that all speak English and maintain the same sex gender in their various lives; that anxieties, conflicts, and fantasy probably account for their stories. The believers will likewise find reasons to support their views.

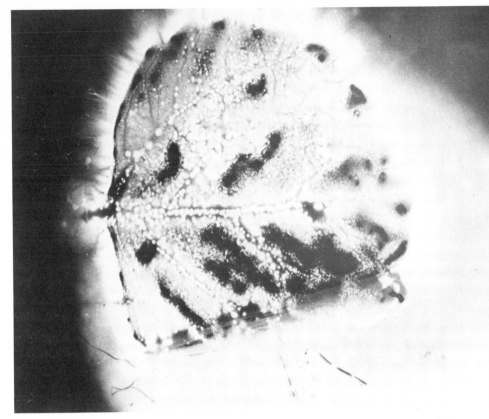

Figure 7.9. Phantom leaf. (Thelma Moss, Neuropsychiatric Institute, UCLA, and Kendall L. Johnson, Paraphysics, Inc. Reprinted by permission of *The Sciences*)

OF HYPNOSIS AND REINCARNATION: THE "INDIAN"

This white male subject was approximately twenty years of age at the time of the hypnotic experiment. During the usual age regression procedures which are elicited in some people's "previous lives" this person manifested the following:

DR. BENTON   What is your name? What is your name? Speak. Say it aloud please, and distinctly.

RESPONDENT	Shini Awa (very softly spoken and with a grunting tone).
DR. BENTON	Where are you?
RESPONDENT	I live north of—north across the big front. North where many elk and many deer. We hunt the deer.
DR. BENTON	What tribe do you belong to?
RESPONDENT	Shoshonee. Many great Shoshonee.
DR. BENTON	How old are you?
RESPONDENT	I am grown up.
DR. BENTON	Who is the chief of your tribe?
RESPONDENT	Chief, Chief of all Shoshonee. Chief of all Shoshonee. He is Crazy Horse. Other chief is Man Afraid of his Own Horse and Bear That Cannot Walk.
DR. BENTON	Relax. Do you have a squaw?
RESPONDENT	A squaw. No, I don't have a squaw. No, tie my horse in front of tepee.
DR. BENTON	Do you have any children?
RESPONDENT	No children.
DR. BENTON	What year is it?
RESPONDENT	It is year when all buffalo go away when railroad comes.
DR. BENTON	What country are you in?
RESPONDENT	Name of Dakota. White man cross territory and once my brother and my father and his horse, they fool me.
DR. BENTON	Are you a great warrior?
RESPONDENT	No, I'm not great warrior. I'm a man who loves his fellow man. Count many cougar and have battle with long knives.
DR. BENTON	Do you know what the Bowie knife is?
RESPONDENT	Bowie—only know long knife. Long knife can——— the people far away.

In normal waking state the subject maintained that he had no knowledge of the Indian tribe mentioned although he had lived in Colorado.

THE "CANADIAN GIRL"

After typical age regression, the following was elicited from a twenty-year-old female:

RESPONDENT   I can't see anything. (In a very tiny, whispy voice) I hear people talking, but I can't see anything.

DR. BENTON   Where are you?

RESPONDENT   Meg—

DR. BENTON   How old are you?

RESPONDENT   I don't know. Not very old.

DR. BENTON   What is your name?

RESPONDENT   Do I have a name?

DR. BENTON   I imagine.

RESPONDENT   I can't see anything. Everything is turning around and around. I hear people talking. I think they're talking about me.

DR. BENTON   What are they saying?

RESPONDENT   I don't know. I think it's about me, though. I must be sick because I can't see anything.

DR. BENTON   The next time I speak, you'll be five years younger than you are now. How old are you?

RESPONDENT   Three years old.

DR. BENTON   What is your name?

RESPONDENT   I don't know. I think it's—

DR. BENTON   The next time I speak, you will be one year older than you are now. How old are you?

RESPONDENT   Four.

DR. BENTON   What is your father's name?

RESPONDENT   Jake Turner.

DR. BENTON   What is your mother's name?

RESPONDENT   I don't have a mother. She died when I was born.

DR. BENTON   Where are you?

RESPONDENT   House—I never go outside the house.

DR. BENTON   The next time I speak, you will be one year older than you are now. How old are you? (pause)

RESPONDENT   Five.

DR. BENTON	What are you doing?
RESPONDENT	Learning to knit.
DR. BENTON	Where do you live?
RESPONDENT	I don't know. I never traveled out of the house. I stay in bed most of the time.
DR. BENTON	Do you ever see?
RESPONDENT	No, I don't know what it is to see. Always black—black and cold.
DR. BENTON	Do you have any brothers?
RESPONDENT	No. My mother died when I was born. My father hates me because he lost her and I'm no good to him because I can't see. I wish I could see.
DR. BENTON	Do you know why you can't see?
RESPONDENT	I don't think I have any eyes.
DR. BENTON	Next time I speak, you're going to be eighteen years old. How old are you?
RESPONDENT	Eighteen.
DR. BENTON	What is your name?
RESPONDENT	Kathy Turner.
DR. BENTON	Where do you live?
RESPONDENT	I live in the same place I always lived in.
DR. BENTON	Do you know the town you live in?
RESPONDENT	It has a funny name. I think it has a "Saint" in it.
DR. BENTON	Which country is it in?
RESPONDENT	In Canada.
DR. BENTON	Do you live in Quebec or Ontario?
RESPONDENT	I live in Vancouver.
DR. BENTON	What year is it?
RESPONDENT	I don't know. I don't go to school. I can't go to school, I don't see. Everyone goes to school except me. I'm no good to anyone because I can't see. (pause)
DR. BENTON	The next time I speak, you will be twenty-one years old.
RESPONDENT	I'm not twenty-one years old. I killed myself when I was nineteen. I took a butcher knife and killed myself. Nobody loved me.

DR. BENTON	What did your daddy say?
RESPONDENT	He didn't cry much. He was glad I was gone. He wanted to leave but he couldn't because I was always alive.
DR. BENTON	Where did he go when you died?
RESPONDENT	He went to the United States.
DR. BENTON	Where?
RESPONDENT	I don't know. To the United States.
DR. BENTON	Okay, where did you go after you died?
RESPONDENT	I don't know. I guess I went to heaven. Where else would I go?
DR. BENTON	You're eighteen years old. Listen closely. The next time I speak, you will feel yourself in a new life. Your mind will move back—turn back, back. You will feel yourself getting smaller and smaller. You will feel yourself going back, back . . . what is your name? (pause)
RESPONDENT	I don't have a name.
DR. BENTON	Who are you?
RESPONDENT	I'm with all the other unborn spirits.
DR. BENTON	Where is this?
RESPONDENT	Way up above everyone else. Way up.
DR. BENTON	Do you see anyone you know?
RESPONDENT	I've known them all. They're all just alike.
DR. BENTON	Do you know when you're going to be born?
RESPONDENT	We never know. We get a summons from God.
DR. BENTON	You get a summons from God?
RESPONDENT	Yes.
DR. BENTON	Where does God stay?
RESPONDENT	He stays in the heavens.
DR. BENTON	What does he look like?
RESPONDENT	We never see God, though.
DR. BENTON	Can you see yourself?
RESPONDENT	No. You can talk to other people but you can't see anything. Not until you're born. Some people are born again.

DR. BENTON	Do you have names in the spirit world?
RESPONDENT	No, I don't think so. I don't have a name.
DR. BENTON	How are you summoned?
RESPONDENT	Oh, I can't—we just know.
DR. BENTON	What does it look like in heaven?
RESPONDENT	It's all white and pink like the sun shining on the clouds. Soft, fluffy, never cold and it's never hot.

THE "SPACE BEING"

In the following male, age regression resulted in the following:

DR. BENTON	Speak. What do you see? Speak clearly. Talk to me clearly. What do you see?
RESPONDENT	I don't know.
DR. BENTON	What does it look like? (pause)
RESPONDENT	It's green.
DR. BENTON	What is green?
RESPONDENT	Saucer. (long pause)
DR. BENTON	What else do you see?
RESPONDENT	Some white and black.
DR. BENTON	What is white and black?
RESPONDENT	Hurts.
DR. BENTON	What shape are they in? Describe to me exactly what you see.
RESPONDENT	Triangle. A triangle. A black-and-white triangle. (heavy breathing and a fearful quality in his voice)
DR. BENTON	What is it used for?
RESPONDENT	(unintelligible)
DR. BENTON	Who lives in it?
RESPONDENT	A great ruler.
DR. BENTON	What is his name?
RESPONDENT	X, X. That's where X lives. (heavy breathing and a morbid, fearful quality in voice)
DR. BENTON	What does he look like?

RESPONDENT   Doesn't have any head, a small head.

DR. BENTON   How did he become ruler? (long pause) What else do you see?

RESPONDENT   A lot of other things.

DR. BENTON   What are they?

RESPONDENT   They are all like X.

DR. BENTON   What shape is their body in?

RESPONDENT   It's all kind, a pointed shape—all kinds of shapes.

DR. BENTON   Do they have arms and legs?

RESPONDENT   Yes, sort of like arms and legs.

DR. BENTON   Are they human?

RESPONDENT   No.

DR. BENTON   Are they metal?

RESPONDENT   No, they're some kind of fiber. A jellylike fiber.

DR. BENTON   What would they eat? Do you see any of them eating?

RESPONDENT   No. (long pause)

DR. BENTON   What else do you see?

RESPONDENT   I see another—

DR. BENTON   What does he look like?

RESPONDENT   The same.

DR. BENTON   What is his name?

RESPONDENT   "C"—I see a "C"—a "C" on the leglike things.

DR. BENTON   What else do you see?

RESPONDENT   I see holes. I see lots of holes.

DR. BENTON   What are they for?

RESPONDENT   Saucers put in the holes—

DR. BENTON   How big are the saucers?

RESPONDENT   They're different sizes.

DR. BENTON   How many people fly in them?

RESPONDENT   Well, there's one room, the room to the saucer.

DR. BENTON   What do they look like?

RESPONDENT   There is a big number on the other type of saucer. Like a cargo.

DR. BENTON   What else do you see?

RESPONDENT   I see "C" again. I see him with a—there's a lot of other one things around here.

DR. BENTON   What are they doing?

RESPONDENT   Killing something. (pause)

DR. BENTON   Do they have males and females?

RESPONDENT   No, they're all alike. They're all alike except for a certain one.

DR. BENTON   Who?

RESPONDENT   "X." (Subject becomes very anxious and fearful.)

A short while later this subject indicated that he, himself, was a "C" and continued to express substantial fear of "X." He subsequently indicated that he lived on another planet, perhaps a moon.

AN OUT-OF-BODY EXPERIENCE

This thirty-five-year-old female describes experiences that bear similarity to those reported by Dr. Moody and Dr. Kübler-Ross; yet, this patient—as far as we know—has not been on the verge of death. Perhaps, many people have these experiences which could include déjà vu.

One theorist has suggested that a reduction of ambient brain-tissue oxygen could foster out-of-body experiences.

DR. BENTON   You were just telling me about some experiences that you had had just as you go to sleep, out-of-body experiences, is that correct?

RESPONDENT   Yes.

DR. BENTON   Would you mind if I record your comments?

RESPONDENT   No . . . I've never talked to anyone about—I haven't read a whole lot on it, either.

DR. BENTON   Why haven't you talked to anyone about it?

RESPONDENT   I guess maybe because they may think I'm odd.

DR. BENTON   What exactly is it that you haven't talked to anyone about and when did you first experience it?

RESPONDENT   Well, I've never talked to anybody about how my body feels, and I've never told anyone about what occurred the day of my first husband's death. The only person I've ever talked to about feeling something bad happening is my mother. But the reason I talked to my mother is because my grandfather was psychic, my father was psychic, and I have a brother that is psychic and they're psychic much stronger than I am.

DR. BENTON   What does psychic mean?

RESPONDENT   Psychic means a feeling of something—the seeing of something for another person. Maybe not seeing, I feel, okay? Now, my brother sees pictures in his mind. All I have is the feeling inside of myself. I don't see a picture, I don't see. The strangest experience of all was when my first husband was killed. He got orders to go to Vietnam the first time around and I knew if he went at that particular time, he was not going to come back. And by that time he'd learned almost to listen when I said, "Don't do such and such or don't go such and such a place. I can't tell you why but just don't do it." He'd learned through a couple of bad experiences when I say it, you know, don't do it because something is going to happen. So, he—at the time he was very strong willed. He was determined to go to Vietnam. He volunteered to go. I understood. I didn't want him to go but at the same time, you know, that's the way he was. And he got orders to go and I was absolutely petrified of his going, you know, because something in me said, "If he goes, he's not going to make it back." So it took me a couple of weeks to persuade him to get out of it. He had a choice to take another job or go which he did. The strangest of all was, when he finally did get orders to go to Vietnam, the second time around, I had no fear, no nothing in me. Actual death of a person, I do not see, I do not feel. I guess my system couldn't cope with it. There was no fear in me. Three months to the day he left, he got killed and this is when it occurred.

DR. BENTON   What occurred?

RESPONDENT   I guess his soul—it has to be, spirit, whatever, basically came to say good-bye.

DR. BENTON   You were asleep?

RESPONDENT   No, I was awake. I had just turned the light off. I had been reading there for a while and just turned the light off. And I was just laying there and like I said, something sat down, waist high—not a word, not a nothing. It was a presence, okay, that's all I felt because the bed went down. You know when somebody sits how the seat will go down? That's what happened. And it stayed there for just a few seconds and it rose back up. It frightened me and I turned the light on but there was nothing there. I didn't know at the time what had happened, but I knew something was there. Then they sent a chaplain and an officer to notify me. And later I got the telegram that stated the time and the day of the death and, I don't know, something just happened in my mind that said that's what it was, you know, he came to say good-bye. I don't know if it was before he was completely dead or if it was after death or what. That I can't say, but I know he came to say good-bye.

DR. BENTON   Now, tell me about this thing where you go to bed and your body—or something seems to leave your body.

RESPONDENT   The first time I remember it happening, I was about fourteen. I had gone to bed. I had turned the light off and I just layed there and the next thing I knew I was looking down on myself. That's the only way I can explain it—I was floating. Or something of me, let's put it that way, was floating right up at the top of the ceiling and I could see myself laying on the bed. But I never leave that spot. I don't float anywhere else. I just stay there. Why I do that, I don't know. And I look down on myself and I just stay there for a few seconds and whatever it is, I have no words for it that leaves me and goes back down inside of my body. I feel something inside of myself that says if I don't get back in my body I'll die. That's what it amounts to because whatever it is up there has to be connected with my body in order for me to live. And I've been doing that ever since. I don't know what to connect it with. I never remember being particularly relaxed or particularly tired or whatever. It just happens. I can't control it.

DR. BENTON	How often does this occur?
RESPONDENT	Oh, I do that every few months. I don't know the reason for it.
DR. BENTON	Now are you awake when this happens or asleep?
RESPONDENT	I'm awake. My eyes are open. I just usually have had the lights off for just a few seconds and it usually takes forty-five minutes to an hour to go to sleep. I see myself going up there and I see myself coming down and when I'm hanging up there I see my body lying down there. It's the weirdest experience. That's the only way I can put it.
DR. BENTON	Do you have any particular kinds of feeling. Any feelings like ultra-relaxation or ecstasy or—
RESPONDENT	None. No, the only feeling that I have is a knowledge that I've got to get back down there. There's no ecstasy, no relaxation.
DR. BENTON	Just a little anxiety occasionally.
RESPONDENT	Just some anxiety, yes, that I know I've got to get back into that shell that's on the bed. And that's what I consider it because I guess the part that makes the shell live basically has left it. Does that make any sense to you? Maybe it would make some sense to somebody that knows what I'm talking about. But it's weird, to me, a strange experience and like I said, I've never discussed it with anybody because it's, I know normal people don't—normal people don't leave their bodies and go float to the ceiling. They don't.

8

Getting in Touch:The Nurse's Response to Death and Dying

Nurses—students and graduates—will in their careers be called upon to assist dying patients. Nonverbal behavior may be as significant in those moments as the spoken word. Tools to sharpen your awareness may assist greatly when you experience uncertainty and anxieties. Accordingly, we have included in this chapter material which we have found useful. We hope you can develop your own creative approaches to getting in touch.

Charles Ross (1976, p. 47), in summarizing the death-education literature, reports that there is ample evidence that professionals dealing with dying patients need assistance in exploring their own attitudes and feelings toward death and dying through death-awareness exercises such as role playing and filling out death certificates. Koestenbaum (1976, p. 199) said, "Techniques to help the dying are meaningless, since death is a philosophical problem rather than a medical one." Worden and Proctor (1976, p. 12) contend that such exercises do alter personal awareness in desirable ways. Several studies testing Frankl's theory on the enhancement of life's meaningfulness through facing anxiety-evoking situations or even suffering seem to support the latter position. In addition, it seems that certain aspects of desensitization training support procedures that encourage controlled measures of exposure.

Seven paper and pencil scales have been evolved that attempt to measure attitudes and orientation toward death.

1. Fear of Death Scale by Sarnoff & Corwin (1959, described in Ross, 1976, p. 48)
2. Boyar Fear of Death Scale (1964)

*Written by R. G. Benton, Ph.D. and Jane Dresser RN, MA, Instructor, Texas Woman's University, Houston.

3. Lester Attitudes toward Death Scale (1967)
4. Collett-Lester Fear of Death Scale (1969)
5. Tolar's Death Anxiety Scale (1969)
6. Templer's Death Anxiety Scale (1969)
7. Dickstein's Death Concern Scale (1972)

Templer's Death Anxiety Scale is often reported in literature about dying (Ross, 1976, p. 51). Some investigators have endeavored to use this scale along with other instruments to assess the constructive or destructive patient coping patterns.

We have included material within this chapter which can be used to help you better understand your attitudes toward death and dying.

How, for example, did your parents or loved ones first explain death to you? With many of us it's hard to remember. Still, as research shows, most of us did ask. Usually, our questions—whether overt or covert—were soft-peddled or embellished with grand metaphors which were difficult for the young to follow, much less for the old. Was it always this way? Were we always so reluctant to speak of such matters? History says no. In early America the families of the deceased often helped prepare the body for burial right in the home. Embalming did not come into burial practice until after the Civil War—when a certain Mr. Holmes—being dismissed from Harvard Medical School, began traveling and offering an embalming service. His technique and service obviously appealed to the early American mentality which desired to preserve as much living likeness and tranquility as possible (Figure 8.1). Embalming didn't have the same wide appeal in Europe and even today is not practiced there on a scale equivalent to that in the United States.

Historians tell us that in bygone eras even the children were present at deathbed scenes. Today most Americans find this horrifying. Since most deaths now occur in hospitals—which refuse young visitors (more for behavioral control purposes)—children have no entreé. Even adult family contact is greatly limited, usually to a very short time. The body is removed from the hospital room (space is at a premium!) to a funeral home or lab for autopsy. Certainly the family is not allowed to witness the autopsy and is almost always excluded from the embalming procedure. The family is generally easily dissuaded from witnessing these procedures. Denial is clearly the less disturbing route.

We are, and perhaps "should" be a life- and living-oriented society. We are much more aware of how many births occur daily than

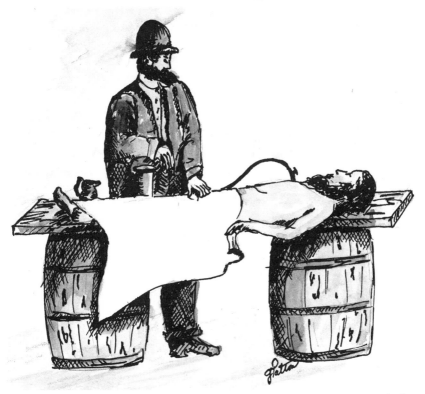

Figure 8.1   An early American embalmer shown with profusion paraphernalia and the "cooling board" on which the body is placed to cool as it becomes rigid. Coins were often placed on eyelids to keep them shut. (Ginny Patton)

deaths. Perhaps our propensity for the denial of death contributes culturally to our personal dilemma with waste materials: we don't think or plan beyond point of utilization. We plan and build all kinds of things and systems but rarely plan past the target function. Thus we have decaying neighborhoods, buildings accumulating atomic waste, piles of garbage.

Freud, Kübler-Ross, and others have suggested that vestiges of personal omnipotence have led to power struggles and war; healthy death attitudes and less denial might well have changed the course of history.

Denial is a useful and perhaps a healthy mechanism. Our argument is not with denial, but rather with our method of employing it as well as other protective defenses. What we shall propose is that you stimulate your coping systems with growth experiences that will give you more flexibility in dealing with living, dying, and death—the complete life cycle. We believe that Dr. Kübler-Ross has identified several significant stages of emotional display which are at the heart of our instinctive detachment pattern. As we gain experience with attachment and detachment, the transitions become increasingly flexible and we are increasingly capable of maintaining an inner state of tranquility and peace. We feel that perhaps some of the experiential approaches we outline and suggest in this chapter will enhance your growth in this area.

Have you denied your death? Let's take a quick inventory of how you use denial.

		YES	NO
1.	Do you have a will?	____	____
2.	Do you plan to donate organs?	____	____
3.	Do you sometimes joke about your death?	____	____
4.	Can you now feel any feeling/emotion about your death?	____	____
5.	In what year do you think you will die?	____	____
6.	Are you afraid of the pain of dying?	____	____
7.	Are you afraid of suffocation?	____	____
8.	Do you realize that your body will decompose after your death?	____	____
9.	Are you going to be embalmed?	____	____
	Cremated?	____	____
10.	Does reading about death depress you?	____	____

In a study which we recently conducted at a major cancer facility, we administered to surgery candidates a "puzzle picture." The picture was simply an outline of a human body with the various major parts segmented and numbered with dark lines. For instance, the lower legs, upper legs, arms, genitalia, mid-torso, chest area, neck, center face, outer face etc., were separated with dark lines. The patients were simply asked to point to those parts of the body which they felt they could do without. The answers varied but invariably each reached the "me point"—a point where they would say, "Well, that's it! I can't take away any more—that's me left!"

To accentuate the perceptual aspects of the test, we actually fabricated the human form in puzzle pieces so that the patient removed each puzzle piece until he reached a point where he felt his life would no longer exist. From this project it became obvious that people tend to maintain a body image with a degree of completeness. Construct your own body-image puzzle. Where is your "me"?

Let's now return to our brief questionnaire above. When are you going to die? You really are going to die. Can you try and guess when? How? Where? Write three brief paragraphs; one which would go into the newspaper about your death, another in "first person" how you think you may die, and the third how you will really probably die. Now, spend a little thought and write your will—

I,_____, being of sound mind do hereby

make my last will and testament on this _____ day of _____, 19___.

It is my desire _____

_____.

Pain. Do you fear pain associated with death? Does it make you "shiver" to think of someone profusing your body? Have you witnessed an embalming or autopsy?

Fear and denial give us the motive and the means of putting distance between ourselves and the unpleasant or unthinkable. Worden and Proctor (1976) have conceptualized a "personal death-awareness index" designed to help people determine their own death-awareness level. Basically, their scale has four points: low, low-moderate, high-moderate, high. A person determines death awareness by recalling the number of times in a day he or she has thought about his or her *own* death (not someone else's). If you had no such thoughts then you would probably score "low." The authors have pointed out that the average person would fluctuate periodically along the scale but that many people would register at the low end. As one's age increases the fluctuations may become more moderate. Personal death awareness beyond an acceptable level results in anxiety, embarassment, death-related humor and other related experiences. These heightened emotive levels may influence our behavior and decisions at the given time, e.g., a nursing student who is in close contact with death may experience avoidance feelings, unmanageable sympathy/empathy, anger.

Low personal death awareness may predispose a man to "ignore" making a will and thereby cause considerable difficulty for his spouse and children. Low personal death awareness tends to reduce or prevent adaptive coping and planning.

We have selected several experientially based inventories which facilitate death awareness in a healthy way. Our selections and a list of information resources are presented in the following pages.

I.   Personal Death Awareness Inventory
II.   Getting Your Financial House in Order
III.   Death Certificate
IV.   Living Bank Donor Forms
V.   Nurses' Attitude Checklist
VI.   Checklist of Religious Rites
VII.   Information Index—A Compilation of Information Resources

I. PERSONAL DEATH AWARENESS INVENTORY

Memories of death:

My first death memories (experiences)_____

The person was (family, friend, other)_____

I was (not) frightened and remember most_____

The first funeral I attended was _____. I remember best _____

Fears

I fear *pain* in death	I fear *suffocation*
I fear *helplessness* in death	I fear *disfigurement*
I fear losing bowel control	I fear *after death*
	a. Burial
	b. Embalming
	c. Other

Interactions: Group experiences/Role playing exercises

The court:

Appoint a Court to probate your will with classmates acting as your heirs.

Speaking of death with a patient:

Encourage participants to verbalize feelings, anxieties, conflicts of knowing.

II. GETTING YOUR FINANCIAL HOUSE IN ORDER

When one knows of impending death, there are several practical matters in the financial area that should be considered:

During the Illness

The Will. Review the will and make necessary changes. Be sure to make a letter of instructions (including location of will). In the letter of instruction you may include wishes not covered in the will, such as designating a funeral home, type of service, preferences for children's school, suggestions on property sales or management.

The Bank Account. Bank funds in the patient's name will be frozen at death. Thus, the dying may wish to consider increasing funds in the survivor's savings and checking accounts. The spouse or survivors may need extra cash. Joint account funds are not frozen, but are considered part of the decedent's taxable estate.

Insurance. There is a three-year contemplation-of-death rule that does not allow one to circumvent insurance policy tax liability if money is converted for use. Such money converted for use and falling under the three-year rule is part of the deceased's taxable estate. This includes a gift of ownership within that period. Review insurance beneficiary clauses.

Estate Taxes. These may be an important consideration for some individuals. Discuss with an attorney the feasibility of setting up a tax-saving trust for survivors.

Investments. Not infrequently a person dies without leaving an inventory of his or her properties. Moreover, the modus operandi that has been used in handling these properties may be impossible to discern unless the decendent leaves some instructions. There may be market situations that should be described as stop orders, stop calls, margin accounts, etc. It may be desirable to convert speculative funds to estate tax saving bonds.

Power of Attorney. Obtain legal advice regarding this important tool. You may want to adopt a general power of attorney that allows a selected survivor to perform transactions if you are incapacitated.

Miscellaneous Matters. Contact insurance companies and review policy benefits. Request claim forms. Contact your company employee benefits department or state agency to determine benefits, claim forms, and beneficiaries, if funds are forthcoming.

Family Functions After a Death

Estate Executor and/or Lawyer. Schedule a meeting with the executor two or three days after funeral services. Speed may be important since probate of the will will soon begin. A meeting before probate begins is often desirable.

Personal Papers of the Deceased. These should be examined. Sometimes there will be unknown burial policies, military discharge papers, or fraternal organization papers that deal with death obligations. Military discharge papers can be used to file a claim with the Veterans Administration for cash death benefits of about $400. Social Security also pays a death benefit.

Miscellaneous Matters after Death. Notify credit card companies and destroy cards. Obtain insurance claim forms. Notify Homeowners Insurance and auto insurance companies. Contact banks, trust departments and others concerned with the deceased's financial matters.

Death and Property*

Almost every person who dies owns some property at the time of death. This may even include "legal paupers" who have no interests except those which may vest after their deaths, such as life insurance policies, survivor's death benefits or properties which may come to them by will or inheritance after their deaths and thus go into their estates.

---

*Written by Mike S. Thorne, Attorney-at-Law, General Practice, 1222 North Loop, P. O. Box 8560, Houston, Texas.

Disposition of Property after Death. A decedent's property is disposed of after death in one of two ways: by will—an instrument made during the lifetime of the decedent directing the disposition of property—and by descent and distribution—the laws applicable to persons who die intestate, that is without a will.

Intestate Succession. Where a person in Texas dies without a will, his property is distributed as follows: If he leaves no spouse, the property goes to his children and their descendants; if there are no children or descendants, then to his father and mother in equal portions if both survive, or half to any one survivor and the other half to any surviving brothers and sisters; or if there are no brothers and sisters, then the entire estate to the surviving parent; if there are no surviving parents, then to the brothers and sisters and their descendants; if there are no parents, brothers or sisters or their descendants, then the inheritance shall be divided into two equal portions, one of which shall go to the paternal and the other to the maternal kin in the following course: to the grandfather and grandmother in equal parts if both survive, but if only one survives, then the estate is divided into two equal parts, one of which shall go to the survivor and the other shall go to the descendant or descendants of the deceased grandfather or grandmother, or if the deceased grandparent has no descendants, then the surviving grandparent receives the entire estate. If no grandparent survives, then the entire estate goes to their descendants, passing to the nearest lineal ancestors and their descendants. (V.A.T.S. Probate Code, Sec. 38 [A].) If the deceased leaves a spouse, the property is disposed of as follows: if the deceased has children or their descendants, the surviving husband or wife receives one-third of the personal property and the balance of the personal property goes to the child or children of the deceased and their descendants. The surviving spouse also receives a life estate in one-third of the real property (land) of the deceased, with the remainder to the child or children of the deceased and their descendants; if the deceased leaves no children or their descendants, then the surviving spouse receives all the personal property and one-half of the real property of the deceased and the other half passes and is inherited according to the rules of descent and distribution unless the deceased has neither surviving parents nor surviving brothers or sisters or their descendants, in which case the surviving spouse receives the entire estate. (V.A.T.S. Probate Code, Sec. 38[B].)

As the foregoing may suggest, the distribution of property without a will is so complicated that it involves a great deal of family research, time, and effort simply to decide who shall receive it. One might rationalize that the probate code disposes of one's property and therefore one does not need a will. This is not strictly true, since the probate code simply outlines who is entitled to the property and thus entitled to *equitable title*—but it does not give that person *legal title*. The law must be invoked in the county or probate court by an application to declare heirship or by an application for administration (the latter of which is necessary if any debts remain to be paid or collected). These actions involve the posting of bonds by administrators and the appointment of attorneys ad litem to represent the "unknown heirs" of the deceased. The process is more time consuming and expensive than if the deceased had left a will.

Disposition of Property by Will. The Texas Probate Code is an outgrowth of the English common law *Statute of Wills,* which directed that a person should have a vehicle for disposition of property after death according to that person's personal preferences. Although people dislike making or even discussing wills because wills suggest death to them, making wills has become necessary to avoid needless expense in legal fees and court costs and also to insure that property will pass according to the deceased's wishes. The Texas Probate Code provides that any person eighteen years of age or older may make a will.

There are four basic kinds of wills:

1. The Formal Self-proving Will. This instrument must be in writing, signed by the testator or testatrix, witnessed by two persons fourteen years of age or older who sign as witnesses in the presence of the testator and at his request and in the presence of a notary public who acknowledges the attached "self-proving affidavit."
2. The Formal Will. This instrument is the same as the formal self-proving will, but does not contain the self-proving affidavit and thus for proof in court requires the testimony of at least one of the attesting witnesses.
3. The Holographic Will. This is a will written wholly in the handwriting of the testator. It is a perfectly good will, but is harder to prove, since it requires the testimony of two witnesses familiar with the handwriting of the testator who can testify that the entire instrument is in the testator's handwriting. Another disadvantage of this type of will is that if the testator uses any words which have legal significance, then his will will be construed as if he had precise legal knowledge of the significance of these words. Theoretically, a will of this type would also be subject

to attack if it were handwritten on a sheet of printed letterhead stationery, since it would not be "wholly in the handwriting of the testator."

4. The Nuncupative Will. This is an oral will made at the time of the last sickness of the deceased at his home or where he has resided for ten days or more preceding the date of the will, except when the deceased becomes ill away from home and dies before he returns home. This will is not valid when the value of the estate exceeds thirty dollars "unless it be proved by three credible witnesses that the testator called on a person to take notice or bear testimony that such is his will, or words of like import." (V.A.T.S. Probate Code, Sec. 65.)

Probate. The word "probate," because of recent popular fiction, has come to have a sinister significance to many people. Actually, all it means is "proof." It is a simple court proceeding wherein the testator's will is proved to be his will and is recorded of record, thus passing record title to the beneficiaries named in the will. There are only three ways to avoid probate. The first is to die without a will, which involves the foregoing hardships of descent and distribution. The second is to give away your property before your death. This is impractical; most persons want to retain title to their property for business or other reasons and even the giving of a remainder interest in their property while retaining a life estate therein effectively ties their hands with regard to the further disposition of their property. The third way to avoid it is to take it with you. Since this is at least as impractical as the former two methods, it is wise to make a will and have the terms of it carried out at your death. It is also important to note that a will is a *death instrument,* as distinguished from a living instrument such as a deed. It does not become operative until the death of the testator and thus may be changed at any time prior to his death.

III DEATH CERTIFICATE*

TYPE OR PRINT IN PERMANENT INK FOR INSTRUCTIONS SEE HANDBOOK

DEPARTMENT OF HEALTH, EDUCATION, AND WELFARE – PUBLIC HEALTH SERVICE – NATIONAL CENTER FOR HEALTH STATISTICS 1978 REVISION

LOCAL FILE NUMBER | STATE FILE NUMBER

DECEDENT

DECEDENT–NAME FIRST	MIDDLE	LAST	SEX	DATE OF DEATH (Mo., Day, Yr.)
1.			2.	3.

RACE—I e.g., White, Black, American Indian, etc.) (Specify)	AGE—Last Birthday (Yrs.)	UNDER 1 YEAR MOS. / DAYS	UNDER 1 DAY HOURS / MINS.	DATE OF BIRTH (Mo., Day, Yr.)	COUNTY OF DEATH
4	5a.	5b.	5c.	6.	7a.

CITY, TOWN OR LOCATION OF DEATH	HOSPITAL OR OTHER INSTITUTION—Name (If not in either, give street and number)	IF HOSP. OR INST. Indicate DOA, OP/Emer. Rm., Inpatient (Specify)
7b.	7c.	7d.

IF DEATH OCCURRED IN INSTITUTION, SEE HANDBOOK REGARDING COMPLETION OF RESIDENCE ITEMS.

STATE OF BIRTH (If not in U.S.A., name country)	CITIZEN OF WHAT COUNTRY	MARRIED, NEVER MARRIED, WIDOWED, DIVORCED (Specify)	SURVIVING SPOUSE (If wife, give maiden name)	WAS DECEDENT EVER IN U.S. ARMED FORCES? (Specify Yes or No)
8.	9.	10.	11.	12.

SOCIAL SECURITY NUMBER	USUAL OCCUPATION (Give kind of work done during most of working life, even if retired)	KIND OF BUSINESS OR INDUSTRY
13.	14a.	14b.

RESIDENCE–STATE	COUNTY	CITY, TOWN OR LOCATION	STREET AND NUMBER	INSIDE CITY LIMITS (Specify Yes or No)
15a.	15b.	15c.	15d.	15e.

PARENTS

FATHER–NAME FIRST MIDDLE LAST	MOTHER–MAIDEN NAME FIRST MIDDLE LAST
16.	17.

INFORMANT–NAME (Type or Print)	MAILING ADDRESS STREET OR R.F.D. NO.	CITY OR TOWN	STATE	ZIP
18a.	18b.			

DISPOSITION

BURIAL, CREMATION, REMOVAL, OTHER (Specify)	CEMETERY OR CREMATORY–NAME	LOCATION CITY OR TOWN STATE
19a.	19b.	19c.

FUNERAL SERVICE LICENSEE Or Person Acting As Such (Signature)	NAME OF FACILITY	ADDRESS OF FACILITY
20a.	20b.	20c.

CERTIFIER

To be Completed by CERTIFYING PHYSICIAN Only

21a. To the best of my knowledge, death occurred at the time, date and place and due to the cause(s) stated.
(Signature and Title)

DATE SIGNED (Mo., Day, Yr.)	HOUR OF DEATH
21b.	21c. M

NAME OF ATTENDING PHYSICIAN IF OTHER THAN CERTIFIER (Type or Print)
21d.

To be Completed by MEDICAL EXAMINER or CORONER Only

22a. On the basis of examination and/or investigation, in my opinion death occurred at the time, date and place and due to the cause(s) stated.
(Signature and Title)

DATE SIGNED (Mo., Day, Yr.)	HOUR OF DEATH
22b.	22c. M

PRONOUNCED DEAD (Mo., Day, Yr.)	PRONOUNCED DEAD (Hour)
22d. ON	22e. AT M

NAME AND ADDRESS OF CERTIFIER (PHYSICIAN, MEDICAL EXAMINER OR CORONER) (Type or Print)
23.

REGISTRAR	DATE RECEIVED BY REGISTRAR (Mo., Day, Yr.)
24a. (Signature)	24b.

CAUSE OF DEATH

CONDITIONS IF ANY WHICH GAVE RISE TO IMMEDIATE CAUSE STATING THE UNDERLYING CAUSE LAST

25. IMMEDIATE CAUSE | [ENTER ONLY ONE CAUSE PER LINE FOR (a), (b), AND (c).] | Interval between onset and death

PART I
(a)

DUE TO, OR AS A CONSEQUENCE OF: | Interval between onset and death
(b)

DUE TO, OR AS A CONSEQUENCE OF: | Interval between onset and death
(c)

PART II | OTHER SIGNIFICANT CONDITIONS—Conditions contributing to death but not related to cause given in PART I (a)

AUTOPSY (Specify Yes or No)	WAS CASE REFERRED TO MEDICAL EXAMINER OR CORONER (Specify Yes or No)
26.	27.

ACC., SUICIDE, HOM., UNDET., OR PENDING INVEST. (Specify)	DATE OF INJURY (Mo., Day, Yr.)	HOUR OF INJURY	DESCRIBE HOW INJURY OCCURRED
28a.	28b.	28c. M	28d.

INJURY AT WORK (Specify Yes or No)	PLACE OF INJURY—At home, farm, street, factory, office building, etc. (Specify)	LOCATION STREET OR R.F.D. No. CITY OR TOWN STATE
28e.	28f.	28g.

HRA-162-1
Rev. 1/78

*Reprinted by permission of U.S. Department of Health, Education, and Welfare. 1978 revision.

The
Living Bank

Uniform Donor Card

EMERGENCY

In the hope that I may help others, I hereby make this anatomical gift, if medically acceptable, to take effect upon my death. The words and marks below indicate my desires.

I give: (a) ☐ any needed organs or parts

(b) ☐ only the following organs or parts

⎯⎯⎯⎯⎯⎯⎯⎯⎯⎯⎯⎯⎯⎯⎯⎯

Specify which organ(s) or part(s) for the purposes of transplantation, therapy, medical research or education;

(c) ☐ my body for anatomical study if needed.

REPRINTED BY PERMISSION OF THE LIVING BANK, HOUSTON, TEXAS.

⎯⎯⎯⎯⎯⎯⎯⎯⎯⎯⎯⎯⎯⎯⎯⎯

Donor's Social Security No.

Print or type next of kin & relationship

Address of next of kin

FOR INFORMATION IN AN EMERGENCY, CONTACT THE LIVING BANK INTERNATIONAL, AREA CODE 713/528-2971, OR WRITE P. O. BOX 6725, HOUSTON, TEXAS 77005.

LIMITATIONS OR SPECIAL WISHES, IF ANY

Signed by the Donor and the following two witnesses in the presence of each other:

Signature of Donor ⎯⎯⎯⎯⎯⎯ Donor's Birthdate

City & State where signed ⎯⎯⎯⎯⎯⎯ Date signed

Witness ⎯⎯⎯⎯⎯⎯ Witness

THIS IS A LEGAL DOCUMENT UNDER THE UNIFORM ANATOMICAL GIFT ACT OR SIMILAR LAWS

The Living Bank

818 Hermann Prof. Bldg.   P. O. Box 6725
Houston, Texas 77005   Phone 713 528 - 2971

Donor's Name (Type or Print)

Social Security No.

Street Address

Date of Birth

City   State   Zip

Donor's Next of Kin

Relationship

Address of Next of Kin

IN THE HOPE THAT I MAY HELP OTHERS, I HEREBY MAKE THIS ANATOMICAL GIFT, IF MEDICALLY AC-
CEPTABLE, TO TAKE EFFECT UPON MY DEATH. THE WORDS AND/OR MARKS BELOW INDICATE MY
DESIRES.

I GIVE:

(a) ☐   Any Needed Organs or Parts

(b) ☐   Only the Following Organs or Parts:

_____

(c) ☐   My Body for Anatomical Study IF NEEDED.

Limitations or Special Wishes _____

By signing this form, the Donor authorizes the physician listed below to furnish the attending physician any pertinent medical information in the event of the Donor's death. If Donor has no physician, please leave the line blank.

Name of Donor's Physician and Address

SIGNED BY DONOR AND THE FOLLOWING TWO WITNESSES IN THE PRESENCE OF EACH OTHER

Signature of Donor

Date Signed

Signature of Witness

Signature of Witness

This or any duplication is a legal document under the Uniform Anatomical Give Act or similar laws.

PLEASE RETURN THIS FORM TO THE OFFICE OF THE LIVING BANK FOR REGISTRATION.

INSTRUCTIONS

The uniform donor card and donor registration form should be completed at the same time so that you will have identical witnesses on both. When possible, please have your next of kin sign as a witness.

The registration form is to be returned to this office. A copy will be made and returned for your files. A copy will also be sent to your physician with a letter of explanation. If you do not have a doctor, just leave the line blank.

The donor card is **FOR YOU** and should be placed with your driver's license for rapid identification. **DO NOT RETURN!**

Parents or legal guardians must sign if the donor is a minor.

If donations are made for transplant purposes only, medically acceptable organs are removed immediately and the body is returned to the family for burial. The usual procedure is for a member of the family, the doctor and/or hospital administrator to notify the nearest medical center or The Living Bank.

There is no cost to the donor when parts are removed for transplantation. Also, there is **no** payment for bodies willed to a medical school.

When "c" is checked, you are signifying that you wish to donate your body to a medical school. Acceptance of the donation depends on the current needs of the medical schools in your area.

Medical schools will not accept a body when an autopsy has been done. The willed body program is full in several states but when the next of kin is willing to pay transportation costs, arrangements may be made to place the donation with a medical school where a need exists. When the donation is refused by the medical school the family of the deceased is responsible for the disposition of the body. Transportation costs vary depending on the distance.

The Uniform Donor Card issued by this office is a legal document in all 50 states. The Living Bank maintains one central office in Houston, Texas and is available on a 24-hour basis. Part of our service is to render assistance at the time of death by helping to make the necessary contacts.

FOR ADDITIONAL IDENTIFICATION, A LIVING BANK PENDANT OR KEY TAG MAY BE PURCHASED AT OUR COST. THE PENDANT IS $3.50 AND THE KEY TAG IS $3.00.

Reprinted by permission of the Living Bank, Houston, Texas.

V NURSES' ATTITUDE CHECKLIST

Death and Dying Attitude Checklist*

Sooner or later you will be expected to treat a patient who is dying. What thoughts and feelings do you have as you think about this? Think about your *true* feelings, not what you think they *ought* to be. For now, try to forget all the things you have learned about how a "professional" must respond to a dying patient, how a "mature" adult must feel about death, and how your family feels about death and dying. To help you do this, complete the following attitude self-check list.

_____ 1.   I expect to feel very uncomfortable when I have to talk to a dying person/patient.

_____ 2.   I wish I knew what to say to a patient who knows he is dying.

_____ 3.   I wouldn't want to be the one to tell a patient he is dying.

_____ 4.   At the point when there's nothing more medical science can do for a patient, then the responsibility of the doctor and nurse is only to make him as comfortable as possible physically.

_____ 5.   I am frankly frightened at the thought of caring for a dying patient. I am afraid the patient will ask me if he is dying—or other questions about his condition—that I am not supposed to answer.

_____ 6.   I think I can help make a patient more comfortable with the fact of his death.

_____ 7.   I worry that I will get too fond of a dying patient and won't be able to control my feelings.

_____ 8.   I can't imagine anyone ever being free of the fear of dying.

_____ 9.   I don't think a person should be told he's dying. There's no point in adding to his suffering.

*From *Nursing the Dying Patient*, Charlotte Epstein, Reston Publishing Company, 1975.

_____10.   I think people are most afraid of death when they're about my age than at any other age.

_____11.   I don't think death should be discussed in front of children.

_____12.   I must admit to a feeling of disgust at the thought of being around a person who is dying.

_____13.   Being around a dying person would just keep reminding me that I will also die.

_____14.   I think people can wish you dead.

_____15.   Being around someone who is sick or dying would make me feel proud of my good physical condition.

Nursing Behaviors That Can Encourage Expression of Patient's Needs*

Encouraging Patient's Expression of Needs:

1.   Sits down at bedside.

2.   Sits for ten minutes.

3.   Come close to the patient without doing medical-technical things.

4.   Asks, "Is there a question you'd like to ask me?"

5.   Invites the patient to ask questions.

6.   Asks, "Is there something you would like to talk about?"

7.   Asks, "How do you feel about being in the hospital?"

*From *Nursing the Dying Patient*, Charlotte Epstein, Reston Publishing Company, 1975.

8. Asks, "How do you feel about the nurses here?"

9. Asks, "How do you feel about the doctors here?"

10. Asks, "How do you feel about the aides here?"

11. Waits at least six seconds for the patient to respond to an invitation to speak.

12. Says, "Tell me more about how you feel."

13. Accepts what the patient says.

14. Says, "I've heard from other people that they feel that way when they come into the hospital."

15. Responds by building on what the patient said.

16. Looks at patient's face when he or she talks, nodding and murmuring understanding.

EMPATHY   17. Says, "Yes, I know. Something like that happened to me."

18. Talks about death.

19. Talks about the patient's family.

20. Expresses sadness to match patient's sadness.

SYMPATHY   21. Expresses anger to match patient's anger.

22. Says, "I am so sorry you have pain."

23. Says, "I'm so sorry I can't change things for you."

24. Can cry when the patient cries.

Neutral Behaviors That Are Part of Nurse's Responsibility:

25. Works efficiently, doing what must be done for the patient's physical comfort.

26. Routine directions.

Discouraging Patient's Expression of Needs:

27. Does not stop work even for a moment when patient is talking.

AVOIDANCE   28. Initiates talk only with casual pleasantry.

29. Responds to patient's casual talk with similar talk.

30. Does not talk to the patient except to give routine directions.

31. Talks zestfully about the weather or view.

FEAR   32. Acts brisk and "healthy," the kind of behavior that makes one say, "She is full of life."

33. Asks a question and does not wait for an answer.

34. Keeps up a steady stream of small talk.

35. Comes in for a quick, "anything you need?" and goes out again.

36. Does not come close to patient except for specific nursing behaviors.

37. Stays with patient for less than five minutes.

38. Does not respond when the patient says something.

39. Leaves without responding when the patient says something.

VI CHECKLIST OF RELIGIOUS RITES*

This is a checklist of religious rites for the three major American faiths. While you will not be tested on these rites, they are important for your work, both now and later, with the terminally ill.

Realizing the importance of meeting religious needs, *RN* has compiled the accompanying chart for handy reference. In this chart are listed the basic rites of the three major religions in the U.S. Here are other basic points to remember about each of these religions:

1. *Judaism.* This includes Orthodox, Conservative, and Reform branches, each varying in its observances. So you'll want to find out which group your Jewish patient belongs to.

2. *Protestantism.* This embraces dozens of denominations with varying theological beliefs. Among them are the so-called "bridge" churches: Episcopalian, Lutheran, and Moravian. While generally referred to as Protestant, such churches actually stand between Protestantism and Catholicism. Their members greatly prefer clergymen of their own church.

3. *Roman Catholicism.* This church has no subdivisions. The Eastern Orthodox, Polish National Catholic, and Anglo-Catholic are separate churches.

By learning the rites listed in this chart, you'll be better able to give religious help to all your patients. And you'll have the satisfaction of knowing you can respond promptly and effectively to spiritual needs as well as to physical needs.

*From *RN*. March 1959, pp. 44–45.

CARE OF THE TERMINALLY ILL PATIENT

Occasion: Birth—General Precepts

Jewish	Protestant	Roman Catholic
Jewish infants aren't baptized. It's a basic ritual among all Jews that male babies be circumcised on the eighth day after birth. (Circumcision of an infant in poor health may be postponed.) If the baby is still in the hospital on the eighth day, the father or another member of the family will want to consult a rabbi with regard to the religious ritual. The nurse will interpret to the family the regulations of the hospital regarding circumcision. There's no rite for Jewish female babies.	Emergency baptism should be performed on all Protestant infants in danger of death, with the exception of Baptists and Disciples of Christ. If possible, a baptized person should be present as sponsor. If none is available, anyone present may serve as witness.	Emergency baptism must be conferred on every Catholic infant in probable danger of death; on every monstrosity; on every stillborn and aborted fetus, whatever its stage and development, unless it is certainly dead. For purposes of baptism the only certain sign of death is noticeable corruption. A baptized fetus should be buried in a Catholic cemetery.

What To Do

Jewish	Protestant	Roman Catholic
Nothing	Call a minister. But if there's danger of death and the minister may not arrive in time, anyone may baptize. Pour water on the infant's head (not merely on the hair), saying simultaneously: "(Name), I baptize you in the name of the Father, and of the Son, and of the Holy Spirit. Amen." If the child hasn't yet been named, use the equivalent of	Call a priest. But if there is danger the infant will die before the priest arrives, anyone may and should baptize. Pour water on the infant's head (not merely on the hair), saying simultaneously: "I baptize you in the name of the Father, and of the Son, and of the Holy Spirit." Water must flow on the skin. Giving a name is not essential. If it's a

Occasion: Birth—General Precepts (Cont.)
What To Do (Cont.)

Jewish	Protestant	Roman Catholic
	"Baby Boy Smith." Excess water is to be poured off on the ground. If cotton was used to wipe the baby's head, it must be burned. Later report all available information about the infant to a clergyman of the specific denomination.	medically dead fetus still enclosed in membranes, immerse it in a basin of water, break the membranes, and pronounce the words while moving the fetus about in the water. In an incomplete delivery, pour water on the presenting part; baptism should later be repeated if a part other than the head was first baptized. If the infant is likely to die in utero, a medically qualified person should attempt baptism in utero with a sterile syringe containing sterile water; the membranes must be pierced before the water is released; after delivery the baptism should be repeated. Following such a baptism, report all available information about the infant to the priest.

What To Prepare

Jewish	Protestant	Roman Catholic
Nothing	A glass of warm water, a spoon, and absorbent cotton.	In most cases, a glass of warm water and absorbent cotton; for baptism in utero, a sterile syringe with sterile water and a sponge; for an aborted fetus, a basin of warm water.

Occasion: Death—General Precepts

Jewish	Protestant	Roman Catholic
When a Jewish patient dies in the hospital, a rabbi, or some responsible member of the Jewish community, will make proper arrangements for burial. Since many Jews are opposed to autopsy for religious reasons, a rabbi, or some responsible member of the Jewish community, should discuss the matter of autopsy with the deceased's family.	Most Protestant denominations don't observe last sacraments. Those that do, administer them before death. There is no moral objection to autopsy among most Protestants.	Every Roman Catholic should receive the last sacraments (penance, Communion, and extreme unction) before death. But penance and extreme unction can be administered conditionally up to several hours after medical death has occurred. The patient's body should not be wrapped in a shroud until after the last rites have been administered. There is no moral objection to autopsy performed in accordance with the provisions of civil law. The deceased Catholic patient should be given Catholic burial. When there are no relatives to claim the body, the Catholic chaplain, or pastor of the parish in which the death occurred, should be asked to arrange for burial.

What To Do

Jewish	Protestant	Roman Catholic
Notify a rabbi or some responsible member of the Jewish community. Provide routine care for the body after death, as prescribed by the hospital.	Call a minister. Provide routine care for the body after death, as prescribed by your hospital. Place arms at the sides, or fold them; close eyes.	Call a priest. When he's finished his ministrations, provide routine care for the body after death as prescribed by your hospital.

Occasion: Death—General Precepts (Cont.)
What To Prepare

Jewish	Protestant	Roman Catholic
Nothing	Nothing	A table covered with a white cloth, preferably of linen, a crucifix, holy water and ritual, two candles (these should not be lit if fire laws prohibit), and six small balls of cotton on a dish (these should afterwards be disposed of by burning separately from other refuse).

Occasion: Serious Illness, Major Surgery, Extreme Old Age—General Precepts

Jewish	Protestant	Roman Catholic
Except where postponement may be harmful, observant Jews may not want to undergo surgery on the Sabbath (after sundown Friday to after sundown Saturday) or on Holy days.	Prayer and pastoral counseling are usually welcome to Protestant patients who are seriously ill or in danger of death. Members of the "bridge" churches (Episcopalians, Lutherans, Moravians) may want the sacraments of Holy Communion, penance, and unction.	Patients in certain danger of death are obliged to receive the sacraments of penance, Holy Communion, and extreme unction. They're entitled to receive unction even when danger of death is only a probability. A hospital's "critical list" designation is roughly equivalent to the theological concept of "probable danger of death." . . . Viaticum (Holy Communion for those in danger of death) doesn't require previous fasting. Major amputated members should, if reasonably possible, be buried in consecrated ground.

Occasion: Serious Illness, Major Surgery, Extreme Old Age—General Precepts (Cont.)

What To Do

Jewish	Protestant	Roman Catholic
Call a rabbi	Call a minister, preferably one of the patient's own denomination, who will tell you what to prepare.	Call a priest, if possible, before any sedatives are administered and while the patient is still conscious. Try to arrange complete privacy for confession (penance). Elevate patient slightly for Communion. Arrange bed covers so that patient's feet may be easily uncovered for annointing.

What To Prepare

Jewish	Protestant	Roman Catholic
A copy of the Jewish Holy Scriptures and a Jewish prayer book, written in both Hebrew and English.	For Holy Communion, a table covered with a clean cloth and whatever else the minister suggests, such as a glass of water.	For communion, a table covered with a white cloth, preferably of linen; a spoon; glass straw; glass of water; crucifix; holy water and ritual; two candles (those should not be lit if fire laws prohibit). For extreme unction, add six small balls of cotton on a dish (these should afterwards be disposed of by burning separately from ordinary hospital refuse).

Occasion: Special Religious Observances

Jewish	Protestant	Roman Catholic
Copies of the Jewish Holy Scriptures and Jewish prayer books, written in both Hebrew and English, should be available for Jewish patients. If the patient or his family requests, the Sabbath and Jewish Holy Days should be kept free of treatments and procedures that can be postponed without injury.	Communion and baptism (penance and unction in the case of the "bridge" churches) are administered at the bedside when requested by the patient. For Communion, offer to hold the patient's breakfast until after the ceremony.	Holy Communion is often administered to Catholic patients on Sunday morning and sometimes daily. Patients in the hospital are subject to no obligation of fasting before Communion.

Dietary Rules

Jewish	Protestant	Roman Catholic
Observant Jews eat only Kosher (permissable) meat, fish, and dairy products. These are prepared in utensils and served in dishes that have been cleaned and kept separate in a ritually prescribed manner; and they're eaten in a prescribed sequence. In a non-Jewish hospital, it's advisable to provide such patients with a protein substitute diet, served on paper plates. If the patient's medical diet requires him to have milk and meat products at the same meal, serve the milk products first. During Passover, the observant Jew will not eat leavened products or drink liquids contain-	Many Protestants observe rules of fasting (only one full meal a day) and abstinence (no meat). It's wise to ask the patient about special dietary rules he prefers to follow, then check with his doctor to see if it's permissable to comply.	On Ash Wednesday and Good Friday, Catholics from the age of fourteen are required to abstain entirely from meat. On these same two days, Catholics between the ages of twenty-one and sixty are also subject to the law of fasting (one full meal, two light meals, nothing between meals.) The truly sick may be exempt from the fast and abstinence if it would be detrimental or exceptionally difficult. It may be taken as a practical rule that patients in hospitals are exempted from this obligation. If in doubt, consult a priest and the physician.

Occasion: Special Religious Observances (Cont.)
Dietary Rules (Cont.)

Jewish	Protestant	Roman Catholic
ing grain alcohol. When dietary problems arise, it's advisable to call a rabbi to discuss the matter with the patient.		

How To Address The Clergy

Jewish	Protestant	Roman Catholic
Rabbi	Mister or Doctor. When in doubt Mister (never Reverend). Lutheran ministers are usually called Pastor. Many Episcopal priests are called Father.	Father

VII. INFORMATION INDEX—A COMPILATION OF INFORMATION RESOURCES
Donor/Recipient Information

Donor information may be obtained from the sources listed below:

American Medical Association
535 N. Dearborn Street
Chicago, Illinois 60610

Continental Association
59 E. Van Buren Street
Chicago, Illinois 60605

Deafness Research Foundation
366 Madison Avenue
New York, New York 10016

Eye Bank Association of America
3195 Maplewood Avenue
Winston-Salem, North Carolina 27103

Eye Bank for *Sight Restoration*
210 East 64th Street
New York, New York 10021

Falconer Foundation Inc. (Radiation Research)
66 W. 87th Street
New York, New York 10024

Living Bank
6631 South Main
P. O. Box 6725
Houston, Texas 77005

Medic Alert
Turlock, California

National Association of Patients on Hemodialysis and Transplantation
P. O. Box 60
Brooklyn, New York 11203

National Kidney Foundation
116 East 27 Street
New York, New York 10010

National Pituitary Agency
Suite 507
210 West Fayette Street
Baltimore, Maryland 21201

National Transplant Information Center
135 Flower Hill Road
Huntington, New York 11743

Project Hear
Rodney Perkins, M.D.
1801 Page Mill Road
Palo Alto, California 94304

Tissue Bank
U.S. Naval Medical Research Institute
Bethesda, Maryland 20014

United Health Foundations, Inc.
150 Fifth Avenue
New York, New York 10011

Counseling, Education and Burial Information Resources Related to Death and Dying

1. Films

Brian's Song, 75 minutes, sound, color. Learning Corporation of America.
This film offers an opportunity to view coping behaviors and defense mechanisms, in addition to experiencing feelings. Since most students may have seen the film previously, they are likely to be more objective.

Death Be Not Proud, 99 minutes, sound, color, 1975. Learning Corporation of America.
This film offers a look at a family in crisis and the opportunity to experience a variety of very intense feelings. Discussion is likely to be lengthy after some time has elapsed.

Larry, 80 minutes, sound, color, 1974. Learning Corporation of America.
This film deals with a young man who was raised in a hospital for the mentally retarded, but was not retarded. It shows his psychological growth and development, in addition to exemplifying caring relationships by professionals. It provides a "life" break while continuing to focus on feelings.

What Man Shall Live and Not See Death, 58 minutes, sound, color. Films, Inc.
This film shows a variety of ways that Americans deal with death. Some of the people interviewed include Dr. Kübler-Ross, some dying patients, Dr. Robert Neale, a woman who had her father's body frozen, and some members of the clergy. The film shows how the bodies are frozen and stored by a cryonic society.

I Heard The Owl Call My Name, 78 minutes, sound, color, 1973. Learning Corporation of America.
This film deals in a very sensitive manner with the learning about life and the death of a young priest. It deals very effectively with the value of life. It is thought provoking and encourages the viewer to feel intensely.

The Family of Man: Series 7—Death, 48 minutes, sound, color, 1971. Time-Life Films.
This film deals rather graphically with cross-cultural differences in the meaning of death and how the bodies of the dead are disposed of. It shows burial in earth graves, tribal rituals, and the burning of bodies on funeral pyres. Expect strong gut-level reactions from the viewers.

Who Shall Survive, 26 minutes, color, 1972.
This stimulating film deals with euthanasia. A panel of experts discusses ethical, legal, and scientific issues when a mongoloid infant is allowed to die.

Perspectives on Dying, Concept Media Inc.
Six films with instructor's manual, roleplaying cards, questionnaire, and text. Appropriate for all allied health care groups.

How Could I Not Be Among You, 30 minutes, color, 1970, Eccentric Circle Cinema Workshop.
This film offers poignant reflections of a young poet dying of leukemia. A theme of love and live when you can.

2.   Manuals and Periodicals

Facts Every Family Should Know (funeral information), Wilbert, Inc., P.O. Box 147, Forest Park, IL 60130

Journal, Death Education Hemisphere Publishing Company, 1025 Vermont Avenue, NW, Washington, D.C., 20005

Journal of Suicide and Life-Threatening Behavior, Human Science Press, 72 5th Avenue, New York, N.Y. 10011

Journal of Thanatology, Foundation of Thanatology, 630 W. 168 Street, New York, N.Y. 10032.

Manual of Death Education and Simple Burial, Cello Press, Brunsville, N.C. 28714 ($1.50)

Omega, 51 Riverside Avenue, Westport, Connecticut, 06880

Price of Death, Consumer Information Center, Dept. 38, Pueblo, CO 81009

Student kit of informational materials. The Euthanasia Educational Council, 240 W. 57th St., New York, NY 10019

Too Personal To Be Private, National Funeral Directors Association, 135 W. Wells St., Milwaukee, WI 53202

3.   Organizations

Make Today Count, Inc.
Burlington, Iowa 52601

Foundation of Thanatology
630 West 168 Street
New York, New York 10032

Center For Aging
North Texas State University
Denton, Texas

Center for Death Education and Research
University of Minnesota
Minneapolis, Minnesota

St. Christopher's Hospital
51–53 Lawrie Park Road
London SE, 26
England

Hospice, Inc.
789 Howard Avenue
New Haven, Connecticut 06504

American Cancer Society
(Most major cities)

Lost Chord—International Association of Laryngectomy
219 E. 42nd Street
New York, N.Y. 10017

Reach For Recovery (Mastectomies)
777 3rd Avenue
New York, N.Y. 10017

Continental Association of Funeral & Memorial Societies
(For information on how to start a memorial society)
1828 L St. NW
Washington, D.C. 20036

Encyclopedia of Associations
Vol. I, Gale Research Company
New York, N.Y.

Cryonics Society
216 Pico Blvd
Santa Monica, California

Bay Area Cryonic Society
1739 Oxford Street
Berkeley, Cal. 94709

American Board of Funeral Service Education
P.O. Box 2098
Fairmont, West Virginia 26554

National Funeral Directors Association
135 West Wells Street
Suite 300
Milwaukee, Wisconsin 53203

The Euthanasia Educational Fund
250 W. 57th Street
New York, N.Y. 10019

Primary Prevention Programs
Public Health Service—NIMH
5600 Fishers Lane
Rockville, Md. 20852

Human Rights and Liberties Information

American Civil Liberties Union
(Most major cities)

Legal Aide Society
(Most major cities)

International League For Human Rights
New York, New York

Amnesty International
London, England

UN Commission on Human Rights
New York, New York

Society for the Right to Die/Euthanasia
Educational Council
250 West Fifty-Seventh Street
New York, N.Y. 10019

Retired Professional Action Group
2000 P Street NW
Washington, D.C. 20009

Right To Life
5227 Lyndale Avenue South
Minneapolis, Minnesota 55419

Planned Parenthood
(Locations in most major cities)

REFERENCES

Boyar, J.I. *The Construction and Partial Validation of a Scale for the Measurement of the Fear of Death*. University of Rochester, 1964.

Collett, L.J., and Lester, D. "The Fear of Death and the Fear of Dying." *Journal of Psychology*, 72 (1969), 179–181.

Dickstein, L.S. "Death Concern: Measurement and Correlates." *Psychological Reports*, 30 (1972), 563–571.

Epstein, C. *Nursing the Dying Patient*. Reston, Va.: Reston, Pub., 1975.

Koestenbaum, P. "The Existential Meaning of Death," in A. Earle, N. Argondizzo, and A. Kutscher, eds., *The Nurse as Caregiver—for the Terminal Patient and His Family*. New York: Columbia University Press, 1976.

Lester, D. "Experimental and Correlational Studies of the Fear of Death." *Psychological Bulleton*, 67 (1967), 27–36.

Mills, G., Reisler, R., Robinson, A., and Vermilye, G. *Discussing Death–A Guide to Death Education*. Hometown, Ill.: E & C Publications, 1976.

Neale, R. E. *The Art of Dying*. New York: Harper & Row, 1971.

RN Magazine, March 1959, 44– 45.

Ross, C. W. *Death Concerns and Responses to Dying Patient Statements* (University of Missouri and Columbia University doctoral dissertation; Xerox available from Xerox University Microfilms, Ann Arbor, Mich. 1976.

Sarnoff, I., and Corwin, S.E. "Castration Anxiety and the Fear of Death." *Journal of Personality*, 27, (1959), 374–385.

Templer, D.I. "The Construction and Validation of a Death Anxiety Scale." *Journal of General Psychology*, 82 (1970), 165–177.

Tolar, A. Unpublished Data, 1966. Cited in Handel, P.J., "The Relationship between Subjective Expectancy, Death Anxiety and General Anxiety." *Journal of Clinical Psychology*, 25 (1969), 39– 42.

Worden, J.W., and Proctor, W. *PDA*; Breaking Free of Fear to Live a Better Life Now*. Englewood Cliffs, N.J.: Prentice Hall, 1976.

GLOSSARY

AGATHANASIA—A good death, a death with dignity.

AMORT—At the point of death.

AMORTALITY—Neither mortal nor immortal.

ARS NORIENDI—Art of dying.

BEREAVE—To deprive as by violence, rob, take away. An emotional state subsequent to a significant loss.

CASKET—A box or enclosure designed to accommodate the bodily remains of the deceased.

CEMETERY—A burial place or, literally, a sleeping ground.

CEREMONY—A religious observance, sacred rite, formality, symbolic behavior.

CODE OF THE HOLY ROMAN EMPIRE (850 A.D.)—A code which banned the practice of burying the dead under the floors of churches. The practice apparently arose from a belief that terrible demons might violate the tomb unless burial was accomplished beneath the church floor.

CORONER—A public official or officer whose principal duty is to inquire into the cause of any death believed to have occurred by other than natural causes. The word derives from "the crown," one who watches over the crown's property.

CORPSE—Dead body.

CORTEGES—A train of attendants or funeral procession. The assemblage of persons who participate in a final rite of burial.

CREMATE—To burn by fire.

CRITCHFIELD-JACOB'S DISEASE—A disease that appears to be impervious to many modern aseptic procedures.

DAKMAS (Towers of Silence)—Ancient Persian Towers which were built in areas apart from human habitation into which the dead were thrown.

DECEASED—Dead person.

DEFENESTRATE—To throw someone or something out of a window; an old Bohemian custom.

DIRGE—A funeral service or hymn, in present usage, a funeral hymn.

EMBALM—To treat the body in such a way as to protect it from decomposition, decay, and odor. The word originated from the use of resin or balm in this context.

EMBALMING—The preservation technique originated among the Egyptians and other early peoples in which complex procedures are employed to preserve bodily remains and retard decomposition.

ENDURA—An ancient Christian practice of hastening death by fasting or bleeding.

EUTHANASIA—This word stems from the Greek words for *easy* and *death*. An easy death accompanied by a lack of worry and inward feeling of tranquility.

EVICERATE—To remove internal organs, a practice usually conducted during autopsies or embalming.

EXHUME—Removal of a body which has been buried.

FUNERAL FEAST—A gathering of survivors of the deceased interpreted as a means of assuring peace for the dead.

FUNERAL ORATION—A sermon or oration, an integral part of modern funeral practices. In Europe, the practice of having orations printed after the funeral became relatively common.

GERONTOLOGY—The study of aging.

GERIATRICS—Health care fields concerned with aspects of human aging.

IATROGENIC—Disease induced by the care giver.

INHUMATION—Burial or interment. One of the more common climaxes to the funeral ceremony. A practice which in earlier times appears to have evolved as a means of protecting the body against ghosts or evil spirits and also of insuring against the return of the dead person's soul or spirit.

LIEBESTOD—The belief that lovers reunite in death.

LOCULI—Shelflike graves located in the catacombs and used for Christian burial.

LUGUBRIA—Black clothing, similar to present-day mourning apparel, worn in ancient Rome by mourners.

MACROBIOSIS—Prolongation of life.

MECROBIOSIS—Physical death of body cells.

MECROLATRY—Worship of dead or dead spirits.

MECROLOGY—Register of deaths; obituary

MOURN—To care for, lament, grieve, and remember.

NECROMANCER—One who practices necromancy.

NECROMANCY—A mode of attempting to contact the dead, considered as witchcraft, sorcery, etc.

NECROPHILISM—An abnormal desire and/or love for the dead.

NECROPHOBIA—An abnormal fear of the dead, death, or dead bodies.

NECROPOLIS—"City of the Dead," cemetery.

NECROPSY—Autopsy.

ORIENTATION—A ritual thought to be as ancient as that of the sun worshippers whereby bodies are formally placed in their graves with feet to the East and heads to the West.

PALL OF LINEN—The materials specially manufactured in ancient times in which dead bodies were wrapped.

RITE—A prescribed form or manner of action usually having numerology or numbered steps that have symbolic or magical meanings repeated in a compulsive fashion.

SURVIVORS SYNDROME—A condition frequently observed in those who do not die in accidents that is characterized by marked guilt.

TAPHOBIA—Fear of being burned alive.

THANATOLOGY—Science of or the study of death.

THANATOPSIS—A view or a contemplation of death.

THANATOTROPISM—A driving toward or being driven toward death.

TODESTRIAB—Death drive or death instinct.

TUMULI—Ancient tombs of northern Europe representing houses of the dead.

UNDERTAKING—A trade now more commonly known as mortuary service carried out by funeral directors.

WAKE—The vigil or the watch over the dead.

WIDOW'S PEAK—Mourning attire originating with Empress Fredricka of Germany.

WIDOW'S WEEPERS—A form of mourning attire that signalled the wearer's ineligibility for marriage.

INDEX